EDINBURGH. Vol. 2. p. 180.

RECOLLECTIONS

OF

A LIFETIME,

OR

MEN AND THINGS I HAVE SEEN:

IN A SERIES OF

FAMILIAR LETTERS TO A FRIEND,

HISTORICAL, BIOGRAPHICAL, ANECDOTICAL, AND
DESCRIPTIVE.

———

BY S. G. GOODRICH.

———

VOL. II.

NEW YORK AND AUBURN:

MILLER, ORTON AND MULLIGAN.

NEW YORK, 25 PARK ROW:—AUBURN, 107 GENESEE-ST.

M DCCC LVI.

R. C. VALENTINE,
STEREOTYPER AND ELECTROTYPIST,
17 Dutch-st., cor. Fulton,
NEW YORK.

C. A. ALVORD, PRINTER,
No. 15 Vandewater Street, N. Y.

CONTENTS.

8   CONTENTS.

LETTER LX.

LETTER LXI.

LETTER LXII.

LETTER LXIII.

RECOLLECTIONS OF A LIFETIME.

LETTER XXXI.

The Hartford Convention—Its Origin—Testimony of Noah Webster—Oath of Roger M. Sherman—Gathering of the Convention—Doings of Democracy thereupon—Physiognomy of the Convention—Sketches of some of the Members—Colonel Jessup—Democracy in the Streets—Report of the Convention—Reception of the Doings of the Convention by Madison and his Party—Its Effect and Example—Comparison of the Hartford Convention with the Nullifiers—The Union forever.

MY DEAR C******

I come now to the "Hartford Convention." Methinks I hear you remark, with an aspect of dismay—are you not venturing into deep water in treating of such a subject, generally regarded as an historical abyss, in which much may be lost and nothing can be gained?

Well, my friend, suppose you do ask this—is it really a good reason why I should not tell what I have seen, what I know, what I believe, in relation to it? The Hartford Convention was in my time: my uncle, Chauncey Goodrich, was one of its prominent members. I was then living with him;* I saw all the

---

* I have stated elsewhere that he had promised to make me one of his aids. Accordingly, H. L. Ellsworth—afterward Indian Agent and Commissioner of Patents—and myself were appointed, with the rank of

persons constituting that famous body, at his house; the image and superscription of the most distinguished individuals are fresh in my recollection. I remember the hue and aspect of the political atmosphere, then and there. Why should I not tell these things? You may, perhaps, entertain the common notion that the Hartford Convention was a congregation of conspirators—traitors—and I shall invite you to abandon this delusion. It may not be pleasant to hear your cherished opinions controverted : it is always a little disagreeable to receive truth, which requires us to sacrifice something of our self-esteem, by giving up errors which have become part of our mental constitution. But certainly you will not silence me on any such narrow ground as this. The time has come when one may speak freely on this subject, and surely without offense. Forty years have passed since the gathering of that far-famed body. Every member of it is dead. I will not insist that you shall say nothing of them which is not good ; but I claim the privilege of saying of them what I know to be true. I am sure you will listen to me patiently, if not approvingly.

major, April 17, 1815. I was not very ambitious of my title, for not long after " *Major Goodridge*," of Bangor, Maine, acquired an infamous notoriety, in consequence of a trial (December, 1816) in which Daniel Webster made a celebrated plea, unmasking one of the most extraordinary cases of duplicity and hypocrisy on record. This Major Goodridge pretended to have been robbed, and the crime was charged upon two persons by the name of Kenniston. In the defense of these, Mr. Webster proved that the charge was false, and that the accuser had himself fabricated the whole story of the robbery. (See Webster's Works, vol. v. page 441.)

You may perhaps suppose that there is but one opinion in the country as to the character of that assembly; but let me observe that there are two opinions upon the subject, and if one is unfavorable, the other is diametrically opposite. In New England, the memories of those who constituted the Convention are held in reverence and esteem, by the great body of their fellow-citizens, including a large majority of those whose opinions are of weight and value, and this has been so from the beginning.

I have said that they are now all gathered to their fathers. As they have gone down, one by one, to their last resting-place, public opinion has pronounced sentence upon their lives and characters. I ask your attention to the historical fact, that in every instance, this has been a eulogy—not for talent only, but the higher virtues of humanity. Of the twenty-six members who constituted the Convention, *every one has passed to an honored grave.* The members of the Hartford Convention were, in effect, chosen by the people, at a time of great trouble and alarm, for the purpose of devising the ways and means to avert threatening— impending evils. All felt the necessity of selecting persons of the highest wisdom, prudence, and virtue, and never was a choice more happily made. Most of these men were indeed of that altitude of talent, piety, dignity, and patriotism, which partisan pigmies naturally hate, by the inherent antipathy of littleness to greatness, and of vice to virtue; but in New England,

the enlightened generation among whom they lived,
estimated them according to their true merits. These
never believed them to be conspirators; they knew,
indeed, the fact to be otherwise. Even the blinding
influence of party spirit has never made the better
class of democrats in New England believe that the
Convention meditated treason. As to the mass of
the people, they held and still hold that the Hartford
Convention was one of the ablest and wisest assemblies ever convened in the country.

I am aware, however, that the prevailing opinion
in the United States at large has been, and perhaps
still is, the reverse of this. Out of New England,
democracy is the dominant party. The war was a
democratic measure, and the Convention was the
work of the federalists, who opposed the war. It is,
doubtless, too much to expect that party spirit will
exercise candor toward those who brave and baffle
it—at least during the conflict. There were many
reasons why the Convention was an unpardonable
sin in the eyes of democracy: it was opposition to
the war, and that itself was treason: the war was
attended with defeat, disaster, disgrace, and to turn
retribution from the heads of the war-makers, it was
considered politic to charge every miscarriage to the
war opposers. In short, it was deemed the best way
for self-preservation, by the democratic leaders, to sink
the federalists in undying infamy. Hence they persisted in denouncing the Convention as an assembly

of conspirators. It is admitted that there was no overt act of treason, but it is maintained that there was treason in their hearts, the development of which was only prevented by the return of peace, and the indignant rebuke of public sentiment.

The foundation of this tenacious calumny is doubtless to be traced to John Quincy Adams, who, having lost the confidence of his political associates—the federalists of Massachusetts—and not being elected to a second term as Senator of the United States, speedily changed his politics, and made a disclosure, real or pretended, to Jefferson, in 1808,* to the effect that the federalists of the North—taking advantage of the uneasiness of the people on account of the distresses imposed upon them by the embargo—were meditating a separation from the Union, and an alliance with Great Britain—of all things the most likely to obtain democratic belief, and to excite democratic horror.

Here was the germ of that clinging scandal against New England, which has been perpetuated for forty years. It certainly had a respectable voucher at the beginning, but its utter want of foundation has long since been proved. For about twenty years, however, the libel was permitted—in secret and of course without contradiction—to ferment and expand and work itself over the minds of Jefferson and his associates.

---

* See note on page 274, vol. i. of this work. Also Hildreth, second series, vol. iii. pp. 79, 117.

It had created such an impression, that Madison—
when President—had only to be told by an unaccred-
ited foreigner, that he had the secret of a federal plot
for disunion in Massachusetts, and he at once bought
it, and paid fifty thousand dollars for it out of the
public treasury.* No doubt he really expected to find
that he had a rope round the necks of half the federalists in New England. He soon discovered, however,
that the biter was bit. John Henry duped the President, who seized the hook, because it was baited with
suspicions, the seeds of which John Q. Adams had
furnished some years before.

It was not till the year 1828, when that person was
a candidate for the presidency a second time, that the
whole facts in regard to this calumny were developed.
He was then called seriously to account,† and such

---

* In March, 1812, Madison sent to Congress certain documents, pretending to disclose a secret plot, for the dismemberment of the Union,
and the formation of the Eastern States into a political connection
with Great Britain. It seems that in the winter of 1809, Sir J. H.
Craig, Governor-general of Canada, employed John Henry to undertake
a secret mission to the United States for this object. Henry proceeded
through Vermont and New Hampshire to Boston. He, however, never
found a person to whom he could broach the subject! As he stated,
the British government refused the promised compensation, and therefore he turned traitor, and sold his secret to our government. The
subject was fully discussed in Parliament, and it appeared that Henry's scheme was not known to or authorized by the British government. The whole substance of the matter was, that our government
was duped by a miserable adventurer. The conduct of Madison, in
this evident greediness to inculpate the federalists, was a lasting ground
of dislike and hostility to him. See *Young's Amer. Statesman*, p. 248.

† I was living in Boston at the time (October, 1828) when the public
first became fully aware of the fact, that, twenty years before, Mr. Adams had planted the seeds of this accusation against the northern fed-

was the effect, that from that time he was silent. In vain did he attempt to furnish evidence of a plausible foundation for his story. He referred to various witnesses, but it was pointedly remarked that all, save one,* were dead. Yet these even seemed to rise up

---

eralists in the eager soil of Mr. Jefferson's mind, where it had flourished in secret, and whence it had been widely disseminated. There was a general—indeed, an almost universal—feeling of indignation and astonishment. The presidential election was at hand, and Mr. Adams was the candidate of the whig party for a second term. Those very persons, whom he had thus maligned—themselves or their descendants—were now his supporters. The election was permitted to pass, and Massachusetts gave her vote for Mr. Adams; he was, however, defeated, and Jackson became his successor.

And now came the retribution. Mr. Adams was addressed by H. G. Otis, T. H. Perkins, William Prescott, Charles Jackson, and others—men of the highest standing, and representing the old federal party, charged with treason by him—demanding the proofs of the accusation for which he stood responsible. I have not space to give here the discussion which followed. Those who wish can find the case clearly stated in *Young's American Statesman*, page 442, &c., &c. The result certainly was, that Mr. Adams showed no grounds, even for suspicion, of what he charged; and that, even if there had been some foundation for his opinion, it referred to an earlier date, and to other individuals, and could not, by any show of fact, reason, or logic, be connected with the Hartford Convention. Indeed, no person can now read the controversy referred to, without coming to this obvious conclusion. It will be remembered, in confirmation of this, that John Henry, the British agent, sent for the purpose of seducing the Boston federalists, by the British governor, Craig, never found an individual to whom he dared even to open his business!

At all events, such was the shock of public feelings, caused by the disclosure of Mr. Adams's charge made to Jefferson, that for a long time, when he walked the streets of Boston, which he occasionally visited, he was generally passed without being spoken to, even by his former acquaintances. The resentment at last subsided, but he never recovered the full confidence of the people of Massachusetts: they were content, however, in view of his great merits, to let the matter pass into oblivion. It is only in obedience to the call of history that I write these facts.

* This individual was William Plumer, a Senator from New Hampshire, who stated that in 1803 and 1804, he was himself in favor of

and speak from their very graves. Sons, brothers, relatives, associates—including some of the first men in the United States—indignantly denied, in behalf of those for whom they had a right to speak, the imputations thus cast upon them. No fair-minded man can read the discussion now, and fail to see that Mr. Adams either invented his story—which, however, is by no means to be presumed—or that, according to the peculiar structure of his mind, having become hostile to the federal leaders in Massachusetts, he really thought he saw evidences of mischief in events which, fairly viewed, furnished not the slightest ground even for suspicion.

Thus, as I think, this foundation, this beginning of the idea that the Hartford Convention originated in treasonable designs on the part of its members, is shown to be absolutely groundless. Not one particle of evidence, calculated to satisfy an honest inquirer after truth, has ever been adduced to sustain the charge. The investigation has been in the highest degree inquisitorial : it was deemed vital to the interests of the democratic party to prove, to establish this allegation of treason. Public documents, newspaper articles, private correspondence, personal

---

forming a separate government for New England, but he abandoned these ideas, and used his influence against them, when, as he says, they were revived in 1809 and 1812. He, too, underwent a close examination, and it appeared that he was unable to produce any reliable evidence whatever, that any plot for disunion was formed, or that any individual, connected with the Hartford Convention, countenanced such a scheme. See *Young's Amer. Statesman*, p. 455, &c.

intercourse — all have been subjected to the rack
and the thumb-screw. The question has been
pushed to the conscience of an individual member
of the Convention, and he has been called to testify,
on oath, as to the origin and intentions of that assembly. Its journal, declared to contain every act,
every motion, every suggestion, that took place,
has been published; and now—after forty years
of discussion, thus urged by hostile parties—sober
history is compelled to say, that not a public document, not a private letter, not a speech, not an act,
secret or open, has been brought to light, which
proves, or tends to prove, the treasonable origin of
the Hartford Convention!

The charge of treason is a serious one: so far
as it may have a just foundation, it is fatal to personal character: it is a stain upon the State to which
it attaches: it is a discredit to human nature, especially in a country like ours, and in a case like that
which we are discussing. It should therefore not be
made—surely it should not be maintained—unless
upon positive, undeniable proof. It should not rest
for its defense upon partisan malice, or that inherent littleness which teaches base minds to accept
suspicion as conclusive evidence of what they believe, only because it coincides with their evil
thoughts. While, therefore, there seems to be no
proof of the alleged treasonable origin of the Hartford Convention—I am able to do more than can-

dor demands, and I here present you with direct testimony from a source that will not be impugned or discredited, showing that the said Convention originated with the people and from the circumstances of the times, and not with conspirators, and that its objects were just, proper, patriotic. I shall hereafter call upon you to admit, that the proceedings of the Convention were in accordance with this its lawful and laudable origin.

I now ask your candid attention to the following statement, made some years after the Convention, by Noah Webster*—a man perhaps as universally

---

* It is certainly not necessary for me to write the biography or certify to the character of Noah Webster: these have been carried all over our country by his Spelling-book and his Dictionary, erecting monuments of gratitude in the hearts of the millions whom he has taught to read, and the millions whom he still teaches, in the perfect use of our language. It has been said, and with much truth, that he has held communion with more minds than any other author of modern times. His learning, his assiduity, his piety, his patriotism, were the groundwork of these successful and beneficent labors. It is the privilege of a great and good man to speak, and when he speaks, to be listened to. The passage here quoted is comprised in his "Collection of Essays," published in 1843: it was written with a sincere and earnest purpose, and it seems no more than due to truth and the justice of logic, to receive it as conclusive proof of the facts it asserts.

Mr. Webster, as is well known, was a native of Hartford, Conn., and was born in Oct. 1758. Among his classmates at Yale College were Joel Barlow, Oliver Wolcott, Uriah Tracy, Zepheniah Swift, and other men of eminence. His life was spent in various literary pursuits. I knew him well, and must mention an incident respecting him, still fresh in my memory. In the summer of 1824, I was in Paris, and staying at the Hotel Montmorency. One morning, at an early hour, I entered the court of the hotel, and on the opposite side, I saw a tall, slender form, with a black coat, black small-clothes, black silk stockings, moving back and forth, with its hands behind it, and evidently in a state of meditation. It was a curious, quaint, Connecticut looking apparition, strangely in contrast to the prevailing forms and aspects in this gay metropolis. I

known and esteemed as any other in our history. He testifies to facts within his own knowledge, and surely no one will deny that, to this extent, he is a competent and credible witness.

Few transactions of the federalists, during the early periods of our government, excited so much the angry passions of their opposers as the Hartford Convention—so called—during the presidency of Mr. Madison. As I was present at the first meeting of the gentlemen who suggested such a convention; as I was a member of the House of Representatives in Massachusetts when the resolve was passed for appointing the delegates, I advocated that resolve; and further, as I have copies of the documents, which no other person may have preserved, it seems to be incumbent on me to present to the public the real facts in regard to the origin of the measure, which have been vilely falsified and misrepresented.

After the War of 1812 had continued two years, our public affairs were reduced to a deplorable condition. The troops of the United States, intended for defending the seacoast, had been withdrawn to carry on the war in Canada; a British squadron was stationed in the Sound to prevent the escape of a frigate from the harbor of New London, and to intercept our coasting-trade; one town in Maine was in possession of the British forces; the banks south of New England had all suspended the payment of specie; our shipping lay in our harbors, embargoed, dismantled, and perishing; the treasury of the United States was exhausted to the last cent; and a general gloom was spread over the country.

In this condition of affairs, a number of gentlemen, in North-

said to myself—"If it were possible, I should say that was Noah Webster!" I went up to him, and found it was indeed he. At the age of sixty-six, he had come to Europe to perfect his Dictionary! It is interesting to know that such tenacity of purpose, such persistency, such courage, were combined with all the refined and amiable qualities which dignify and embellish domestic and private life.

ampton, in Massachusetts, after consultation, determined to invite some of the principal inhabitants of the three counties on the river, formerly composing the old county of Hampshire, to meet and consider whether any measure could be taken to arrest the continuance of the war, and provide for the public safety. In pursuance of this determination, a circular letter was addressed to several gentlemen in the three counties, requesting them to meet at Northampton. The following is a copy of the letter:

NORTHAMPTON, Jan. 5, 1814.

Sir: In consequence of the alarming state of our public affairs, and the doubts which have existed as to the correct course to be pursued by the friends of peace, it has been thought advisable by a number of gentlemen in this vicinity, who have consulted together on the subject, that a meeting should be called of some few of the most discreet and intelligent inhabitants of the old county of Hampshire, for the purpose of a free and dispassionate discussion touching our public concerns. The legislature will soon be in session, and would probably be gratified with a knowledge of the feelings and wishes of the people ; and should the gentlemen who may be assembled recommend any course to be pursued by our fellow-citizens, for the more distinct expression of the public sentiment, it is necessary the proposed meeting should be called at an early day.

We have therefore ventured to propose that it should be held at Col. Chapman's, in this town, on Wednesday, the 19th day of January current, at 12 o'clock in the forenoon, and earnestly request your attendance at the above time and place for the purpose before stated.

With much respect, I am, sir, your obedient servant,

JOSEPH LYMAN.

In compliance with the request in this letter, several gentlemen met at Northampton, on the day appointed, and after a free conversation on the subject of public affairs, agreed to send to the several towns in the three counties on the river, the following circular address:

Sir: The multiplied evils in which the United States have been involved by the measures of the late and present administrations, are subjects of general complaint, and in the opinion of our wisest statesmen call for some effectual remedy. His excellency, the Governor of the Commonwealth, in his address to the General Court, at the last and present session, has stated, in temperate, but clear and decided language, his opinion of the injustice of the present war, and intimated that measures ought to be adopted by the legislature to bring it to a speedy close. He also calls the attention of the legislature to some measures of the general government, which are believed to be unconstitutional. In all the measures of the general government, the people of the United States have a common concern, but there are some laws and regulations, which call more particularly for the attention of the Northern States, and are deeply interesting to the people of this Commonwealth. Feeling this interest, as it respects the present and future generations, a number of gentlemen from various towns in the old county of Hampshire, have met and conferred on the subject, and upon full conviction that the evils we suffer are not wholly of a temporary nature, springing from the war, but some of them of a permanent character, resulting from a perverse construction of the Constitution of the United States, we have thought it a duty we owe to our country, to invite the attention of the good people of the counties of Hampshire, Hampden, and Franklin, to the radical causes of these evils.

We know indeed that a negotiation for peace has been recently set on foot, and peace will remove many public evils. It is an event we ardently desire. But when we consider how often the people of the country have been disappointed in their expectations of peace, and of wise measures ; and when we consider the terms which our administration has hitherto demanded, some of which, it is certain, can not be obtained, and some of which, in the opinion of able statesmen, ought not to be insisted upon, we confess our hopes of a speedy peace are not very sanguine.

But still, a very serious question occurs, whether, without an amendment of the Federal Constitution, the northern and commercial States can enjoy the advantages to which their wealth, strength, and white population justly entitle them. By means of the representation of slaves, the Southern States have an influence in our national councils altogether disproportionate to their wealth, strength, and resources ; and we presume it to be a fact capable of demonstration, that for about twenty years past the United States have been governed by a representation of about two-fifths of the actual property of the country.

In addition to this, the creation of new States in the South, and out of the original limits of the United States, has increased the southern interest, which has appeared so hostile to the peace and commercial prosperity of the Northern States. This power assumed by Congress of bringing into the Union new States, not comprehended within the territory of the United States at the time of the federal compact, is deemed arbitrary, unjust, and dangerous, and a direct infringement of the Constitution. This is a power which may hereafter be extended, and the evil will not cease with the establishment of peace. We would ask, then, ought the Northern States to acquiesce in the exercise of this power? To what consequences would it lead? How can the people of the Northern States answer to themselves and to their posterity for an acquiescence in the exercise of this power, that augments an influence already destructive of our prosperity, and will in time annihilate the best interests of the northern people?

There are other measures of the general government, which, we apprehend, ought to excite serious alarm. The power assumed to lay a permanent embargo appears not to be constitutional, but an encroachment on the rights of our citizens, which calls for decided opposition. It is a power, we believe, never before exercised by a commercial nation; and how can the Northern States, which are habitually commercial, and whose active foreign trade is so necessarily connected with the interest of the farmer and mechanic, sleep in tranquillity under such a violent infringement of their rights? But this is not all. The late act imposing an embargo is subversive of the first principles of civil liberty. The trade coastwise between different ports in the *same State* is arbitrarily and unconstitutionally prohibited, and the subordinate offices of government are vested with powers altogether inconsistent with our republican institutions. It arms the President and his agents with complete control of persons and property, and authorizes the employment of military force to carry its extraordinary provisions into execution.

We forbear to enumerate all the measures of the federal government which we consider as violations of the Constitution, and encroachments upon the rights of the people, and which bear particularly hard upon the commercial people of the North. But we would invite our fellow-citizens to consider whether peace will remedy our public evils, without some amendments of the Constitution, which shall secure to the Northern States their due weight and influence in our national councils.

The Northern States acceded to the representation of slaves as a matter of compromise, upon the express stipulation in the Constitution that they should be protected in the enjoyment of their commercial rights. These stipulations have been repeatedly violated; and it can not be expected that the Northern States should be willing to bear their portion of the burdens of the federal government without enjoying the benefits stipulated.

If our fellow-citizens should concur with us in opinion, we would suggest whether it would not be expedient for the people in town meetings to address memorials to the General Court, at their present session, petitioning that honorable body to propose a convention of all the Northern and commercial States, by delegates to be appointed by their respective legislatures, to consult upon measures in concert, for procuring such alterations in the federal Constitution as will give to the Northern States a due proportion of representation, and secure them from the future exercise of powers injurious to their commercial interests; or if the General Court shall see fit, that they should pursue such other course, as they, in their wisdom, shall deem best calculated to effect these objects. The measure is of such magnitude, that we apprehend a concert of States will be useful and even necessary to procure the amendments proposed; and should the people of the several States concur in this opinion, it would be expedient to act on the subject without delay.

We request you, sir, to consult with your friends on the subject, and, if it should be thought advisable, to lay this communication before the people of your town.

In behalf, and by direction of the gentlemen assembled,

JOSEPH LYMAN, *Chairman.*

In compliance with the request and suggestions in this circular, many town meetings were held, and with great unanimity, addresses and memorials were voted to be presented to the General Court, stating the sufferings of the country in consequence of the embargo, the war, and arbitrary restrictions on our coasting trade, with the violations of our constitutional rights, and requesting the legislature to take measures for obtaining redress, either by a convention of delegates from the Northern and commercial States, or by such other measures as they should judge to be expedient.

These addresses and memorials were transmitted to the General Court then in session, but as commissioners had been sent to Europe for the purpose of negotiating a treaty of peace, it was judged advisable not to have any action upon them till the result of the negotiation should be known. But during the following summer, no news of peace arrived; and the distresses of the country increasing, and the seacoast remaining defenseless, Governor Strong summoned a special meeting of the legislature in October, in which the petitions of the towns were taken into consideration, and a resolve was passed appointing delegates to a convention to be held in Hartford. The subsequent history of that convention is known by their report.

The measure of resorting to a convention for the purpose of arresting the evils of a bad administration, roused the jealousy of the advocates of the war, and called forth the bitterest invectives. The convention was represented as a treasonable combination, originating in Boston, for the purpose of dissolving the

Union. But citizens of Boston had no concern in originating the proposal for a convention; it was wholly the project of the people in old Hampshire county—as respectable and patriotic republicans as ever trod the soil of a free country. The citizens who first assembled in Northampton, convened under the authority of the *bill of rights*, which declares that the people have a right to meet in a peaceable manner and consult for the public safety. The citizens had the same right then to meet in convention as they have now; the distresses of the country demanded extraordinary measures for redress; the thought of dissolving the Union never entered into the head of any of the projectors, or of the members of the Convention; the gentlemen who composed it, for talents and patriotism have never been surpassed by any assembly in the United States, and beyond a question the appointment of the Hartford Convention had a very favorable effect in hastening the conclusion of a treaty of peace.

All the reports which have been circulated respecting the evil designs of that Convention, I know to be the foulest misrepresentations. Indeed, respecting the views of the disciples of Washington and the supporters of his policy, many, and probably most of the people of the United States in this generation, are made to believe far more falsehood than truth. I speak of facts within my own personal knowledge. We may well say with the prophet—" Truth is fallen in the street, and equity can not enter." Party spirit produces an unwholesome zeal to depreciate one class of men for the purpose of exalting another. It becomes rampant in propagating slander, which engenders contempt for personal worth and superior excellence; it blunts the sensibility of men to injured reputation; impairs a sense of honor; banishes the charities of life; debases the moral sense of the community; weakens the motives that prompt men to aim at high attainments and patriotic achievements; degrades national character, and exposes it to the scorn of the civilized world.

Such is the testimony—direct, positive, documentary—of Noah Webster, as to the origin of the Hartford Convention.* This, be it remembered, is evidence furnished by one outside of that assembly: let me now present you with the testimony of Roger Minot Sherman—a member of that body, and a worthy bearer of one of the most honored names in American history.

[From the Norwalk Gazette, January, 1831.]

To the Editor of the Gazette:

Previous to the trial of Whitman Mead, on the charge of libel, of which you gave a brief notice in your last number, the pris-

---

* This statement, on the part of Mr. Webster, does not exclude the supposition that the idea of a convention of the New England States may have been previously suggested by others. Such a thing was very likely to occur to many minds, inasmuch as New England had been accustomed, from time immemorial, to hold conventions, in periods of trouble and anxiety. His testimony, however, shows clearly that the actual, efficient movement which resulted in the Hartford Convention, originated, as he states, with the citizens of Hampshire county. Other testimony shows that some prominent federalists did not at first favor it, and only yielded at last to a feeling of prudence, in following this lead of the people.

The following letter from Harrison Gray Otis to Mrs. Willard, written in reply to a request from her, for information on the subject, will be seen to correspond with Mr. Webster's statement, and also with the proceedings of the Convention, and all other known facts relating to it, in such a manner as to satisfy every honest mind of its truth.

"The Hartford Convention, far from being the original contrivance of a cabal for any purpose of faction or disunion, was a result growing, by natural consequences, out of existing circumstances. More than a year previous to its institution, a convention was simultaneously called for by the people in their town meetings, in all parts of Massachusetts. Petitions to that effect were accumulated on the tables of the legislative chamber. They were postponed for twelve months by the influence of those who now sustain the odium of the measure. The adoption of it was the consequence, not the source of a popular sentiment; and it was intended by those who voted for it, as a safety-valve, by which the

oner moved the Court for a subpœna, to Mr. Sherman, of Fairfield, Mr. Goddard, of Norwich, and others, as witnesses in
his behalf. It was allowed by the Court, and was served on
Mr. Sherman, but could not be, seasonably, on Mr. Goddard, on
account of the lateness of his application. One of the articles
charged as libellous, compared a recent political meeting at Hartford with the Hartford Convention, and the prisoner supposed
that a full development of the proceedings of that Convention
would furnish a legal vindication of the article in question. With
a view to such development, he wished the testimony of the gentlemen above named. At the instance of the prisoner, Mr. Sherman testified on the trial of the case, and the inclosed paper contains his testimony, exact in substance, and very nearly in his
language—which you are at liberty to publish.—[The trial took
place at Fairfield, Connecticut, the place of Mr. Sherman's residence, in January, 1831.]

State of Connecticut,)
              vs.   }
    Whitman Mead.   )   *Hon. Roger Minot Sherman's Testimony.*

Question by the Prisoner. What was the nature and object of the
Hartford Convention?

Answer. I was a member of that Convention. It met on the 15th of
December, 1814. The United States were then at war with Great Britain. They had, in their forts and armies, twenty-seven thousand effective men : of these about thirteen hundred only were employed in
New England. The war had been in operation two years and a half.
We had a seacoast of almost seven hundred miles to protect, and with
the exception of about thirteen hundred men, had the aid of no military force from the United States. By internal taxes, all others having
become unproductive by reason of the war, the national government
raised large sums from the people within our territory. Direct taxation
was the only resource of the State governments, and this had been carried to as great an extreme in Connecticut as could be sustained. The
banks, which furnished all our currency, either withheld their accommodations or stopped payment, and the people were embarrassed by a
general stagnation of business. Powerful fleets and armies lay off our

---

steam arising from the fermentation of the times might escape, not as
a boiler by which it is generated." (See *Willard's History of the United
States*, p. 851.)

coasts, and were making or threatening invasions in all parts of our defenseless sea-board. Commodore Decatur, with his squadron, had taken refuge in the waters of Connecticut, and attracted a powerful concentration of the enemy's forces on our borders. Castine, if I mistake not, and some other parts of the territory of Massachusetts, had fallen into the hands of the British. The New England States, under all these disadvantages, were obliged to protect themselves by their own militia, at their own expense. The expenses of Connecticut greatly exceeded our resources. The duration of the war could not be foreseen, and our credit was exhausted. Attempts were made to borrow money, but without any adequate success. The national Constitution prohibited the emission of bills of credit. In this extremity, while the legislature was in session at New Haven, in October, 1814, a communication was received from the legislature of Massachusetts, proposing a convention of delegates from the New England States, to consult on the adoption of measures for their common safety. This communication was referred to a joint committee of both houses. General Henry Champion and myself were appointed from the Upper House. He was chairman of the committee. I drew the report, recommending a compliance with the proposal made by the State of Massachusetts, and assigning the reasons at length. This report was published by order of the legislature, and extensively circulated in the newspapers of this and other States. Seven delegates were appointed to represent the Convention. As soon as it was organized, Mr. Otis, a delegate from Massachusetts, proposed, after some prefatory remarks, that it should be recommended to our several legislatures to present a petition to the Congress of the United States, praying that they would consent that the New England States, or so many of them as should agree together for that purpose, might unite in defending themselves against the public enemy ; that so much of the national revenue as should be collected in these States, should be appropriated to the expense of that defense ; that the amount so appropriated should be credited to the United States ; and that the United States should agree to pay whatever should be expended beyond that amount. This proposal was approved by the Convention. The same views had been stated here before the meeting of the delegates. By the Constitution of the United States, no such compact for mutual defense could be formed, without the consent of Congress. By thus augmenting our immediate resources, and obtaining the national guaranty that the expenses of the war, to be increased by the States thus uniting, should be ultimately paid out of the national treasury, it was supposed that our credit, as well as our present pecuniary resources, would be enhanced. A debate was had in the Convention as to certain amendments to the Constitution of the United States, to be proposed for adoption by the State legislatures. One was, that Congress should not have power to declare war without the concurrence of two-thirds of both houses. I can not, from recollection, detail the proposed amendments ;

but they appear on the printed report of the Convention, of which I have a copy at my office, which the prisoner may use on the trial, if he pleases. A committee, of whom I was one, was appointed by the Convention to draw up that report to present to their respective legislatures. The proposal of Mr. Otis was adopted with little variation. This report was immediately printed by order of the Convention, and was circulated throughout the country.

Among other things, as may be seen by that report, it was recommended to the legislatures represented in the Convention, to adopt measures to protect their citizens from such conscriptions or impressments as were not authorized by the Constitution of the United States. This resolution originated from a project of the then Secretary of War, which I believe was not adopted by Congress. The secretary of the Convention kept a journal of their proceedings. This, as I understand, was deposited by Mr. Cabot, the President, in the office of the Secretary of State of Massachusetts, and a copy transmitted to Washington, and lodged in the office of the Secretary of State of the United States. It was afterward published in certain newspapers. I saw it in the American Mercury, a newspaper published at Hartford, by Mr. Babcock. The legislatures of Massachusetts and Connecticut, pursuant to the recommendation of the Convention, sent a delegation to Washington, to present their respective petitions to the Congress of the United States. The gentlemen sent from Connecticut were Mr. Terry, Mr. Goddard, and, I think, Mr. Dwight. On their arrival, the Treaty of Peace, concluded at Ghent, reached the national government, and further measures became unnecessary.

This is an outline of the origin and proceedings of the Hartford Convention. There was not, according to my best recollection, a single motion, resolution, or subject of debate, but what appears in the printed journal or report. If any further particulars are requested, I will state them.

Question by the Prisoner. Was it not an object of the Convention to embarrass and paralyze the government of the United States in the prosecution of the war with Great Britain?

Answer. It was not. Nothing of the kind was done or entertained by the Convention, or, so far as I know or believe, by those by whom it was originated. On the contrary, its principal object was a more effectual co-operation in that war, as to the defense of the New England States.

Question by the Prisoner. Has not that Convention been generally reputed in the United States to be treasonable?

Answer. Much has been said and published to that effect, but without the least foundation. I believe I know their proceedings perfectly; and that every measure, done or proposed, has been published to the world. No one act has ever been pointed out, to my knowledge, as inconsistent with their obligations to the United States, nor was any such act ever contemplated by them.

Here is the testimony of a great and good man—a member of the Convention—*under oath*. Who will venture to gainsay it? Certainly no individual who feels the claims of truth, and appreciates the requisitions of logic, unless he is armed with proofs, clear, indisputable, demonstrative; he must bring facts sufficient to destroy the direct testimony of such men as Noah Webster and Roger M. Sherman, and, indeed, a cloud of other witnesses of equal weight and responsibility.

It seems to me that every candid mind, upon these statements, will be constrained to admit that the Convention thus originated in public necessity, and not in treason; I think the additional evidence I am about to present will satisfy you that their proceedings were in harmony with the wise and worthy motives that brought the members together.

If you look into certain partisan histories of the times, you might be led to suppose that on the day of the gathering of the Convention at Hartford—the 15th of December, 1814—the heavens and the earth were clothed in black; that the public mind was filled with universal gloom; that the bells—tremulous with horror—tolled in funereal chimes; that the flag of the country everywhere was at half-mast; and that the whole American army marched with muffled drums and inverted arms, and all this in token of the quaking terror of the public mind, at the ominous gathering of a committee of some two dozen mild, respect-

able, gray-haired old gentlemen, mostly appointed
by the legislatures of Massachusetts, Connecticut,
and Rhode Island, to investigate and report upon
the state of public affairs! Such, I recollect, was the
picture of Hartford, that was circulated over the
country by the democratic papers* remote from the

---

* The following is from the American Mercury, the democratic organ at Hartford—Dec. 18, 1815, a year after the Convention. There
can be little doubt that, at the outset, many of the democrats really felt
that the Convention meditated treason. I have already shown that the
leaders of democracy had been made, by the revelations of John Q.
Adams, to suspect the northern federalists; and there is no doubt
that Madison and his cabinet, for a time, apprehended that the Hartford Convention was to be the fulfillment of Adams's prediction. But
the maledictions here poured out by the Mercury—a year after the gathering of the Convention, and when its innocence, to say the least, was
universally known and understood—were mere electioneering devices.
They are interesting, however, as showing the means by which the
obstinate prejudice against the Convention was wrought into the minds
of the mass of the democratic party.

"The fifteenth of December is an epoch in the history of America
which can never be passed over by Republicans, without mingled emotions of regret and exultation: of regret, that we have among us 'men
—freeborn men—men born, nursed, and brought up by our firesides—
Americans—American citizens,' who are so depraved, so wicked, as to
aim a dagger at the vitals of their already bleeding country, and to attempt to subvert the liberties of the people; of exultation, that the grand
designs of these hellish conspirators have been frustrated with infamy,
and that the Union has triumphed over their mischievous machinations!

"Impressed with these sentiments, the Republicans of Hartford, on
Friday last (being the day of the first meeting of the Convention), displayed the flag of the Union at half-mast during the early part of the
day, as expressive of their sorrow for the depravity of those, who, one
year since, were plotting in our city, in conjunction with Britain, the
destruction of the liberties of the Republic. In the afternoon, the flag
was raised to the masthead, as emblematical of the complete discom-
fiture of their designs, and the triumph of the Constitution. In the
rueful countenance of the federalists, it was plain to discover the mortification and chagrin which they experienced. They say, let us bury in
oblivion's dark bastile all bitter recollection! But so long as New England is cursed with federal rulers, till she emerges from the darkness

scene of action.   The whole is very well reflected in
the inspired pages of Charles Jared Ingersoll,* who
may be considered as the Jeremiah of democracy, for
this period of our history.   He seems to have regarded
himself as specially raised up to prophesy against
New England.   " The sin of Judah"—that is, of federalism—he has written " with a pen of iron," though
not " with the point of a diamond."

Now I perfectly well remember the day of the
gathering of the Convention.†   There was in the city

---

which has for years enveloped her, till republicanism reigns triumphant throughout New England (which we trust in God is close at hand),
it becomes the imperious duty of Republicans to hold up to the contempt of the people, their wicked and nefarious designs. * * *

" We think it a duty we owe to our country, to publish annually the
names of those who composed the ' Hartford Convention,' that they may
never be forgotten."   Here follows a list of the names.

Not only the Hartford Mercury, but the Boston Patriot, and probably
other democratic journals, made a similar pledge to hold up to eternal
disgrace this black list of conspirators.   All this was, however, a mere
electioneering game, and after two or three years, the pledge was forgotten.

* " *Historical Sketch of the Second War between the United States and
Great Britain*, by Charles Jared Ingersoll."

† The following are the names of the members of the so-called Hartford Convention : those from Massachusetts, Connecticut, and Rhode
Island were appointed from the State legislatures ; those from New
Hampshire, by county conventions ; the delegate from Vermont was
chosen by persons in the county of Windham.   These were all appointed " *for the purpose of devising and recommending such measures for the
safety and welfare of these States as may be consistent with our obligations
as members of the National Union*."

From Massachusetts—George Cabot, Nathan Dane, William Pres-
cott, Harrison Gray Otis, Timothy Bigelow, Joshua Thomas, Samuel
Sumner Wilde, Joseph Lyman, Stephen Longfellow, Jr., Daniel Waldo,
Hodijah Baylies, George Bliss.

From Connecticut—Chauncey Goodrich, John Treadwell, James Hillhouse, Zephaniah Swift, Nathaniel Smith, Calvin Goddard, Roger M.
Sherman.

a small squad of United States recruits—I think some two dozen in number. These, assisted no doubt by others, ran up the American flag at their rendezvous, with the British flag at half-mast, beneath it. They also—these two dozen, more or less—marched through the streets with reversed arms and muffled drums. A few persons, I believe, got hold of the bell-rope of the Baptist meeting-house, and rang a funereal chime. All this—chiefly the work of the rabble—was the scoff of the great body of the people; nevertheless, it was reported in the democratic papers abroad, as if some black and mighty portent had signalized the arrival of the Convention. The simple truth was, that the six and twenty gray-haired men—legislators, senators, judges—honored for long years of service—came quietly into town, and were welcomed by the mass of the citizens, according to their standing and their mission, with respect, esteem, and confidence.

Let us take a sketch of what followed from the prophet Jared: "On the 15th of December, 1814, with excited sentiments of apprehension, mingled approval and derision, the inhabitants of Hartford awaited the nefandous Convention, which takes its bad name from that quiet town." "One of their number, Chauncey Goodrich, was mayor of Hartford, *by whose arrangements the Convention was disposed of*

From Rhode Island—Daniel Lyman, Samuel Ward, Edward Manton, Benjamin Hazard.

From New Hampshire—Benjamin West, Mills Olcott.

From Vermont—William Hall, Jr.

*in the retirement of the second story of an isolated stone
building, in which the little State Senate or Council sat,
when, in rotation, Hartford was the seat of government.
Locking themselves up stairs, there, in awfully obscure
concealment, for three weeks, twice every day, except Sunday, Christmas and New Year's-day, they were continually in conclave,"* &c.

What an accumulation of horrors! Tell me, my
dear C...., does not your hair bristle at the grisly
picture? It indeed sounds like a tale of the Inquisition. What a pity it is to spoil it! And yet, this
infernal Rembrandt coloring—this violent contrast of
light and shade—is wholly imaginary. The Convention met in the council-chamber of the State-
house, which the gazetteers tell us—and tell us truly
—is a very handsome building. It is in the center
of the city, and the most prominent edifice in the
place. The room in which they met is still the
senate-chamber, and is neither isolated nor obscure:
on the contrary, it is one of the best and most conspicuous rooms in the building: at the time, it was
probably the finest public hall in the State.*

It is true that the Convention sat with closed doors,
as probably every similar convention had done be-

---

* The Hon. R. R. Hinman, the historian of Connecticut during the
Revolutionary period, and several years Secretary of State, once told me a
good anecdote in relation to this dark, dismal hiding-place of the "nefandous" Convention. One day, a man from the South—I believe a South
Carolinian—some one doubtless who had been reading Ingersoll's history, came into the office of the Secretary, and desired to be shown the
place where the Hartford Convention sat. Mr. Hinman accordingly

fore. The State Council—in whose room the Convention met—had furnished this example from time immemorial. The General Assembly of Connecticut had always done the same, at periods of difficulty and danger. The Convention that framed the Constitution of the United States had done likewise. The Continental Congress did the same, through the whole period of the war of the Revolution. A great part of the executive business of the United States Senate is now done in secret session, and is never known to the public. The archives of the State Department, at Washington, are under the lock and key of the Executive. The legislature of every State has the capacity to hold secret sessions, and nobody questions their right to exercise it according to their discretion. Both houses of Congress discussed, resolved upon, and voted the war of 1812, in secret session! And yet, what was useful, proper, and of good re-

---

took him into the room. The stranger looked around with much curiosity, and presently he saw Stuart's likeness of Washington—for in this chamber is one of the most celebrated of the full-length portraits of the Father of his Country.

The stranger started. "And was this picture here, when the Convention held its sittings?" said he.

"Yes, certainly," said the secretary.

"Well," replied the man — observing the high color which Stuart had given to the countenance of Washington, in the picture—"well, I'll be d——d if he's got the blush off yet!"

This is a sharp joke; but yet, it is natural to ask—if Washington's picture should blush for the Hartford Convention—which above all things advocated the preservation of the Union—what should it have done in the presence of that Convention in South Carolina, November, 1832, which resulted in an open, avowed opposition to the Union, and has perhaps laid the foundation for its overthrow, in establishing the doctrine of Secession?

port in all other similar bodies, was "*nefandous*" in the Hartford Convention ! So saith Jared, the historian, whose account seems to consist largely of the prejudices and exaggerations of the democratic papers of that day—raked together in one undigested heap. As such it is amusing—nay, instructive—but alas, how is history degraded, when such a mass of incongruities assumes its sacred name !

I have told you that I was at this time living with my uncle, Chauncey Goodrich—then a member of the Convention. His house, of course, became the frequent rendezvous of the other members, and here I often saw them. On one occasion, in the evening, they all met at his house, by invitation—the only instance in which they partook of any similar festivity. At this time, the other persons present, so far as I recollect, were William Coleman,* editor of the

---

* William Coleman was a native of Massachusetts, and was born in 1766. He studied law, and settled at Greenfield about 1794, where he erected a house, noted for its architectural beauty. Here he also edited a newspaper. Buckingham—vol. ii. p. 319—says that he was remarkable for his vigor in skating, having passed in one evening from near Greenfield to Northampton, a distance of about twenty miles. As I recollect him, he was a large man, of robust appearance, with a vigorous and manly countenance. His nose was bony and prominent, and in connection with a strongly defined brow, gave his face an expression of vigor and sagacity. His eye was gray, his hair light brown, and at the time I speak of, was slightly grizzled. He removed to New York, where he published some law books, and in 1801 (Nov. 16), founded the Evening Post, which became a leading federal paper, and so continued for many years. Its columns were distinguished for ability, as well in its political discussions as its literary essays and criticisms. In general, he set a good example of dignity of style and gentlemanly decorum, though he was drawn into some violent altercations with Cheetham and Duane. It is sufficient eulogy of Mr. Coleman to say that he enjoyed the con-

New York Evening Post, Theodore Dwight, secretary of the Convention, my cousin, Elizur Goodrich, now of Hartford, and myself. The majority of
the members were aged men, and marked not only
with the gravity of years, but of the positions which
they held in society—for some of them had been governors, some senators, some judges. I do not recollect ever to have seen an assemblage of more true
dignity in aspect, manner, and speech. They were
dressed, on the evening in question, somewhat in
the ancient costume—black coats, black silk waist-
coats, black breeches, black silk stockings, black
shoes. I wonder that this universal black has not
been put into the indictment against them! Perhaps
the silvery-whiteness of their heads—for the majority
were past fifty, several past sixty—may have pleaded
in extenuation of this sinister complexion of their dress.

The most imposing man among them, in personal
appearance, was George Cabot,* the president. He
was over six feet in height, broad-shouldered, and of
a manly step. His hair was white—for he was past
sixty—his eye blue, his complexion slightly florid. He
seemed to me like Washington—as if the great man,

---

fidence of Hamilton, King, Jay, and other notabilities of that day, and
that he made the Evening Post worthy of the editorial successorship of
Leggett (1829) and of Bryant (1836).

* George Cabot was a native of Salem, Mass., born in 1752. He was
originally a shipmaster, but he rose to various stations of eminence.
He became a senator of the United States, and in 1798 was appointed
the first Secretary of the Navy, but declined. His personal influence
in Boston was unbounded. He died in that city, 1823.

GEORGE CABOT. Vol. 2, p. 36.

as painted by Stuart, had walked out of the canvas, and lived and breathed among us. He was, in fact, Washingtonian in his whole air and bearing, as was proper for one who was Washington's friend, and who had drunk deep at the same fountain—that of the Revolution—of the spirit of truth, honor, and patriotism. In aspect and general appearance, he was strikingly dignified, and such was the effect of his presence, that in a crowded room, and amid other men of mark—when you once became conscious that he was there, you could hardly forget it. You seemed always to see him—as the traveler in Switzerland sees Mont Blanc towering above other mountains around him, wherever he may be. And yet he was easy and gracious in his manners, his countenance wearing a calm but radiant cheerfulness, especially when he spoke. He was celebrated for his conversational powers, and I often remarked that when he began to converse, all eyes and ears turned toward him, as if eager to catch the music of his voice and the light of his mind. He came to my uncle's almost every morning before the meeting of the Convention, and I have never felt more the power of goodness and greatness, than in witnessing the intercourse between these two men.

The next person as to prominence, in the Massachusetts delegation, was Harrison Gray Otis,* then in

* Harrison Gray Otis, son of Samuel A. Otis, the first Secretary of the Senate of the United States, was born in 1765, and died 1848. He

the zenith of his years and his fame. He had a name
honorable by tradition, and a position—social as well
as political—due to his great wealth, his eminent talents, and his various accomplishments. He was
doubtless the most conspicuous political character in
New England—for the sun of Webster was but just
rising in the horizon. He was deemed ambitious,
and hence was regarded by the democrats as the
arch instigator of the traitorous Convention. Such
an opinion, however, shows the greatest ignorance of
his character and the actual state of things. Mr.
Otis was a far-seeing politician, and knew there was
no treason in the hearts of the people of New England: he stood at the highest point to which ambition could lead him, and any step in that direction
must be downward. Besides, he was of the cautious, not the dashing school of statesmanship, as well
by constitution as training. To suppose him a plotter of treason, is to divest him of all his attributes—
inherent and conventional. It is, furthermore, historical and beyond dispute, that he was averse to the
Convention. By his influence, it was delayed, long
after it was proposed and almost clamored for by the

---

was one of the most eminent of the Massachusetts bar, even by the side
of Ames, Parsons, Lowell, and Gore. He succeeded Ames in Congress,
in 1797. In 1817, he became a senator of the United States. To learning and vigor of intellect, he added great powers of oratory, captivating
alike to the simple and the refined. He held various other offices, and
in these, discharged his duties with distinguished ability. His residence was at Boston. He retained his mental faculties, his cheerfulness,
and his amenity of demeanor, to the last.

people. He objected to being a member of it, and only yielded at last, that he might use his influence to secure to it a safe and tranquilizing direction. At the very opening of the Convention, he signalized himself by proposing the safe and discreet measures which were finally adopted. Hence, he always felt, with a keen sense of injustice, the imputation which long hung about him, as being the leader in a treasonable enterprise.

The impression he made on my mind upon the occasion I am describing, was deep and lasting. He had not the lofty Washingtonian dignity of George Cabot, nor the grave suavity of Chauncey Goodrich; he was, in fact, of quite a different type—easy, polished, courtly—passing from one individual to another, and carrying a line of light from countenance to countenance, either by his playful wit or gracious personal allusions. He seemed to know everybody, and to be able to say to each precisely the most appropriate thing that could be said. He was one of the handsomest men of his time; his features being classically cut, and still full of movement and expression. To me—who had seen little of society beyond Connecticut, and accustomed therefore to the rather staid manners of public men—Mr. Otis was an object of strange, yet admiring curiosity. I knew him well, some years after and when I was more conversant with the world, and he still seemed to me a very high example of the finished gentleman of the assiduous and

courtly school. He lowered himself, no doubt, in the
public estimation by his somewhat restive and quer-
ulous — though masterly and conclusive—vindica-
tions of the Convention; while all the other members,
conscious of rectitude, scorned to put themselves in
the attitude of defense. We may forgive what seemed
a weakness in Mr. Otis, while we must pay homage to
that dignity in his associates, which would not stoop
to ask in life, the justice which they knew posterity
must render them, in their graves.

Of the other members of the Massachusetts delegation, I have less distinct personal reminiscences.
Mr. Prescott, father of the historian,* and Mr. Longfellow,† father of the poet—worthy, by their talents,
their virtues, and their position, of such descendants
—I only remember as two grave, respectable old
gentlemen, seeming, by a magic I did not then comprehend, to extort from all around them peculiar

---

* William Prescott was a native of Pepperell, Mass., born 1762. His
father, Colonel Prescott, commanded at the battle of Bunker Hill. He
became one of the most eminent lawyers in the State, and filled various
public stations. Mr. Webster said of him at the time of his death, in
1844: "No man in the community, during the last quarter of a century, felt himself too high, either from his position or his talents, to ask
counsel of Mr. Prescott."

† Stephen Longfellow, of Portland, Maine, was an eminent lawyer,
and ranked among the most distinguished and estimable citizens of New
England. He was noted for unsullied purity of life and character, an
inflexible devotion to his convictions, great powers of conversation,
and winning amenity of manners, always mingling an elevated piety
with a kindly charity to all other sects. While Maine was a part of
Massachusetts, he exercised great influence in the State: after the separation, he was one of the leading men of this new member of the
Union. He died in 1849.

marks of deference and respect. Since I have known their history, I have ascertained the secret.*

One of the oldest, and in some respects the most re-

---

* The other members from Massachusetts were all eminent for their virtues and their talents.

Few names in our history are more honorably remembered than that of Nathan Dane. He was a native of Ipswich, Massachusetts, born in 1754. He was a lawyer of great eminence, and a statesman of distinguished patriotism and wisdom. He was a member of Congress under the Confederation, and was the framer of the famed ordinances of 1787, for the government of the territory of the United States northwest of the Ohio river; an admirable code of law, by which the principles of free government, to the exclusion of slavery, were extended to an immense region, and its political and moral interests secured on a permanent basis. He published some useful works, and founded a professorship of law in Harvard University. His life is a long record of beneficent works. He died in Feb. 1835.

Timothy Bigelow was a learned, eloquent, and popular lawyer, born in 1767, and died in 1821. For more than twenty years he was a member of the Massachusetts legislature, and for eleven years he was Speaker of its House of Representatives. His residence was at Medford. Mrs. Abbott Lawrence was one of his daughters.

Joseph Lyman, of Northampton, was born in 1767, and died in 1847. He was the person associated with Noah Webster and others, in the first movement for the Hartford Convention, as previously noticed. He held many important offices, and enjoyed, in an unbounded degree, the confidence of the community. He was an eminently dignified and handsome man, of the old school of manners, and mingling in his countenance and demeanor a certain seriousness, with kindness and condescension. He never failed to attend the polls, and deposited his fifty-ninth ballot the year of his death !

Joshua Thomas, born 1751, and died 1821, held for many years the office of Judge of Probate for the county of Plymouth.

Samuel Sumner Wilde, born 1771 and died 1855, was an eminent lawyer, and several years judge of the Supreme Court—the same in which Parsons, Story, Sedgwick, and Sewall had officiated. He was a man of unbending integrity, and the utmost dignity and purity of life. He was the father-in-law of Caleb Cushing—the present Attorney-general of the United States.

George Bliss, born 1764, died 1830, was a distinguished lawyer of Springfield. He enjoyed in an eminent degree the respect and confidence of all who knew him.

Daniel Waldo was born in 1763 at Boston : he settled at Worcester,

markable member of the Convention, was Mr. West,*
of New Hampshire. I recollect him distinctly, partly
because of his saintly appearance, and partly because
of the terms of affection and respect in which my
uncle spoke of him. He, too, was often at our house,

---

and devoted himself to mercantile affairs with great success. He acquired in a high degree the confidence of the community around him.
He was distinguished for integrity, justice, and punctuality, in all the
affairs of life. He died in 1845.

Thomas Handyside Perkins, born in Boston, 1764, and died in 1854.
He was an eminent merchant of that city, and having amassed a large
fortune, was distinguished for his liberality. Several literary and charitable institutions owe their existence to him. In person, he was a large
man, with a grave countenance, but with an expression indicative of his
large and generous heart.

Hodijah Baylies was born in 1757. He served during the Revolutionary war, and was at one time aid to General Lincoln, and afterward to
Washington. He held various public offices, and was noted as combining, in a high degree, the Christian character with that of the gentleman. He died in 1843.

The four members from Rhode Island were among the most respectable citizens of that State.

Daniel Lyman was a native of Connecticut, born in 1776 and died in
1830. He served through the Revolutionary war, and rose to the rank
of major. He afterward settled in Rhode Island, became eminent as a
lawyer, and was finally chief-justice of the Supreme Court of that State.

Samuel Ward, son of Gov. Ward, of that State, was born in —— and
died in ——. In the Revolution he was a soldier, and accompanied Ar-
nold in his perilous march against Quebec. After the peace he devoted
himself to commerce. As a soldier, patriot, and citizen, his character
was without a stain.

Benjamin Hazard was among the ablest lawyers of his day, enjoying
the highest esteem for his private worth. He was very swarthy, with
long frizzled hair, and I particularly noticed him, among the other members, for the singularity of his appearance. He was often called by the
people of his neighborhood "Black Ben." He was born in 1776 and died
in 1841. He was elected to the Assembly of Rhode Island sixty-two times!

Edward Manton was a merchant of Johnston, and distinguished for
his probity and moral worth. He was born in 1760 and died in 1820.

* Benjamin West was a native of Massachusetts, son of Rev. T.
West, and born in 1746. He was graduated at Harvard College, studied
law, and settled at Charlestown, N. H., where he died, July 27, 1817.

and seldom have I seen a man who commanded such ready love and admiration. He was then sixty-eight years old: his form tall but slender, his hair white, long, and flowing, his countenance serene, his voice full of feeling and melody. His appearance indicated the finest moral texture; but when his mind was turned to a subject of interest, his brow flashed with tokens of that high intellectual power which distinguished him. His character and his position were well displayed in a single passage of his history: " He was chosen a member of Congress under the old Confederation; a member of the convention which framed the Constitution of his adopted State, and a member of Congress under the Constitution; he was appointed Attorney-general and Judge of Probate, and yet all these offices he refused, owing to his aversion to public life, and his sincere, unambitious love of domestic peace and tranquillity." His great abilities, however, were not hidden in a napkin. He devoted himself to the practice of the law, which he pursued with eminent success, for the space of thirty years. It was in the evening of his days that he accepted his first prominent public station, and that was as member of the Hartford Convention. This he did, under a conviction that it was a period of great difficulty and danger, and he felt that duty called upon him to sacrifice his private comfort to public exigencies. Who will

For a full and touching biography of him, see Knapp's Biographical Sketches of Eminent Lawyers, Statesmen, &c., p. 245.

believe that man to have been a conspirator, or that the people who designated him for this place were traitors?

As to the Connecticut members of the Convention, I could easily gather up pages of eulogy. There are, indeed, few such men now; I am afraid that in this age of demagogism, there are few who can comprehend them. I shall, however, present you with brief delineations of their lives and characters from the sober records of the historian.

" At the head of the Connecticut delegation stood his honor, Chauncey Goodrich,* whose blanched locks and noble features had long been conspicuous in the halls of national legislation; a gentleman whose character is identified with truth and honor in all parts of the Union; a gentleman of whom Albert Gallatin was wont to say, that when he endeavored to meet the arguments of his opponents, he was accustomed to select those of Mr. Goodrich, as containing the entire strength of all that could be said upon that side—feeling that if he could answer him, he could maintain his cause; a man whom Jefferson—no mean judge of intellectual strength—used playfully to say, ' That white-headed senator from Connecticut is by far the most powerful opponent I have, to my administration.'

" Next to him was James Hillhouse,† the great financier of the

---

* For a sketch of the life of Chauncey Goodrich, see page 526, vol. i. of this work.

† James Hillhouse was one of the most remarkable men of his time. He was born in 1754, entered upon the practice of the law, engaged in the Revolutionary war, became a member of Congress, and was sixteen years a senator. He possessed an iron frame, and his industry and devotion to his duties knew no bounds. He usually slept but four or five hours in twenty-four. His personal appearance was remarkable. He was over six feet high, of a large bony frame: his complexion was swarthy, and his eye black and keen. He was thought to have something

State, who found our School Fund in darkness, and left it in light; the scholar and the father, who superintended the early culture of that poet-boy, and laid the foundation of that bright and glorious intellect, which in the bowers of 'Sachem's Wood' saw, as in a vision, the magnificent scenes of Hadad, and received as guests in western groves, the spirits of oriental oracle and song; Hillhouse—the man of taste, who planted the New Haven elms; the native American, with Irish blood in his veins —the man who, like Washington, never told a lie.

"John Treadwell* was the third delegate, whose life was filled

---

of the Indian in his physiognomy and his walk, and he humorously favored this idea. He was once challenged by a Southerner, for something uttered in debate, in the Senate. He accepted the challenge, but added, that as the choice of weapons fell to him, he selected tomahawks! He was full of wit, and it is said that one day, as he was standing on the steps of the Capitol with Randolph, a drove of asses chanced to be going by—these animals being then raised in Connecticut for the South. "There are some of your constituents!" said Randolph. "Yes," said Hillhouse; "they are going to be schoolmasters in Virginia!" This story is sometimes told of Uriah Tracey, to whom, perhaps, it really belongs.

Hillhouse always scoffed at the abuse heaped upon the Hartford Convention. Several years after the meeting of this body, he had some business at Boston, which required several advertisements in a newspaper. These he had inserted in the Patriot—a democratic paper, which had been furious against the Convention. When he went to pay the bill, he desired to see the editor. Being introduced to him, he said—"Sir, my name is Hillhouse, and I was a member of the Hartford Convention. You inserted the names of the members for several years, and promised to keep them in eternal remembrance. I am very proud of having been a member of that body, and feel that I owe you a debt of gratitude. So I have selected your paper as the object of my patronage. I owe you sixteen dollars and sixty-seven cents, and there, sir, is the money. I have to remark, however, that for several years you have neglected your promise to keep us before the world." This led to a hearty laugh, and the two gentlemen parted. The history of Connecticut is full of this man's good works. He died in 1832.

* John Treadwell, of Farmington, was born in 1745, and died in 1823. He studied law, and afterward was employed for thirty years in public stations, rising finally to the office of Governor of the State. He was a man of learning, and received the title of LL.D. from Yale College. He was distinguished as a consistent professor of religion, and a firm supporter of its interests. He was the first President of the American For-

with honors and usefulness." He was then on the verge of threescore and ten, and the oldest man in the Convention.

"The fourth was Chief-justice Swift,* the first commentator upon the laws of our little republic, of whom no lawyer in the United States would dare to feign ignorance, lest he should put at risk his professional reputation.

"Nathaniel Smith† was the fifth, whom the God of nature chartered to be great by the divine prerogative of genius; a jurist wiser than the books; whose words were so loaded with convincing reasons that they struck an adversary to the earth like blows dealt by a hand gauntleted in steel; to listen to whom, when he spoke in the Convention, Harrison Gray Otis turned back as he was leaving the chamber, and stood gazing in silent admiration, unconscious of the flight of time.

"The sixth was Calvin Goddard,‡ who long enjoyed the repu-

---

eign Missionary Society, and for thirty years was deacon of the church —thus mingling the humble with the higher offices of life, and discharging the duties of each with the most exemplary fidelity. In person, he was short and bulbous about the waist, with a certain air of importance in his face and carriage. Some little weaknesses can be forgiven in one whose life is so full of honors.

* Zephaniah Swift was born in 1759; having been a member of Congress, he accompanied Oliver Ellsworth, ambassador to France in 1798, as his secretary. In 1801 he was appointed judge of the Superior Court, and was chief-justice from 1806 to 1819. He was a large man, of strong manly features; in conversation he spoke rapidly, without grace of manner or expression, but with force and perspicuity. His mind was eminently fitted for juridical duties. He died while on a visit to Ohio in 1823.

† For a sketch of the life and character of Nathaniel Smith, see page 308, vol. i. of this work.

‡ Calvin Goddard was born 1768, and died 1842. He filled various public offices, and was mayor of Norwich for seventeen years. It is difficult to say which predominated, his learning, his wit, or his amenity. I chanced to be with him and Gen. Terry in the stage-coach from New Haven to New York, when, in January, 1815, they were proceeding to Washington, to carry the proceedings of the Convention. Gen. Terry slept nearly all the way, nor could Mr. Goddard's ceaseless wit arouse him. When they got to Washington, the news of peace had just arrived, and their "occupation was gone." They experienced some gibes, but it is said that Goddard paid back with compound interest. No man was more competent.

tation of being the most learned and successful lawyer east of the Connecticut river: an upright judge, a wise counselor, an honest man.

"Last, but not least of the Connecticut delegation, was Roger Minot Sherman,* a profound metaphysician, a scholar equal to the younger Adams, one of the principal oracles of the New York city bar for the last twenty years of his life, who seemed more fitly than any other man to represent the lawgiver, Roger Ludlow, and to inhabit the town which he had planted, whose level acres he had sown with the quick seeds of civil liberty, and then left the up-springing crop to be harvested by the sickle of his successor."

This is the verdict—not of the apologist, not of the partisan—but of the historian, in a sober review of the past, with all the light which time has thrown

---

* Roger Minot Sherman, nephew of the celebrated Roger Sherman, was a native of Woburn, Mass., and born in 1773. He established himself as a lawyer at Fairfield, Conn., and rose to the first rank of his profession. He was distinguished for acute logical powers, and great elegance of diction—words and sentences seeming to flow from his lips as if he were reading from the Spectator. He was a man of refined personal appearance and manners; tall, and stooping a little in his walk; deliberate in his movements and speech, indicating circumspection, which was one of his characteristics. His countenance was pale and thoughtful, his eye remarkable for a keen, penetrating expression. Though a man of grave general aspect, he was not destitute of humor. He was once traveling in Western Virginia, and stopping at a small tavern, was beset with questions by the landlord, as to where he came from, whither he was going, &c. At last said Mr. Sherman—"Sit down, sir, and I will tell you all about it." The landlord sat down. "Sir," said he, "I am from the Blue Light State of Connecticut!" The landlord stared. "I am deacon in a Calvinistic church." The landlord was evidently shocked. "I was a member of the Hartford Convention!" This was too much for the democratic nerves of the landlord; he speedily departed, and left his lodger to himself. Mr. Sherman filled various offices, and in 1840, became judge of the Superior Court. To a mind at once brilliant and profound, he added the embellishments of literature and science and the graces of Christianity. He died Dec. 30, 1844.

upon the lives of those whom he thus characterizes.*

And now, my dear C . . . ., let me ask you to look
at the Hartford Convention, through these Connecticut delegates—all grave and reverend seigniors—
one of them sixty-nine years of age, and having been
governor of the State; one of them, at the time,
chief-justice of the State; another a judge of the Superior Court; two of them grown gray in the Senate
of the United States: all past fifty, all distinguished
for prudence, caution, sobriety; all of the Washington
school in politics, morals, manners, religion.   Look at
these men, and then tell me if there was treason, conspiracy, dismemberment of the Union, either in their
hearts, or the hearts of the people who elected them?
If there be any thing holy in truth, any thing sacred
in justice, degrade not the one, desecrate not the
other, by calling these men traitors!   Say rather
that their presence in the Hartford Convention is
proof—clear, conclusive, undeniable, in the utter
absence of all evidence to the contrary—that it was
an assembly of patriots, chosen by a patriotic people,
wisely seeking the best good of the country.   If this
be not so, then there is no value in a good name, no
ground for faith in human virtue.   Treason is the
highest crime against society: is there not something
shocking to the universal sense of decency in char-

---

* Hollister's History of Connecticut, vol. ii. p. 303.

ging this upon men thus signalized for their virtues? Such perverse logic would make Judas a saint, and the eleven true disciples, betrayers.

But I must leave discussion, and proceed with my narrative. As the Convention sat with closed doors, the world without, despite their eager curiosity, were kept in general ignorance as to their proceedings. There was a rumor, however, that Mr. Otis opened the debate, and was followed, first by Chauncey Goodrich and then by Nathaniel Smith—the latter making one of those masterly speeches for which he was renowned, and which shook even this assembly of great men with emotions of surprise and admiration. The first day's debate was said to have brought all minds to a general agreement as to the course to be adopted —that of mild and healing measures, calculated to appease the irritated minds of their constituents, to admonish the national government of the general feeling of danger and grievance, and thus to save the country from an example either of popular outbreak or organized resistance to the laws. Subsequent events showed that these rumors were well founded.

While such was the course of things in the Convention, some curious scenes transpired without and around it. I cannot do better, in order to give you an idea of these, than to transcribe part of a letter, which I recently received from a friend in Hartford, to whom I had written for some details, to refresh and confirm my own recollections. This was hastily written, and with no idea of its publication; but it is, nevertheless, graphic, and coming from an old democrat, will be received as good authority for the facts it presents, even by the contemners of the Convention and its federal supporters.

"Previous to the war, Captain Morgan recruited in Hartford a company of light dragoons. Elijah Boardman was his lieutenant, and Owen Ranson—afterward Major Ranson—was cornet. When war was declared, and an army was to be raised, the first thing was to appoint officers, and the *respectables*—that is, the federalists—being to a man opposed to the war, none of them applied for commissions; so that the administration was compelled—nothing loth—to officer the army from the democrats. Having a great number of appointments to make, and little time to examine the qualifications of the applicants, and, as I have remarked, having only the democrats to select from, many men received commissions who were hardly qualified to carry a musket in the ranks. Among the appointments was a general of brigade in the Vermont militia—Jonas Cutting, a boatman on the Connecticut river—who obtained his appointment of colonel through the influence of J. and E. L . . . ., good democrats, for whom he boated. He was ordered to Hartford on recruiting service, where he established the head-quarters of the 25th regiment. He was a rude, boorish, uncouth man, and received but little attention from the citizens generally, and none from the respectables—the federalists: he was, however, successful in raising recruits. After a time he was sent to the lines, and was succeeded by Lieutenant-colonel Jos. L. Smith, of Berlin—a large, handsome man, of some talents, but a good deal of a fire-eater. He assumed the command at Hartford, but was not kindly received by the federalists. There was in fact no love lost between him and them.

"This brings us near the time of the Hartford **Convention,** the winter of 1814, preparatory to another campaign on the frontier. A very considerable force of regular troops were in cantonment in Hartford. The federalists, who were a large majority, as you know, hated the democrats, denounced the war, and detested the troops generally, and Lieutenant-colonel Smith in particular—for he thought it a part of his duty to make himself as odious to them as possible. His recruiting parties were constantly parading the city, and monopolizing the sidewalks, in all the pomp and circumstance of glorious war. With gun, drum, trumpet, blunderbuss, and thunder, they crowded the ladies into the gutters, frightened horses, and annoyed the citizens. Some of them called on Colonel Smith, as the commanding officer, and begged of him, as a gentleman, to keep his recruiting parties from Main-street—our principal avenue. I need not say that by this time an intensely bitter feeling had grown up between the two political parties, and the democrats were overjoyed that Colonel S. took pains to show his hatred and contempt for the anti-war party, and so they encouraged him to persevere, and do his duty by flouting the feds, and in raising recruits for the glorious war. So the more the citizens requested him to desist, the more he would not.

"In this state of things, the city council assembled, and passed and published an ordinance that no military parties should be permitted to march on the sidewalks, but should confine themselves to the streets. The democrats and Col. S. scouted the idea that the council had the power to regulate the march of United States troops, and so the troops persisted in this annoyance. The Governor's Foot Guard, one hundred muskets strong, composed of our most respectable young men, and all federalists, commanded by Nathaniel Terry, Esq., now prepared a quantity of ball cartridges, which, with their arms, were deposited in the old Hartford Bank. The men were required to be always ready to act when necessary. The government recruits not heeding the ordinance, Capt. Boardman and some other officers and non-commissioned officers were arrested and imprisoned.

The United States troops, reinforced by all the out parties in the neighboring towns, now came into the city, and completely monopolized the streets by night and by day.

" The Superior Court was in session at this time, and each day during the session, the military bands, with divers supernumerary bass-drums, incessantly marched around the Courthouse with so much din that the court was obliged to adjourn.   This was repeated daily, and matters had arrived at a terrible pass, when the administration at Washington saw the necessity of interfering.   It was obvious that the difficulty arose chiefly from the impertinence and vulgarity of the army officers ; so they ordered Colonel Jessup to come to Hartford and assume the command, and packed off Smith to the lines or somewhere else.

" Colonel Jesup on his arrival called at once on Chauncey Goodrich, the mayor, and begged him to let him know how matters stood.   Jesup was a man of sense and a gentleman, and all difficulties speedily vanished.   The troops were kept in their cantonments, a certain distance out of town ; and only a few at a time, of the most orderly, were permitted to come into the city, and without military parade.   Colonel Jesup was received into society, and caressed by the better class of citizens, and became a great favorite.   He was dined and tea'd to his heart's content by the federalists, after which the democracy rather cut him.   So ended this little war.

" The celebrated Hartford Convention assembled here about this time, and Mr. Thomas Bull, a large, portly, courtly old gentleman, was the doorkeeper and messenger.   As it was proper that this dignified body should have all things done decently and in order, Mr. Bull was directed to call on the reverend clergy, in turn, to pray with the Convention.   Dr. Strong made the first prayer, and Dr. Perkins and other eminent clergymen followed.   The Rev. Philander Chase*—afterward Bishop Chase

---

* Philander Chase was a native of Vermont, born 1775, and died 1852. He was a man of imposing personal appearance and manners.   He became bishop of Ohio in 1819, and afterward was elected bishop of Illinois.

—was at this time rector of Christ Church—a high Church-
man, who probably never in all his ministry offered an extem-
poraneous prayer. He was, in his turn, called on by Mr. Bull,
who in his blandest manner informed him of the honor conferred
on him, and begged his attendance to pray at the opening of the
morning session. What must have been his horror, when Mr.
Chase declined, saying that he knew of no form of prayer for
rebellion! Mr. Chase himself related this anecdote to me soon
after. Major J. M. Goodwin was present and heard it. Nevertheless, I believe this speech was hardly original: some of the
tory Episcopal clergymen had said the same thing during the
Revolution. They had forms of prayer for the king, but none
for liberty.

"No annoyance was offered to the Convention. A body of
United States troops, under command of Jemmy Lamb, a facetious old Irishman, and the town-crier, in a fantastic military
dress, marched around the State-house, while they were in session—the music playing the 'Rogues' March.' The Convention,
however, excited less attention in Hartford than in other places.
' 'Tis distance lends enchantment,' &c. Very little more notice
was taken of their proceedings by the people here—exclusive of
violent partisans—than of those of the Superior Court."

This sketch gives a clear insight into the state of
popular feeling at this period, in Hartford, which has
been the theme of much discussion and gross mis-
representation. It is obvious that, had there been
no other reason for it, the danger of intrusion and
interruption from the irritated United States recruits,
led by incendiary officers and encouraged by reckless
mischief-makers, rendered it a matter of prudence for
the Convention to sit with closed doors. The State
court had been braved and insulted, and the far more

obnoxious Convention would doubtless have experienced still more emphatic demonstrations of rudeness. Had the sessions been open, a guard of a hundred men would scarcely have protected them from interruption, perhaps violence.

It is creditable to all parties that Col. Jesup was sent thither : it showed a disposition on the part of the administration to afford no ground of offense; it proved that the citizens—the federalists—sought no quarrel, and would interpose no difficulties to the government troops or their officers in the lawful discharge of their duties. It showed, moreover, that they could appreciate gentlemanly qualities, and were ready to bestow honor on a gallant soldier who had fought and bled in battle for the country, even although they disapproved of the war.

As to Colonel Jesup*—Brigadier-general Jesup now—I must say a few words. At the time I speak of, he was some thirty years old. He had recently come from the northern frontier, where he had won laurels by the side of Scott, Miller, Brown, Ripley, and other gallant soldiers. He was of modest demeanor, pleasing address, and gentlemanly tastes : it was no disparagement to his agreeable appearance that he

---

* Thomas S. Jesup was a native of Virginia, and holding the rank of Major, distinguished himself at Chippewa, Niagara, &c., during the campaign of 1814. While he was at Hartford, in the winter of 1814–15, there was a public ball, in which I was one of the managers. I recollect that he was present, and was dressed in blue undress military coat with epaulettes, white small-clothes, and white silk-stockings, and was quite a favorite with the ladies—a proper homage to the brave.

had his arm in a sling—a touching testimonial of his merits brought from the field of battle. He was the complete antipode of the J. L. Smiths and Joseph Cuttings who had preceded him, and who thought it a part of their democratic duty to be conspicuously vulgar. He did not seek to promote democracy by rendering it disgusting to all who held opposite opinions. He mingled in amicable intercourse with the citizens; sought interviews with the leading inhabitants—with the mayor of the city, and the governor of the state when he chanced to be on a visit there. I know he took counsel with my uncle and became acquainted with members of the Convention, and thus found means not only to smooth away the difficulties which had been engendered by his rude and reckless predecessors in the military command of that station, but gained correct information as to the actual state of things.

It was perfectly well understood, at this time, that he was not only a military officer, but that he was the diplomatic agent of the government at Washington, and communicated his observations to the Executive. He was not, for this reason, either shunned or depreciated. It is evident, from his letters sent almost daily to Madison—and the substance of which has transpired, at least in part—that the real intentions of the Convention were penetrated by him almost from the beginning. It is evident that he never found the lightest proof of treasonable intentions on the part

of that assembly.* It has been reported that he in-
tends publishing his personal memoirs, and that in
these he will give some interesting revelations respecting the Convention: I trust he will fulfill his
design, and I am equally confident that his report
will be in unison with the views I have here presented. As a matter of principle—regarding it from
his point of view—he will doubtless condemn that

---

* Mr. Ingersoll, in his history of the " Late War," professes to report
the substance of Jesup's letters to the President: in one of these he
says, among other things, that after an interview which he had with
Gov. Tompkins, of New York, on his way to Hartford, he thinks the
" Convention will complain, remonstrate, and probably address the people, but that its proceedings will neither result in an attempt to sunder
the Union, nor in a determination to resist by force the measures of the
general government."

This is sensible. Thus Col. Jesup, even before he reached Hartford,
had discovered the actual state of things in New England. I can testify
that, living in the very midst of the members of the Convention, I never
heard such a thing as disunion advocated, or even suggested, as probable or possible. In confirmation of this, Mr. Ingersoll adds:

" *Colonel Jesup soon ascertained that the Connecticut members of the
Convention were opposed to disunion, to disorder; that every throb of the
people's heart was American,*" &c., &c. Surely no sensible man needed
a ghost to tell him that; and yet, strange to say, there are persons who
still believe that the Convention, pushed on by the people of New England, were a band of traitors, at least in their hearts!

Mr. Ingersoll states that one member of the Convention—Chauncey
Goodrich—listened favorably to Jesup's counterplot, which was, that
New England should put her shoulder to the war, capture Halifax and the
adjacent territories, and these, with Canada, should be annexed to New
England! That the ardent young lieutenant-colonel should have made
such a suggestion, is very possible, but those who knew the parties, will
smile at the idea that a scheme so utterly preposterous—so hopeless
in the actual state of the country, so opposed to public sentiment, so
certain to protract and aggravate the war—should have been entertained
for a moment by the far-sighted person to whom it was proposed. If
such a plot was ever seriously suggested, it was no doubt respectfully
listened to as a matter of courtesy, but in no other sense could it have
been received.

assembly, but as to matters of fact, I am certain he will never furnish the slightest support to the charge of treason, either secret or open.

But I must draw this long letter to a close. The result of the Hartford Convention is well known. After a session of three weeks, it terminated its labors, and, in perfect conformity with public expectation and public sentiment at the North, it issued an address, full of loyalty to the Constitution, recommending patience to the people, and while admitting their grievances, still only suggesting peaceable and constitutional remedies. The authors of this document knew well the community for which it was intended: their purpose was to allay anxiety, to appease irritation, to draw off in harmless channels the lightning of public indignation. They therefore pointed out modes of relief, in the direction of peace, and not in the direction of civil war. They were federalists, as were the people who supported them; they belonged to that party who founded the Constitution, in opposition to the democracy.* Leaving it for democracy, which opposed the Constitution in its cradle, to fur-

---

* The sincere seeker for truth should read the history of the parties of this period, in connection with their previous annals. " It is a remarkable fact," says Noah Webster, in his history of political parties in the United States, "that the democratic party, with few or no exceptions, opposed the ratification of the Constitution ; and beyond a question, had that opposition succeeded, anarchy or civil war would have been the consequence. The federalists made the form of government, and with immense efforts procured it to be ratified, in opposition to nearly one-half of the citizens of the United States, headed by some of the ablest men in the Union."

nish the first examples of Nullification, Disunion, Secession—with a discretion and a patriotism which does them infinite credit—they found the means of removing the cloud from the minds of their constituents, and yet without in any degree shaking the pillars of the Union, which was their ark of the covenant of national honor and glory and prosperity.

It is said Mr. Madison laughed when he heard the result: it is very likely, for he had really feared that the Convention meditated treason; he perhaps felt a little uneasy in his conscience, from a conviction that his administration had afforded serious grounds for discontent. He, as well as those who shared his views, were no doubt relieved, when they found the cloud had passed. Some of the democratic editors satisfied themselves with squibs, and some found relief in railing. Those especially who had insisted that the Convention was a band of traitors, seemed to feel personally affronted that it did not fulfill their evil prophecies. There is perhaps no greater offense to a partisan who has predicted evil of his adversary, than for the latter to do what is right, and thus turn the railer into ridicule. At all events, so bitter was the disappointment of the fanatical portion of the democrats, on the occasion in question, that they sought relief in declaring that if the Convention did not act treason, they at least felt it! Perhaps in consideration of their disappointment, we may pass over this obliquity as one of those frailties of human nature, which time teaches us to forget and forgive.

As to the general effect of the course adopted by the Convention, no reasonable man can deny that it was eminently salutary. It immediately appeased the irritation and anxiety of the public mind in New England; it taught the people the propriety of calm and prudent measures in times of difficulty and danger; and more than all, it set an example worthy of being followed for all future time, by holding the Constitution of the United States as sacred, and by recommending the people to seek remedies for their grievances by legal and not by revolutionary means. "Blessed are the peacemakers, for they shall see God." I know of no similar benediction upon the promoters of civil war.

And now I have done. The treaty of Ghent speedily came to smooth the ruffled waters. Monroe succeeded to Madison, and an era of good feeling seemed to dawn upon the country. It is true the promised millennium was not fully realized: the dying flurries of the old federal party, under the harpooning of triumphant democracy, caused some froth upon the sea of politics. Connecticut passed through the spasms of Toleration, in which that hard old federalist, Oliver Wolcott, became the candidate of democracy, and overturned the Charter of Charles II., and with it all his early political associations—public and personal. It was a strange dance, and with a curious arrangement of partners. Similar movements took place in other parts of the country—the result of which was, a new crystallization of parties, in which the terms federalist and democrat lost their original signification. I have before adverted to this fact, and have stated that—in application to present parties—they are little more than names to discriminate between conservatives and radicals.

I have thus deemed it due to truth, in giving my recollections of the war, to give them frankly and fearlessly. Believing the old federalists — especially those of Connecticut, for with them my acquaintance was personal—to have been honest and patriotic, as I knew them to be virtuous and wise, so I have said, and given my reasons for the faith that is in me. While doing them this justice, I do not affirm that in all things their measures were right. I contend, however, that they were true men, and, on the whole, have left memories behind them which every dictate of virtue and patriotism teaches us to cherish. By the side of their opponents—and the very best of them—they may claim at least equal respect. As time advances and the mists of party are cleared from the horizon, I doubt not their images will be seen and recognized by all, as rising higher and higher among the nobler monuments of our history. One truth will stand—they were of those who reared the glorious fabric of the Union, and under all circumstances taught the people to regard it as sacred. Before any man presumes to call them traitors, let him see that his own hands are equally pure, his own spirit equally exalted.

LETTER XXXII.

The Count Value—Lessons in French, and a Translation of René—Severe Retribution for Imprudence—The End of the Pocket-book Factory—Napoleon returns to Paris and upsets my Affairs—Divers Experiences and Reflections upon Dancing—Visit to New York—Oliver Wolcott and Archibald Gracie—Ballston and Saratoga—Dr. Payson and the three Rowdies—Illness and Death of my Uncle—Partnership with George Sheldon—His Illness and Death.

MY DEAR C******

I must now go back and take up a few dropped stitches in my narrative. I have told you that my apprenticeship terminated in the summer of 1814. Previous to that time, I had made some advances in the study of the French language under M. Value, or, to give him his title, the Count Value. This person had spent his early life in Paris, but he afterward migrated to St. Domingo, where he owned a large estate. In the insurrection of 1794, he escaped only with his life. With admirable cheerfulness and serenity, he devoted himself to teaching French and dancing, as means of support. He settled for a time at New Haven, where, at the age of seventy, he was captivated and captured by a tall, red-haired schoolmistress of twenty. She accounted to me, for her success, by stating that, at the time, she was called the "Rose of Sharon"—she being a native of a town in Litchfield county bearing the latter name.

The Count finally established himself at Hartford, and I became one of his pupils. I pursued my studies with considerable assiduity, and to practice myself in French, I translated Chateaubriand's René. One of my friends had just established a newspaper at Middletown, and my translation was published there. About this time my health was feeble, and my eyes became seriously affected in consequence of my night studies. Unaware of the danger, I persevered, and thus laid the foundation of a nervous weakness and irritability of my eyes, which has since been to me a rock ahead in the whole voyage of life. From that time, I have never been able to read or write, but with pain. As if by a kind of fatality, I seemed to be afterward drawn into a literary career, for which I was doubly disqualified—first, by an imperfect education, and next, by defective eyesight. Oh! what penalties have I paid for thus persisting in a course which seems to have been forbidden to me by Providence. After a long and laborious life, I feel a profound consciousness that I have done nothing well; at the same time, days, months, nay years, have I struggled with the constant apprehension that I should terminate my career in blindness! How little do we know, especially in the outset of our existence, what is before us! It is indeed well that we

do not know, for the prospect would often overwhelm us.

In the autumn of 1814, as already stated, I established, in company with a friend, a pocket-book factory at Hartford ; but the peace put a speedy termination to that enterprise. We got out of it with a small
loss, and my kind-hearted partner pocketed this, "for
he had money, and I had none." He forgave me,
and would have done the same, had the defalcation
been more considerable—for he was a true friend.

Early in the following spring, I made an arrangement to go to Paris as a clerk in a branch of the im-
porting house of Richards, Taylor & Wilder, of New
York. About a month after, the news came that Bonaparte had suddenly returned from Elba, and as business was prostrated by that event, my engagement
failed. For nearly a year, my health continued indifferent, and my eyes in such a state that I was incapable of
undertaking any serious business. I spent my time
partly at Berlin,* with my parents, and partly at Hart-

---

* I have already said that my father, having asked a dismission from
his parochial charge at Ridgefield, was settled—1811—in Berlin, eleven
miles south of Hartford. It is a pleasant village, situated on a slight
elevation, rising from a fertile valley, bounded on the south by a range
of mountains. The town embraces three parishes, which, thirty years
ago, were the principal seat of the tin manufacture, from which the
whole country was long supplied by peddlers. The arts of these became proverbial ; not confining themselves to the sale of tin-ware, they
occasionally peddled other articles. In the Southern States, it is pretended, they palmed off upon the people " wooden nutmegs," " oak-leaf
cigars," &c.

Berlin was the birthplace of Isaac Riley—a noted bookseller of New
York—forty years ago. He was a man of fine personal address and

ford. I read a little, and practiced my French with
Value and his scholars. I also felt the need of disci-
plining my hands and feet, which about these days
seemed to me to have acquired a most absurd development—giving me an awful feeling of embarrassment
when I entered into company. I therefore took lessons in dancing, and whether I profited by it or not,
as to manners, I am persuaded that this portion of
my education was highly beneficial to me in other
points of view.

As many good people have a prejudice against
dancing, I am disposed to write down my experience
on the subject. In the winter, our good old teacher
had weekly cotillion parties, for the purpose of practi-
cing his scholars. The young men invited the young
ladies, and took them to these gatherings, and after
the exercises, conducted them home again. I know
this will sound strange to those who only understand
metropolitan manners at the present day ; but let
me tell you that I never knew an instance, in my
own experience or observation, in which the strictest
propriety was departed from. These parties took

---

striking intellectual activity, but was marked with great vicissitudes of
fortune. One of the Berlin peddlers, by the name of B...., chanced
to be at one of Riley's book-auction sales, when he bid off a thousand
copies of a cheap edition of Young's Night Thoughts. These he peddled in the South and West as *bad books*, getting five dollars apiece for
them ! When remonstrated with for imposition, he insisted that it was
a good moral and religious operation !

At the present day, New Britain, one of the parishes of Berlin, is
noted for extensive brass and iron foundries, and various other manufactures.

place in the evening: they began at eight o'clock, and continued till ten or eleven—sometimes till twelve. The company consisted entirely of young persons— from fifteen to twenty years of age: they included the children of the respectable inhabitants, with a number of young ladies from the boarding-schools. Some of these I have since seen the wives of bishops, senators, and governors of States—filling indeed the first stations to which the sex can aspire in this country.

I have had enough experience of the world to know that such things could not be in the great cities of Europe or America—perhaps nowhere out of New England. The division of society into castes in monarchical countries, no doubt involves the necessity of keeping young ladies jealously aloof from companionship with the other sex, because they might entangle themselves in engagements which would defeat the system of building up families and estates by politic marriages. In this state of society, it might be found dangerous for young persons of opposite sexes to be left even casually together, for a spirit of intrigue is always indigenous under a system of restraint and espionage. But however this may be, I am satisfied that these Hartford parties, under the auspices of our amiable and respectable old teacher, were every way refining and elevating: not only did they impart ease of manner, but, as I think, purity of sentiment. The earlier emotions of youth are delicate, modest, conservative ; and if acquaintance with life be made at this period, these stamp their refinements upon the feelings, and form a safe, conservative basis of future habits of thought and conduct. I do not mean to favor latitudinarianism of manners ; I do not, indeed, say that this system can be adopted in large cities, but I believe that dancing parties, consisting of young persons of both sexes, under proper guidance—as, for instance, under the eye of parents, either in a public hall, or by the domestic fireside— have a refining influence, beneficial alike to manners and morals. I believe that even public assemblies for dancing, regulated by the presence of good people, are eminently useful.

I have been in Catholic countries, where the system is to keep girls in cloisters, or schools resembling them, till they are taken out by their parents or guardians to be married ; and it is precisely in these countries, where education is the most jealous, and discipline the most rigorous, that intrigue is the great game of life—especially with the upper classes—of both sexes. I have seen society where Puritan ideas prevailed, and where religious people held dancing to be a device of the devil; and here I have often found that practices, secret or open, quite as exceptionable as dancing, were current in society. If in the earlier ages of our New England history, a hard, self-denying system was profitable, it is not so in the present state of society. We are created with social feelings, which demand indulgence. No system of religion, no code or contrivance of state policy, has been able to get over this fact. We can not kill the voice of God and nature in the soul : we can only regulate it, and by using common sense and the lights of religion, give it a safe and beneficent development. Is it not time for society to cast off prejudice, and to be governed by truth and experience? It must be remembered that what is condemned by the good and wise, often thereby becomes evil, though in itself it may be beneficial. Has not this wrong been done among us? It seems to me that good people, pious people, may at least inquire whether it may not be well for them to take under their patronage, that branch of education which proposes at once to perfect the manners and refine the sentiments of youth. It is not to dictate, but to aid in this inquiry, that I give you with some minuteness my observations on this subject; hence I offer you my testimony to the fact that in the course of three winters, during which I attended these cotillion parties at Hartford, I never saw or heard of an instance of impropriety in word or deed.

Let me further suggest that there is a principle here which it is important to recognize and appreciate. These young people were brought together at a period when their emotions were still sheltered in the folds of that sensitive and shrinking modesty, designed to protect them at the period of their first adventure into mixed society. This modesty is to the heart of youth, like the envelope in which nature enshrines the choicest products of the vegetable kingdom, till they are ripened and prepared for the harvest. This shrinking delicacy of feeling is conservative; to this, license is offensive, and if suggested, is repelled. If young people associate together at this period—under the restraints which necessarily exist in an assembly such as I am contemplating—habits of delicacy, in thought and manner, are likely to be established. A person who has been thus trained, seems to me armed, in some degree at least, against those coarse seductions which degrade, and at last destroy, so many young persons of both sexes. To young men, an early familiarity with the refined portion of the gentler sex, placing them at ease in their society and making this a sort of necessity to them, I conceive to be one of the greatest safeguards to their morals and manners in after life. And as a preparation for this— as an introduction, an inducement to this—I conceive that the art of dancing, practiced by young people of both sexes, together, is to be commended.

I am aware that I am treading upon delicate ground. You may share the idea entertained by many good, pious people, that dancing is always degrading and vicious in its tendencies. This, however, I think, arises from considering it in its abuses. I am not contending for juvenile balls, as a pursuit fit to absorb the whole thought and attention. Remember,

I am speaking of dancing as a part of education—to
be conducted with propriety—in order to train young
people of both sexes to habits of easy and delicate
intercourse.   As to the practice of dancing, afterward, this must be regulated by the judgment of
parents.   One custom may be proper in one place,
and not in another.   In this country, our habits are
different from those of others: in Asia, where woman
is designed for the harem, and in Europe, where she
is trained to be the make-weight of a bargain, jealousy becomes the sentinel of society; in the United
States, woman is comparatively free, and here confidence must be the guardian of society.   I am inclined
to think, in this respect, our system has the advantage, provided it be not abused by license on the one
hand, nor bigotry on the other.

In respect to the case I am describing in my early
experience, in which the young gentlemen conducted
the young ladies to and from the dancing hall—the
confidence of parents, thus reposed in their children,
fortified and recommended by the purer suggestions
of the heart—appealed to motives of honor, and was
usually responded to by scrupulous rectitude of demeanor.   If you doubt the justice of this philosophy,
I ask your attention to the fact that, at this day—
forty years subsequent to the period to which I refer
—in this very city of Hartford, with a population of
twenty thousand people, women, young and old, of
all classes, walk the streets till midnight, with as

much sense of security and propriety, as at noonday! Where will you find higher evidence of a refined state of society than this?

In the spring of 1815 I paid a visit to New York, and having letters of introduction to Oliver Wolcott and Archibald Gracie, I called on these gentlemen. Mr. Wolcott lived in Pine-street, nearly opposite where the custom-house is now, and at a short distance was John Wells, an eminent lawyer of that day. But a considerable number of the higher aristocracy was gathered toward the lower part of the city, the Battery being pretty nearly the focus of fashion. Streets now desecrated by the odor of tar and turpentine, were then filled with the flush and the fair. Nath'l Prime lived at No. 1 Broadway; Mr. Gracie in the Octagon House, corner of Bridge and State streets. Near by was his son-in-law, Charles King, now president of Columbia College, and his son, Wm. Gracie, who had married the second daughter of Oliver Wolcott. In this quarter, also, were Wm. Bayard, Gen. Morton, Matthew Clarkson, J. B. Coles, Moses Rogers, &c., all eminent citizens.

My lodgings were at the City Hotel, situated on the western side of Broadway, between Thames and Cedar streets—the space being now occupied by warehouses. It was then the Astor House of New York, being kept by a model landlord, whose name was Jennings, with a model barkeeper by the name of Willard. The latter was said never to sleep—night or day—for at all hours he was at his post, and never forgot a customer, even after an absence of twenty years.

It was late in the spring, and Mr. Gracie called for me and took me to his country-seat, occupying a little promontory on the western side of Hurlgate—a charming spot, now cut up into some thirty city lots. Contiguous to it, toward the city, were the summer residences of J. J. Astor, Nathaniel Prime, and Wm. Rhinelander; on the other side were the seats of Commodore Chauncey, Joshua Jones, and others.

Here I spent a fortnight very agreeably. Mr. Gracie was at this period distinguished alike on account of his wealth, his intelligence, and his amiable and honorable character. Never have I witnessed any thing more charming—more affectionate, dignified, and graceful—than the intercourse of the family with one another. The sons and daughters, most of them happily connected in marriage—as they gathered here —seemed, to my unpracticed imagination, to constitute a sort of dynasty, something like the romance of the middle ages. Not many years after, Mr. Gracie lost his entire fortune by the vicissitudes of commerce, but his character was beyond the reach of accident. He is still remembered with affectionate respect by all those whose memories reach back to the times in which he flourished, and when it might be said, without disparagement to any other man, that he was the first merchant in New York.

I must not omit to mention two other celebrities

whom I saw during this visit to New York. You must recollect I was on my travels, and so, as in duty bound, I sought to see the lions. Of course I went to the court-house, and there I saw two remarkable men—Judge Kent, and Thomas Addis Emmet—the first, chancellor of the State of New York, and the latter one of the most eminent lawyers in the city, perhaps in the United States.

Judge Kent* I had seen before, at my uncle's house. He had been educated at Yale College, was my father's classmate, and formed an early acquaintance with our family, resulting in a friendly intercourse which was maintained throughout his whole life. It would be difficult now to point to a man so universally honored and esteemed. To the most extensive learning, he added a winning simplicity of manners and transparent truthfulness of character. All this was written in his countenance, at once irresistible by its beaming intelligence, and its not less impressive benevolence. The greatness and goodness of his character shone full in his face.

I remember perfectly well the scene, when I saw Emmet† and the judge together. The former was

---

* James Kent was born in Putnam county, N. Y., 1763. He rose to eminence in the profession of the law, and was appointed by John Jay, then governor, judge of the supreme court. He was afterward chief-justice, and, in 1814, chancellor. He died in New York, which had been his residence, in 1847—an ornament to human nature, to the bar, the bench, and the Christian profession.

† Thomas Addis Emmet, a native of Cork, in Ireland, was born in 1764. He was one of the Committee of the Society of United Irishmen,

arguing a case, but there were only half a dozen persons present, and it was rather a conversation than a plea. Emmet was a somewhat short but very athletic man, with large, rosy cheeks, an enormous mouth, and full, expressive eyes. His Irish brogue, rich and sonorous, rolled from his lips like a cataract of music. Kent listened, but frequently changed position, and often broke into the argument with a question, which sometimes resulted in a dialogue. His whole manner was easy, familiar, and very different from the statue-like dignity of other judges I had seen. The whole spectacle left on my mind the impression that two great men were rather consulting together, than that one was attempting to win from the other an opinion to suit an interested client. I recollect to have seen, listening to this discussion, a large, florid, handsome man, with a dark, eloquent eye; I inquired his name, and was told that it was John Wells, the renowned lawyer, already mentioned.

As I thus saw the lions of the town, I also heard the thunderers of the pulpit. On one occasion I listened to a discourse from Dr. J. B. Romeyn*—a tall, thin, eloquent man—I think in Cedar-street. He was celebrated in his day; and, if I understood him cor-

---

and was involved in the unfortunate rebellion of 1798. Mr. Emmet was imprisoned, but was finally set free, and came to the United States. His great learning, his extraordinary talents, his powerful eloquence, soon gave him a place among the first lawyers of the country. He died in 1827.

* John B. Romeyn was settled first at Rhinebeck, then at Schenectady, and finally at New York. He was born in 1769, and died 1825.

rectly, he maintained the doctrine of election in such rigor as to declare that if he knew who the elect were, he would preach only to them, inasmuch as it would be useless to preach to other persons!

In a new church in Murray-street, I heard Dr. Mason,* then regarded as the Boanerges of the city. Instead of a pulpit—which serves as a sort of shelter and defense for the preacher—he had only a little railing along the edge of the platform on which he stood, so as to show his large and handsome person, almost down to his shoe-buckles. He preached without notes, and moved freely about, sometimes speaking in a colloquial manner, and then suddenly pouring out sentence after sentence, glowing with lightning and echoing with thunder. The effect of these outbursts was sometimes very startling. The doctor was not only very imposing in his person, but his voice was of prodigious volume and compass. He was sometimes adventurous in his speech, occasionally passing off a joke, and not unfrequently

---

* John M. Mason, D. D.—son of Dr. John Mason of the Scotch Church —was born in 1770, and died in 1829. He was alike distinguished for his wit, his intellectual powers, and his eloquence. He was the author of several religious works of great ability. I have heard the following anecdote of him : A certain parishioner of his, after the establishment of a Unitarian church in New York, joined it. One day, when the Doctor chanced to meet him, the former said—

"Mr. S . . . ., it is some time since I have seen you at Murray-street."

"I have not been there lately, it is true," was the reply—"and I will tell you the reason. I think you make religion too difficult; I prefer rather to travel on a turnpike, than on a rough and thorny road."

"Yes," said the Doctor; "but you must look out, and see that you don't have a Hell of a toll to pay !"

verging on what might seem profane, but for the solemnity of his manner. When I heard him, in speaking of some recent Unitarian point of faith, he said, "This is damnable doctrine—I say it is damnable doctrine!"—the deep, guttural emphasis giving to the repetition a thrilling effect.

Early in the ensuing summer, my uncle, Chauncey Goodrich, being in bad health, paid a visit to Saratoga* and Ballston for the benefit of the waters, and I accompanied him. We soon returned, however, for

---

* I remember a striking incident which occurred at the hotel in Saratoga where we lodged. One Sunday morning, as the company sat down to breakfast at a long table, a small, dark, and rather insignificant looking minister said grace. As soon as he began, and his voice attracted notice, most of the persons gave respectful attention to his words; but three gay young men took pains to signify their superiority to such a vulgar custom by clashing the knives and forks, calling upon the waiters, and proceeding to their work. After breakfast, a notice was given to the lodgers that a sermon would be preached in the dining-hall at 10 o'clock. At this hour the lodgers generally gathered there, and among them the three young men—these, however, with a decided Gallio air and manner. Indeed, it was pretty evident that they had come to quiz the little parson. The latter soon entered, with a peculiarly noiseless, unostentatious step and demeanor. He sat down and meditated for a few minutes, and then rose to pray. The first tones of his voice were faint, but they grew in strength; and as we took our seats, all began to look with strange interest upon the countenance of that little, dark, unpretending preacher. He read a familiar hymn, but it seemed new and striking; he read a familiar chapter in the Bible, but it had a depth and meaning not realized before. He took his text, and preached such a sermon as seldom falls from the lips of man. Every heart was thrilled, and even the three young men who came to scoff, remained to pray. Never have I seen such alternations of feelings as passed over their countenances—first of ridicule, then of astonishment, then of shame, and at last, of consternation and contrition. "And who is this strange man—so insignificant in appearance, so seemingly inspired in fact?" said the people. It was Edward Payson, afterwards D. D., of Portland, one of the most pious, devoted, and eloquent ministers of his day. He was born at Rindge, in New Hampshire, in 1783, and died in 1827.

it was now apparent that he had a disease of the heart, which was rapidly tending to a fatal result. Experiencing great suffering at intervals, he gradually yielded to the progress of his malady, and at last, on the 18th of August, 1815—while walking the room, and engaged in cheerful conversation—he faltered, sank into a chair, and instantly expired. "His death," says the historian, "was a shock to the whole community. Party distinctions were forgotten, under a sense of the general calamity; and in the simple but expressive language which was used at his funeral, 'all united in a tribute of respect to the man who had so long been dear to us, and done us so much good.'" To me, the loss was irreparable—leaving, however, in my heart a feeling of gratitude that I had witnessed an example of the highest intellectual power united with the greatest moral excellence—and that, too, in one whose relationship to me enforced and commended its teachings to my special observance. Alas, how little have I done in life that is worthy of such inspiration!

Not long after this, my friend George Sheldon having established himself as a bookseller and publisher, he invited me to become his partner—and this I did, early in the year 1816. We pursued the business for nearly two years, during which time we published, among other works, Scott's Family Bible, in five volumes quarto—a considerable enterprise for that period, in a place like Hartford. In the autumn of

1817 I had gone to Berlin, for the purpose of making a short excursion for the benefit of my health, when a messenger came from Hartford, saying that my partner was very ill, and wished me to return. I immediately complied, and on entering the room of my friend, I found him in a high fever, his mind already wandering in painful dreams. As I came to his bedside he said—"Oh, take away these horrid knives; they cut me to the heart!" I stooped over him and said—

"There are no knives here; you are only dreaming."

"Oh, is it you?" said he. "I am glad you have come. Do stay with me, and speak to me, so as to keep off these dreadful fancies."

I did stay by him for four days and nights—but his doom was sealed. His mind continued in a state of wild delirium till a few minutes before his death. I stood gazing at his face, when a sudden change came over him: the agitated and disturbed look of insanity had passed—a quiet pallor had come over his countenance, leaving it calm and peaceful. He opened his eyes, and, as if waking from sleep, looked on me with an aspect of recognition. His lips moved, and he pronounced the name of his wife; she came, with all the feelings of youth and love—aye, and of hope, too, in her heart. She bent over him: he raised his feeble and emaciated arms and clasped her to his heart: he gave her one kiss, and passed to another life!

LETTER XXXIII.

The Famine of 1816 *and* 1817—*Panic in New England*—*Migrations to Ohio*—*T'other Side of Ohio*—*Toleration*—*Downfall of Federalism*—*Oliver Wolcott and the Democracy*—*Connecticut upset*—*The new Constitution*—*Gov. Smith and Gov. Wolcott*—*Litchfield*—*Uriah Tracey*—*Frederick Wolcott*—*Tapping Reeve*—*Col. Talmadge*—*James Gould*—*J. W. Huntington*—*The Litchfield Centennial Celebration.*

MY DEAR C********

I must now ask your attention to several topics having no connection, except unity of time and place : the cold seasons of 1816 and 1817, and the consequent flood of emigration from New England to the West ; the political revolution in Connecticut, which was wrought in the magic name of Toleration, and one or two items of my personal experience.

The summer of 1816 was probably the coldest that has been known here, in this century. In New England—from Connecticut to Maine—there were severe frosts in every month. The crop of Indian corn was almost entirely cut off : of potatoes, hay, oats, &c., there was not probably more than half the usual supply. The means of averting the effects of such a calamity—now afforded by railroads, steam navigation, canals, and other facilities of intercommunication—did not then exist. The following winter was severe, and the ensuing spring backward. At this time I made a journey into New Hampshire, pass-

ing along the Connecticut river, in the region of
Hanover. It was then June, and the hills were almost as barren as in November. I saw a man at Or-
ford, who had been forty miles for a half bushel of
Indian corn, and paid two dollars for it!

Along the seaboard it was not difficult to obtain a
supply of food, save only that every article was dear.
In the interior it was otherwise : the cattle died for
want of fodder, and many of the inhabitants came
near perishing from starvation. The desolating effects of the war still lingered over the country, and at
last a kind of despair seized upon some of the people.
In the pressure of adversity, many persons lost their
judgment, and thousands feared or felt that New
England was destined, henceforth, to become a part
of the frigid zone. At the same time, Ohio—with its
rich soil, its mild climate, its inviting prairies—was
opened fully upon the alarmed and anxious vision.
As was natural under the circumstances, a sort of
stampede took place from cold, desolate, worn-out
New England, to this land of promise.

I remember very well the tide of emigration through
Connecticut, on its way to the West, during the summer of 1817. Some persons went in covered wagons—
frequently a family consisting of father, mother, and
nine small children, with one at the breast—some on
foot and some crowded together under the cover, with
kettles, gridirons, feather-beds, crockery, and the family Bible, Watts' Psalms and Hymns, and Webster's

Spelling-book—the lares and penates of the household. Others started in ox-carts, and trudged on at
the rate of ten miles a day. In several instances I
saw families on foot—the father and boys taking
turns in dragging along an improvised hand-wagon,
loaded with the wreck of the household goods—occasionally giving the mother and baby a ride. Many of
these persons were in a state of poverty, and begged
their way as they went. Some died before they
reached the expected Canaan ; many perished after
their arrival, from fatigue and privation ; and others,
from the fever and ague, which was then certain to
attack the new settlers.

   It was, I think, in 1818, that I published a small
tract, entitled "T'other side of Ohio"—that is, the
other view, in contrast to the popular notion that it
was the paradise of the world. It was written by
Dr. Hand—a talented young physician of Berlin—
who had made a visit to the West about these days.
It consisted mainly of vivid but painful pictures of
the accidents and incidents attending this wholesale
migration. The roads over the Alleghanies, between
Philadelphia and Pittsburg, were then rude, steep,
and dangerous, and some of the more precipitous
slopes were consequently strewn with the carcases
of wagons, carts, horses, oxen, which had made shipwreck in their perilous descents. The scenes on
the road—of families gathered at night in miserable
sheds, called taverns—mothers frying, children cry-

EMIGRATION IN 1817.   Vol. 2, p. 80.

ing, fathers swearing—were a mingled comedy and tragedy of errors. Even when they arrived in their new homes—along the banks of the Muskingum or the Scioto—frequently the whole family—father, mother, children—speedily exchanged the fresh complexion and elastic step of their first abodes, for the sunken cheek and languid movement, which marks the victim of intermittent fever.

The instances of home-sickness, described by this vivid sketcher, were touching. Not even the captive Israelites, who hung their harps upon the willows along the banks of the Euphrates, wept more bitter tears, or looked back with more longing to their native homes, than did these exiles from New England —mourning the land they had left, with its roads, schools, meeting-houses—its hope, health, and happiness! Two incidents, related by the traveler, I must mention—though I do it from recollection, as I have not a copy of the work. He was one day riding in the woods, apart from the settlements, when he met a youth, some eighteen years of age, in a hunting-frock, and with a fowling-piece in his hand. The two fell into conversation.

"Where are you from?" said the youth, at last.

"From Connecticut," was the reply.

"That is near the old Bay State?"

"Yes."

"And have you been there?"

"To Massachusetts? Yes, many a time."

"Let me take your hand, stranger. My mother was from the Bay State, and brought me here when I was an infant. I have heard her speak of it. Oh, it must be a lovely land! I wish I could see a meeting-house and a school-house, for she is always talking about them. And the sea—the sea—oh, if I could see that! Did you ever see it, stranger?"

"Yes, often."

"What, the real, salt sea—the ocean—with the ships upon it?"

"Yes."

"Well"—said the youth, scarcely able to suppress his emotion—"if I could see the old Bay State and the ocean, I should be willing then to die!"

In another instance the traveler met—somewhere in the valley of the Scioto—a man from Hartford, by the name of Bull. He was a severe democrat, and feeling sorely oppressed with the idea that he was no better off in Connecticut under federalism than the Hebrews in Egypt, joined the throng and migrated to Ohio. He was a man of substance, but his wealth was of little avail in a new country, where all the comforts and luxuries of civilization were unknown.

"When I left Connecticut," said he, "I was wretch-ed from thinking of the sins of federalism. After I had got across Byram river, which divides that State from New York, I knelt down and thanked the Lord for that he had brought me and mine out of such a priest-ridden land. But I've been well punished, and I'm now preparing to return ; when I again cross Byram river, I shall thank God that he has permitted me to get back again !"

Mr. Bull did return, and what he hardly anticipated had taken place in his absence : the federal dynasty had passed away, and democracy was reigning in its stead ! This was effected by a union of all the dissenting sects—Episcopalians, Methodists, Baptists —co-operating with the democrats to overthrow the old and established order of things. Up to this period, Connecticut had no other constitution than the colonial charter granted by Charles II. This was a meager instrument, but long usage had supplied its deficiencies, and the State had, practically, all the functions of a complete political organization. It had begun in Puritanism, and even now, as I have elsewhere stated—notwithstanding gradual modifications—the old Congregational orthodoxy still held many privileges, some traditionary and some statutory. Yale College—an institution of the highest literary standing—had been from the beginning, in its influence, a religious seminary in the hands of the Congregational clergy. The State had not only chartered it, but had endowed and patronized it. And besides, the statute-book continued to give preference to this sect, compelling all persons to pay taxes to it, unless they should declare their adhesion to some other persuasion.

All this was incompatible with ideas and interests

that had now sprung up in the community. The Episcopalians had become a large and powerful body, and though they were generally federalists, they now clamored—as an offset to the endowments of Yale College—for a sum of money to lay the foundation of a " Bishops' Fund." The Methodists and Baptists had discovered that the preference given to orthodoxy, was a union of Church and State, and that the whole administration was but the dark and damning machinery of privileged priestcraft. To all these sources of discontent, the democracy added the hostility which it had ever felt toward federalism—now intensely embittered by the aggravations of the war and the Hartford Convention.

It was clear that the doom of federalism was at hand, even in Connecticut. Many things had conspired to overthrow it in other parts of the country. Jefferson had saddled it, in the popular mind, with a tendency to monarchy and a partiality for England— a burden which it was hard to bear—especially near the revolutionary period, when the hearts of the people still beat with gratitude to France and aggravated hostility to Great Britain. John Adams, the candidate of the federalists, gave great strength to this charge by his conduct, and having thus nearly broken down his supporters, did what he could to complete their destruction, by at last going over to the enemy. John Quincy Adams followed in the footsteps of his father. Washington was early withdrawn from the scene of action: Hamilton was shot: Burr proved treacherous and infamous. The pillars of federalism were shaken, and at the same time two mighty instruments were at work for its final overthrow. The great body of the people had got possession of suffrage, and insisted, with increasing vehemence, upon the removal of every impediment to its universality. The conservatives, in such a contest, were sure to be at last overwhelmed, and this issue was not long delayed. One thing more—the foreign element in our population, augmenting every year, was almost wholly democratic. Democracy in Europe is the watchword of popular liberty; the word is in all modern languages, the idea in all existing masses. This name was now assumed by the radical or republican party, and to its standard, as a matter of course, the great body of the European immigrants—little instructed in our history or our institutions—spontaneously flocked, by the force of instinct and prepossession. And still further—as I have before intimated, nearly all foreigners hate England, and in this respect they found a ready and active sympathy with the democratic party—the federalists being of course charged with the damning sin of love for that country and its institutions.

To these and other general influences, which had shattered the federal party in the Southern and Middle States, was now added, in Connecticut, the local difficulties founded in sectarian discontent. But it is probable that a revolution could not have been speed-

ily consummated, but for an adventitious incident.
Oliver Wolcott, who had been one of Washington's
cabinet, and of the strictest sect of federalism, had resided some years in New York, where he had acquired
a handsome fortune by commercial pursuits. For a
number of years he had taken no part in politics,
though I believe he had rather given support to the
war. No doubt he disapproved of the course of the
federalists, for I remember that shortly before the
Hartford Convention he was at my uncle's house—
the two being brothers-in-law—as I have before stated. In allusion to the coming assembly, I recollect
to have heard him say, interrogatively—

"Well, brother Goodrich, I hope you are not about
to breed any mischief?"

"Sir," said my uncle, somewhat rebukingly, "you
know me too well to make it necessary to ask that
question!"

I recollect at a later period, when he was governor
of Connecticut, to have heard him speak reproachfully
of both political parties in New York. Said he—

"After living a dozen years in that State, I don't
pretend to comprehend their politics. It is a labyrinth of wheels within wheels, and is understood only
by the managers. Why, these leaders of the opposite
parties, who—in the papers and before the world—
seem ready to tear each other's eyes out, will meet some
rainy night in a dark entry, and agree, whichever way
the election goes, they will share the spoils together!"

At all events, about this time Oliver Wolcott removed to Litchfield, his native place, and in 1817 was nominated for governor by the malcontents of all parties, rallying under the name of Toleration. To show the violent nature of the fusion which united such contradictory elements into one homogeneous mass, it may be well to quote here an extract from a Connecticut democratic organ—the American Mercury. This paper, with others, had charged Oliver Wolcott with burning down the War and Treasury Departments at Philadelphia, in order to cover up the iniquities he had committed while Secretary of War. The following was its language, Feb. 3, 1801:

" An evening paper asks the editor for his knowledge : the editors of that paper, if they will apply to Israel Israel, Esq., may have full and perfect knowledge of the accounts published. To conceal fraud and rob the public; to conceal dilapidation and plunder, while the public are paying enormous interest for money to support wicked and unnecessary measures ; to conceal as much as possible the amount and names of the robbers, and the plans and evidences of the villainy—these the editor believes to have been the true causes of the conflagration. When did it take place ? At the dusk of night, and in the rooms in which the books were kept, in which were contained the registers of public iniquity !"

A short time after this—February 26—the same paper copies from the Philadelphia Aurora an article, of which the following are extracts :

" The Honorable Mr. Wolcott, ex-Secretary of the Treasury, successor to the virtuous Hamilton and predecessor to the equally virtuous Dexter, has lately honored our city with his presence. Having done enough for his ungrateful country, he is retiring to the place from whence he came, to enjoy the *otium cum digni-tate*. It is to be hoped he will have enough of the former, to afford him an opportunity of nursing what little he has of the latter.

" This representative of Mr. Hamilton was very fortunate in escaping the federal bonfires at Washington ; even his papers and private property were *providentially* saved—but his fair fame sustained a *slight singeing* between the two fires : his friends in Congress, it is presumed, will pass a vote which shall operate as a cataplasm to the burn.

" Our federal worthies, justly appreciating the services of this valuable man, and wisely considering that nothing can afford more pleasure than eating or drinking, resolved to treat him to a din-ner ; and as it is proper the world should know that Mr. Wolcott had something to eat in Philadelphia, their proceedings on the occasion, at least such parts of them as will bear the light, are published in the federal prints."

Such were the opinions—at least such were the representations — of the leading democratic organs, respecting Oliver Wolcott, the federalist, in 1801. In 1817, he was the champion of the democratic party in Connecticut, and the idol of the American Mer-cury! What transformations are equal to those which the history of political parties, for the short space of twenty years, brings to our view ?

It is needless to tell you in detail what immediately followed. The struggle was one of the most violent that was ever witnessed in Connecticut. It was cu-rious as well as violent—for we saw fighting side by side, shoulder to shoulder, democracy, Methodism,

Episcopacy, Pedobaptism, Universalism, radicalism, infidelity—all united for the overthrow of federalism and orthodoxy; and Oliver Wolcott was the leader in this onset! The election took place in April, 1817, and the federalists were routed, according to the established phrase, " horse, foot, and dragoons." John Cotton Smith,* the most popular man in the State,

---

* John Cotton Smith was born in 1765, became member of Congress in 1800, where he remained six years. Being a federalist, he was nearly the whole time in the minority, yet such were his character and address, that he presided more frequently, and with more success, over the House, when in Committee of the Whole, than any other member. "To the lofty bearing of a Roman senator," says the historian, " he added a gentleness so conciliating and persuasive, that the spirit of discord fled abashed from his presence."

He was my mother's cousin, and I saw him several times at our house. He was tall, slender, and graceful in form and manner. His hair, a little powdered, was turned back with a queue, and a slight friz over the ears. His dress was of the olden time—with breeches, black silk stockings, and shoe-buckles. His address was an extraordinary mixture of dignity and gentle persuasive courtesy. He was made judge of the Superior Court in 1809, and soon after lieutenant-governor; in 1812, he became acting-governor, upon the death of the lamented Griswold. In 1813, he was elected governor, and led the State through the war, and until 1817, when he was defeated by the election of Wolcott.

Governor Smith was the last of those stately, courtly Christian gentlemen of the " Old School," who presided over Connecticut: with him passed away the dignity of white-top boots, queues, powder, and pomatum. His successor, Oliver Wolcott, though a federalist in the days of Washington, was never courtly in his manners. He was simple, direct, almost abrupt in his address, with a crisp brevity and pithiness of speech. His personal appearance and manner, contrasting with those of his predecessors, represented well enough the change of politics which his accession to the gubernatorial chair indicated.

Governor Smith was the first president of the Connecticut Bible Society, President of the American Board of Commissioners for Foreign Missions, President of the American Bible Society, and received from Yale College the degree of LL.D. He lived at Sharon with patriarchal liberality and dignity, to the age of eighty, where he died, beloved and honored by all who knew him.

was defeated : federalism was in the dust, toleration
was triumphant !

I remember that at that time, William L. Stone was
editor of the Connecticut Mirror. Nearly the whole
paper, immediately preceding the election, was filled
with pungent matter. I think I filled a column or
two myself. The feelings of the federalists were
very much wrought up, but after it was all over,
they took it good-naturedly. A new Constitution
for the State—1818—and a very good one, was the
first fruit of the revolution. Wolcott continued governor for ten years, and taking a moderate course,
in the end, satisfied reasonable men of both parties.
He was no radical, and inasmuch as a political change
in Connecticut was inevitable, it is probable that no
better man could have been found, to lead the people
through the emergency.*

---

* Oliver Wolcott was the third governor of Connecticut in a direct
line from father to son. Roger, his grandfather, was a native of Windsor, born in 1679 and died in 1767. He was a clever author, a conspicuous Christian, and governor of his native State from 1751 to 1754. His
son, Oliver W., was born about 1727. He was a member of Congress in
1776, when the Declaration of Independence was made. Barlow, in his
Columbiad, thus speaks of him :

> " Bold Wolcott urged the all-important cause—
> With steady hand the solemn scene he draws ;
> Undaunted firmness with his wisdom join'd—
> Nor kings, nor worlds, could warp his steadfast mind."

He was elected governor in 1796, but died the next year.

His son Oliver was born 1759, and became Secretary of the Treasury,
under Washington, upon the retirement of Hamilton, in 1795. He was
continued in this office till the close of Adams's administration. After
twelve years of public service, he retired, with but six hundred dollars
in his pocket ! He devoted himself to commerce in New York from
1801 to 1815. His correspondence, in two volumes octavo, has been

During the period in which Oliver Wolcott was governor, I was several times at Litchfield, and often at his house. My sister, Mrs. Cooke, had married his brother, Frederick Wolcott, living in the old family

---

published by his grandson Gibbs, and is a valuable and interesting work. When he ceased to be governor, he returned to New York, where he died, in 1833. He was an able statesman, possessed of considerable literary attainments, and in conversation was full of sagacity, wit, and keen observations upon the world.

His sister, Maryanne, wife of Chauncey Goodrich—born 1765—was one of the most accomplished women of her time. A portrait of her—though doing no justice to her beauty—is given in Dr. Griswold's "Republican Court." It is among the household anecdotes of the family, that during the Revolution, a leaden statue of George III. was taken from New York to Litchfield, and there cast into bullets, and that these were formed into cartridges by this lady and others in the neighborhood, for the army. I never saw her, as she died in 1805, before I went to Hartford.

Of Frederick Wolcott, my brother-in-law, I find the following obituary notice in the Philadelphia United States Gazette, July 11, 1837:

"Died on the 28th of June, at his residence in Litchfield, Conn., in the 70th year of his age, the Hon. Frederick Wolcott, one of the most distinguished citizens of that State: a patriot of the old school, a gentleman of great moral and intellectual worth, a sincere, humble, consistent Christian. It has been well said of Judge Wolcott, that he was one of 'nature's noblemen.' They who knew him personally, will appreciate the correctness and significance of the remark. His noble form, dignified yet affable and endearing manners, intelligence and purity of character, magnanimity of soul and useful life, were in grand and harmonious keeping, uniting to make him distinguished among men— greatly respected, beloved, and honored.

"Judge Wolcott was descended from one of the most eminent families in New England, being the son of Oliver Wolcott, former governor of Connecticut and one of the immortal signers of the Declaration of Independence, and grandson of Roger Wolcott, a still former governor of that State, who, together with the late Gov. Oliver Wolcott, Secretary of the Treasury under Washington's administration, and brother of the deceased, were lineal descendants of Henry Wolcott, an English gentleman of Tolland, in Somersetshire, who came to this country in 1628, and soon after undertook the first settlement in Connecticut, at Windsor. After graduating at Yale College, at an early age, with the highest honors of his class, Mr. Wolcott directed his studies to the law, and was soon called to various offices of important civil trust, the chief of which he held through every fluctuation of party, during a long life. His

mansion near by, and as I have intimated, my uncle, Chauncey Goodrich, had married his sister — thus making a double connection in the family. Uriah Tracy,* one of the most distinguished men in the

---

integrity inflexible, his perception ready, his judgment sound, his deportment always courteous, exemplary, and pleasing, he discharged all the public duties to which he was called with distinguished reputation. After his profession of faith in Christ, his life, morally correct and seemingly without defect before, was pre-eminently that of an enlightened and devoted follower of the Lord Jesus.

"In all the various relations which he sustained, his character as a great and good man shone with peculiar luster. In the church, he was not simply a member, but a pillar. No one could command more respect, no one possessed more influence. In the great schemes of benevolence which distinguish the present age, he ever lent a helping hand, and over several beneficent institutions was called to preside. A decided, though unostentatious Christian, he was ready to do every good work, and by his counsels and efforts, the weight of his character, and the beautiful consistency of his piety, did much to promote the cause which he espoused, and to recommend the religion he professed. It may be truly said of him, that 'he walked with God.'

"In private and social life, his character had charms of still greater endearment and loveliness. Here he loved most to move, and here his more intimate friends will love to contemplate him. Modest and unassuming, frank and generous, cordial and cheerful, he was eminently formed for friendship, and none knew him but to love and honor him. His mansion was always the abode of hospitality, his heart was always open, delighting in those varied duties which pertain to the friend, the neighbor, the relative, the father, and head of his family. In these several relations, his example was noble, beautiful, lovely indeed!

"The closing scene corresponded with the tenor of his long and useful life. It was calm, dignified, of steadfast faith, meekness, patience, and Christian hope. He died in the full possession of his mental faculties, leaving behind him a truly enviable reputation, and coming to his grave, 'as a shock of corn fully ripe, in its season.'"

* Uriah Tracy was born in 1754 and died in 1807. He was many years a leading member of Congress, and distinguished for his eloquence, learning, and wit. I have heard of him the following anecdote : Toward the latter part of Adams's administration, the latter nominated to office a connection of his family, by the name of Johnson, formerly a federalist, but recently turned democrat. This was offensive to the federalists, and Tracy, then of the Senate, being regarded as a skillful diplomat, was appointed to go and remonstrate with the President. He

history of Connecticut, had been dead for several years, but others of great eminence were still living— giving to Litchfield a remarkable prominence in the State. Among these were Tapping Reeve,* at one time chief-justice of Connecticut, and founder of the law school, which was long the first institution of the kind in the United States; Colonel Talmadge, distinguished as a gallant officer in the Revolution, and a manly, eloquent debater in Congress; James Gould, a learned judge, an elegant scholar, and successor of Reeve in the law school; Jabez W. Huntington—law lecturer, judge, senator—and distinguished in all these eminent stations; Lyman Beecher,† an able theolo-

---

accordingly went, and having put his Excellency in excellent humor, by some of his best stories, at last said—

"By the way, we have been thinking over this nomination of Johnson, and find there is a good deal of objection to him. The democrats will oppose him, because you nominated him; and some of the federalists will oppose him, because he is a democrat. We fear that if he goes to a vote, he will fail of a confirmation. As it would be unfortunate, just now, to have the administration defeated, your friends have requested me to suggest to your Excellency whether it would not be best to withdraw his name and substitute another?"

The President thrust his hands into his breeches pockets, and strode fiercely across the room: then coming up to Tracy, he said—"No, sir, no—that —— Boston Junto will never be satisfied till they drive me and my family back to Braintree to dig potatoes. No, sir—I'll not withdraw it!"

* Judge Reeve was born in 1744, and died in 1823. His law school was founded in 1784: in 1794, he associated Judge Gould with him. In 1820, Judge Reeve left it, and Mr. Huntington became connected with it. More than eight hundred persons have here had their legal education: among these there have been fifteen United States senators —five have been cabinet members; ten governors of States; two judges of the Supreme Court; and forty judges of State courts. Judge Gould died in 1838, aged 67: Judge Huntington died in 1847, aged 59.

† Dr. Beecher was born at New Haven, in 1775, was educated at Yale

gian and eloquent preacher, and even now more wide-ly known through his talented family, than his own genius. Litchfield Hill was in fact not only one of the most elevated features in the physical conforma-of Connecticut, but one of the focal points of litera-ture and civilization. You will readily suppose that my visits here were among the most interesting events of my early life.

In August, 1851, there was at Litchfield a gather-ing of distinguished natives of the county, convened to celebrate its organization, which had taken place a century before. Appropriate addresses were made by Judge Church, Dr. Bushnell, F. A. Tallmadge, D. S. Dickinson, George W. Holley, George Gould, Henry Dutton, and other persons of distinction. Among

College, settled at Hampton, Long Island, 1798; in 1810, at Litchfield; in 1826, in the Hanover-street church, Boston; in 1832, became Presi-dent of the Lane Theological Seminary, Cincinnati, which office he re-signed in 1842, returning to Boston, where he still resides. He has published several volumes on theological subjects. He has devoted his long life, with prodigious activity and vigor, to the promotion of religion, learning, and the larger humanities of life. As a preacher he was very effective, possessing surpassing powers of statement, illustration, and argument.

His spirit and genius seem to have been imparted to his large family, of whom Edward Beecher, Miss Catherine Beecher, Mrs. Stowe, Henry Ward Beecher, and others—all celebrated for their works—are members.

At the time I was in Litchfield I heard the following anecdote of Dr. B. He was one evening going home, having in his hand a volume of Ree's Encyclopædia, which he had taken at the bookstore. In his way, he met a skunk, and threw the book at him, upon which the animal re-torted, and with such effect that the doctor reached home in a very shocking plight. Some time after he was assailed, rather abusively, by a controversialist, and a friend advised the doctor to reply. "No," said he—"I once discharged a quarto at a skunk, and I got the worst of it. I do not wish to try it again!"

the performances was a poem by Rev. J. Pierpont,* alike illustrative of the local history of Litchfield and the manners and character of New England.

---

* I can not deny myself the pleasure of making a few extracts from this admirable performance, vividly portraying my own observations and recollections. Having described the boundaries of New England, the poet adds:

> Here dwells a people—by their leave I speak—
> Peculiar, homogeneous, and unique—
> With eyes wide open, and a ready ear,
> Whate'er is going on to see and hear;
> Nay, they do say, the genuine Yankee keeps
> One eye half open, when he soundest sleeps.
>
> * * * * *
>
> He loves his labor, as he loves his life;
> He loves his neighbor, and he loves his wife:
> And why not love her? Was she not the pearl
> Above all price, while yet she was a girl?
> And, has she not increased in value since,
> Till, in her love, he's richer than a prince?
> Not love a Yankee wife! what, under *Heaven*,
> Shall he love, then, and hope to be forgiven?
> So fair, so faithful, so intent to please,
> A "help" so "meet" in health or in disease!
>
> * * * * *
>
> And then, such housewives as these Yankees make;
> What can't they do? Bread, pudding, pastry, cake,
> Biscuit, and buns, can they mould, roll, and bake.
> *All* they o'ersee; their babes, their singing-birds,
> Parlor and kitchen, company and curds,
> Daughters and dairy, linens, and the lunch
> For out-door laborers—instead of punch—
> The balls of butter, kept so sweet and cool—
> All the boys' heads, before they go to school,
> Their books, their clothes, their lesson, and the ball,
> That she has wound and covered for them—all,
> All is o'erseen—o'erseen!—nay, it is *done*,
> By these same Yankee wives:—If you have run
> Thus far without one, toward your setting sun,
> Lose no more time, my friend—go home and speak for one!
>
> * * * * *
>
> The Yankee boy, before he's sent to school,
> Well knows the mysteries of that magic tool,

I think it may be safely said that there are few
counties in the United States, which could furnish
either such a poet or such materials for poetry, as this.

The pocket-knife.   To that his wistful eye
Turns, while he hears his mother's lullaby;
His hoarded cents he gladly gives to get it,
Then leaves no *stone* unturned, till he can whet it:
And, in the education of the lad,
No little part that implement hath had.
His pocket-knife to the young whittler brings
A growing knowledge of material things.
Projectiles, music, and the sculptor's art,
His chestnut whistle, and his shingle dart,
His elder pop-gun with its hickory rod,
Its sharp explosion and rebounding wad,
His corn-stalk fiddle, and the deeper tone
That murmurs from his pumpkin-leaf trombone,
Conspire to teach the boy.   To these succeed
His bow, his arrow of a feathered reed,
His windmill, raised the passing breeze to win,
His water-wheel that turns upon a pin;
Or, if his father lives upon the shore,
You'll see his ship, "beam-ends" upon the floor,
Full-rigged, with raking masts, and timbers stanch,
And waiting, near the washtub, for a launch.
Thus by his genius and his jack-knife driven,
Ere long he'll solve you any problem given;
Make any gimcrack, musical or mute,
A plow, a coach, an organ, or a flute—
Make you a locomotive or a clock,
Cut a canal, or build a floating-dock,
Or lead forth Beauty from a marble block;
Make any thing, in short, for sea or shore,
From a child's rattle to a seventy-four:—
Make *it*, said I?—Ay, when he undertakes it,
He'll make the thing, and the machine that makes it.
And, when the thing is made—whether it be
To move on earth, in air, or on the sea,
Whether on water o'er the waves to glide,
Or upon land to roll, revolve, or slide,
Whether to whirl, or jar, to strike, or ring,
Whether it be a piston or a spring,
Wheel, pulley, tube sonorous, wood or brass—

It has not only produced the eminent men already noticed, but it has been the birthplace of thirteen United States senators, twenty-two representatives

---

The thing designed shall surely come to pass;
For, when his hand's upon it, you may know,
That there's *go* in it, and he'll make it go!

    *   *   *   *   *

  'Tis not my purpose to appropriate
All that is clever to our native State:
The children of her sister States, our cousins,
Present their claims :—allow them—though by dozens;

    *   *   *   *   *

But when we've weighed them, in a balance true,
And given our cousins *all* that is their due,
Will not themselves acknowledge that the weight
Inclines in favor of "the Nutmeg State?"

    *   *   *   *   *

  What if her faith, to which she clings as true,
Appears, to some eyes, slightly tinged with *blue?*
With blue *as* blue, aside from any *ism*,
We find no fault; the spectrum of a prism,
The rainbow, and the flowers-de-luce, that look
At their own beauty in the glassy brook,
Show us a blue, that never fails to please;
So does yon lake, when rippled by a breeze;
In morning-glories blue looks very well,
And in the little flower they call "blue-bell."
No better color is there for the sky,
Or, as *I* think, for a blonde beauty's eye.
It's very pretty for a lady's bonnet,
Or for the ribbon that she puts upon it;
But in her faith, as also in her face,
Some will insist that blue is out of place;
As all agree it would be in the rose
She wears, and, peradventure, in—*her hose.*
  Still, for her shrewdness, must the "Nutmeg State"
As Number One among her sisters rate;
And which, of all *her* counties, will compare,
For size, or strength, for water, soil, or air,
With our good Mother County—which has sown
Her children, broadcast, o'er a wider zone,
Around the globe? And has she not, by far,
Outdone the rest in giving to the bar,

in Congress from the State of New York, alone, fifteen judges of the supreme courts of other States, nine presidents of colleges, and eighteen professors of colleges!

And to the bench—for half of all her years—
The brightest names of half the hemispheres?
  Our Mother County! never shalt thou boast
Of mighty cities, or a sea-washed coast!
Not thine the marts where Commerce spreads her wings,
And to her wharves the wealth of India brings;
No field of thine has e'er been given to fame,
Or stamp'd, by History, with a hero's name;
For, on no field of thine was e'er displayed
A hostile host, or drawn a battle-blade.
The better honors thine, that wait on Peace.
Thy *names* are chosen, not from martial Greece,
Whose bloody laurels by the sword were won,
Platea, Salamis, and Marathon—
But from the pastoral people, strong and free,
Whose hills looked down upon the Midland sea—
The Holy Land. Thy *Carmel* lifts his head
Over thy *Bethlehem*—thy "house of bread;"
Not Egypt's land of *Goshen* equaled thine,
For wealth of pasture, or "well-favored kine,"
While many a streamlet through thy *Canaan* flows,
And in thy *Sharon* blushes many a rose.
  But, Mother Litchfield, thou hast stronger claims
To be called holy, than thy holy names
Can give thee. Reckon as thy jewels, then,
Thy saintly women, and thy holy men.
Scarce have thine early birds from sleep awoke,
And up thy hillsides curls the cottage smoke,
When rises with it, on the morning air,
The voice of household worship and of prayer;
And when the night-bird sinks upon her nest,
To warm her fledglings with her downy breast,
In reverent posture many a father stands,
And, o'er his children, lifting holy hands,
Gives them to God, the Guardian of their sleep;
While round their beds their nightly vigils keep,
Those Angel ministers of heavenly grace,
Who "always do behold their Father's face."

LETTER XXXIV.

Stephen R. Bradley—My Pursuit of the Vocation of Bookseller and Publisher—Scott's Poems—General Enthusiasm—Byron's Poems—Their Reception—The Waverley Novels—Their amazing Popularity—I publish an Edition of them—Literary Club at Hartford—J. M. Wainwright, Isaac Toucey, William L. Stone, &c.—The Round Table—Original American Works—State of Opinion as to American Literature—Publication of Trumbull's Poems—Books for Education—Rev. C. A. Goodrich—Dr. Comstock—Woodbridge's Geography.

MY DEAR C******

Early in the year 1818 I was married to the daughter of Stephen Rowe Bradley,* of Westminster, Vermont. Thus established in life, I pursued the business of bookseller and publisher at Hartford for

---

* General Bradley was a native of Cheshire, Connecticut, where he was born, Oct. 20, 1754. He graduated at Yale College in 1775, and as before stated, was aid to Gen. Wooster, at the time he fell, in a skirmish with the British, near Danbury, in 1777. He removed to Vermont about the year 1780, and devoting himself to the bar, acquired an extensive practice. Having popular manners, and a keen insight into society, he became a prominent political leader, and exercised a large influence in laying the foundations of the State of Vermont, then the Texas of this country—Ethan Allen, Ira Allen, Seth Warner, and Thomas Chittenden — all from Connecticut — being the Austins and Houstons of its early history. At the period to which I refer it was rising from the chaos of the Revolutionary war, and the still more disorganizing contests with colonial claimants for sovereignty over her territories. In 1791, that State having come into the Union, Gen. Bradley was chosen one of its first senators. With an interval of six years—from 1795 to 1801—he continued in the Senate till 1813, a period of sixteen years. He was a member of the democratic party, and called, "*by virtue of powers vested in him*," the caucus which nominated Madison, and resulted in his election to the presidency. He was distinguished for political sagacity, a ready wit, boundless stores of anecdote, a large acquaintance with mankind, and an extensive range of historical knowledge. His conversation was exceedingly attractive, being always illustrated by pertinent anecdotes and apt historical references. His devel-

four years. My vocation gave me the command of
books, but I was able to read but little, my eyes con-
tinuing to be so weak that I could hardly do justice
to my affairs. By snatches, however, I dipped into a
good many books, and acquired a considerable knowledge of authors and their works.

During the period in which Scott had been enchanting the world with his poetry—that is, from 1805 to
1815—I had shared in the general intoxication. The
Lady of the Lake delighted me beyond expression,
and even now, it seems to me the most pleasing and
perfect of metrical romances. These productions
seized powerfully upon the popular mind, partly on
account of the romance of their revelations, and
partly also because of the pellucidity of the style
and the easy flow of the versification. Everybody
could read and comprehend them. One of my
younger sisters committed the whole of the Lady
of the Lake to memory, and was accustomed of an
evening to sit at her sewing, while she recited it
to an admiring circle of listeners. All young poets
were inoculated with the octa-syllabic verse, and news-

opments of the interior machinery of parties, during the times of
Washington, Jefferson, and Madison; his portraitures of the political leaders of these interesting eras in our history—all freely communicated at a period when he had retired from the active arena of
politics, and now looked back upon them with the feelings of a philosopher—were in the highest degree interesting and instructive. He received the degree of LL.D., and having removed to Walpole, in New
Hampshire, a few years before, died Dec. 16, 1830, aged 76. His son,
W. C. Bradley—still living, at the age of 74—has also been a distinguished lawyer and member of Congress.

papers, magazines, and even volumes, teemed with imitations and variations inspired by the "Wizard Harp
of the North." Not only did Scott* himself continue to
pour out volume after volume, but others produced set

---

* Scott experienced the fate of most eminent writers who have acquired a certain mannerism, recognized by the community at large—
that is, he was laughed at by burlesques of his works. George Col-
man, the Younger, though not *very* young, travestied the *Lady of the
Lake* under the title of the *Lady of the Wreck*—the latter of about the
same dimensions as the former. It is an Irish story, full of droll extravagance and laughable imitations of the original, at which they are
aimed.

In 1812, appeared the "Rejected Addresses" of James and Horace
Smith, and in these the principal poets of the day were imitated, and
their peculiarities parodied. They may, in fact, be considered as masterly criticisms of the several authors, in which their weak points are
strongly suggested to the reader. The laughable imitations of the "Lake
Poets"—Wordsworth, Southey, and Coleridge—probably had as much
effect in curing them of their affectations, as the scoffing ridicule of the
Edinburgh Review. Even Byron, who actually gained the prize offered
by the manager of Drury Lane Theater, on the occasion of its opening
in the new building, received a staggering blow from the imitation of
Childe Harold, which was so close in manner as to seem as if extracted
from that poem, while the spirit of the composition is strongly and effectively ridiculed. The following are two characteristic stanzas :

" Sated with home, with wife and children tired,
  The restless soul is driven abroad to roam—
  Sated abroad, all seen, yet naught admired—
  The restless soul is driven to ramble home.
  Sated with both, beneath new Drury's dome,
  The fiend Ennui a while consents to pine—
  There growls and curses like a deadly Gnome,
  Scorning to view fantastic Columbine,
Viewing with scorn the nonsense of the Nine !
        *   *   *   *   *
" For what is Hamlet, but a hare in March ?
  And what is Brutus, but a croaking owl ?
  And what is Rolla ? Cupid steep'd in starch,
  Orlando's helmet in Augustine's cowl !
  Shakspeare—how true thine adage, ' fair is foul'—
  To him whose soul is with fruition fraught,
  The song of Braham is an Irish howl—
  Thinking it but an idle waste of thought,
And naught is every thing and every thing is naught !"

poems, in his style, some of them so close in their imitation, as to be supposed the works of Scott himself, trying the effect of a disguise. At last, however, the market was overstocked, and the general appetite began to pall with a surfeit, when one of those sudden changes took place in the public taste, which resemble the convulsions of nature—as a whirlwind or a tempest in the tropics—by which a monsoon, having blown steadily from one point in the compass, for six months, is made to turn about and blow as steadily in the opposite direction.

It was just at the point in which the octa-syllabic plethora began to revolt the public taste, that Byron produced his first canto of Childe Harold's Pilgrimage. In London, the effect was sudden, and the youthful poet who went to bed a common man, woke up in the morning and found himself famous. This

---

It is a point of the highest interest in my recollections, that during the period in which Scott and Byron were rising into notice, and afterward, in the full tide of success, were thrilling the whole reading world with their masterly productions, that the Edinburgh Review, under the leadership of Jeffrey, was at its zenith. His criticisms were undoubtedly the most brilliant and profound that had appeared at that period; nor has any thing superior to them been written since. About the same time Wordsworth and his friends, Southey and Coleridge, attempted to make the world believe that bathos is pathos, weakness strength, and silliness sublimity. On this experiment they wasted a large amount of genius. While the Edinburgh Review found a noble scope for its highest efforts in illustrating the beauties of the Waverley novels, and setting forth as well the faults as the sublimities of Byron, it also gave full exercise to its incomparable ridicule and raillery, in noticing the harlequinisms of the Lake triumvirate. At this period, a new number of "the Edinburgh" created as much sensation as a new instalment of Macauly's history, at the present day.

ready appreciation there, arose in a great degree from the fact that the author was a man of fashion and a lord. In this country, these adventitious attributes were less readily felt, and therefore the reception of the new poem was more hesitating and distrustful. For some time, only a few persons seemed to comprehend it, and many who read it, scarcely knew whether to be delighted or shocked. As it gradually made its way in the public mind, it was against a strong current both of taste and principle.

The public eye and ear — imbued with the genius of Scott—had become adjusted to his sensuous painting of external objects, set in rhymes resonant as those of the nursery books. His poems were, in fact, lyrical romances, with something of epic dignity of thought and incident, presented in all the simplicity of ballad versification. A person with tastes and habits formed upon the reading of these productions, opening upon Childe Harold's Pilgrimage, was likely to feel himself—amid the long-drawn stanzas and the deep, mystic meditations—in somewhat of a labyrinth. Scott's poems were, moreover, elevating in their moral tone, and indeed the popular literature of the day—having generally purified itself from the poisons infused into it by the spirit of the French Revolution—was alike conservative in manners and morals. Campbell's Pleasures of Hope and Rogers' Pleasures of Memory, were favorite poems from 1800 to 1815; and during the same period,

Thaddeus of Warsaw, the Scottish Chiefs, the Pastor's Fireside, by Jane Porter; Sandford and Merton, by Day; Belinda, Leonora, Patronage, by Miss Edgeworth; and Cœlebs in Search of a Wife, by Hannah More—were types of the popular taste in tales and romances. It was therefore a fearful plunge from this elevated moral tone in literature, into the daring if not blasphemous skepticisms of the new poet.

The power of his productions, however, could not be resisted : he had, in fact—in delineating his own moody and morbid emotions—seemed to open a new mine of poetry in the soul; at least, he was the first to disclose it to the popular mind. By degrees, the public eye—admitted to these gloomy, cavernous regions of thought—became adjusted to their dim and dusky atmosphere, and saw, or seemed to see, a majestic spirit beckoning them deeper and deeper into its labyrinths. Thus, what was at first revolting, came at last to be a fascination. Having yielded to the enchanter, the young and the old, the grave and the gay, gave themselves up to the sorceries of the poet-wizard. The struggle over, the new-born love was ardent and profound, in proportion as it had dallied or resisted at the beginning. The very magnitude of the change—in passing from Scott's romantic ballads to Byron's metaphysical trances—when at last it was sanctioned by fashion, seemed to confirm and sanctify the revolution. Thus in about

five or six years after the appearance of the first canto
of Childe Harold's Pilgrimage—the others having
speedily followed—the whole poetic world had become Byronic.   Aspiring young rhymers now affected the Spenserian stanza, misanthropy, and skepti-
cism.   As Byron advanced in his career of profligacy,
and reflected his shameless debaucheries in Don Juan,
Beppo, and other similar effusions, the public—seduced, bewildered, enchanted—still followed him, and
condescended to bring down their morals and their
manners to his degraded and degrading standard.

The secret of the power thus exercised lay in various elements.   In England, the aristocratic rank of
Byron added greatly to his influence over the public
mind, and this was at last reflected in America.
With little real feeling of nature, he had, however,
an imagination of flame, and an amazing gift of poetic expression.   The great fascination, however—
that which creates an agonizing interest in his principal poems—is the constant idea presented to the
reader that, under the disguise of his fictitious heroes,
he is unconsciously depicting his own sad, despairing
emotions.   We always feel—whether in perusing
Childe Harold, or Manfred, or Cain, or any of his
more elaborate works—as if we were listening to the
moans of Prometheus struggling with the vultures,
or of Ixion toiling at his wheel.   We could not, if
we would, refuse our pity for such suffering, even in
a demon; how deep, then, must be our sympathy,

5*

when this is spoken to us in the thrilling tones of humanity, using as its vehicle all the music and melody of the highest lyrical art!

In vain, therefore, was it that the moralist resisted the diffusion of Byron's poems over the country. The pulpit opened its thunders against them—teachers warned their pupils, parents their children. I remember, even as late as 1820, that some booksellers refused to sell them, regarding them as infidel publications. About this time a publisher of Hartford, on this ground, declined being concerned in stereotyping an edition of them. It was all in vain. Byron could no more be kept at bay, than the cholera. His works have had their march over the world, and their victims have been probably not less numerous than those of that scourge of the nations. Byron may be, in fact, considered as having opened the gates to that tide of infidelity and licentiousness which sometimes came out boldly, as in the poems of Shelly, and more disguisedly in various other works, which converted Paul Clifford and Dick Turpin into popular heroes. He lowered the standard of public taste, and prepared a portion of the people of England and America to receive with favor the blunt sensualities of Paul de Kock, and the subtle infiltrations of deism by Madame George Sand. Happily, society has in its bosom the elements of conservatism, and at the present day the flood of license has subsided, or is subsiding. Byron is still read, but his immoralities, his atheism, have lost their relish, and are now deemed offenses and blemishes, and at the same time the public taste is directing itself in favor of a purer and more exalted moral tone in every species of literature. Longfellow, Bryant, and Tennyson are the exponents of the public taste in poetry, and Hawthorne, Dickens, Thackeray, in romance. All the varied forms of light reading are taking a corresponding tone of respect for morals and religion.

Scott speedily appreciated the eclipse to which his poetical career was doomed by the rising genius of Byron. He now turned his attention to prose fiction, and in July, 1814, completed and published Waverley, which had been begun some eight or ten years before. It produced no sudden emotion in the literary world. It was considered a clever performance—nothing more. I recollect to have heard it criticised by some veteran novel-readers of that day, because its leading character, Waverley, was only a respectable, commonplace person, and not a perfect hero, according to the old standards of romance. Guy Mannering came out the next year, and was received with a certain degree of eagerness. The Antiquary, Black Dwarf, Old Mortality, Rob Roy, and the Heart of Mid-Lothian, followed in quick succession. I suspect that never, in any age, have the productions of any author created in the world so wide and deep an enthusiasm. This emotion reached its height upon the appearance of Ivanhoe in 1819, which, I think, proved the most popular of these marvelous productions.

At this period, although there was a good deal of mystery as to their authorship, the public generally referred them to Scott.* He was called the "Great Unknown"—a title which served to create even an adventitious interest in his career. The appearance of a new tale from his pen, caused a greater sensation in the United States than did some of the battles of Napoleon, which decided the fate of thrones and empires. Everybody read these works; everybody— the refined and the simple—shared in the delightful trances which seemed to transport them to remote ages and distant climes, and made them live and breathe in the presence of the stern Covenanters of Scotland, the gallant bowmen of Sherwood Forest, or even the Crusaders in Palestine, where Cœur de Lion and Saladin were seen struggling for the mastery! I can testify to my own share in this intoxication. I was not able, on account of my eyes, to read these works myself, but I found friends to read

---

* It is a fact worthy of being noted, that while the evidence that Scott was the author of the Waverley Novels was clear and conclusive, various writers asserted the contrary. Some contended that they were written by Sir Walter's brother, Thomas, in Canada; some, that they were the productions of a certain—or rather an *uncertain*—Dr. Greenfield, &c. The subject was discussed with great vehemence, and something like partisan bitterness. It was proved to demonstration, over and over again, by some of these wiseacres, from internal, external, moral, religious, and political evidence, that Sir Walter Scott could not be the author. The foundation of all this was that envy, inherent in some minds, which is offended by success. Persons of this class invented, and at last believed, the absurdities which they propagated. The fact is instructive, for it teaches us the danger of following the lead of littleness and malignity. Candor is a safer guide than envy or malice.

them to me. To one good old maid—Heaven bless her!—I was indebted for the perusal of no less than seven of these tales.

Of course, there were many editions of these works in the United States, and among others, I published an edition, I think in eight volumes, octavo—including those which had appeared at that time. About this period—that is, in 1819—I was one of a literary club, of which J. M. Wainwright,* Isaac Toucey, William L. Stone, Jonathan Law, S. H. Huntington, and others, were members. The first meeting was at my house, and I composed a poem for the occasion,

---

* Dr. Wainwright was born at Liverpool, in 1792, of parents who were citizens of the United States, but who at that date were on a visit to England. He came to this country at the age of 11, was educated at Cambridge, and was instituted rector of Christ Church at Hartford, in 1815. He came to New York about 1820, and after filling various important stations, was in 1852 elected provisional bishop of the diocese of New York. He was an accomplished scholar and gentleman, and an earnest and successful laborer in the various fields to which his life was devoted.

Mr. Toucey studied law at Newtown, and came to Hartford about 1812, and has since resided there. He is an eminent lawyer, and has filled the offices of governor and senator of the United States. The latter place he still holds.

William L. Stone, born at Esopus, New York, 1792, was first a printer, and afterward became distinguished as an editor—first in conducting a political paper at Albany, and then at Hudson. When Theodore Dwight, who had founded the Connecticut Mirror, left for Albany, in 1816, Mr. Stone succeeded him. In 1821, he succeeded to the editorship of the Commercial Advertiser, at New York, which place he filled till his death, in 1844. He published various works, among which were the Life of Brant, Memoir of Red Jacket, Letters on Masonry and Antimasonry, &c. He wrote with great rapidity and fluency, and had a remarkable talent in collecting materials and making compilations. In personal character he was exceedingly amiable, giving his warm sympathy to all things charitable and religious.

Jonathan Law was the postmaster of Hartford; he was a good scholar,

entitled "A Vision"—afterward published, with other poems, in 1836. I also published three or four numbers of a small work entitled the "Round Table," the articles of which were written by different members of the club.

About this time I began to think of trying to bring out original American works. It must be remembered that I am speaking of a period prior to 1820. At that date, Bryant, Irving, and Cooper—the founders of our modern literature—a trinity of genius in poetry, essay, and romance—had but just commenced their literary career. Neither of them had acquired a positive reputation. Halleck, Percival, Brainard, Longfellow, Willis, were at school—at least, all were unknown. The general impression was that we had not, and could not have, a literature. It was the precise point at which Sidney Smith had uttered that bitter taunt in the Edinburgh Review— "Who reads an American book?" It proved to be that "darkest hour just before the dawn." The successful booksellers of the country—Carey, Small, Thomas, Warner, of Philadelphia; Campbell, Duyckinck, Reed, Kirk & Mercein, Whiting & Watson, of New York; Beers & Howe, of New Haven; O. D.

a man of refined feelings, with a sensitive, shrinking delicacy of manners in the intercourse of life.

Mr. Huntington has been judge of the county court, and has filled other responsible offices. He is now clerk of the Court of Claims, at Washington, though he resides at Hartford.—Such were some of the members of our little club.

Cooke, of Hartford; West & Richardson, Cummings & Hilliard, R. P. & C. Williams, S. T. Armstrong, of Boston—were for the most part the mere reproducers and sellers of English books. It was positively injurious to the commercial credit of a bookseller to undertake American works, unless they might be Morse's Geographies, classical books, school-books, Watts' Psalms and Hymns, or something of that class.

Nevertheless, about this time I published an edition of Trumbull's poems, in two volumes, octavo, and paid him a thousand dollars, and a hundred copies of the work, for the copyright. I was seriously counseled against this by several booksellers—and, in fact, Trumbull had sought a publisher, in vain, for several years previous. There was an association of designers and engravers at Hartford, called the "Graphic Company,"* and as I desired to patronize the liberal arts there, I employed them to execute the embellishments. For so considerable an enterprise, I took the precaution to get a subscription, in which I was tolerably successful. The work was at last produced, but it did not come up to the public expectation, or the patriotic zeal had cooled, and more than half the subscribers declined taking the work.

---

* The designer of the establishment was Elkanah Tisdale, a fat, facetious gentleman—a miniature painter by profession, but a man of some literary taste, and admirable humor in anecdote. He illustrated, with great cleverness, the handsome edition of the Echo, published by Isaac Riley—brother-in-law of Dwight and Alsop, two of the principal authors —though it professes to be from the Porcupine Press, and by Pasquin Petronius.

I did not press it, but putting a good face upon the affair, I let it pass, and—while the public supposed I had made money by my enterprise, and even the author looked askance at me in the jealous apprehension that I had made too good a bargain out of him—I quietly pocketed a loss of about a thousand dollars. This was my first serious adventure in patronizing American literature.

About the same period I turned my attention to books for education and books for children, being strongly impressed with the idea that there was here a large field for improvement. I wrote, myself, a small arithmetic, and half a dozen toy-books, and published them, though I have never before confessed their authorship. I also employed several persons to write school histories, and educational manuals of chemistry, natural philosophy, &c., upon plans which I prescribed—all of which I published; but none of these were very successful at that time. Some of them, passing into other hands, are now among the most popular and profitable school-books in the country.*

---

* Among these was *A History of the United States of America*, by Rev. C. A. Goodrich: this was the first of the popular school histories of the United States, now in circulation—and, in fact, the first of my brother's numerous publications. Previous to this time, the history of the United States was not one of our school studies. Other works of a similar kind, after this example, soon followed, but this work has continued to be one of the most popular. Several hundred thousand copies of it have been sold.

Another was an educational treatise on *Natural Philosophy*, by J. L. Comstock, which is now a popular and standard work in the schools, and has been republished in England. Dr. Comstock also wrote, upon plans which I indicated, an educational work on Chemistry, another on

William C. Woodbridge, one of the teachers of the Deaf and Dumb Asylum, at this time projected a school geography, in which I assisted him—mostly in preparing the details of the work for the press, and in the mechanical department. When an edition of it was finally ready—after long and anxious labor, both on his part and mine—the state of my health compelled me to relinquish it. This work acquired great popularity, and became the starting-point of a new era in school geographies, both in this country and in England.

Mineralogy, &c., which I published. Thus this excellent and useful author began that series of treatises, designed to popularize science, which has placed his name among the eminent benefactors of education in this country. I am happy to say, that he is still living at Hartford, in the enjoyment of the respect and friendship which his amiable character and useful life naturally inspire—and, I may add, in the enjoyment also of that independence which is but a just compensation of well-directed industry and talent.

Mr. Woodbridge was born in 1795, graduated at Yale in 1811, and, having studied theology, became one of the teachers of the deaf and dumb, at Hartford. He was a man of the greatest amenity of manner and purity of life ; he showed also a complete devotion to what he deemed his duty, viewed through a religious light. He gave his attention to education, and may be considered as one of the pioneers in the great improvements lately made in the art of instruction. He traveled in Europe, visiting the most celebrated educational establishments, and holding intercourse with the most enlightened friends of educational progress and improvement. The result of his researches and reflections he gave to the public in numerous valuable and profound treatises. He was a little too much of a perfectionist to be immediately practical, and hence his books—two geographical treatises—were somewhat beyond the age in which he lived ; but still they exercised a powerful influence in suggesting valuable ideas to others. His first geography I took to England in 1823, and got it published there, for his benefit. It still continues to be published in London. Mr. Woodbridge was a man of feeble health, yet struggled manfully till 1845, when he expired, at Boston—loved and admired by all who knew him.

LETTER XXXV.

Sketches of the " Hartford Wits"—Dr. Hopkins—Trumbull, author of Mc-
Fingal—David Humphries—Dr. Strong—Theodore Dwight—Thomas H.
Gallaudet—Daniel Wadsworth—Dr. Coggswell—Mrs. Sigourney.

My dear C*******

In order to complete the panorama of my life at
Hartford, I must give you a brief sketch of some of
the persons whom I knew there, and who had become
conspicuous by their words or works. I have already said that Hopkins,* who in point of genius
stood at the head of the noted literary fraternity of
" Hartford Wits," was not living when I went to reside at that place. Trumbull, the author of McFingal, was still living, and I knew him well. He was at
that time an old man, and—always small of stature—
was now bent, emaciated, and tottering with a cane.
His features were finely cut, and he must have been

---

* Dr. Lemuel Hopkins was born at Waterbury, 1750 : he practiced
physic at Litchfield, and afterward at Hartford, where he died in 1801.
He left a strong impression upon the public mind, as well by the eccentricity of his personal appearance and habits, as by his learning and genius. He was often described to me as long and lank, walking with
spreading arms and straddling legs. His nose was long, lean, and flexible ; his eyes protruding, and his whole expression a strange mixture
of solemnity and drollery. He was of a social disposition, and often in
talking at a neighbor's house, would forget his business engagements.
He was intimate with Theodore Dwight, and his daughter has told me
that she recollects his coming to their house, and being very much fa-
tigued, he laid himself down on the floor, and put a log of wood under
his head for a pillow. Here he began to dictate poetry, which her father wrote down, being very likely one of those poems which has placed
his name among the most vigorous of our satirists.

handsome in his younger days. His eye was keen and bright, his nose slightly aquiline, his mouth arching downward at the corners, expressive of sarcastic humor. There was something about him that at once bespoke the man of letters, the poet, and the satirist.*

---

* John Trumbull—the poet—belonged to one of those remarkable families in Connecticut which, through several generations, have possessed talents that carried them to the highest stations in society. Jonathan Trumbull, of Lebanon, born in 1710, was elected governor in 1769, and continued to be annually elected till 1783, when he resigned, having been thirty years, without interruption, in public employment. His services, rendered to the country during the war, were regarded as almost next those of Washington. It is said that the name given to our country of "Brother Jonathan," came from him, in an allusion to his co-operation with Washington in the Revolution. He died in 1785. His son Jonathan, born at Lebanon, 1740, was Washington's secretary and aid, member of Congress in 1789, speaker of the House in 1791, in 1794 senator, and in 1798, governor of the State. He died in 1809. Joseph Trumbull, nephew of the preceding, and still living, has filled various offices, and been senator of the United States and governor of the State. Benjamin Trumbull, the distinguished historian—born in 1735 and died in 1820—was nephew of the first Gov. Trumbull. Jonathan Trumbull, son of the second governor of that name, and aid to Washington, was an eminent painter and elegant gentleman, and died in 1843, aged 87. A collection of his paintings, valuable as historical and biographical mementoes, belongs to Yale College.

John Trumbull, the poet, son of the Rev. John T. of Watertown, a connection of this family, was born 1750. At seven he was admitted at college, but did not enter upon his studies there till thirteen. I have heard him say that when he went to enter at Yale, he rode on horseback behind his father, and wore his mother's cloak and hood. He studied law, mingling the composition of poetry with legal pursuits. Having been in the law office of John Adams, at Boston, he settled as a lawyer at Hartford in 1781, and became distinguished in his profession. He wrote several poems, the most noted of which was McFingal, an imitation of Hudibras, and in some passages not inferior to the best portions of that famous production. Trumbull was, no doubt, the most conspicuous literary character of his day, in this country. I published a revised edition of his works in 1820, as elsewhere stated. His society was much sought, and he was the nucleus of a band of brilliant geniuses, including Dwight, Hopkins, Alsop, Humphries, &c.

The latter I often saw at Hartford, usually on visits to Trumbull. He

Dr. Strong was the minister of the Middle Brick Church—the principal Congregational church in the city. He was now near threescore and ten—large, infirm, and shuffling along as if afflicted with gout in the feet. His life and character had been marked with eccentricities—with worldliness, wit, and social aptitudes. Nevertheless, he was an eloquent and devout preacher: it was said of him that when in the pulpit, it seemed that he ought never to leave it, and when out of it, that he ought never to go into it. All his levity, however, had passed when I knew him. He was indeed fast approaching that bourne whence no traveler returns. With all his early

---

was then old, and living in his native town of Derby, where he had established a woolen manufactory. He had been one of the handsomest men of his time, and was now large, portly, powdered, with a blue coat and bright buttons, a yellow waistcoat, drab breeches, and white-top boots. His complexion was florid, showing a little more appreciation of Sherry than was orthodox in Connecticut—a taste he brought with his wife and her fortune from Lisbon, or Madrid, in both which places he had been ambassador. He was in truth a splendid mixture of the old Continental soldier, and the powdered and pomatumed diplomat. Though past sixty, he still affected poetry, and on one occasion—perhaps about 1810—came in his coach-and-four, to get Trumbull to aid him in finishing his Fable of the Monkey, who, imitating his master in shaving, cut his own throat. He had nearly completed it, but wished a pointed, epigrammatic termination. Trumbull took it and read to the end, as it was written, and then added, without stopping—

> " Drew razor swift as he could pull it,
> And cut, from ear to ear, his gullet!"

This completed the fable, and it so stands to this day. This anecdote was told me by Trumbull himself, and I gave it to Kettell, who inserted it in the notice of the poet, in his "Specimens of American Poetry." Humphries died in 1818 ; Trumbull in 1841, having been a judge of the Superior Court from 1801 till 1819, when he was disqualified by age, under a law of the State.

faults, he had a very strong hold of the affections and confidence of his people. His face was remarkably expressive, his eye keen, his lips firm, his nose arched, and his long, thick, gray hair turned back and rolled in waves upon his shoulders. I am not sure that his reputation as a man of wit and worldly taste, now that these were cast aside, did not deepen the impression made by his preaching at this period. I am certain that I have never heard discourses more impressive, more calculated to subdue the pride of the heart, and turn it to religious submission, than these. He was considered a man of remarkable sagacity, especially in penetrating the motives of mankind, and he was at the same time esteemed by his clerical brethren as a very able divine. He published two volumes of sermons, but they furnish little evidence of the genius which was imputed to him. His reputation is now merely traditional, but it is impossible not to perceive that, with such eccentricities, he must have been a man of remarkable qualities, inasmuch as he gathered into his congregation the first minds in the city, and left a name which still seems a bond of union and strength to the church over which he presided.*

---

* Nathan Strong, D. D., was born at Coventry, 1748, and graduated at Yale : during the Revolution, he was a chaplain in the army. After he was settled as a minister, he became a partner in the firm of Strong & Smith, and engaged in the manufacture of gin. As was fit and proper, one of his deacons, good old Mr. Corning, was a grocer, and sold New England rum. As this article was frequently wanted after the store was shut, he kept a barrel on tap at his house, so that the people need

Theodore Dwight, a younger brother of Dr. Dwight, was born at Northampton, in 1764. His early life was spent upon the farm, and at that period when the wolf, wild-cat, and Indian were occasionally seen in the forest—furnishing him with ample materials for interesting descriptions of adventure in after-

---

not suffer for the want of this staff of life! The firm of Strong & Smith failed, and the minister shut himself up in his house to avoid the sheriff, but as no writ could be served on Sundays, he then went forth and preached to his congregation. All this took place toward the close of the last century. There was nothing in it disgraceful, then. Let those who deny that society has made progress in its standard of propriety, compare this with the universal tone of public sentiment now.

Of the numerous anecdotes of Dr. Strong, I give you one or two specimens. The first of these is connected with the Missionary Society of Connecticut, of which he was a principal founder. The Rev. Mr. Bacon—father of the present celebrated Dr. Leonard Bacon, of New Haven—had been employed as a missionary to that part of Ohio called the Western Reserve. Some deeply interesting letters, detailing his operations, had been received, and on the Sabbath, after the service, Dr. Strong invited Theodore Dwight into the pulpit, to read them. This he performed, and the letters made a deep impression upon the audience. One old man, by the name of Z... P...., who was not only hard of hearing, but hard of head and heart, actually wept. As Mr. Dwight was about to descend, the doctor whispered to him—"You have done in thirty minutes what I have not been able to accomplish in thirty years: you have made old Z... P.... cry!"

Dr. S. had issued a prospectus for his sermons, when one day he met Trumbull the poet. "When are your sermons to be out?" said the latter. "I cannot exactly tell," said the doctor. "I am waiting to find a text to suit a man who never comes to church, except when he has a child to be baptized"—a palpable allusion to Trumbull's neglect of the sanctuary about those days.

Dr. Mason, of New York, once called on Dr. Strong, and as he was about to depart, he stumbled, and almost fell, in consequence of a defect in one of the door-steps. "Why don't you mend your ways?" said he, somewhat peevishly. "I was waiting for a Mason," was the ready reply.

One of Dr. S.'s deacons came to him with a difficulty. "Pray, doctor," said he, "tell me how it happens: all my hens hatch on Sunday." "The reason is," said the doctor, "that you set them on Sunday!"

time. When nearly twenty, he injured his wrist, and being disqualified for the labors of a farmer, he turned his attention to study, and finally selected the profession of the law. He established himself at Hartford,* and rose to eminence in his profession. He had, however, a strong bias toward literature, and

---

* When I went to reside at Hartford, Mr. Dwight was living next door to my uncle, and was on intimate terms with him. He was a tall, handsome man, with an exceedingly black, flashing eye, and a lip that curled easily in laughter or satire. He had an infinite fund of anecdote, great learning, an abundant acquaintance with literature, and lively powers of description. He wrote with facility, and dashed off verses almost by improvisation.

In early life, he had written sentimental poetry, specimens of which may be found in " American Poems," published at Litchfield, in 1793. The lines, " Alfred to Philena," are his—Philena being Mrs. Morton. They sound strongly Della Cruscan—at this day—for the productions of Theodore Dwight. As an editor, he was chiefly devoted to politics, pursuing democracy with the unsparing vigilance of a falcon in chase of its prey. Some of his pasquinades became very popular, and greatly irritated the opposite party. His lines in ridicule of a Jeffersonian festival at New Haven, March, 1803—beginning as follows, and consisting of some dozen similar stanzas—were said and sung all over the country.

> Ye tribes of Faction, join—
> Your daughters and your wives:
> Moll Cary's come to dine,
> And dance with Deacon Ives.
> Ye ragged throng
> Of democrats,
> As thick as rats,
> Come join the song.
>
> Old Deacon Bishop stands,
> With well-befrizzled wig,
> File-leader of the band,
> To open with a jig—
> With parrot-toe
> The poor old man
> Tries all he can
> To make it go, &c.

When the Non-intercourse act—the last of the so-called " *Restrictive Measures*," and which by way of ridicule had been nick-named the

wrote verses and political essays. Such was the reputation he soon acquired, that he was selected by Wolcott, Hamilton, and others, to preside over the Evening Post, established in 1801. This offer was declined, and William Coleman filled the place. Mr. Dwight was elected a member of the State Coun-

---

"*Terrapin System*," was repealed—Dwight wrote the following. It pretends to be a lyrical lament sung by the democrats at Washington, with whom this system had been a great favorite.

DIRGICAL HYMN.

Mourn! sons of democratic woe!
   In sadness bow the head:
Bend every back with sorrow low—
   Poor TERRAPIN is dead.

And see his dying bed, around
   His weeping friends appear:
Low droops his grandsire to the ground;
   His father drops a tear.

Old Clopton begs the twentieth god,
   The victim's life to spare:
Calhoun and Johnson kiss the rod,
   And Troup and Johnson swear.

Good old Long Tom stands sniveling by,
   His dying eyes to close;
While Jemmy heaves a bitter sigh,
   And wipes his mournful nose.

Let sharks exult with savage joy,
   The wallowing porpoise spout:
No more his fangs their peace annoy,
   Nor dread their ribs his snout.

Mud-turtles, paddle at your ease
   In every pond and pool;
Ye tadpoles, settle on your lees,
   And in the slime-bed cool.

Ye British weavers, shout and sing;
   Ye tinkers, join the chorus;
Cobblers and tailors, make a ring,
   And dance a jig before us!

Tell old King George the glorious tale:
   Amid his dire offences,
Perhaps 'twill light his visage pale,
   And bring him to his senses.

cil, and in 1806, a member of Congress. Soon after he established the Connecticut Mirror, and from that time followed the career of an editor. He was secretary of the Hartford Convention in 1814. In 1815, he removed to Albany, and conducted the Albany Daily Advertiser: in 1817, he

> The time will shortly come, when we
> Like Terrapin must wander;
> And our poor eyes will nothing see
> But death's cold Gerrymander!

The "Gerrymander" here alluded to, originated in a division of Massachusetts, by the democrats, in the time of Governor Gerry, into Congressional Districts, so as to give that party the ascendency. It was a violent disregard of geographical and political propriety, and the federalists retaliated by having a huge monster—with tail and claws, resembling, in outline, the state of Massachusetts, as thus distorted—engraved and circulated, with an exceedingly piquant natural history of the animal. It took such effect that for a long time it gave a new word to the American political vocabulary. It is said by Buckingham, that Gilbert Stuart, the artist, suggested this clever caricature.

The following will serve as a specimen of Mr. Dwight's New-Year's Carrier's verses, which appeared annually, and acquired great popularity. This extract is from the Connecticut Mirror, January 6, 1813.

> * * * * *
> Survey our desolated shores,
> Our grass-grown wharves and empty stores—
> Our arts and industry depress'd,
> The wealthy cramp'd, the poor distress'd:
> Our cities wrapp'd in deepest gloom.
> Our commerce buried in the tomb.
> No hum of business meets the ear,
> No songs of joy the bosom cheer;
> The sailor hears the whistling blasts
> Murmur through sullen groves of masts—
> The billows dash, the useless sail
> Flap mournful to the rising gale—
> Then turns and views the dismal shed
> Where his young offspring cry for bread.
> And as the nightly breezes blow,
> Curses the authors of his woe!
>   Naught but exterminating war
> Could all this nation's blessings mar—
> Naught but an arm of Vandal power

established the Daily Advertiser in New York, of which he was the chief editor till 1836, when he removed to Hartford. He afterward returned to New York, where he died, in 1846.

Among the Hartford notables was Daniel Wadsworth, son of Col. Jeremiah Wadsworth, who had

> The harvest of its hopes devour.
> Where is that virtuous patriot band,
> The pride, the bulwark of our land,
> Form'd to uphold the nation's sway—
> Pinckney, and Strong, and King, and Jay—
> Whose counsels might our country shield,
> And guide our armies in the field?
> By party zeal and passions base,
> Exiled from power, and driven from place!
>   Who fill the void? What names succeed?
> Read the bright list—exult and read!
> Alston and Johnson, Fisk, Desha,
> Porter and Piper, Pond and Rhea,
> Grundy, and Hufty, and Lefevre,
> Sammons and Stow, and Shaw, and Seaver,
> Newton, McCoy, McKim, McKee,
> Smilie, and Troup, and Widgery!—
> And shall our nation's courage sink,
> E'en on perdition's awful brink,
> When such a constellated train
> Her highest interests sustain?

I have already alluded to the "Hartford wits," of whom Mr. Dwight was one. Their reputation was chiefly founded upon a series of articles which appeared in various papers, and were collected and published in 1807, under the title of the Echo—including other pieces. They consisted of satires, mostly in the form of parodies and burlesques—with occasional passages of a more serious character. They attracted great attention at the time, and had a wholesome effect in curing the public of a taste for ridiculous bombast, which then prevailed. The principal writers were Mr. Dwight, his brother-in-law Richard Alsop, of Middletown, and Dr. Hopkins, of Hartford. Mr. Theodore Dwight, now of New York, the son of the author I am noticing, has shown me a volume in which the lines contributed by each of these persons are marked, in the handwriting of his father. This suggests the manner in which the whole was written—one composing a few stanzas, then another taking the pen, and then another. The characteristics of each of these several writers are clearly indicated, in compositions having a general aspect of homogeneity.

been a distinguished member of Congress. He had
traveled in Europe, and was not only a man of large
wealth, but he had a taste for literature and art. His
wife was daughter of the second Governor Trumbull,
and a very excellent example of the refined and dignified lady of the olden time. She had been at Phil-

---

I am indebted to Mr. Dwight for the following, which is copied
from a memorandum in his father's handwriting, in relation to the
Echo :

"In the year 1829 a work was published in Boston, called 'Specimens of American Poetry,' &c., by S. Kettell. In a biographical sketch of Richard Alsop, a
minute and circumstantial account is given by Mr. Kettell, and which has been
frequently referred to as a correct narrative of that publication. It seems no
more than an act of justice to individuals, that a true history of it should be
published.

"The first number of the Echo appeared in the American Mercury, at Hartford,
in August, 1791. It was written at Middletown, by Richard Alsop and Theodore
Dwight. The authors, at the time of writing it, had no expectation of its being
published; their sole object was to amuse themselves, and a few of their personal
friends. The general account of its origin is given in the preface of the volume in
which the numbers were afterward collected, and published in New York. A few
lines in the course of it were written by three of their literary friends, viz.: Dr.
M. F. Coggeswell, Elihu H. Smith, and Lemuel Hopkins. Dr. Hopkins wrote
more than these two others; a considerable part of ten numbers were by him.
With these exceptions, the entire work was the production of Messrs. Alsop and
Dwight. Judge Trumbull never wrote a line of it. Mr. Kettell's account is incor-
rect in almost every essential particular.

"The 'Political Green-House' was written by Alsop, Hopkins, and Dwight, in
unequal proportions."

I think it may be remarked that, in these compositions, Dwight shows
the most brilliant fancy and playful wit, Alsop the broadest humor,
and Hopkins the most original and crushing satire. French Jacobin-
ism, with all its brood of infidelity, radicalism, and licentiousness, is
the especial object of attack throughout, and is justly and unsparingly
ridiculed.

Though Mr. Dwight is perhaps chiefly known as the author of satirical
verses, and as a somewhat severe though able political writer, he was in
private life one of the most pure, disinterested, and amiable of men. He
had an almost womanly sensibility to human suffering; he was true to
friendship, and inflexibly devoted to what he deemed the cause of truth,
honor, and patriotism. He furnishes an instance of what has often happened before, in which the literary man seems a vindictive satirist, while
the social man—friend, neighbor, father, husband—is full of the milk

adelphia when her father was member of Congress, and recited many interesting anecdotes of Washington and Hamilton, and other great men, whom she had there seen. I was often at the house, and here frequently saw her brother, Col. Trumbull, the artist, with his European wife, about whom there was an impenetrable mystery. She was a beautiful woman, and of elegant manners: her features are well preserved in her husband's portrait of her, in the Trumbull Gallery, at Yale College. It was rumored that she was the daughter of an English earl, but her name and lineage were never divulged.*

---

of human kindness. He had great abilities, and only missed a permanent reputation by setting too light a value upon his performances, and thus not bringing them up to a higher standard of criticism. He wrote too much and too rapidly for lasting fame.

* Mr. Wadsworth was one of the few rich men who know how to make a good distribution of their wealth. His charities during his lifetime were numerous, and bestowed with kindness and judgment. He founded at Hartford the Wadsworth Atheneum, which is an interesting and useful institution, including many antiquities, works of art, and a valuable historical library.

Among the interesting objects connected with the city of Hartford, is his country-seat on Talcott's mountain—embracing a lake, a tower, and other attractions. The situation is beautiful, and the whole is tastefully arranged. To the west of it lies the valley of Farmington river, exhibiting a varied landscape of winding streams, swelling hills, and cultivated fields, all seen through the enchanting azure of distance. To the east is the Connecticut, rolling proudly through its borders, crowned with the richest cultivation, and dotted with towns and villages, presenting some thirty spires in a single view.

The scene presented to the eye from the top of this tower—which rises seventy feet above its platform, situated upon a high point of rock—is indeed unrivaled. The immediate objects beneath—the tasteful villa, the quiet lake, and, rising up from its shores—

"Rocks, mounds, and knolls, confusedly hurled,
The fragments of an earlier world"—

suggesting a resemblance to the wild borders of Loch Katrine, consti-

It was, I believe, through Mr. Wadsworth's influence that Miss Huntly, now Mrs. Sigourney, was induced to leave her home in Norwich, and make Hartford her residence. This occurred about the year 1814. Noiselessly and gracefully she glided into our young social circle, and ere long was its presiding genius. I shall not write her history, nor dilate upon her literary career—for who does not know them both by heart? Yet I may note her influence in this new relation—a part of which fell upon myself. Mingling in the gayeties of our social gatherings, and in no respect clouding their festivity, she led us all toward intellectual pursuits and amusements. We had even a literary cotery under her inspiration, its first meetings being held at Mr. Wadsworth's. I believe one of my earliest attempts at composition was made here. The ripples thus begun, extended over the whole surface of our young society, producing a lasting and refining effect. It could not but be beneficial thus to mingle in intercourse with one who has the angelic faculty of seeing poetry in all things, and good everywhere. Few persons living have exercised a wider influence than Mrs. Sigourney; no one that I now know, can look back upon a long and earnest career of such unblemished beneficence.

---

tute a rare assemblage of beautiful and striking groups. It is sad to reflect that "lands and manors pass away," yet it is consoling to know that others live to enjoy them. Mr. Wadsworth is gone—but it gives me pleasure to state that my old friend, D. W., a thriving manufacturer of axes, is his successor.

In the immediate vicinity of Mr. Wadsworth, lived Dr. Coggeswell, a renowned surgeon and excellent physician. He was, withal, a man of refined tastes, and exceedingly easy and gracious address. In early life he had been associated with the "Hartford wits," and occasionally wrote verses, though more frequently of the sentimental than the satirical kind. His daughter, Alice, was deaf and dumb, if we speak of the ear and the lip; yet her soul heard and spoke in her eyes and her countenance. She excited universal interest by her sweetness of character, manners, and appearance; she was, in truth, an eloquent and persuasive lecturer upon the language, and beauty, and immortality of the soul—that lives above and beyond the senses.

Mr. Gallaudet, the founder of the Deaf and Dumb Asylum at Hartford, was a person of very diminutive stature, with a smooth, placid physiognomy—irradiated, however, by a remarkably large, expressive eye, rolling at you over his spectacles. Of a frail and feeble constitution, and a mind of no great compass, he still possessed two faculties which rendered his career glorious. He had a clearness and precision in his perceptions, which rendered his mental operations almost as exact and certain as the movements of mechanism. It was this which enabled him to master the elements of the art of teaching the deaf and dumb, and to carry that art—in its uses as well as its philosophy—greatly beyond its condition when he entered upon it. This principle in the head was impelled to action by another in the heart—a deep conviction that it was his duty to be useful to his fellow-men. It is pleasing to observe how wide and ample a field may be harvested by a good man, even though he may not be a giant or a genius!

I must here tell you an anecdote still fresh in my recollection. When President Monroe made his tour through the New-England States, in the summer of 1817, the asylum was a novelty, and naturally enough was the pride of the good citizens of Hartford. Of course, the President was invited to see the performances of the new institution. He was scarcely out of his carriage, and delivered from the noise and confusion of his reception—for all the world turned out to see him—before he was hurried down to the place where the school was then kept.

A high central platform was prepared, like a throne, for the great man, and here he took his seat. Around were the spectators; on one side was Mr. Gallaudet, and Mr. Clerc, the well-known deaf and dumb professor from the school of the Abbé Sicard, in Paris. Mr. Gallaudet was a man of admirable address, and all being ready, he said to the President, in his smooth, seductive way—

" If your Excellency will be so kind as to ask some question, I will repeat it to Mr. Clerc on my fingers, and he will write an answer on the slate, to show the manner and facility of conversation by signs."

The President, who was exceedingly jaded by his journey, looked obfuscated; but he changed the position of his legs, showing a consciousness of the question, and then fell into a very brown study. Everybody expected something profound—equal to the occasion, and worthy of the chief magistrate of the greatest nation on the face of the globe. We waited a long time, every minute seeming an hour, through our impatience. At last it became awkward, and Mr. Gallaudet insinuated—

" If your Excellency will be so kind as to ask some question, I will repeat it on my fingers to Mr. Clerc, and he will write an answer on the slate, to show the manner and facility of conversing by signs."

The President again changed the position of his legs, and again meditated. We all supposed he was at the very bottom of the abyss of philosophy, hunting up some most profound and startling interrogation. Expectation was on tiptoe; every eye was leveled at the oracular lips, about to utter the amazing proposition. Still, he only meditated. A long time passed, and the impatience became agonizing. Again Mr. Gallaudet, seeming to fear that the great man was going to sleep, roused him by repeating his request. The President at last seemed conscious; his eye twinkled, his lips moved, sounds issued from his mouth—

"Ask him—how old he is !"—was the profound suggestion.

LETTER XXXVI.

Dr. Percival—His early Life—His Father's attempt to cure his Shyness—College Life—His First Love—His Medical Experience—His Poetical Career—An awkward Position—The Saddle on his own Back—Cooper and Percival at the City Hotel — Publication of his Poems at New York—The Edition in England—Other Literary Avocations—His Station at West Point—His great Learning—Assistance of Dr. Webster in his Dictionary—State Geologist in Connecticut—In Wisconsin—His Death—Estimate of his Character.

MY DEAR C******

I am glad to find, by your recent letter, that you approve of my hasty sketches of the men I have seen and known—even though they are not all of that general celebrity which creates, in advance, an interest in their behalf. No doubt the portrait of a man, whose renown has filled our ears, is more gratifying than one which merely presents the lineaments of an unknown, unheard-of individual. Yet every picture which is life-like—which possesses an obvious verisimilitude—is pleasing, especially if it seems to represent a type of some class of men, which we have seen in life. It is mainly upon this principle that the fictitious heroes and heroines of romance, interest us as deeply as even the celebrities of history. As I describe things I have seen, I hope my delineations may have so much seeming truth as to amuse you, even though they possess only that interest which attaches to all true pictures of humanity. I say this, not as an introduction, especially suited to this chapter, for I am now going to speak of names that are familiar to you: I make these reflections upon your letter, only as a precaution against any criticisms you may offer upon the less pretentious miniatures scattered through these pages.

The news comes, even while I write, that Percival, the poet, is dead! Yes—one by one, those I have known and cherished, are falling around me. Few of my early acquaintances are left, and I am but a lingerer among the graves of early friendship and love!

James Gates Percival was a native of Berlin,* the residence of my family, and I knew him well. His father was a physician—a man of ability, and of resolute and energetic character. His mother was by nature of a susceptible and delicate organization, and she seems to have imparted to her son these qualities, with a tendency to excessive mental development. He early manifested a morbid shyness and shrinking sensitiveness, which his father sought to cure by harsh measures. On one occasion he put the child behind him on horseback, and rode into the thickest of a sham fight, during a regimental muster. The result was, that the boy was almost thrown into convulsions.

Dr. Percival died when James was still young, and

---

* Berlin consists of three parishes—Worthington, where my father resided, New Britain, and Kensington. The latter was Percival's birthplace.

after a time his mother married a respectable farmer of the village by the name of Porter. The young Percival made extraordinary progress in his studies, but was little understood by those around him. He entered college at the age of sixteen, and speedily attracted attention by his acquisitions and his compositions. At this period he was often at my father's house, in Berlin, and being subject to paroxysms of great depression of spirits, he deeply excited the interest of my mother. Although, on the whole, he pursued his education with avidity and ambition, yet he often wandered forth in lonesome places, nursing a moody melancholy, and at one period, he actually contemplated suicide. From this he was diverted—mainly, I believe, by my mother's timely counsel and other kindly offices.

About this time he was frequently in the society of a beautiful and accomplished young lady of the neighborhood ; he botanized with her in the fields, and poetized with her in the library, and at last he thought himself in love. Months thus ran pleasantly on, when one day he made up his mind to give her a delicate hint of his condition. He did so, I believe, in verse. The young lady replied in plain prose, that she was engaged, and was speedily to be married ! The poet came to the conclusion that this was a deceitful world, and wrote Byronic verses. In 1820 he published a volume of poems, including the first part of his Prometheus.

Having studied medicine, he went to South Caro-

lina the same year, and established himself at Charleston, as a physician. He told me afterward, that, at
the end of some months, he had one patient, afflicted
with sore lips. He prescribed a dose of salts, gratis,
and this was a pretty fair example of his practice.

"I had got my name up for writing verses," said
he, "and found myself ruined."

"How so?" said I.

"When a person is really ill, he will not send for
a poet to cure him," was his answer.

Having little else before him, he directed his attention to literature, and published the first number
of his Clio, 1822. Soon after, he returned to the
North, and produced some miscellanies in prose and
verse. At this period, he had excited a deep interest
in the public mind, as well by his writings as his
somewhat eccentric life and manners. The melancholy which pervaded his poetry, with fugitive pieces
of great feeling and tenderness, together with a certain
wildness in his air and manner, rendered him an object of general curiosity, and in many cases of deep
sympathy. Of all this he seemed unconscious, and
walked the world like one who neither accepted nor
desired its friendship.

In the spring of 1823, I was walking up Broadway
in New York, and met him. I had been intimate
with him for several previous years, having often
seen him at my father's house; but I now observed,
that on seeing me, he turned aside, and evidently

PERCIVAL.   Vol 2, p. 132.

sought to avoid me. This was what I expected, for such was his habit of shrinking shyness, that it embarrassed him to meet even an old friend. I put myself in his way, and, after a few words of recognition, perceiving something more than usually downcast in his appearance, I asked him what was the occasion of it. At first he denied that any thing had happened, but at length, with some reluctance, he told me he had been making a tour to the North, and was out of money. His trunk was consequently detained on board the packet in which he had come down from Albany!

Percival had some patrimony, and though his means were narrow, they might have been sufficient for his comfort, with good management. But common sense —in the economy of life—was, unhappily, not one of his endowments. When he was about fifteen years old, his friends gave him fifty dollars, mounted him on a horse, and told him to ride till he had spent half his money, and then turn about and come home—thinking him competent to fulfill this simple programme. He rode on for two or three days, when he found that the horse's back was sadly galled. Shocked at what seemed an inhumanity—for his feelings were exquisitely tender—he resolved immediately to return. He would not mount the animal, for this would but aggravate its misery; so he set out on foot, and led the creature behind him. The saddle, however, still irritated the wound, and Percival, taking it from the animal's back, threw it over his own shoulder, and thus trudged home. I was familiar with this and other similar anecdotes. Thus knowing his imbecility in the common affairs of life, it did not surprise me to find him now without money, and in a state of complete bewilderment as to what should be done.

I gave him ten dollars, which he received and put into his pocket, making no reply—for such was his undemonstrative habit and manner. I asked him to dine with me the next day at the City Hotel, to which he agreed. I invited Mr. Cooper—the novelist—to meet him, and he came. It is not easy to conceive of two persons more strongly contrasting with each other. As they sat side by side at the table, I noted the difference. Mr. Cooper was in person solid, robust, athletic : in voice, manly ; in manner, earnest, emphatic, almost dictatorial—with something of self-assertion, bordering on egotism. The first effect was unpleasant, indeed repulsive, but there shone through all this a heartiness, a frankness, which excited confidence, respect, and at last affection.

Percival, on the contrary, was tall and thin, his chest sunken, his limbs long and feeble, his hair silken and sandy, his complexion light and feminine, his eye large and spectral, his whole air startled, his attitudes shy and shrinking, his voice abashed and whispering. Mr. Cooper ate like a man of excellent appetite and vigorous digestion : Percival scarce seemed to know that he was at the table. Cooper took his wine as if his lip appreciated it : Percival swallowed his, evidently without knowing or caring whether it was wine or water. Yet these two men conversed pleasantly together. After a time Percival was drawn out, and the stores of his mind were poured forth as from a cornucopia. I could see Cooper's gray eye dilate with delight and surprise.

I had a design in bringing these two men together, and this was to have a handsome edition of Percival's poems published for his benefit, and under such influences as to make it profitable to him. The matter was talked over between us, and before we parted, it was all arranged. I at once drew up a prospectus, and had it printed. I wrote a contract between Percival and the publisher, Charles Wiley, and had it duly signed. Mr. Cooper took the prospectus in hand, and aided by the powerful assistance of Mr. Bronson, Percival's college classmate, the subscription was actively pushed. The fairest ladies of New York gave a helping hand, and before I left the city, three hundred subscribers were secured. Provision had also been made for Percival's immediate comfort ; lodgings were furnished, and he was forthwith to prepare the copy for the promised volume. I returned to Hartford, but in a fortnight, got a letter asking me if I knew what had become of our poet ? Some weeks passed, during which time he was among the missing. At last it was discovered that he had been annoyed by a fiddling Frenchman, near his

room, and had fled to New Haven. There he had
entered into another contract for the publication of
his poems!

It required some weeks to disentangle the affair from
all these difficulties. At last, however, after many
delays and annoyances, the copy was furnished, and
the book printed. At that time I was on the point
of going to Europe. I delayed a fortnight to get a
perfect copy, so that I might take it with me—in order to secure its publication in England, for Percival's benefit. At last I departed, having obtained the
unbound sheets of a single copy. I sailed from New
York in the packet ship Canada—Percival accompanying me in the steamboat Nautilus, from White-
hall, to the vessel, which lay out in the stream. I
believe he regarded me as one of his best friends, but
as we shook hands, and I bade him farewell, he said
coldly, "Good-by"—his pale and spectral countenance showing not a ray of emotion.

Soon after reaching London, however, I received a
copy of the New York Commercial Advertiser, dated
Nov. 17, 1823, in which I read the following—there
being a small "P." in ink, at the bottom. I copy it
from the file of the New York Spectator of Nov. 17,
1823—then edited by W. L. Stone.

The Canada.—We never saw a ship spread her broad wings
to the breeze and go out to sea in finer style than did the ship
Canada yesterday. We received this morning the following
effusion from a gentleman who accompanied a friend on board,

and had watched the vessel from the steamboat till she was lost in the blue distance, and have no doubt that our friends will recognize the author.

TO THE CANADA ON GOING TO SEA.

The gallant ship is out at sea,
　Proudly o'er the water going ;
Along her sides the billows flee,
　Back in her wake a river flowing.
She dips her stem to meet the wave,
　And high the toss'd foam curls before it :
As if she felt the cheer we gave,
　　She takes her flight,
　　Where the sea looks bright,
And the sun in sparkles flashes o'er it.

Gallantly as she cuts her way—
　And now in distance far is fleeting,
There are some on board whose hearts are gay,
　And some whose hearts are wildly beating.
Loud was the cheer her seamen gave,
　As back they sent our welcome cheering—
Many a hand was seen to wave,
　　And some did weep
　　And fondly keep
Their gaze intent, when out of hearing.

They have parted, and now are far at sea—
　Heaven send them fine and gentle weather !
They parted not for eternity—
　Our hands shall soon be link'd together !
The sea was smooth and the sky was blue,
　And the tops of the ruffled waves were glowing—
As proudly on the vessel flew
　　Like the feather'd king
　　On his balanced wing,
To a distant land o'er the ocean going.

I knew Percival too well to feel hurt at his cool good-by—nevertheless, it was a pleasure to have this evidence of his feeling and his friendship. On reaching London, I made a contract with John Miller for

the publication of the poems in two volumes 12mo—
half the profits to go to the author. I also wrote for
it a brief biographical notice. A very handsome
edition soon appeared, and attracted some attention,
but excited no enthusiasm in London. On the whole,
the publication was a failure. The edition of one
thousand copies was not sold, but I subsequently induced Miller to send to Percival one hundred copies,
as his share of the proceeds. This was all he ever
received from the English edition.

After my return to America, I frequently met Percival, but never under circumstances which renewed
our intimacy. Indeed, by this time he had become
confirmed in his habits of abstraction in life and
manner, which rendered it difficult to enter into his
thoughts or feelings. He even seemed misanthrop-
ical, and repelled, as an offense, every thing that
jealousy could suspect to be either interested or intended as a gratuity or a favor. There were many
persons ready—nay desirous—to render him efficient
service, but they did not know how to approach him.

In 1824 he was appointed assistant surgeon in the
United States army, and professor of chemistry in
the Military Academy at West Point. This station
he soon abandoned, being disgusted, as he told me,
with one part of his duty—which was to examine
recruits, by inspection of their persons, and ascertain-
ing their weight, height, &c. About this time he was
employed and liberally paid by Mr. Samuel Walker,

of Boston, in editing an extensive edition of "Elegant
Extracts," both in verse and in prose; and afterward
in editing Malte Brun's large Geography, adding
thereto numerous useful notes. About this period
he was also engaged in assisting Dr. Webster, in preparing his quarto dictionary. In 1836, he received
from Connecticut a government appointment to assist
in a geological survey of the State. He entered upon
this duty, and his report was published in 1842. In
1852, he received a similar appointment for the State
of Wisconsin, and made his first report in 1855. He
was still engaged in this duty, when his career was
suddenly terminated by death, which took place at
Hazelgreen, in the State of Wisconsin, May, 1856.

With all the knowledge I possess of Dr. Percival's
life and character, he is still, to me, somewhat of an
enigma. That he was a man of powerful imagination and an intellect of great capacity, is manifest:
his poems prove the one—his amazing acquisitions,
the other. That his understanding was even of larger scope and measure than his fancy, is, I think,
apparent, for he not only had a vast range of knowledge—precise and reliable obedient to recollection
as the stores of a cyclopedia—yet his powers of combination, his judgment, were of the very first order.
This was evinced, not only in his connection with
Dr. Webster's Dictionary, already alluded to, by the
nice discrimination he displayed in philological inquiries, and the exactitude with which he rendered

the shadings of sense and meaning, in giving the definitions of words, but in the larger and grander surveys of geology—the largest and grandest of practical sciences. Such compass and such precision of knowledge—such power of exact as well as vast combination—are indeed marvelous. When we consider him in this aspect, and at the same time remember that thirty years ago he was captivating the world with his imaginative effusions, we have indeed a character of remarkable and almost contradictory elements.

Yet it must be added that, on the whole, his life was a complete shipwreck. He lived to excite admiration and wonder; yet in poverty, in isolation, in a complete solitude of the heart. He had not, I think, a single vice; his life was pure, just, upright. How then did he fail? The truth seems to be, that he was deficient in that sympathy which binds man to man, and hence he was an anomaly in the society among which he dwelt—a note out of tune with the great harmony of life around him. He was a grand intellect, a grand imagination, but without a heart. That he was born with a bosom full of all love and all kindness, we can not doubt; but the golden bowl seems to have been broken, almost at the fountain. By the time he was twenty, he began to stand aloof from his fellow-man. I think he had been deeply injured—nay ruined—by the reading of Byron's works, at that precise age when his soul was in all the sensitive bloom of spring, and its killing frost of atheism, of misanthropy, of pride, and scorn, fell upon it, and converted it into a scene of desolation.   The want of a genial circle of appreciation, of love and friendship, around his early life, left this malign influence to deepen his natural shyness into a positive and habitual self-banishment from his fellow-man.   Such is the sad interpretation I put upon his career.*

LETTER XXXVII.

A few Wayside Notes—The Poet Brainard—His first Introduction—Ripley's Tavern—Aunt Lucy—The little back-parlor—Brainard's Office—Anecdote—The Devil's Dun—The Lines on Niagara—Other Poems—One that is on the Sea—The Sea-bird's Song—Publication of Brainard's Poems—General Remarks—His Death.

MY DEAR C******

I have told you that in the autumn of 1823 I set out to visit Europe; but a few previous events are needful to bring my narrative to that epoch.   In 1821, clouds and darkness began to gather around my path.   By a fall from a horse, I was put upon crutches

---

* The notice of Dr. Percival in Kettell's Specimens of American Poets, was written at my request by Rev. Royal Robbins, of Kensington parish, Berlin, in which the poet lived.   It is a beautiful and just appreciation of his character at that time.   I know of no person so competent as he to give the world a biography of Percival.   He is familiar with the details of his whole career, and especially with the earlier portions of his life, and is, moreover, master of all the qualifications requisite to give interest and value to such a work.

for more than a year, and a cane for the rest of my
life. Ere long death entered my door, and my home
was desolate. I was once more alone—save only that
a child was left me, to grow to womanhood, and to
die a youthful mother, loving and beloved*—leaving
an infant soon to follow her to the tomb. My affairs
became embarrassed, my health failed, and my only
hope of renovation was in a change of scene.

---

* Sweet Spirit passed! 'Tis not for thee
　　Our bitter tears unmeasured flow—
Thy path to Heaven is traced, but we,
　　With grieving heart, must writhe below!

We mourn thy lost yet loving tone,
　　That made endearing names more dear,
And touched with music all its own
　　The warm fond hearts that clustered near.

We mourn thy form—thy spirit bright,
　　Which shone so late mid bridal flowers—
And yet could pour angelic light
　　Across the last tempestuous hours!

We mourn for thee—so sudden-flown,
　　When least we thought from thee to sever—
As if some star we deemed our own,
　　At brightest hour had set forever!

Unpitying Fate! thy dark designs
　　Can spare the weary, wasted, bent,
Yet crush the fairest thing that shines
　　Where peace and joy have pitched their tent!

Could not the youthful mother claim
　　Exemption from thy stern decree?
Could not the child that lisped her name,
　　Extort one pitying tear from thee?

Ah, human woes are not thy care!
　　The lightning, in its plunge of wrath,
Turns not, with heedful thought, to spare
　　The buzzing insect in its path!

But before I give you a sketch of my experience and observations abroad, I must present one portrait more—that of my friend Brainard.* He came to Hartford in February, 1822, to take the editorial charge of the Connecticut Mirror—Mr. Stone, as I have stated, having left it a short time before. He was now twenty-six years old, and had gained some reputation for wit and poetical talent. One day a young man, small in stature, with a curious mixture of ease and awkwardness, of humor and humility, came into my office, and introduced himself as Mr. Brainard. I gave him a hearty welcome, for I had heard very pleasant accounts of him. As was natural, I made a complimentary allusion to his poems,

> Forgive us, Heaven! if thus we mourn
>   The lost on earth—the blest above—
> So rudely from our bosom torn,
>   With all its clinging ties of love!
>
> One bright, blest spot of sunshine played
>   Upon the landscape's varied breast—
> Yet there the clouds have cast their shade
>   And there the deepest shadows rest!

* John Gardiner Caulkins Brainard was the youngest son of Jeremiah G. Brainard, of New London, judge of the supreme court, whom I have already mentioned in the history of my military adventures in 1813. His two elder brothers, William F., a lawyer, and Dyer, a physician, were both men of wit and learning; the first died some years since, the latter is still living. John, of whom I now write, was born in 1795, educated at Yale, prepared for the law, and settled at Middletown 1819. He died at New London, in 1828. The portrait of him in Messrs. Duyckincks' "Cyclopædia of American Literature," is from an engraving in the Token for 1830, and that is taken from a miniature I had painted of him, by our mutual friend, Tisdale. It was from recollection, but gives a pretty good idea of the sad yet humorous, boyish yet manly, countenance of the original.

which I had seen and admired. A smile, yet shaded with something of melancholy, came over his face, as he replied—

"Don't expect too much of me; I never succeeded in any thing yet. I never could draw a mug of cider without spilling more than half of it!"

I afterward found that much truth was thus spoken in jest: this was, in point of fact, precisely Brainard's appreciation of himself. All his life, feeling that he could do something, he still entertained a mournful and disheartening conviction that, on the whole, he was doomed to failure and disappointment. There was sad prophecy in this presentiment —a prophecy which he at once made and fulfilled.

We soon became friends, and at last intimates. I was now boarding at "Ripley's"—a good old-fashioned tavern, over which presided Major Ripley, respected for revolutionary services, an amiable character, and a long Continental queue. In the administration of the establishment he was ably supported by his daughter, Aunt Lucy—the very genius of tavern courtesy, cookery, and comfort. Here Brainard joined me, and we took our rooms side by side. Thus for more than a year we were together, as intimate as brothers. He was of a child-like disposition, and craved constant sympathy. He soon got into the habit of depending upon me in many things, and at last—especially in dull weather, or when he was sad, or something went wrong with him—he crept into my bed, as if it was his right. At that period of gloom in my own fortunes, this was as well a solace to me as to him. After my return from Europe we resumed these relations, and for some months more we were thus together.

Brainard's life has been frequently written. The sketch of him in Kettell's "Specimens," I furnished, soon after his death. Mr. Robbins, of Berlin, wrote a beautiful biographical memoir of him for Hopkins' edition of his poems, published at Hartford, in 1842. A more elaborate notice of his life, character, and genius, had been given in Whittier's edition of his "Remains," 1832. To this just and feeling memoir, by a kindred spirit—one every way qualified to appreciate and to illustrate his subject—I have now nothing to add, except a few personal recollections— such as were derived from my long intercourse and intimacy with him.

Perhaps I cannot do better than to begin at once, and give you a sketch of a single incident, which will reflect light upon many others. The scene opens in Miss Lucy's little back-parlor—a small, cozy, carpeted room, with two cushioned rocking-chairs, and a bright hickory fire. It is a chill November night, about seven o'clock of a Friday evening. The Mirror —Brainard's paper—is to appear on the morning of the morrow, it being a weekly sheet, and Saturday its day of publication. The week has thus far passed, and he has not written for it a line. How the days

have gone he can hardly tell. He has read a little—
dipped into Byron, pored over the last Waverley
novel, and been to see his friends; at all events, he
had got rid of the time. He has not felt competent
to bend down to his work, and has put it off till the
last moment. No further delay is possible. He is
now not well; he has a cold, and this has taken the
shape of a swelling of the tonsils, almost amounting
to quinsy, as was usual with him in such attacks.

Miss Lucy, who takes a motherly interest in him,
tells him not to go out, and his own inclinations suggest the charms of a quiet evening in the rocking-
chair, by a good fire—especially in comparison with
going to his comfortless office, and drudging for the
inky devils of the press. He lingers till eight, and
then suddenly rousing himself, by a desperate effort,
throws on his cloak and sallies forth. As was not
uncommon, I go with him. A dim fire is kindled
in the small Franklin stove in his office, and we sit
down. Brainard, as was his wont, especially when
he was in trouble, falls into a curious train of reflections, half comic and half serious.

" Would to heaven," he says, " I were a slave. I
think a slave, with a good master, has a good time
of it. The responsibility of taking care of himself—
the most terrible burden of life—is put on his master's shoulders. Madame Roland, with a slight altera-
tion, would have uttered a profound truth. She
should have said—' Oh, liberty, liberty, thou art a

humbug!' After all, liberty is the greatest possible slavery, for it puts upon a man the responsibility of taking care of himself. If he goes wrong—why he's damned! If a slave sins, he's only flogged, and gets over it, and there's an end of it. Now, if I could only be flogged, and settle the matter that way, I should be perfectly happy. But here comes my tormentor."

The door is now opened, and a boy with a touseled head and inky countenance, enters, saying curtly—"Copy, Mr. Brainard!"

"Come in fifteen minutes!" says the editor, with a droll mixture of fun and despair.

Brainard makes a few observations, and sits down at his little narrow pine table—hacked along the edges with many a restless penknife. He seems to notice these marks, and pausing a moment, says—

"This table reminds me of one of my brother William's stories. There was an old man in Groton, who had but one child, and she was a daughter. When she was about eighteen, several young men came to see her. At last she picked out one of them, and desired to marry him. He seemed a fit match enough, but the father positively refused his consent. For a long time he persisted, and would give no reason for his conduct. At last, he took his daughter aside, and said—'Now, Sarah, I think pretty well of this young man in general, but I've observed that he's given to whittling. There's no harm in that, but the point is this: he whittles and whittles, and never makes nothing! Now I tell you, I'll never give my only daughter to such a feller as that!' Whenever Bill told this story, he used to insinuate that this whittling chap, who never made any thing, was me! At any rate, I think it would have suited me, exactly."

Some time passed in similar talk, when at last Brainard turned suddenly, took up his pen and began to write. I sat apart, and left him to his work. Some twenty minutes passed, when, with a radiant smile on his face, he got up, approached the fire, and taking the candle to light his paper, read as follows:

"THE FALL OF NIAGARA.

" The thoughts are strange that crowd into my brain,
   While I look upward to thee. It would seem
   As if God pour'd thee from his ' hollow hand,'
   And hung his bow upon thy awful front ;
   And spoke in that loud voice that seem'd to him
   Who dwelt in Patmos for his Saviour's sake,
   ' The sound of many waters ;' and had bade
   Thy flood to chronicle the ages back,
   And notch his cent'ries in the eternal rocks !"

He had hardly done reading, when the boy came. Brainard handed him the lines—on a small scrap of rather coarse paper—and told him to come again in half an hour. Before this time had elapsed, he had finished, and read me the following stanza :

" Deep calleth unto deep. And what are we,
   That hear the question of that voice sublime ?

BRAINARD WRITING "THE FALL OF NIAGARA."   Vol. 2, p. 148.

Oh! what are all the notes that ever rung
From war's vain trumpet by thy thundering side?
Yea, what is all the riot man can make,
In his short life, to thy unceasing roar?
And yet, bold babbler, what art thou to Him
Who drown'd a world, and heap'd the waters far
Above its loftiest mountains? A light wave,
That breathes and whispers of its Maker's might."

These lines having been furnished, Brainard left
his office, and we returned to Miss Lucy's parlor. He
seemed utterly unconscious of what he had done. I
praised the verses, but he thought I only spoke warmly from friendly interest. The lines went forth, and
produced a sensation of delight over the whole country. Almost every exchange paper that came to the
office had extracted them: even then he would scarce
believe that he had done any thing very clever. And
thus, under these precise circumstances, were composed the most suggestive and sublime stanzas upon
Niagara, that were ever penned. Brainard had never,
as he told me, been within less than five hundred
miles of the cataract, nor do I believe, that when he
went to the office, he had meditated upon the subject. It was one of those inspirations which come to
the poet—and often come like the lightning—in the
very midst of clouds and darkness.

You will readily see, from the circumstances I have
mentioned, that I knew the history of most of Brainard's pieces, as they came out, from time to time, in
his newspaper. Nearly all of them were occasional

—that is, suggested by passing events or incidents in the poet's experience. The exquisite lines beginning,

> "The dead leaves strew the forest walk,
> And wither'd are the pale wild-flowers"—

appeared a few days after he had taken leave of a young lady from Savannah, who had spent a month at our hotel, and had left an impression upon his sensitive heart, which the lines, mournful and touching as they are, only reveal to those who witnessed his emotions. Many were struck off in the extreme exigencies of the devil's dun—his very claws upon him. In these cases, he doubtless resorted to the treasures of his mind, which seems to have been largely stored with the scenery of his native State, and the legends connected with them. Two elements, in nearly equal proportion, seemed to fill his soul—the humorous and the sublime—and often in such contiguity, or even mixture, as to heighten the effect of each—this, however, being more noticeable in his conversation than his writings. It was sometimes amazing to watch the operations of his mind—even in moments of familiarity, often starting from some trivial or perhaps ludicrous incident, into a train of the most lofty and sublime thought. I have compared him, in my own mind, to a child playing upon the sea-beach, who by chance picks up and winds a Triton's shell, or wandering into some cathedral, lays his finger upon the clavier of the organ, and falling upon the key-note of his heart, draws from the instrument all its sounding melody.

I trust you will pardon me if I give the history of one or two other poems, connected with my own observation. I have told you that in the autumn of 1823, I went to Europe, and was absent for a year. On parting with Brainard, we mutually promised to write each other, often. Yet I received not a line from him during my absence. I knew his habits and forgave him—though I was certainly pained by such neglect. On meeting him after my return, I alluded to this. Without saying a word, he went away for a short time: on his return, he put into my hands a copy of the Mirror, which had appeared a few days before, and pointing to the lines—which I extract below— he left me. His reply, thus indicated, was indeed gratifying. You will understand that at the time, Lafayette had just arrived in the country.

ONE THAT'S ON THE SEA.

With gallant sail and streamer gay,
Sweeping along the splendid bay,
That, throng'd by thousands, seems to greet
The bearer of a precious freight,
The Cadmus comes; and every wave
Is glad the welcomed prow to lave:
 What are the ship and freight to me?
 I look for One that's on the sea.

"Welcome Fayette," the million cries:
From heart to heart the ardor flies,

And drum and bell and cannon noise,
In concord with a nation's voice,
Is pealing through a grateful land,
And all go with him. Here I stand,
  Musing on One that's dear to me,
  Yet sailing on the dangerous sea.

Be thy days happy here, Fayette!
Long may they be so—long—but yet
To me there's one that, dearest still,
Clings to my heart and chains my will.
His languid limbs and feverish head
Are laid upon a sea-sick bed :
  Perhaps his thoughts are fix'd on me,
  While toss'd upon the mighty sea.

I am alone. Let thousands throng
The noisy, crowded streets along :
Sweet be the beam of beauty's gaze—
Loud be the shout that freemen raise—
Let patriots grasp thy noble hand,
And welcome thee to Freedom's land—
  Alas! I think of none but he
  Who sails across the foaming sea!

So when the moon is shedding light
Upon the stars, and all is bright
And beautiful; when every eye
Looks upward to the glorious sky;
How have I turn'd my silent gaze,
To catch one little taper's blaze :
  'Twas from a spot too dear to me—
  The home of him that's on the sea.

Ought I not to have been satisfied? If you will
compare these lines with those by Percival, under

circumstances not altogether dissimilar, you will have the means of comparing the two poets—the one feeling through the suggestions of his imagination, the other exercising his imagination through the impulse of his feelings. Percival was a poet of the fancy—Brainard, of the heart.

Still one more passing note. The "Sea-Bird's Song" appears to me one of the most poetical compositions in Brainard's collection, and the history of it can not be uninteresting. It was written some time after my return from England, and when I was again married and settled at Hartford. He was a frequent—almost daily visitor at our house, and took especial pleasure in hearing my wife sing. He had no skill in music, but, as with most persons of a sentimental turn, his choice always fell upon minors. One evening his ear caught up the old Welsh tune of "Taffy Morgan," which is, in point of fact, a composition of great power, especially when it is slowly and seriously executed. He was greatly affected by it, and some one suggested that he should compose a song to suit it. I remarked that I had often thought the song of a sea-bird, if treated with ballad simplicity and vigor, might be very effective. He began to ponder, and the next day brought a verse to try its rhythm with the music. This being approved, he went on, and two days after, came with the whole poem, which he slightly altered and adapted upon hearing it sung. Having said thus much, pardon me

7*

for reciting the lines, and asking you to get some good ballad-singer to give it to you, in the cadence of the old Welch melody I have mentioned. Thus sung, it is one of the most thrilling compositions I have ever heard.

THE SEA-BIRD'S SONG.

On the deep is the mariner's danger—
  On the deep is the mariner's death:
Who, to fear of the tempest a stranger,
    Sees the last bubble burst of his breath?
    'Tis the sea-bird, sea-bird, sea-bird,
      Lone looker on despair:
    The sea-bird, sea-bird, sea-bird,
      The only witness there!

Who watches their course, who so mildly
  Careen to the kiss of the breeze?
Who lists to their shrieks, who so wildly
  Are clasped in the arms of the seas?
    'Tis the sea-bird, &c.

Who hovers on high o'er the lover,
  And her who has clung to his neck?
Whose wing is the wing that can cover
  With its shadow the foundering wreck?
    'Tis the sea-bird, &c.

My eye in the light of the billow,
  My wing on the wake of the wave,
I shall take to my breast, for a pillow,
  The shroud of the fair and the brave!
    'Tis the sea-bird, &c.

My foot on the iceberg has lighted
  When hoarse the wild winds veer about;

My eye, when the bark is benighted,
  Sees the lamp of the lighthouse go out!
I'm the sea-bird, sea-bird, sea-bird,
    Lone looker on despair;
  The sea-bird, sea-bird, sea-bird,
    The only witness there!

Where is there a song of more wild and impressive imagery—exciting more deep and touching emotions, than this?

These stanzas were written in the spring of 1826. The year before I had persuaded Brainard to make a collection of his poems, and have them published. At first his lip curled at the idea, as being too pretentious; he insisted that he had done nothing to justify the publication of a volume. Gradually he began to think of it, and at length—March 14, 1825—I induced him to sign a contract, authorizing me to make arrangements for the work. He set about the preparation, and at length—after much lagging and many lapses—the pieces were selected and arranged. When all was ready, I persuaded him to go to New York with me, to settle the matter with a publisher. I introduced him to Bliss & White, and they readily undertook it, on the terms of joint and equal profits. Thus appeared the little volume, with Bunyan's quaint rhyme for a motto—

  "Some said, 'John, print it'—others said, 'Not so;'
  Some said, 'It might do good'—others said, 'No!'"

I must note a slight incident which occurred at

New York, illustrative of Brainard's character. He was keenly alive to every species of beauty, in nature and art. His appreciation of the beauties of literature amounted to passion. That he had a craving for pathos and sublimity, is manifest from his works; yet he seemed to feel the nicer and more latent touches of wit and humor with a greater intensity of delight, than any other species of literary luxury. He was hence a special admirer of Halleck, and more than once remarked that he should like to see him. I proposed to introduce him; but he was shy of all formal meetings, and seemed indeed to feel that there would be a kind of presumption in his being presented to the leading poet of the great metropolis.

I was therefore obliged to give up the idea of effecting a meeting between these two persons, both natives of Connecticut, and peculiarly fitted to appreciate and admire each other. One morning, however, fortune seemed to favor me. As we entered the bookstore of Messrs. Bliss & White—then on the eastern side of Broadway, near Cedar-street—I saw Halleck at the further end of the room. Incautiously, I told this to Brainard. He eagerly asked me which was the poet, among two or three persons that were standing together. I pointed him out. Brainard took a long and earnest gaze, then turned on his heel, and I could not find him for the rest of the day!

His little volume was very favorably received by the public, and he was universally recognized as a true poet. These effusions, however, were regarded rather in the light of promise than fulfillment, and therefore people generally looked forward to the achievement of some greater work. I felt this, and frequently urged him to undertake a serious poem, which might develop his genius and establish his fame. He thought of it, but his habitual inertness mastered him. I returned to the subject, however, and we frequently conversed upon it. At last, he seemed to have resolved on the attempt, and actually wrote a considerable number of stanzas. After a time, however, he gave it up in despair. He told me, frankly, that it was impossible for him to sustain the continuity of thought and consistency of purpose indispensable to such an achievement. What he had actually done was merely an introduction, and was afterward published under the title of "*Sketch of an Occurrence on board a Brig.*" Whoever has read these lines, can not fail to lament that weakness in the author—constitutional and habitual—which rendered him incompetent to continue a flight so nobly begun.

One anecdote—in addition to those already before the public—and I shall close this sketch. Brainard's talent for repartee was of the first order. On one occasion, Nathan Smith, an eminent lawyer, was at Ripley's tavern, in the midst of a circle of judges and lawyers, attending the court. He was an Episcopalian, and at this time was considered by his political adversaries—unjustly, no doubt—as the paid agent of that persuasion, now clamoring for a sum of money from the State, to lay the foundation of a "Bishops' Fund." He was thus regarded somewhat in the same light as O'Connell, who, while he was the great patriot leader of Irish independence, was at the same time liberally supported by the "rint." By accident, Brainard came in, and Smith, noticing a little feathery attempt at whiskers down his cheek, rallied him upon it.

"It will never do," said he; "you can not raise it, Brainard. Come, here's sixpence—take that, and go to the barber's and get it shaved off! It will smooth your cheek, and ease your conscience."

Brainard drew himself up, and said, with great dignity—as Smith held out the sixpence on the point of his forefinger—"No, sir, you had better keep it for the Bishops' Fund!"

I need not—I must not—prolong this sketch. What I have said, is sufficient to give you an insight into the character of this gifted child of genius. In person he was very short, with large hands and feet, and a walk paddling and awkward. His hair was light-brown, his skin pallid, his eye large and bluish-gray, his lips thick, his forehead smooth, white, and handsome; his brow beautifully arched, and edged with a definite, narrow line. His general appearance was that of a somewhat clumsy boy. His countenance was usually dull, yet with a wonderful power of expression—wit, drollery, seriousness, chasing each other in rapid succession. Its changes were at once sudden and marvelous. At one moment he looked stupid and then inspired. His face was like a revolving light—now dull and dark—now radiant, and shedding its beams on all around. His manners were subject to a similar change; usually he seemed uncouth, yet often have I seen him seductively courteous. In short, he was a bundle of contradictions : generally he was ugly, yet sometimes handsome; for the most part he was awkward, yet often graceful; his countenance was ordinarily dull, yet frequently beaming with light.

Thus with a look and appearance of youth—with indeed something of the waywardness and improvidence of boyhood, even when he had reached the full age of manhood—he was still full of noble thoughts and sentiments. In his editorial career—though he was negligent, dilatory, sometimes almost imbecile from a sort of constitutional inertness—still a train of inextinguishable light remains to gleam along his path. Many a busy, toiling editor has filled his daily columns for years, without leaving a living page behind him; while Brainard, with all his failings and irregularities, has left a collection of gems, which loving, and tender, and poetic hearts will wear and cherish to immortality. And among all that he wrote—be it remembered, thus idly, recklessly, as it might seem—there is not a line that, "dying, he could wish to blot." His love of parents, of home, of kindred, was beautiful indeed; his love of nature, and especially of the

scenes of his childhood, was the affection of one never
weaned from the remembrance of his mother's breast.
He was true in friendship, chivalrous in all that belonged to personal honor. I never heard him utter a
malignant thought—I never knew him to pursue an
unjust design. At the early age of eight-and-twenty
he was admonished that his end was near. With a
submissive spirit he resigned himself to his doom,
and, in pious, gentle, cheerful faith, he departed on
the 26th of September, 1828.

> Weep not for him, who hath laid his head
>   On a pillow of earth in the cypress shade;
> For the sweetest dews that the night airs shed,
>   Descend on the couch for that sleeper made.
>
> Weep not for him, though the wintry sleet
>   Throw its chill folds o'er his manly breast—
> That spotless robe is a covering meet
>   For the shrouded soul in its home of rest!
>
> Weep not for him, though his heart is still,
>   And the soul-lit eye like a lamp grown dim—
> Though the noble pulse is an icy rill,
>   By the hoar-frost chained—Oh, weep not for him!
>
> The diamond gathers its purest ray
>   In the hidden grot where no sun is known—
> And the sweetest voices of music play
>   In the trembling ear of silence alone:
>
> And there in the hush of that starless tomb
>   A holier light breaks in on the eye,
> And wind-harps steal through the sullen gloom,
>   To woo that sleeper away to the sky!

LETTER XXXVIII.

My first Voyage across the Atlantic—England—London—My Tour on the Continent—Return to England—Visit to Barley Wood—Hannah More —Inquiries as to Books for Education—Ireland—Dublin—The Giant's Causeway—Scotland—Scenery of the Lady of the Lake—Glasgow—Edinburgh.

MY DEAR C******

It was, as I have already told you, on the 16th of November, 1823, that I set sail in the Canada, Captain Macy, on my first visit to Europe. I have now before me four volumes of notes made during my tour; but be not alarmed—I shall not inflict them upon you. I might, perhaps, have ventured to publish them when they were fresh, but since that period the world has been inundated with tales of travels. I shall therefore only give you a rapid outline of my adventures, and a few sketches of men and things, which may perchance interest you.

Our voyage was—as usual at that season of the year—tempestuous. As we approached the British Islands, we were beset by a regular hurricane. On the 5th of December, the captain kindly informed us that we were almost precisely in the situation of the Albion,* the day before she was wrecked on the rocky

---

* The Albion was a packet ship plying between New York and Liverpool. She sailed from the former port April 1, 1822, and went ashore on the 22d of the same month. She had twenty-four seamen and twenty-eight passengers : seven of the former and two of the latter, only, were saved.

headland of Kinsale—at the southeast extremity of Ireland—an event which had spread general gloom throughout the United States. As night set in, we were struck with a squall, and with difficulty the vessel was brought round, so as to lie to. The storm was fearful, and the frequent concussions of the waves upon the ship, sounding like reports of artillery, made her reel and stagger like a drunken man. The morning came at last, and the weather was fair, but our deck was swept of its boats, bulwarks, and hen-coops. Our old cow in her hovel, the covering of the steerage, and that of the companion-way, were saved. We had, however, some gratis sea-bathing in our berths —terribly suggestive of the chill temperature of that abyss which might soon be our grave. The next morning we took a pilot, and on the 8th of December entered the dock at Liverpool.

As this was my first experience at sea, I beg you to forgive this brief description. I had suffered fearfully by sea-sickness, and had scarce strength to walk

---

Among the persons lost was Alexander W. Fisher, Professor of Mathematics in Yale College. He was a young man—twenty-eight years old —of fine genius, and great expectations were entertained as to his future achievements. A person who escaped from the wreck, whom I chanced to meet, told me that the last he saw of Mr. Fisher, he was in his berth with a pocket-compass in his hand, watching the course of the vessel. A moment after she struck, and he saw him no more.

The ship went to pieces on the rocks, in face of high perpendicular cliffs. The people of the neighborhood rendered all possible assistance, but their efforts were but partially successful. The struggles of the sufferers, clinging to ropes, yards, and points of the rocks, in the very sight of persons on shore, were fearful, and the details given of these scenes, rendered the event one of the most agonizing on record.

ashore. I felt such horror—such disgust of the sea, that I could easily have pledged myself never to venture upon it again. Strange to say, this all passed away like a dream: my strength revived, and even my constitution, shattered by long suffering, seemed to be renovated. With the return of health and spirits, my journey to London seemed like a triumphal march. Though it was December, the landscape was intensely green, while the atmosphere was dark as twilight. The canopy of heaven seemed to have come half way down, as if the sky had actually begun to fall. Yet this was England! Oh, what emotions filled my breast as I looked on Kenilworth, Warwick, and Litchfield, and at last on London!

I remained at the latter place about a month, and then went to Paris. In April I departed, and visiting Switzerland, and a portion of Germany, followed the Rhine to Cologne. Thence I traveled through Flanders and Holland, and taking a sloop at Rotterdam, swung down the Maese, and in May reached London, by way of the Thames.

I soon after departed for Bristol—taking the renowned cathedral at Salisbury and the Druidical ruin of Stonehenge in my way. Having reached that city and seen its sights, I hired a post-coach, and went to Barley-wood—some ten miles distant. Hannah More was still there! The house consisted of a small thatched edifice—half cottage and half villa—tidily kept, and garnished with vines and trellices, giving it a

cheerful and even tasteful appearance. Its site was on
a gentle hill, sloping to the southeast, and commanding a charming view over the undulating country
around, including the adjacent village of Wrington,
with a wide valley sloping to the Bay of Bristol—the
latter sparkling in the distance, and bounded by the
Welch mountains, in the far horizon. Behind the
house, and on the crown of the hill, was a small copse,
threaded with neat gravel walks, and at particular
points embellished with objects of interest. In one
place there was a little rustic temple, with this motto—
Audi Hospes, contemnere opes; in another, there was a
stone monument, erected to the memory of Bishop
Porteus, who had been a particular friend of the proprietor of the place. A little further on, I found another monument, with this inscription: *"To John
Locke, born in this village, this monument is erected by
Mrs. Montague, and presented to Hannah More."* From
this sequestered spot, an artificial opening was cut
through the foliage of the trees, giving a view of the
very house—about a mile distant—in which Locke
was born! In another place was a small temple built
of roots, which might have served for the shrine of
some untamed race of Dryads.

Mrs. More was now seventy-nine years of age,* and

---

* Hannah More was born at Stapleton, in 1744. She and her sisters
established a boarding-school in this village, but afterward it was removed to Bristol, and became very successful. Hannah More early became a writer, and at the age of seventeen, she published a pastoral
drama, entitled "Search after Happiness." Being intimate with Gar-

was very infirm, having kept her room for two years. She was small, and wasted away. Her attire was of dark-red bombazine, made loose like a dressing-gown. Her eyes were black and penetrating, her face glowing with cheerfulness, through a lace-work of wrinkles. Her head-dress was a modification of the coiffure of her earlier days—the hair being slightly frizzed, and lightly powdered, yet the whole group of moderate dimensions.

She received me with great cordiality, and learning that I was from Hartford, immediately inquired about Mrs. Sigourney, Mr. Gallaudet, and Alice Coggswell : of the latter she spoke with great interest. She mentioned several Americans who had visited her, and others with whom she had held correspondence. Her mind and feelings were alive to every subject that was suggested. She spoke very freely of her writings and her career. I told her of the interest I had taken, when a child, in the story of the Shepherd of Salisbury Plain, upon which she recounted its history, remarking that the character of the hero was modeled from life, though the incidents were fictitious. Her tract, called "Village Politics, by Will Chip," was written at the request of the British Ministry,

---

rick, she wrote several plays, which were performed. Afterward she regretted these works, her new religious views leading her to condemn the stage. She amassed a handsome fortune, and purchasing Barleywood, she fitted it up as I have described it. Soon after I was there, in consequence of the frauds of her servants, her means were so diminished, that she was obliged to leave it. She removed to Clifton, near Bristol, and died September, 1833.

and two million copies were sold the first year. She showed me copies of Cœlebs in Search of a Wife— the most successful of her works—in French and German, and a copy of one of her sacred dramas— "Moses in the Bullrushes"—on palm-leaves, in the Cingalese tongue—it having been translated into that language by the missionary school at Ceylon. She showed me also the knife with which the leaf had been prepared, and the scratches made in it to receive the ink. She expressed a warm interest in America, and stated that Wilberforce had always exerted him-self to establish and maintain good relations between Great Britain and our country. I suggested to her that in the United States, the general impression— that of the great mass of the people—was that the English were unfriendly to us. She said it was not so. I replied that the Americans all read the Eng-lish newspapers, and generally, the products of the British press ; that feelings of dislike, disgust, ani-mosity, certainly pervaded most of these publications, and it was natural to suppose that these were the reflections of public opinion in Great Britain. At all events, our people regarded them as such, and hence inferred that England was our enemy. She express-ed great regret at this state of things, and said all good people should strive to keep peace between the two countries : to all which I warmly assented.

My interview with this excellent lady was, on the whole, most gratifying. Regarding her as one of the greatest benefactors of the age—as, indeed, one of the most remarkable women that had ever lived—I looked upon her not only with veneration but affection. She was one of the chief instruments by which the torrent of vice and licentiousness, emanating from the French Revolution and inundating the British Islands, was checked and driven back : she was even, to a great extent, the permanent reformer of British morals and manners, as well among the high as the humble. And besides, I felt that I owed her a special debt, and my visit to her was almost like a pilgrimage to the shrine of a divinity. When I left America, I had it in mind to render my travels subservient to a desire I had long entertained of making a reform —or at least an improvement—in books for youth. I had made researches in London, France, and Germany, for works that might aid my design. It is true I had little success, for while scientific and classical education was sedulously encouraged on the continent as well as in England, it seemed to be thought, either that popular education was not a subject worthy of attention, or that Dilworth and Mother Goose had done all that could be done. In this interview with the most successful and most efficient teacher of the age, I had the subject still in mind; and discerning by what she had accomplished, the vast field that was open, and actually inviting cultivation, I began from this time to think of attempting to realize the project I had formed. It is true that, in some respects, the example I had just contemplated was different from my own scheme. Hannah More had written chiefly for the grown-up masses; I had it in contemplation to begin further back—with the children. Her means, however, seemed adapted to my purpose: her success, to encourage my attempt. She had discovered that truth could be made attractive to simple minds. Fiction was, indeed, often her vehicle, but it was not her end. The great charm of these works which had captivated the million, was their verisimilitude. Was there not, then, a natural relish for truth in all minds, or at least was there not a way of presenting it, which made it even more interesting than romance? Did not children love truth? If so, was it necessary to feed them on fiction? Could not history, natural history, geography, biography, become the elements of juvenile works, in place of fairies and giants, and mere monsters of the imagination? These were the inquiries that from this time filled my mind.

Taking leave of Barley-wood and its interesting occupant, I traversed Wales, and embarking at Holyhead, passed over to Ireland. Having seen Dublin, with the extraordinary contrasts of sumptuousness in some of its streets and edifices, with the fearful squalidness and poverty in others—I passed on to the North. Having taken a wondering view of the Giants' Causeway, I returned to Belfast, embarked in a steamboat, and went over to Greenock. Thence I proceeded toward Dumbarton, and in the early evening, as I approached the town in a small steamer, I actually realized, in the distance before me, the scene of the song—

> "The sun has gone down behind lofty Ben Lomond,
>   And left the red clouds to preside o'er the scene."

On the morrow I went to Loch Lomond, crossing the lake in a steamboat; thence on foot to Callender, and spent two days around Loch Katrine, amid the scenery of the Lady of the Lake. With a copy of that poem in my hand, which I had bought of a peasant on the borders of Loch Lomond, I easily traced out the principal landmarks of the story: "Ellen's Isle," nearly in the middle of the lake; on the northern shore, "the Silver Strand," where the maiden met Fitz James; far to the east, Benain, rearing its "forehead fair" to the sky; to the south, the rocky pyramid called "Roderick's Watch-tower;" and still beyond, the "Goblin's Cave." Leaving the lake, I passed through the Trosachs, a wild rocky glen, and the scene of the most startling events in the poem. At last I came to Coilantogle Ford, where the deadly struggle took place between the two heroes of the poem—Roderick and Fitz James. Finally, I went to the borders of Loch Achray—a placid sheet of water—beautiful by nature, but still more enchanting through the delightful associations of poetic art.

> "The minstrel came once more to view
>   The eastern ridge of Benvenue,

> For ere he parted he would say,
> Farewell to lovely Loch Achray.
> Where shall he find, in foreign land,
> So lone a lake, so sweet a strand!"
>
> *   *   *   *   *

But I must forbear. I have pledged myself not to weary you with descriptions of scenery, and especially with that which is familiar to you in twenty books of travels. Forgive me this instance of weakness, and I will try not to sin again—at least till I get out of Scotland. Having spent two days in this region of poetry and romance, I left for Glasgow, and at last reached Edinburgh.

LETTER XXXIX.

Edinburgh—The Court of Sessions—Cranstoun, Cockburn, Moncrief—Lockhart—Jeffrey—Sir Walter Scott.

MY DEAR C******

Think of being in Edinburgh, and Scott, Jeffrey, Chalmers, Dugald Stuart, Lockhart, there! It was then decidedly the literary metropolis of the Three Kingdoms—not through the amount of its productions, but their superiority. The eloquent, sparkling, trenchant Edinburgh Review was the type of Scottish genius; the heavy Quarterly represented London. I had several letters of introduction—among

them one to Blackwood, another to Constable, another to Miss Y .... The latter proved fortunate.
Her father was a Writer to the Signet—an elderly
gentleman of excellent position, and exceedingly fond
of showing off "Auld Reekie." Well indeed might
he be, for of all the cities I have seen, it is, in many
respects, the most interesting. I am told it is gloomy
in winter, but now it was the zenith of spring. The
twilight did not wholly disappear till twelve, and the
dawn was visible at one. If nature, in these high
latitudes, falls into a harsh and savage humor in winter, it makes ample amends in summer.

The very day after delivering my letters, Mr. Y ....
called on me, and showed me the lions of the town.
Many of them, all indeed, were interesting, but I pass
them by, and shall only linger a short time at the
Court of Sessions, which is the supreme civil court
of Scotland. This, with the High Court of Justi-
tiary—the supreme criminal court—forms the College of Justice, and constitutes the supreme judicial
system of Scotland. Their sessions are held in the
old Parliament House, situated in the center of the
Old Town.

We entered a large Gothic hall, opening, as I observed, into various contiguous apartments. Here I
saw a considerable number of persons, mostly lawyers and their clients—some sauntering, some meditating—some gathered in groups and conversing
together. I noticed that many of the former, and

more especially the older members of the bar, wore gowns and wigs; others wore gowns only, and still others were in the ordinary dress. I afterward was told that it was wholly at the option of individuals to adopt this costume, or not; in general, it was regarded as going out of fashion. There was a large number of people distributed through the several apartments, and in the grand hall there was a pervading hum of voices which seemed to rise and rumble and die away amid the groinings of the roof above.

Among the persons in this hall, a man some thirty years of age, tall and handsome, dressed in a gown but without the wig, attracted my particular attention. He was walking apart, and there was a certain look of coldness and haughtiness about him. Nevertheless, for some undefinable reason, he excited in me a lively curiosity. I observed that his eye was dark and keen, his hair nearly black, and though cut short, slightly curled. He carried his head erect, its largely developed corners behind, giving him an air of self-appreciation. His features were small, but sharply defined; his lips were close, and slightly disdainful and sarcastic in their expression.

There was a striking combination of energy and elegance in the general aspect of this person; yet over all, I must repeat, there was something also of coldness and pride. Upon his face, expressive of vigor and activity—mental and physical—there was a visible tinge of discontent.

"Who is that gentleman?" said I, to my guide.

"That large, noble-looking person, with a gown and wig? That is Cranstoun, one of our first lawyers, and the brother-in-law of Dugald Stuart."

"No: that person beyond and to the left? He is without a wig."

"Oh, that's Cockburn—a fiery whig, and one of the keenest fellows we have at the bar."

"Yes: but I mean that younger person, near the corner."

"Oh, that small, red-faced, freckled man? Why that's Moncrief—a very sound lawyer. His father, Sir Harry Moncrief, is one of the most celebrated divines in Scotland."

"No, no: it is that tall, handsome, proud-looking person, walking by himself.

"Oh, I see: that's Lockhart—Sir Walter Scott's son-in-law. Would you like to know him?"

"Yes."

And so I was introduced to a man* who, at that time, was hardly less an object of interest to me than

---

* J. G. Lockhart was a native of Scotland, and born in 1794. In 1826, he became editor of the Quarterly Review, and removed to London. In 1853, he resigned this situation in consequence of ill health. His biography of his father-in-law—Sir Walter Scott—is well known and highly appreciated. The latter part of his life, Lockhart was afflicted with deafness, which withdrew him much from society. He died in 1854: his wife had died in London, 1837. His son, John Hugh Lockhart, to whom Scott dedicated his History of Scotland, under the title of Hugh Littlejohn, died early. Lockhart had a daughter, who also has a daughter, and these two are now the only living descendants of Sir Walter.

Scott himself. Though a lawyer by profession, he had devoted himself to literature, and was now in the very height of his career. "Peter's Letters to his Kinsfolk," "Valerius," and other works, had given him a prominent rank as a man of talent; and besides, in 1820, he had married the eldest daughter of the "Great Unknown." My conversation with him was brief at this time, but I afterward became well acquainted with him.

My guide now led me into one of the side-rooms, where I saw a judge and jury, and a lawyer addressing them. The latter was a very small man, without gown or wig, apparently about forty years of age, though he might be somewhat older. He was of dark complexion, with an eye of intense blackness, and almost painfully piercing expression. His motions were quick and energetic, his voice sharp and penetrating—his general aspect exciting curiosity rather than affection. He was speaking energetically, and, as we approached the bar, my conductor said to me in a whisper—"Jeffrey!"

We paused, and I listened intently. The case in itself seemed dry enough—something, I believe, about a *stoppage in transitu*. But Jeffrey's pleading was admirable—clear, progressive, logical. Occasionally, in fixing upon a weak point of his adversary, he displayed a leopard-like spring of energy, altogether startling. He seized upon a certain point in the history of the case, and insisted that the property in question rested at that period in the hands of the defendant's agent, for at least a fortnight. This he claimed to be fatal to his adversary's plea. Having stated the facts, with a clearness which seemed to prove them, he said, turning with startling quickness upon his antagonist— "Now, I ask my learned brother to tell me, what was the state of the soul during that fortnight?" To a jury of Scotch Presbyterians, familiar with theological metaphysics, this allusion was exceedingly pertinent and effective.

We passed into another room. Three full-wigged judges were seated upon a lofty bench, and beneath them, at a little table in front, was a large man, bent down and writing laboriously. As I approached, I caught a side-view of his face. There was no mistaking him—it was Sir Walter himself!

Was it not curious to see the most renowned personage in the three kingdoms, sitting at the very feet of these men—they the court, and he the clerk? They were indeed all "lords," and their individual names were suggestive to the ear: one was Robertson, son of the historian of Charles V.; another was Gillies, brother of the renowned Grecian scholar of that name; another, Mackenzie, son of the author of the Man of Feeling. These are high titles—but what were they to the author of Waverley?

Mr. Y.... introduced me to him at once, breaking in upon his occupation with easy familiarity. As he arose from his seat, I was surprised at his robust, vigorous frame. He was very nearly six feet in height, full chested, and of a farmer-like aspect. His complexion seemed to have been originally sandy, but now his hair was gray. He had the rough, freckled, weather-beaten skin of a man who is much in the open air; his eye was small and gray, and peered out keenly and inquisitively from beneath a heavy brow, edged with something like gray, twisted bristles—the whole expression of his face, however, being exceedingly agreeable. He wore a gown, but no wig. It would have been a sin to have covered up that wonderful head, towering, as we have all seen it in his portraits —the throne of the richest intellect in the world.*

He greeted me kindly—the tone of his voice being hearty, yet with a very decided Scotch accent. I told him I had been to the Highlands. "It is a little too early," said he; "I always wish my friends to wait till the middle of June, for then the ash is in its glory. Here in the north, summer, as you know, is a laggard. In America it visits you in better season?"

"I am from New England, and our forests are not in full leaf till June."

---

* Scott was born in 1771—so at this time, 1824, he was fifty-three years old, at the highest point of his fame, and in the full vigor of his genius. In 1826 he was involved in the failure of the Ballantynes— printers and publishers—to an extent of $700,000. He made prodigious efforts to liquidate this immense debt, and had laid the foundation for its payment, when his overwrought brain gave way, and he died of paralysis, September 21, 1832. He married Miss Carpenter in 1797, and had four children: Walter, Sophia, who married Lockhart, Ann, and Charles. All are now dead. Abbotsford remains in the family.

Sir Walter Scott, as Clerk of the Court of Sessions.   Vol. 2, p. 175.

"Yes, your climate there is somewhat like ours. Are you from Boston?"

"I am from Hartford, in Connecticut—of which you have perhaps never heard."

"My American geography is not very minute; yet Connecticut is a familiar name to my ear. Do you know Mr. Irving?"

"I have never seen him but once."

"Mr. Cooper?"

"Yes, I know him well."

"Do you stay long in Edinburgh?"

"A few weeks."

"We shall meet again, then, and talk these matters over."

So I had seen the author of Waverley! I leave you to guess my emotions, for I could not describe them.

———◆———

LETTER XL.

Preparations for a Ride—Mr. Jeffrey in a Rough-and-tumble—A Glance at Edinburgh from the Braid Hills—A Shower—The Maids of the Mist— Durable Impressions.

My dear C******

I found a note—May 31st—at my hotel, from Miss Y...., inviting me to breakfast. I went at ten, and we had a pleasant chat. She then proposed a ride, and I accepted. She was already in her riding-habit,

8*

and putting on a hat and collar—both of rather masculine gender, yet not uncomely—we went forth. We were in Queen-street, No. 48; passing along a short distance, we turned a corner to the left, mounted the steps of a fine house, and rang. We entered, and I was introduced to the proprietor, Mrs. Russell. She led us into another room, and there, on the floor, in a romp with her two boys, was a small, dark man. He arose, and behold, it was Francis Jeffrey!* Think of the first lawyer in Scotland—the lawgiver of the great Republic of Letters throughout Christendom—having a rough-and-tumble on the floor, as if he were himself a boy! Let others think as they will—I loved him from that moment; and ever after, as I read his criticisms—cutting and scorching as they often were—I fancied that I could still see a kind and genial spirit shining through them all. At least it is certain that, behind his editorial causticity, there was in private life a fund of gentleness and geniality

---

* Mr. Jeffrey was born in Edinburgh in 1773. He was admitted to the bar at the age of twenty-one; having little practice for a time, he sedulously pursued the study of belles-lettres, history, ethics, criticism, &c. In 1802, at the age of twenty-nine, he founded the Edinburgh Review, of which he continued as principal editor till 1829—placing it above every other work of the kind which had ever appeared. In 1816 he was acknowledged to be at the head of the Scottish bar as an advocate. Having held other high stations, he was appointed, in 1830, Lord-Advocate of Scotland, and became a member of Parliament. In 1834 he was raised to the bench as one of the judges of the Court of Sessions. He died at Edinburgh in 1850. He married in 1813, at New York, Miss Wilkes, grand-niece of the celebrated John Wilkes of England. In 1815 he became the occupant of the villa of Craigcrook, near Edinburgh, anciently a monastery, but improved and beautified. Here he was residing at the time I saw him.

which endeared him to all who enjoyed his intimacy.
I was now introduced to him, and he seemed a totally
different being from the fierce and fiery gladiator of
the legal arena, where I had before seen him. His
manners were gentle and gentlemanly—polite to the
ladies and gracious to me.

Jeffrey's house was some two miles from town.
His custom was to come to the city on horseback—
and Mrs. Russell being his friend, he frequently
stopped at her house, leaving his horse in her stable.
Some gossiping scandal arose from this intimacy, but
it was, of course, not only idle, but absurd. We
found Mrs. Russell in a riding-dress, and prepared to
accompany us in our excursion. Taking leave of
Mr. Jeffrey, we went to the stable, where were nearly
a dozen horses, of various kinds and adapted to various uses. Miss Y .... chose a shaggy gray pony,
half savage and half pet; Mrs. Russell mounted a
long, lean, clean-limbed hunter; and I, at her suggestion, took Mr. Jeffrey's mare—a bay, rollicking
cob, with a gait like a saw-mill—as I found to my
cost.

We walked our steeds gently out of town, but on
leaving the pavements the ladies struck into a vigorous trot. Up and down the hills we went, the turnpike gates flying open at our approach, the servant
behind, paying the tolls. We passed out of the city
by Holy Rood, and swept round to the east of Arthur's seat, leaving Portobello on the left. We rode

steadily, noting a few objects as we passed, until at last, reaching an elevated mound, we paused, and the ladies directed my attention to the scenes around. We were some two miles south of the town, upon one of the slopes of the Braid Hills. Ah, what a view was before us! The city, a vast, smoking hive, to the north; and to the right, Arthur's Seat, bald and blue, seeming to rise up and almost peep into its streets and chimneys. Over and beyond all, was the sea. The whole area between the point where we stood and that vast azure line, blending with the sky, was a series of abrupt hills and dimpling valleys, threaded by a network of highways and byways—honeycomb-ed in spots by cities and villages, and elsewhere sprin-kled with country-seats.

It is an unrivaled scene of varied beauty and in-terest. The natural site of Edinburgh is remarkable, consisting of three rocky ledges, steepling over deep ravines. These have all been modified by art; in one place a lake has been dried up, and is now cov-ered with roads, bridges, tenements, gardens, and lawns. The sides of the cliffs are in some instances covered with masses of buildings, the edifices occa-sionally rising tier upon tier—in one place present-ing a line of houses a dozen stories in height! The city is divided by a deep chasm into two distinct parts, the Old Town, dun and smoky, and justifying the popular appellation of "Auld Reekie," or Old Smoky; the other the New Town, with all the fresh

architecture and all the rich and elaborate embellishments of a modern city.   Nearly from the center of
the old town rises the Castle, three hundred and
eighty feet above the level of the sea—on one side
looking down almost perpendicularly, two hundred
feet into the vale beneath—on the other holding communication with the streets by means of a winding
pathway.   In the new town is Calton Hill, rich with
monuments of art and memorials of history, and suggesting to the mind a resemblance to the Acropolis
of Athens.   From these two commanding positions,
the scenes are unrivaled.

But I forget that I have taken you to the Braid
Hills.   The panorama, from this point, was not only
beautiful to the eye, but a rich harvest to the mind.
My amiable guides directed my attention to various
objects—some far and some near, and all with names
familiar to history or song or romance.   Yonder mass
of dun and dismal ruins was Craigmillar's Castle, once
the residence of Queen Mary.   Nearly in the same
direction, and not remote, is the cliff, above whose
bosky sides peer out the massive ruins of Roslin
Castle ; further south are glimpses of Dalkeith Palace, the sumptuous seat of the Duke of Buccleugh ;
there is the busy little village of Lasswade, which
takes the name of "Gandercleugh" in the "Tales of
my Landlord ;" yonder winds the Esk and there the
Galawater—both familiar in many a song ; and there
is the scenery of the "Gentle Shepherd," presenting

the very spot where that inimitable colloquy took
place between Peggy and her companion, Jenny—

> " Gae farer up the burn to Habbie's How,
>   Where a' the sweets o' spring an' summer grow:
>   Between twa birks, out o'er a little linn,
>   The water fa's and makes a singan din:
>   A pool, breast deep, beneath as clear as glass,
>   Kisses wi' easy whirls the bordering grass.
>   We'll end our washing while the morning's cool,
>   And when the day grows hot, we'll to the pool,
>   There wash oursels—it's healthful now in May,
>   An' sweetly caller on sae warm a day."

While we were surveying these unrivaled scenes,
the rain began to fall in a fine, insinuating mizzle:
soon large drops pattered through the fog, and at last
there was a drenching shower. I supposed the ladies
would seek some shelter: not they—maids of the
mist—accustomed to all the humors of this drizzly
climate, and of course defying them. They pulled off
their green vails, and stuffed them into their saddle-
pockets; then chirruping to their steeds, they sped
along the road, as if mounted on broomsticks. I was
soon wet to the skin, and so, doubtless, were they—
if one might suggest such a thing. However, they
took to it as ducks to a pond. On we went, the water—accelerated by our speed—spouting in torrents
from our stirrups. In all my days, I had never such
an adventure. And the coolness with which the ladies took it—that was the most remarkable. Indeed,

it was provoking—for as they would not accept sympathy, of course they could not give it, though my reeking condition would have touched any other heart than theirs. On we went, till at last coming to the top of a hill, we suddenly cropped out into the sunshine —the shower still scudding along the valley beneath us. We continued our ride, getting once more soaked on our way, and again drying in the sun. At last we reached home, having made a circuit of fifteen miles. Scarcely a word was said of the rain. I saw my mermaid friends to their residences, and was thankful when I got back to the hotel. What with the shower, and a slight cold which ensued—I did not get the trot of Jeffrey's mare out of my bones for a fortnight. Indeed, long after, during rough weather, when the gust and rain dashed against my window, the beast sometimes visited me in sleep, coming in the shape of a nightmare, carrying me at a furious rate, with two charming witches before, beckoning me on to a race. As a just moral of this adventure—I suggest to all Americans, who ride with Scotch ladies around Edinburgh, not to go forth in their best dresscoat, and pantaloons having no straps beneath the boot.

LETTER XLI.

William Blackwood—The Magazine—A Dinner at Blackwood's—James Ballantyne—Lord Byron and Lady Caroline Lamb—The General Assembly of Scotland—Dr. Chalmers.

MY DEAR C******

One or two more selections from my journal, and we will leave Edinburgh. I had delivered my letter of introduction to Blackwood, and he had treated me very kindly. He was, professionally, a mere bookseller and publisher—a plain, short, stocky person, with a large head, bald and flat on the top. He spoke broad Scotch, or rather sang it, for although all spoken language, in every country, has its cadences, in Scotland it is a veritable song. This is more noticeable among the illiterate, and especially the old women. I sometimes thought they were mocking me, so emphatic were their inflexions and modulations. I have since observed similar intonations in other countries, especially in Italy, where the rising and falling of the voice is so marked as to appear like an affectation of musical cadenzas, even in conversation.

Nevertheless, Mr. Blackwood was an exceedingly intelligent and agreeable gentleman. The Magazine* which bears his name, was then in its glory,

---

* Blackwood's Magazine was founded in April, 1817, the office of publication being the proprietor's bookstore, 17 Prince-street. The founder, William Blackwood, died some years since, and the Magazine is

and of course a part of its radiance shone on him.
He was a man of excellent judgment, even in literary
matters, and his taste, no doubt, contributed largely
to the success of the Magazine. He was in familiar
intercourse with the celebrities of the day—and a
bright constellation they were. He spoke as familiarly of great names—Scott, Lockhart, Hogg, Wilson
—sacred to me, as Appleton and Putnam and the Harpers do of Irving, Halleck, and Bryant, or Ticknor &

---

continued by his sons. In general, its tone has not been friendly to
America, and while I was there an article in the May number, 1824,
upon our country, then just issued, excited some attention, and I was
frequently interrogated respecting it. It was entitled the "Five Presidents of the United States," and though it was written as by an Englishman, perhaps in order to secure its insertion, Blackwood told me it
was from the pen of a distinguished American, then in London. It was
a somewhat slashing review of the administrations of the presidents,
from Washington to Monroe, the latter being then in office. It embraced sketches of Adams, Clay, Crawford, and Jackson—the prominent candidates for the presidency. The following is part of the notice
of Adams.

Supposing a European ambassador to visit Washington, and is introduced into the President's house, "He sees a little man writing at a
table, nearly bald, with a face quite formal and destitute of expression;
his eyes running with water—his slippers down at the heel—his fingers
stained with ink—in summer wearing a striped sea-sucker coat, and
white trowsers, and dirty waistcoat, spotted with ink—his whole dress
altogether not worth a couple of pounds; or in a colder season, habited
in a plain blue coat, much the worse for wear, and other garments in
proportion—not so respectable as we may find in the old-clothes bag of
almost any Jew in the street. This person, whom the ambassador mistakes for a clerk in a department, and only wonders, in looking at him,
that the President should permit a man to appear before him in such
dress, proves to be the President of the United States himself!"

The article was written with vigor and discrimination, and excited a
good deal of attention. Though free, and by no means dainty in its
criticisms, it was, on the whole, just, and produced a favorable impression in our behalf. The author, whoever he was, evidently possessed
eminent qualifications for magazine writing.

Fields of Prescott and Longfellow. Was not that a time to be remembered?

Of course I was gratified at receiving from him a note, inviting me to dine with him the next day. His house was on the south of the old town—nearly two miles distant. The persons present were such as I should myself have selected : among them Lockhart and James Ballantyne. I sat next the latter, and found him exceedingly agreeable and gentlemanlike. He was a rather large man, handsome, smooth in person and manner, and very well dressed. You will remember that at this time, it was not acknowledged by Scott or his friends that he was the author of the Waverley novels. Perhaps the mystery was even promoted by them, for, no doubt, it added adventitious interest to his works. However, the vail was not closely preserved in the circle of intimacy. Ballantyne said to me, in the course of a conversation which turned upon the popularity of authors, as indicated by the sale of their works—" We have now in course of preparation forty thousand volumes of Scott's poems and the works of the author of Waverley"—evidently intimating the identity of their authorship.

There was nothing remarkable about our meal : it was like an English dinner, generally—ample, substantial, administered with hospitality, and discussed with relish. There was a certain seriousness and preparation about it, common in Europe, but uncommon in our country. We rush to the table as if eating was an affair to be dispatched in the shortest possible time : to linger over it would seem to be an indecency. The Englishman, on the contrary, arranges his business for his dinner; he prepares his mind for it; he sets himself to the table, and adjusts his legs beneath, for it; he unfolds his napkin and lays it in his lap, or tucks a corner within his waistcoat, for it; he finally qualifies himself the better to enjoy it, by taking a loving survey of the good things before him and the good friends around him. He begins leisurely, as if feeling that Providence smiles upon him, and he would acknowledge its bounties by prolonging the enjoyment of them. As he proceeds, he spices his gratification by sips of wine, exchanges of compliments with the ladies and convivial chat, right and left, with his neighbors. The host is attentive, the hostess lends a smiling countenance, the servants are ubiquitous, and put your wishes into deeds, without the trouble of your speaking to them.

The first half hour has a certain earnestness about it, apparently occupied in reducing the Malakoffs of beef, Mamelons of mutton, and Redans of poultry— that come one after another. The victory is, at last, substantially won : all that remains is to capture the pies, cakes, tarts, ices, creams, fruits, &c., which is usually done with a running artillery of light wit. Conversation ensues; now and then all listen to some good talker; perhaps a story-teller catches, for a time, the attention of the company, and then again all around resolves itself into a joyous and jovial confusion of tongues. An hour is past, and the ladies retire. The gentlemen fill their glasses, and offer them a parting toast; then they drink "The Queen," and give themselves up to social enjoyment.

And so it was on this occasion—only that we drank the King, instead of the Queen, for George IV. was then upon the throne. Mr. Blackwood was living in a plain but comfortable style, and garnished his entertainment with a plain, simple hospitality—which lost nothing by his occasional interjections of very broad Scotch. It was delightful to see the easy intimacy of the persons present: they frequently called each other by their Christian names—using terms of endearment, which with us would seem affected, perhaps absurd. "Jammy, dear, tak some wine yoursel, and hand it to me!" said Blackwood to Ballantyne, and the latter answered in a similar tone of familiar kindness. The whole intercourse of the company seemed warmed and cheered by these simple, habitual courtesies. Our own manners, I think, under similar circumstances, must appear bald and chilling, in comparison.

Nor was there any thing remarkable in the conversations—save only what related to Byron. The news of his death at Missolonghi, on the 19th of April, had reached Scotland a few weeks before, and produced a profound sensation. Even while I was there, the interest in the subject had not subsided. Mr. Lockhart had not known Byron, personally, but he was in London soon after his departure for the continent, and at several subsequent periods, and he gave us many interesting details respecting him. He was frequently at Lady Caroline Lamb's soirées, where he met the literary celebrities of London, and especially the younger and gayer portion of them. Her ladyship had flirted with the lordly poet in the heyday of his fame, and it was said, condescended to visit him in the guise of a page—her reputation being of that salamander quality, which could pass through such fire and suffer no damage. Her lover proved fickle, and at last ungrateful, and she retaliated in the novel of "Glenarvon"—venting her rage upon him by depicting him as "having an imagination of flame playing around a heart of ice."

At the time Lockhart thus mingled in Lady Caroline's circle, Byron was the frequent theme of comment. She had a drawer-full of his letters, and intimate friends were permitted to read them. She had also borrowed of Murray the poet's manuscript autobiography given to Moore, and had copied some of its passages. This was soon discovered, and she was obliged to suppress them—but still passages of them got into circulation. The work was written in a daring, reckless spirit, setting at defiance all the laws of propriety, and even of decency. One of the chapters consisted of a rhyming list of his acquaintances, at the period of his highest fashionable success, in London— dashed off with amazing power—yet in such terms of profanity as to forbid repetition, at least in print. It was obvious, from what was said by Mr. Lockhart and others, that such were the gross personalities, the shameful outrages of decorum, and the general licentiousness of this production, that it was impossible for any respectable publisher to be concerned in giving it to the world. The consignment of it to the flames, by his friends, was as much dictated by regard to their own characters, as to the fame of the author, which was in a certain degree committed to their keeping.

We sat down to dinner at seven, and got up at eleven. After a short conversation with the ladies, we took our departure. As I was getting into my carriage, Mr. Lockhart proposed to me to walk back to town, a distance of a mile and a half. I gladly accepted this proposition, and we had a very interesting conversation. Upon intimacy, Lockhart's coldness wholly disappeared. He spoke in an easy, rattling way, very much in the manner of the freer portions of Peter's Letters. The good dinner had doubtless cheered him a little; but not only on this, but other occasions I had evidence of a more genial nature than might have been supposed to exist beneath the haughty armor which he seemed to wear toward the world.

The next day I went to St. Giles's Church,* to see the General Assembly, then holding its annual session there. This body consisted of nearly four hundred members, chosen by different parishes, boroughs, and universities. The sessions are attended by a Commissioner appointed by the crown, but he is seated outside of the area assigned to the assembly, and has no vote, and no right of debate. He sits under a pavilion, with the insignia of royalty, and a train of gaily-dressed pages. He opens the sessions in the name of the King, the Head of the Church : the moderator then opens it in the name of the Lord Jesus Christ, *the only true Head of the Church !* It appears that the Scotch, in bargaining for a union with England, took good care to provide for their religious independence, and this they still jealously preserve : the Irish, on the contrary, were sold out, and treated like a conquered people. The commissioner, at this time, was Lord Morton—who, according to all the accounts I heard, was a disgrace to human nature.

The aspect of the Assembly was similar to that of the House of Commons—though somewhat graver. I observed that the debates were often stormy, with scraping of the floor, laughing aloud, and cries of "hear, hear!" The members were, in fact, quite disorderly, showing at least as little regard for decorum

---

* In 1844 a fine church, called Victoria Hall, was erected for the meetings of the General Assembly. It is of rich Mediæval Gothic architecture, with a spire two hundred and forty-six feet in height.

as ordinary legislatures. Sir Walter Scott once remarked, in my hearing, that it had never yet been
decided how many more than six members could
speak at once!

The persons here pointed out to me as celebrities
were Dr. Chalmers, the famous pulpit orator, Dr.
Cook, the ecclesiastical historian, and Dr. Baird, principal of the University, and caricatured in the print-
shops under a rude portrait of his large face, nearly
covered with hair, the whole labeled, *Principal Beard*.
The first of these was now at the height of his fame.
He had already begun those reforms which, some
years later, resulted in a disruption of the Scottish
Church. At this period the Assembly was divided
into two opposite parties, the *Moderate*, and the *Sound*
—the former contending for the old doctrine, that
presbyteries were bound to receive and accept every
qualified preacher, presented by the crown, or others
exercising the right of such preferment, and the latter opposing it. The importance of the question lay
in the fact that a large number of the places in the
Church were in the gift of the crown, and many others
in the hands of lay-patrons, and these were frequently bestowed in such a manner as to accumulate
two or more benefices in the hands of one person.
The great point made by Chalmers was, that one
church, one congregation, however small, was enough
to occupy and absorb the attention of one minister;
and that a plurality of benefices was both corrupting

to the Church, by making it subservient to patronage, and destructive of the apostolic spirit, which demands the devotion of the whole soul to the work of the ministry.

I had the good fortune to hear Chalmers speak for a few moments, but with great energy and power, so as to give me an idea of his appearance and manner. He was a large man, and as he rose he seemed rather heavy, slow, and awkward. His face was large, its outline being nearly circular. His lips, when closed, were thin, giving a certain sharpness and firmness to his countenance. His forehead was large and expansive, his brow finely arched, his eye gray, and its expression ordinarily heavy. Altogether his appearance, as he first rose to my view, was unpromising. His speech, his articulation, was even worse, at the outset, for he had the Fifeshire dialect—the harshest and most unintelligible in Scotland. He had, however, spoken but a few sentences, when the whole man was transformed. That heaviness which marked his appearance, had wholly passed away. Upon his countenance there was an animated yet lofty expression—firm and fearless, benevolent and winning—while his voice, pouring out a vast flow of thought, had in it a tone at once of love and command, of feeling and of authority, absolutely irresistible. I felt myself borne along in the torrent—compelled, yet lending myself gratefully to the movement. Sentence after sentence fell from his lips, thought accumulated upon thought,

illustration upon illustration, and yet the listener com-
passed every conception and treasured every word.
There was something in his voice so musical, so
touching, that the whole sank into the soul like a
hymn. The general effect was aided by his gestures
and movements, for though by no means graceful,
they harmonized so well with the emotions of the
speaker as at once to illustrate and enforce the general tenor of his address.

On another occasion I heard Dr. Chalmers preach,
in one of the churches of the city. The crowd was
so great, however, that I saw and heard very imper-
fectly. It seemed to me that he was rather calculated
to produce an effect by his oratory, than his writings.
He had evidently wonderful powers of amplification:
he often started topics apparently barren and unsug-
gestive, but soon he called around them a crowd of
thoughts and associations of the highest interest. The
common labors of the minister of the Gospel—entering into the hearts and homes of the rich and the
poor; now leading to the stately hall, and now to the
squalid dens of vice, poverty, and crime; now to the
administration of baptism, and now to the sacrament
—this hackneyed routine, by force of his vivid imagination and ardent spirit, presented pictures to the
mind and awoke emotions in the heart, quite overwhelming. He seemed, indeed, like a magician, capable of converting even the sand and stones of the desert into images of life and power; but it appeared

to me that in order to do this, the voice and gesture
and presence of the sorcerer, were indispensable. I
have never, in reading any thing he has written—
noble as are his works—at all realized the emotions
produced by the brief, but startling speech I heard
from him in the Assembly.

———————

LETTER XLII.

*A Dinner at Lockhart's—Conversation about Byron—Mrs. Lockhart—Ir-
ving—Professor Ticknor—Music—The Pibroch and Miss Edgeworth—
Anecdotes of the Indians—Southey and Second Sight—Cooper's Pioneers—
The Pilot—Paul Jones—Brockden Brown—Burns—Tricks of the Press
—Charles Scott—The Welsh Parson—The Italian Base-viol Player—
Personal Appearance of Sir Walter—Departure for London—Again
in Edinburgh in 1832—Last Moments of Sir Walter—The Sympathy of
Nature.*

MY DEAR C*******

I hope you fully comprehend that, in these
sketches I am only dipping into my journal here
and there, and selecting such memoranda as I think
may amuse you. Most of these passages refer to
individuals who have now passed to their graves.
It is mournful—to me it is suggestive of feelings inex-
pressibly sad and solemn—to reflect that of the long
list of distinguished persons who, at the period I
refer to, shed a peculiar glory upon Edinburgh, not
one survives. Scott, Lockhart, Jeffrey, Chalmers—
these, and others who stood beside them, either shar-

ing or reflecting the blushing honors of genius and fame, falling around them—all are gone from the high places which they then illumined with their presence. I am speaking only of the dead—yet I remember them as living, and—though their history, their works, their fame, are familiar to you—it may still interest you to go back and participate in recollections of them—their persons, speech, manner—and thus, in some degree, see them as they were seen, and know them as they were known. I pray you to accept these passages from my journal, as glimpses only of what I saw, and not as pretending at all to a regular account of my travels and observations, at the time referred to.

On Wednesday, June 2, I dined with Mr. Lockhart—25 Northumberland-street. Besides the host and hostess, there were present Sir Walter Scott, his son, Charles Scott, Mr. Blackwood, Mr. Robinson, and three or four other persons. At dinner I sat next Sir Walter—an arrangement made, I believe, in compliment to myself. Every thing went off pleasantly —with the usual ease, hospitality, and heartiness of an English dinner. The house and furniture were plain and handsome—such as were common to people of good condition and good taste.

The meal was discussed with the usual relish, and with the usual garnish of wit and pleasantry. After the ladies had retired, the conversation became general and animated. Byron was the engrossing topic.

Sir Walter spoke of him with the deepest feeling of admiration and regret. A few weeks before, on the receipt of the news of his death, he had written an obituary notice of him, in which he compared him to the sun, withdrawn from the heavens at the very moment when every telescope was leveled to discover either his glory or his spots. He expressed the opinion that Byron was "dying of home-sickness"—that being his phrase. For a long time he had flouted England, and seemed to glory alike in his exile and his shame. Yet all this time his heart was devoured with "the fiend ennui." He went to Greece, in the hope of doing some gallant deed that would wipe out his disgrace, and create for him such sympathy in the breasts of his countrymen, as would enable him to return—his "faults forgiven and his sins forgot."

Lockhart and Blackwood both told stories, and we passed a pleasant half hour. The wine was at last rather low, and our host ordered the servant to bring more. Upon which Scott said—"No, no, Lokert"—such was his pronunciation of his son-in-law's name—"we have had enough : let us go and see the ladies." And so we gathered to the parlor.

Mrs. Lockhart was now apparently about two and twenty years old—small in person, and girl-like in manner. Her hair was light-brown, cut short, and curled in her neck and around her face. Her cheeks were blooming, and her countenance full of cheerfulness. Her address was at once graceful and gracious

—indicating a lively, appreciative nature and the finest breeding. She had a son, four years old, and at my request, he was brought in. He was a fine boy, "very like his father," but alas, doomed to an early death.*

Mrs. Lockhart spoke with great interest of Mr. Irving, who had visited the family at Abbotsford. She said that he slept in a room which looked out on the Tweed. In the morning as he came down to breakfast, he was very pale, and being asked the reason, confessed that he had not been able to sleep. The sight of the Tweed from his window, and the consciousness of being at Abbotsford, so filled his imagination—so excited his feelings, as to deprive him of slumber. She also spoke of Professor Ticknor—laying the accent on the last syllable—as having been at Abbotsford, and leaving behind him the most agreeable impressions.

Our lively hostess was requested to give us some music, and instantly complied—the harp being her instrument. She sang Scotch airs, and played several pibrochs—all with taste and feeling. Her range of tunes seemed inexhaustible. Her father sat by, and entered heartily into the performances. He beat time vigorously with his lame leg, and frequently helped out a chorus, the heartiness of his tones making up for some delinquencies in tune and time.

* He died at London, Dec. 15, 1831; his mother followed him, May 17, 1837.

Often he made remarks upon the songs, and told anecdotes respecting them. When a certain pibroch had been played, he said it reminded him of the first time he ever saw Miss Edgeworth. There had come to Abbotsford, a wild Gaelic peasant from the neighborhood of Staffa, and it was proposed to him to sing a pibroch, common in that region. He had consented, but required the whole party present, to sit in a circle on the floor, while he should sing the song, and perform a certain pantomimic accompaniment, in the center. All was accordingly arranged in the great hall, and the performer had just begun his wild chant, when in walked a tall, stately lady, and announced herself as Miss Edgeworth!

Mrs. Lockhart asked me about the American Indians—expressing great curiosity concerning them. I told the story of one who was tempted to go into the rapids of the Niagara river, just above the Falls, for a bottle of rum. This he took with him, and having swam out to the point agreed upon, he turned back and attempted to regain the land. For a long time the result was doubtful: he struggled powerfully, but in vain. Inch by inch, he receded from the shore, and at last, finding his doom sealed, he raised himself above the water, wrenched the cork from the bottle, and putting the latter to his lips, yielded to the current, and thus went down to his doom.

Mrs. Lockhart made some exclamations of mingled admiration and horror. Sir Walter then said that he had read an account of an Indian, who was in a boat, approaching a cataract; by some accident, it was drawn into the current, and the savage saw that his escape was impossible. Upon this he arose, wrapped his robe of skins around him, seated himself erect, and with an air of imperturbable gravity, went over the falls.

"That is sublime," said Mrs. Lockhart: "as if he were preparing to meet the Great Spirit, and he thought it proper to enter his presence with dignity!"

"The most remarkable thing about the American Indians," said Blackwood, "is their being able to follow in the trail of their enemies, by their footprints left in the leaves, upon the grass, and even upon the moss of the rocks. The accounts given of this seem hardly credible."

"I can readily believe it, however," said Sir Walter. "You must remember that this is a part of their education. I have learned at Abbotsford to discriminate between the hoof-marks of all our neighbors' horses, and I taught the same thing to Mrs. Lockhart. It is, after all, not so difficult as you might think. Every horse's foot has some peculiarity—either of size, shoeing, or manner of striking the earth. I was once walking with Southey—a mile or more from home—across the fields. At last we came to a bridle-path, leading toward Abbotsford, and here I noticed fresh hoof-prints. Of this I said nothing; but pausing and looking up with an inspired expression, I said to Southey—'I have a gift of second sight : we shall have a stranger to dinner !'

" ' And what may be his name ?' was the reply.

" 'Scott,' said I.

" ' Ah, it is some relation of yours,' he said ; ' you have invited him, and you would pass off as an example of your Scottish gift of prophecy, a matter previously agreed upon !'

" ' Not at all,' said I. ' I assure you that till this moment I never thought of such a thing.'

" When we got home, I was told that Mr. Scott, a farmer living some three or four miles distant, and a relative of mine, was waiting to see me. Southey looked astounded. The man remained to dinner, and he was asked if he had given any intimation of his coming. He replied in the negative : that indeed he had no idea of visiting Abbotsford when he left home. After enjoying Southey's wonder for some time, I told him that I saw the tracks of Mr. Scott's horse in the bridle-path, and inferring that he was going to Abbotsford, easily foresaw that we should have him to dinner."

Mrs. Lockhart confirmed her father's statement, and told how, in walking over the country together, they had often amused themselves in studying the hoof-prints along the roads.

Mr. Lockhart returned to the Indians. "I have lately been reading an exceedingly clever American novel, entitled the Pioneers, by Cooper. His descriptive power is very great, and I think he has opened a new field of romance, especially in the hunters along the frontiers, who, in their intercourse with savages, have become half savage themselves. That border life is full of incident, adventure, poetry; the character of Leatherstocking is original and striking."

"I have not seen the Pioneers," said Scott; "but I have read the Pilot by the same author, which has just been published. It is very clever, and I think it will turn out that his strength lies in depicting sea life and adventure. We really have no good sea-tales, and here is a wide field, open to a man of true genius."

"But, papa," said our hostess, "I should think it rather a narrow field. Only a few persons go to sea, and the language of sailors is so technical as to be hardly understood by people generally. It seems to me that sea-tales can never excite the sympathy of the great mass of readers, because they have had no experience of its life and manners."

"It is no doubt a task of some difficulty," said Sir Walter, "to bring these home to the hearts of the reading million; nevertheless, to a man of genius for it, the materials are ample and interesting. All our minds are full of associations of danger, of daring, and adventure with the sea and those who have made that element their home. And besides, this book to which I refer—the Pilot—connects its story with the land. It is perhaps more interesting to me,

because I perfectly well recollect the time when Paul
Jones—whose character is somewhat reflected in the
hero of the story—came up the Solway in 1778 in
the Ranger, though I was then less than ten years old.
He kept the whole coast in a state of alarm for some
time, and was in fact the great scarecrow of that age
and generation."

"Mr. Cooper is a man of genius," said Lockhart :
"no one can deny that; but it seems to me that
Brockden Brown was the most remarkable writer of
fiction that America has produced. There is a similar-
ity in his style to that of the Radcliffe school, and in
the tone of mind to Godwin's Caleb Williams ; but in
his machinery, he is highly original. In his display
of the darker passions, he surpasses all his models."

"That may be true," said Sir Walter, "but it is
neither a wholesome nor a popular species of literature.
It is almost wholly ideal; it is not in nature; it is in
fact contrary to it. Its scenes, incidents, characters,
do not represent life : they are alien to common experience. They do not appeal to a wide circle of
sympathy in the hearts of mankind. The chief emotion that it excites is terror or wonder. The suggestive manner of treating every subject, aims at keeping
the mind constantly on the rack of uncertainty. This
trick of art was long ago exhausted. Brown had
wonderful powers, as many of his descriptions show ;
but I think he was led astray by falling under the
influence of bad examples, prevalent at his time.

Had he written his own thoughts, he would have been, perhaps, immortal : in writing those of others, his fame was of course ephemeral."

The conversation turned upon Burns. Scott knew him well. He said that Tam O'Shanter was written to please a stonecutter, who had executed a monument for the poet's father, on condition that he should write him a witch-story, in verse. He stated that Burns was accustomed, in his correspondence, more especially with ladies, to write an elaborate letter, and then send a copy of it to several persons— modifying local and personal passages to suit each individual. He said that of some of these letters, he had three or four copies thus addressed to different persons, and all in the poet's handwriting.

The tricks of the London newspapers were spoken of, and he mentioned the following instance. A pop- ular preacher there, had caused a church to be built, in which he was to officiate. The time was fixed for its dedication; but two days before this, an article appeared in one of the city prints, describing the building, and speaking well of it, but suggesting that the pillars which supported the gallery were entirely too slight, and it must be exceedingly dan- gerous for any congregation to assemble there! This of course produced a general alarm, and to appease this, the proprietor found it necessary to have a sur- vey made by an architect. This was done, and the architect declared, that, as the pillars were of iron, there was not the slightest danger. The proprietor took this statement to the editor of the paper, and begged him to retract his false and injurious statement. The reply was—

" This is doubtless an important matter to you, but not of the slightest interest to me."

" But, sir," was the reply, " you have stated what is not true : will you not correct your own error ?"

" Yes, but we must be paid for it."

" What, for telling the truth ?"

" That depends upon circumstances : do you suppose we can tell every truth that everybody desires us to ? No, sir ; this is a matter of interest to you : you can afford to pay for it. Give us ten guineas, and we will set it all right."

The proprietor of the church had no other resource, and so he paid the money.

Charles Scott, Sir Walter's second son, a rosy-cheeked youth of about eighteen, was present. He had recently come from Wales, where he had been under the teaching of a Welch clergyman. This subject being mentioned, Blackwood asked Mr. Robinson—a very sober, clerical-looking gentleman—to give the company a sample of a Welch sermon. Two chairs were placed back to back : Blackwood sat in one—his bald, flat pate for a desk, and the performer mounted the other—taking one of Mrs. Lockhart's songs for his notes. It seems he was familiar with the Welch language, and an admirable mimic. His performance was exceedingly amusing. When he became animated, he slapped the music down on Blackwood's bald pate, and in capping his climaxes, gave it two or three smart thumps with his fist. Blackwood must have had a substantial skull, or he could not have borne it. At last, even he had enough of it, and when he perceived another climax was coming, he dodged, and the sermon was speedily brought to a close.

Mr. Robinson was then called upon to imitate an Italian player on the bass-viol. He took a pair of tongs for his bow, and a shovel for the viol, and mounting a pair of spectacles on the tip-end of his nose, he began imitating the spluttering of the instrument by his voice. It was inimitably droll. Sir Walter was quite convulsed, and several of the ladies absolutely screamed. As to myself, I had the side-ache for four-and-twenty hours.

And thus passed the evening—till twelve o'clock. I have not told you the half of what is indicated in the notes before me. These specimens will suffice, however, to give you some idea of the manner in which good people unbent in the family circle of Edinburgh, thirty years ago. You will readily suppose that my eye often turned upon the chief figure in this interesting group. I could not for a moment forget his presence, though nothing could be more unpretending and modest than his whole air and bearing.

His features are doubtless impressed upon you by his portraits, for they have all a general resemblance.

There was in Mr. Lockhart's parlor, where we were sitting, a copy of Chantry's bust of him—since repeated a thousand times in plaster. I compared it again and again with the original. Nothing could possibly be better as a likeness. The lofty head, the projecting brows, the keen, peering glance of the eye, the long, thick upper lip, the dumpy nose, the rather small and receding chin—each feature separately homely, yet all combined to form a face of agreeable expression. Its general effect was that of calm dignity; and now, in the presence of children and friends, lighted by genial emotions, it was one of the pleasantest countenances I have ever seen. When standing or walking, his manly form, added to an aspect of benevolence, completed the image—at once exciting affection and commanding respect.

As to his manners, I need only add that they were those of a well-bred English gentleman—quiet, unpretending, absolutely without self-assertion. He appeared to be happy, and desirous of making others so. He was the only person present, who seemed unconscious that he was the author of Waverley. His intercourse with his daughter, and hers in return, were most charming. She called him "papa," and he called her "my child," "my daughter," "Sophia," and in the most endearing tone and manner. She seemed quite devoted to him, watching his lips when he was speaking, and seeking in every thing to anticipate and fulfill his wishes. When she was singing,

his eye dwelt upon her, his ear catching and seeming
to relish every tone. Frequently, when she was silent, his eye rested upon her, and the lines came to
my mind—

> "Some feelings are to mortals given,
>   With less of earth in them, than Heaven:
>   And if there be a human tear
>   From passion's dross refined and clear,
>   A tear so limpid and so meek
>   It would not stain an angel's cheek—
>   'Tis that which pious fathers shed
>   Upon a duteous daughter's head!"

After a stay of about three weeks in Edinburgh,
I took a reluctant leave of it, and went to London.
Eight years later, September, 1832, I was again there.
Scott was on his death-bed, at Abbotsford. Over-
burdened with the struggle to extricate himself from
the wreck of his fortunes, his brain had given way,
and the mighty intellect was in ruins. On the morning of the 17th, he woke from a paralytic slumber—
his eye clear and calm, every trace of delirium having
passed away. Lockhart came to his bedside. "My
dear," he said, "I may have but a moment to speak
to you. Be a good man; be virtuous—be religious:
be a good man. Nothing else will give you any comfort, when you are called upon to lie here!"

Oh, what a bequest were these words, uttered by
the dying lips of the mightiest genius of the age!
We may all do well to heed them. Few more words
did he speak; he soon fell into a stupor, which, on

the 21st, became the sleep of death. Thus he expired, all his children around him. "It was a beautiful day," says his biographer—"so warm that every
window was wide open, and so perfectly still that
the sound of all others most delicious to his ear, the
gentle ripple of the Tweed over its pebbles, was distinctly audible as we knelt around the bed, and his
eldest son kissed and closed his eyes!"

The signs and symbols of mourning that spread
over Great Britain on account of the death of the
great and good man, were like those which commemorate the decease of a sovereign. Bells were
tolled, sermons were preached, flags of ships were at
half-mast, nearly every newspaper was clothed in
black. In Edinburgh, every lip trembled in speaking of the melancholy event.

Two days after this, I departed with my companion for the Highlands. On reaching Stirling, we
found it enveloped in the drapery of dark, impenetrable clouds. We passed on to Callender; we proceeded to Loch Katrine. All around seemed to be in
mourning. Huge masses of dim vapor rolled around
the pinnacle of Benain; the shaggy brows and rocky
precipices of Benvenue were all shrouded in gloomy
mist. The hoary forests of the Trosachs heaved sad
and moaning in the breeze. The surface of the lake
was wrinkled with falling spray. All around seemed
to wail and weep, as if some calamity had fallen upon
nature itself. He who had endowed these scenes with

immortality, was dead; his body was now being borne to its tomb. While a nation wept, it was meet that the mountain and the lake, the stream and the glen—which his genius had consecrated—should also weep.

> "Call it not vain; they do not err
>   Who say, that when the poet dies,
> Mute nature mourns her worshiper,
>   And celebrates his obsequies;
> Who say, tall cliff and cavern lone,
> For the departed bard make moan;
> That mountains weep in crystal rill;
> That flowers in tears of balm distill;
> Through his loved groves that breezes sigh,
> And oaks, in deeper groans, reply;
> And rivers teach their rushing wave
> To murmur dirges round his grave!"

LETTER XLIII.

Journey to London—Remarks on England, as it appears to the American Traveler—The Climate—The Landscape—Jealousies between the English and Americans—Plan for securing Peace.

My dear C******

Early in June, I set out for London. My route led me through the village of Dalkeith, and the possessions of the Duke of Buccleugh, extending for thirty miles on both sides of the road. We were constantly meeting objects which revived historical or poetic reminiscences. Among these was Cockpen, the scene of the celebrated ballad, and as I rode by, the whole romance passed before my mind. I fancied that I could even trace the pathway along which the old laird proceeded upon his courtship, as well as the residence of

"The pennyless lass with a lang pedigree;"

and who was so daft as to reject his offer, although

"His wig was well powthered and as gude as new;
His waistcoat was red, and his coat it was blue;
A ring on his finger, his sword and cocked hat—
And who could refuse the auld laird wi' a' that?"

We crossed the Galawater and the Ettrick, and traveled along the banks of the Tweed—formed by the union of these two streams. We passed Abbotsford, rising at a little distance on the left—its baronial dignity being lost in the spell of more potent associations. Further on, we saw the Eildon Hills, "cleft in three" by the wondrous wizzard, Michael Scott—as duly chronicled in the Lay of the Last Minstrel. We procceded along the banks of the Teviot—a small limpid stream, where we observed the barefooted lassies washing, as in the days of Allan Ramsay. We saw Netherby Hall, and a little beyond Cannobie Lea, the scenes of the song of Young Lochinvar. All these, and many more localities of legendary name and fame, were passed in the course of a forenoon's progress in the stage-coach. Scotland is indeed a charmed land!

One day's journey brought me to Carlisle: thence I traveled westward, looking with all due delight upon Wendermere, and Rydal, and Grassmere, and Helvellyn, and Derwentwater, and Skiddau. Then turning eastward, I traveled over a hilly and picturesque country, to the ancient and renowned city of York. Having lingered, half entranced amid its antiquities, and looked almost with worship upon its cathedral— the most beautiful I have ever seen—I departed, and soon found myself once more in London.

As I shall not return to the subject again, allow me to say a few words as to the impression England makes upon the mind of an American, traveling over its surface. I have visited this country several times within the last thirty years, and I shall group my impressions in one general view. The whole may be summed up in a single sentence, which is, that England is incomparably the most beautiful country in the world! I do not speak of it in winter, when incumbered with fogs; when there is

> "No sun, no moon, no morn, no noon,
>   No dusk, no dawn—no proper time of day;
>   No sky, no earthly view, no distance looking blue;
>   No road, no street, no t'other side the way!"

I take her as I do any other beauty who sits for her portrait—in her best attire; that is, in summer. The sun rises here as high in June, as it does in America. Vegetation is just about as far advanced. The meadows, the wheat-fields, the orchards, the forests, are in their glory. There is one difference, however, between the two countries—the sun in England is not so hot, the air is not so highly perfumed, the buzz of the insects is not so intense. Every thing is more tranquil. With us, all nature, during summer, appears to be in haste, as if its time was short—as if it feared the coming frost. In England, on the contrary, there seems to be a confidence in the seasons, as if there were time for the ripening harvests; as if the wheat might swell out its fat sides, the hops amplify its many-plaited flowers, the oats multiply and increase its tassels—each and all attaining their perfection at leisure. In the United States, the period of growth of most vegetables is compressed into ten weeks; in Great Britain, it extends to sixteen.

If we select the middle of June as a point of comparison, we shall see that in America there is a spirit, vigor, energy in the climate, as indicated by vegetable and animal life, unknown in Europe. In the former, the pulse of existence beats quicker than in the latter. The air is clearer, the landscape is more distinct, the bloom more vivid, the odors more pungent, the perceptions of the mind even, I doubt not, are more intense. A clover-field in America, in full bloom, is by many shades more ruddy than the same thing in England—its breath even is sweeter: the music of the bees stealing its honey is of a higher key. A summer forest with us is of a livelier green than in any part of Great Britain; the incense breathed upon the heart, morning and evening, is, I think, more full and fragrant. And yet, if we take the summer through, this season is pleasanter in England than with us. It is longer, its excitements are more tranquil, and, being spread over a larger space, the heart has more leisure to appreciate them, than in the haste and hurry of our American climate.

There is one fact worthy of notice, which illustrates this peculiarity of the English summer. The trees there are all of a more sturdy, or, as we say, *stubbed* form and character. The oaks, the elms, the walnuts, beeches, are shorter and thicker, as well in the trunks as the branches, than ours. They have all a stocky, John Bull form and stature. The leaves are thicker, the twigs larger in circumference. I have noticed particularly the recent growths of apple-trees, and they are at once shorter and stouter than in America. This quality in the trees gives a peculiarity to the landscape. The forest is more solid and less graceful than ours. If you will look at an English painting of trees, you notice the fact I state, and perceive the effect it gives, especially to scenes of which trees constitute a prevailing element. All over Europe, in fact, the leaves of the trees have a less feathery appearance than in America; and in general the forms of the branches are less arching, and, of course, less beautiful. Hence it will be perceived that European pictures of trees differ in this respect from American ones—the foliage in the for-

SCENE IN ENGLAND. Vol. 2, p 214.

mer being more solid, and the sweep of the branches more angular.

But it is in respect to the effects of human art and industry, that the English landscape has the chief advantage over ours. England is an old country, and shows on its face the transforming influences of fifteen centuries of cultivation. It is, with the exception of Belgium, the most thickly-settled country of Europe—nearly three hundred and fifty inhabitants to the square mile, while in the United States we have but seven. Massachusetts, the most thickly-settled State in America, has but one hundred and thirty.

England, therefore, is under a garden-like cultivation; the plowing is straight and even, as if regulated by machinery; the boundaries of estates consist for the most part of stone mason-work, the intermediate divisions being hedges, neatly trimmed, and forming a beautiful contrast to our stiff stone walls and rail fences. The public roads are nicely wrought, the sides being turfed with neat and convenient footways. The railway stations are beautiful specimens of architecture; the sides of the railways are all sodded over, and often are blooming with patches of cultivated flowers. In looking from the top of a hill over a large extent of country, it is impossible not to feel a glow of delight at the splendor of the scene— the richness of the soil, its careful and skillful cultivation, its green, tidy boundaries checkering the scene, its teeming crops, its fat herds, its numberless and full-fleeced sheep.

Nor must the dwellings be overlooked. I pass by the cities and the manufacturing villages, which, in most parts, are visible in every extended landscape— sometimes, as in the region of Manchester, spreading out for miles, and sending up pitchy wreaths of smoke from a thousand tall, tapering chimneys. I am speaking now of the country, and here are such residences as are unknown to us. An English castle would swallow up a dozen of our shingle or brick villas. The adjacent estate often includes a thousand acres—and these, be it remembered, are kept almost as much for ornament as use. Think of a dwelling that might gratify the pride of a prince, surrounded by several square miles of wooded park, and shaven lawn, and winding stream, and swelling hill, and all having been for a hundred, perhaps five hundred years, subjected to every improvement which the highest art could suggest! There is certainly a union of unrivaled beauty and magnificence in the lordly estates of England. We have nothing in America which at all resembles them.

And then there is every grade of imitation of these high examples, scattered over the whole country. The greater part of the surface of England belongs to wealthy proprietors, and these have alike the desire and the ability to give an aspect of neatness, finish, and elegance, not only to their dwellings and the immediate grounds, but to their entire estates. The prevailing standard of taste thus leads to a universal beautifying of the surface of the country. Even the cottager feels the influence of this omnipresent spirit; the brown thatch over his dwelling, and the hedge before his door, must be neatly trimmed; the green ivy must clamber up and festoon his windows, and the little yard in front must bloom with roses and lilies, and other gentle flowers, in their season.

And thus cold, foggy England is made the paradise of the earth—at least during this charming month of June. Nature now, in compensation for her ill humor at other seasons, aids in this universal decoration. Through the whole summer—nay, in autumn, and even in winter—the verdure of the English landscape is preserved. Not in July nor August, not even in December, do we here see the grass parched with heat or grown gray in the frost. It is true the leaves of the trees fall, as they do with us, in November—not having first clothed the hills in red and purple and gold as in America, but, as the English poet tells us—

> " —— the fading, many-colored woods,
> Shade deep'ning over shade, the country round
> Imbrown; a crowded umbrage, dusk and dun,
> Of every hue, from wan, declining green,
> To sooty dark"—

thus, for a time, seeming to prelude the coming winter, with a drapery of mourning woven of the faded

glories of summer. Nothing can indeed be more dismal than the aspect of England, when the black, crum-
pled leaves are falling in the forests—some yet flut-
tering on the branches, and others strewn on the
ground. But even then the sod retains its living
hue, and when at last the leaves have fallen, there is
still a universal mantle of verdure over the fields—
thus redeeming winter from a portion of its gloom.

So much for the common aspect of England as the
traveler passes over it. The seeker for the picturesque may find abundant gratification in Devon-
shire, Derbyshire, Westmoreland, though Wales and
Scotland, and parts of Ireland, are still more renowned for scenic beauty. So far as combinations of nature are concerned, nothing in the world can surpass
some of our own scenery—as along the upper waters
of the Housatonic and the Connecticut, or among the
islands of Lake George, and a thousand other places
—but these lack the embellishments of art and the
associations of romance or song, which belong to the
rival beauties of British landscapes.

You will notice that I confine these remarks to a
single topic—the aspect of England, as it meets the
eye of an American traveler. The English, with all
their egotism, do not appreciate that wonderful display of wealth and refinement, which the surface of
their country presents. They do not and can not
enjoy the spectacle as an American does, for they are
born to it, and have no experience which teaches

them to estimate it by common and inferior standards. Having said so much on this subject, I shall
not venture to speak of English society—of the lights
and shadows of life beneath the myriad roofs of towns
and cities. The subject would be too extensive, and
besides, it has been abundantly treated by others. I
only say, in passing, that the English people are best
studied at home. John Bull, out of his own house, is
generally a rough customer: here, by his fireside, with
wife, children, and friends, he is generous, genial,
gentlemanly. There is no hospitality like that of an
Englishman, when you have crossed his threshold.
Everywhere else he will annoy you. He will poke
his elbow into your sides in a crowded thoroughfare;
he will rebuff you if, sitting at his side in a locomotive, you ask a question by way of provoking a little
conversation; he will get the advantage of you in
trade, if he can; he carries at his back a load of prejudices, like that of Christian in Pilgrim's Progress,
and instead of seeking to get rid of them, he is always
striving to increase his collection. If he becomes a
diplomat, his great business is to meddle in everybody's affairs; if an editor, he is only happy in
proportion as he can say annoying and irritating
things. And yet, catch this same John Bull at home,
and his crusty, crocodile armor falls off, and he is the
very best fellow in the world—liberal, hearty, sincere—the perfection of a gentleman.

The relations of America to England are a subject

of great interest to both countries. It would seem that by every dictate of prudence, as well as of propriety, they should remain friends. We are of the same kith and kin, have the same language, the same faith, the same moral and social platform, the same, or at least similar institutions. All these ties seem to bind us in the bonds of peace and amity. To this may be added the myriad relations of commercial interest. To do good to each other is virtually to earn and bless our daily bread. And yet we have been twice at war. There is a social war always being waged between us. The presses of England and America seem to conceive that they say their best things when they say their worst, of the two countries. We must not, then, put too much faith in consanguinity. Family quarrels are proverbially the fiercest. It is a mournful truth that the first murder was a fratricide.

What then is to be done? One thing could and should be done, in England. The press there is in the hands of the ruling people. If, as is asserted in England, there is a general feeling of good-will there toward America, that should be made manifest by the common vehicles of public opinion. Certainly this has never yet been done. From the very beginning, the British press has been supercilious, hypercritical, condemnatory of our country, its manners, principles, institutions. Is it possible—so long as this state of things shall continue—for the American people to believe that the English nation do not, in their hearts, cherish hostility toward this country?

It may, indeed, be said that the American press is as little conciliatory toward England as that of England toward America. But, certainly, the good example should come from them. They are the older people—the mother country : their journals are more immediately within the control and influence of leading minds and influential men, than ours. And besides, all that is wanted on our part, to a good understanding, is an assurance, a conviction of good-will, toward us on the other side of the water. Amid all our scolding at England, there is at the bottom of the American heart, a profound respect for her. We care very little what the French, or Dutch, or Germans, or Russians, or Chinese, or Japanese, say or think of us; but if the English say any thing bad of us, we are sure to resent it. Why can not something be done to bring this mischievous war to an end?

And yet how can it be effected? Let me venture upon a suggestion : if the London Times—that mighty personification of John Bull—would always be a gentleman, when he speaks of America, such would be the influence of this high example, that I should have some hope of seeing, even in my life-time, a millennial spirit in the intercourse of the two countries.

LETTER XLIV.

London Thirty Years Ago—Its Great Increase—George IV.—Ascot Races —The Duke of Wellington—Jacob Perkins and the Steam-gun—The Duke of Sussex—Duke of York—Hounslow Heath—Parliament—Canning—Mackintosh—Brougham—Palmerston— House of Lords — Lord Eldon—Rhio Rhio—Catalani—Signorina Garcia—Edward Irving—Byron's Coffin.

My dear C******

It is said that Mr. Webster remarked, while in London, that his constant and predominant feeling was that of wonder at its enormous extent : fourteen thousand streets, two hundred thousand houses, fifteen hundred places of public worship, three millions of human beings—all crowded within the space of seven miles square !

Yet London, when I first knew it, was not what it is now. Its population has at least doubled since 1824. At that time Charing Cross was a filthy, triangular thoroughfare, a stand for hackney-coaches, a grand panorama of showbills pasted over the surrounding walls, with the king's mews in the immediate vicinity : this whole area is now the site of Trafalgar-Square—one of the most imposing combinations of magnificent architecture and tasteful embellishments in the world. This is an index of other and similar changes that have taken place all over the city. London has been nearly as much improved as New York within the last thirty years. I know a portion of it, nearly a mile square, now covered with buildings, which consisted of open fields when I first visited the city. At the present day, London not only surpasses in its extent, its wealth, its accumulations of all that belongs to art—the richness of its merchandises, the extent of its commerce, the vastness of its influence— all the cities that now exist, but all that the world has before known. What were Nineveh, or Babylon, or Rome—even if they had an equal population—when their relations were confined to the quarter of a single hemisphere, and their knowledge did not embrace the telescope, the mariner's compass, the steam-engine, nor the telegraph—neither railroads nor the printing-press;—what were they in comparison with the metropolis of a kingdom, whose colonies now belt the world, and whose influence, reaching every state and nation under the sun, extends to the thousand millions of mankind!

But what of London in 1824? King George IV. was then on the throne, and though he was shy of showing himself in public, I chanced to see him several times, and once to advantage—at Ascot Races. This was a royal course, and brought together an immense crowd of the nobility and gentry, as well as an abundant gathering of gamblers and blacklegs. For more than an hour his majesty stood in the pavilion, surrounded by the Duke of Wellington, the Duke of York, the Marquis of Anglesea, and other persons of note. He was a large, over-fat man, of a rather sour and discontented countenance. All the arts of the toilet could not disguise the wrinkles of age, and the marks of dissipation and dilapidation. His lips were sharp, his eye grayish-blue, his wig chestnut-brown. His cheeks hung down pendulously, and his whole face seemed pallid, bloated, and flabby. His coat was a blue surtout, buttoned tight over the breast; his cravat, a huge black stock, scarcely sufficient to conceal his enormous, undulating jowl. On his left breast was a glittering star. He wore a common hat, the brim a little broader than the fashion. But for the star and the respect paid to him, he might have passed as only an overdressed and rather sour old rake. I noticed that his coat set very close and smooth, and was told that he was trussed and braced by stays, to keep his flesh in place and shape. It was said to be the labor of at least two hours to prepare him for a public exhibition, like the present. He was a dandy to the last. The wrinkles of his coat, after it was on, were cut out by the tailor, and carefully drawn up with the needle. He had the gout, and walked badly. I imagine there were few among the thousands gathered to the spectacle, who were really less happy than his majesty— the monarch of the three kingdoms.

I not only saw the Duke of Wellington on this, but on many subsequent occasions. I think the portraits give a false idea of his personal appearance. He was really a rather small, thin, insignificant looking man, unless you saw him on horseback. His profile was indeed fine, on account of his high Roman nose, but his front face was meager, and the expression cold, almost mean. His legs were too short, a defect which disappeared when he was in the saddle. He then seemed rather stately, and in a military dress, riding always with inimitable ease, he sustained the image of the great general. At other times, I never could discover in his appearance any thing but the features and aspect of an ordinary, and certainly not prepossessing, old man. I say this with great respect for his character, which, as a personification of solid sense, indomitable purpose, steady loyalty, and unflinching devotion to a sense of public duty, I conceive to be one of the finest in British history.

At this period, our countryman, Jacob Perkins, was astonishing London with his steam-gun. He was certainly a man of extraordinary genius, and was the originator of numerous useful inventions. At the time of which I write, he fancied that he had discovered a new mode of generating steam, by which he was not only to save a vast amount of fuel, but to obtain a marvelous increase of power. So confident was he of success, that he told me he felt certain of being able, in a few months, to go from London to Liverpool, with the steam produced by a gallon of oil. Such was his fertility of invention, that while pursuing one discovery, others came into his mind, and, seizing upon his attention, kept him in a whirl of experiments, in which many things were begun and comparatively nothing completed.

Though the steam-gun never reached any practical result, it was for some time the admiration of London. I was present at an exhibition of its wonderful performances in the presence of the Duke of Sussex, the king's youngest brother, and the Duke of Wellington, with other persons of note. The general purpose of the machine was to discharge bullets by steam, instead of gunpowder, and with great rapidity—at least a hundred a minute. The balls were put in a sort of tunnel, and by working a crank back and forth, they were let into the chamber of the barrel— one by one—and expelled by the steam. The noise of each explosion was like that of a musket, and when the discharges were rapid, there was a ripping uproar, quite shocking to tender nerves. The balls—carried about a hundred feet across the smithy—struck upon an iron target, and were flattened to the thickness of a shilling piece.*

---

* Jacob Perkins was a native of Newburyport, Mass., born in 1776. He was apprenticed to a goldsmith, and soon was noted for his ingenuity. Before the establishment of a national mint, he was employed, and with success, in making dies for copper coin. At the age of twenty-four, he invented the machine for cutting nails, which had a great effect over the whole world. He next invented a stamp for preventing counterfeit bills, and then a check-plate, which was long adopted by law in Massachusetts. He now discovered a mode of softening steel, by decarbonization, which led to the use of softened steel for engraving. The results of this discovery have been extensive—the bank-note engraving, now brought to such perfection, being one of the most prominent. Steel

The whole performance was indeed quite formidable, and the Duke of Sussex—who was an enormous, red-faced man—seemed greatly excited. I stood close by, and when the bullets flew pretty thick and the discharge came to its climax, I heard him say to the Duke of Wellington, in an under-tone—" Wonderful, wonderful—d——d wonderful ; wonderful, wonderful—d——d wonderful ; wonderful, wonderful—d——d wonderful !" and so he went on, without variation. It was in fact, save the profanity, a very good commentary upon the performance.

---

engraving for fine pictures, was another, and this led to the *Souvenirs*—making books the most desirable articles for presents—instead of rings, necklaces, shawls—thus producing not only a new generation of publications, but a revolution in the taste of society. This discovery Mr. Perkins carried to England, and here he remained till his death in 1849. His other inventions are very numerous : among these are the chain-pump, the bathometer, to measure the depth of water, the pleometer, to measure the velocity of ships, together with a multitude of improvements in various devices, from house-stoves to steam-engines.

After I left London, he so far improved his steam-gun, that he sent balls through eleven planks of deal, an inch thick ! A report of his experiments in 1825, before a committee, of which the Duke of Wellington was the head, describes the power exerted, as absolutely terrific.

Mr. Perkins's establishment was in Fleet-street, 69, when I was in London. One of the superintendents of this was Mr. Charles Toppan, now so well known in connection with the eminent firm of Toppan, Carpenter & Co. To his intelligence and kindness I was indebted for much of the pleasure and profit of my first visit to London. Here also was Asa Spencer—originally a watchmaker of New London, and the inventor of the geometric lathe, for copying medals, as well as other ingenious and useful devices. He was a man of true genius—full of goodness, modesty, and eccentricity.

The house of Mr. Perkins, at this period, was a familiar gathering place of Americans in London—his charming daughters giving a sort of American life and grace to all around them. His son, Angier M. Perkins, a gentleman of great talent, worth, and kindliness, continues his father's establishment in London.

Having thus spoken of the Duke of Sussex, I must say a few words of his brother, the Duke of York, whom I had seen, dressed in a green frock-coat and white pantaloons, at Ascot. He was there interested in the race, for he had entered a famous courser by the name of Moses, for one of the prizes. Some person reflected upon him for this, inasmuch, as among other titles, he held that of bishop.* His ready reply was, that he was devoted to *Moses and the profits*. Despite his disgrace in the Flanders campaign, and his notorious profligacy, both as a gambler and a roué, he was still a favorite among the British people. There was about him a certain native honorableness and goodness of heart, which survived, even in the midst of his debaucheries. English loyalty has the faculty of seeing the small virtues of its princes through the magnifying power of the telescope ; their vices are dwindled into comparative insignificance by being observed with the instrument reversed. And besides, the Duke of York was now heir-apparent to the throne, and thus stood next the king himself.

I saw him not only at Ascot, but on other occasions—especially in a review of the first regiment of foot-guards, at Hyde Park, and again at a review of four thousand horse-guards, at Hounslow Heath. The foot-guards were grenadiers, and their

---

* It is a curious item in ecclesiastical history, that the Duke of York was *Bishop of Osnaburgh*, a district in the kingdom of Hanover.

caps were of enormous height. The duke himself
wore the same kind of cap, with a red coat of
course. Like all his brothers, he was a large man,
and of full habit, though not up to the dimensions
of the Duke of Sussex. He had a red, John Bull
face, without expression, save that of good feeding.
The Duke of Wellington, at this time, was among
the spectators. He was now in military dress, on a
fine chestnut-colored horse. His motions were quick,
and frequently seemed to indicate impatience. His
general aspect was highly martial. Several ladies
as well as gentlemen on horseback, were admitted to
the review and within the circle of the sentries stationed to exclude the crowd. I obtained admission
for a crown—five shillings, I mean—for I had learned
that in England cash is quite as mighty as in America. The privileged group of fair ladies and brave
men, gathered upon a grassy knoll, to observe the
evolutions of the soldiers, presented an assemblage
such as the aristocracy of England alone can furnish. Those who imagine that this is an effem-
inate generation, should learn that both the men
and women, belonging to the British nobility, taken
together, are without doubt the finest race in the
world. One thing is certain, these ladies could stand
fire—for, although the horses leaped and pranced at
the discharges of the troops, their fair riders seemed
as much at ease as if upon their own feet. Their
horsemanship was indeed admirable, and suggested

those habits of exercise and training, to which their full rounded forms and blooming countenances gave ample testimony.

The review at Hounslow Heath, some eight miles from London—and at the present day nearly covered with buildings—comprised seven regiments of cavalry, including the first and second of the horse-guards. The latter were no doubt the finest troops of the kind in the world—all the horses being large and black, and finely groomed. The caparisons were of the most splendid description, and the men picked for the purpose. All the officers were men of rank, or at least of good family.

The performances consisted of various marches and countermarches—sometimes slow and sometimes quick—across the extended plain. The evolutions of the flying-artillery excited universal admiration. When the whole body—about four thousand horse—rushed in a furious gallop over the ground, the clash of arms, the thunder of hoofs, the universal shudder of the earth—all together created more thrilling emotions in the mind than any other military parade I ever beheld. I have seen eighty thousand infantry in the field, but they did not impress my imagination as forcibly as these few regiments of cavalry at Hounslow Heath. One incident gave painful effect to the spectacle. As the whole body were sweeping across the field, a single trooper was pitched from his horse and fell to the ground. A hundred hoofs passed over him, and trampled him into the sod. On swept the gallant host, as heedless of their fallen companion, as if only a feather had dropped from one of their caps. The conflict of cavalry in real battle, must be the most fearful exhibition which the dread drama of war can furnish. On this occasion both the king and the Duke of York were present, so that it was one of universal interest. About fifty ladies on horseback rode back and forth over the field, on the flanks of the troops, imitating their evolutions.

You have no doubt heard enough of Parliament; but I shall venture to make a few extracts from my note-book respecting it, inasmuch as these present slight sketches of persons of eminence who have now passed from the scene. I have been often at the House of Commons, but I shall now only speak of a debate in July, 1824, upon the petition, I believe, of the city of London, for a recognition of the independence of some of the South American States. Canning was then secretary of foreign affairs, and took the brunt of the battle made upon the ministry. Sir James Mackintosh led, and Brougham followed him on the same side.

I shall not attempt to give you a sketch of the speeches: a mere description of the appearance and manner of the prominent orators will suffice. Sir James—then nearly sixty years old—was a man rather above the ordinary size, and with a fine, philanthropic face. His accent was decidedly Scotch, and his voice shrill and dry. He spoke slowly, often hes-

itated, and was entirely destitute of what we call eloquence. There was no easy flow of sentences, no gush
of feeling, no apparent attempt to address the heart or
the imagination. His speech was a rigid lecture, rather
abstract and philosophical, evidently addressed to the
stern intellect of stern men. He had a good deal of
gesture, and once or twice was boisterous in tone and
manner. His matter was logical, and occasionally
he illustrated his propositions by historical facts, happily narrated. On the whole, he made the impression upon my mind that he was a very philosophical,
but not very practical, statesman.

Brougham, as you know, is one of the ugliest
men in the three kingdoms. His nose is long, and
the nostrils, slightly retreating, seem to look at you
—sometimes to mock you. The mouth is hooked
downward at either corner; the brow is rolled in
folds, like the hide of a rhinoceros. And yet, strange
to say, this odd composition of odd features makes
up a face of rather agreeable, and certainly very effective expression. His figure is a little above the common size, and at the time I speak of, was thin and
wiry—a characteristic which time has since kindly
converted into a moderate degree of portliness. He
had abundance of words, as well as ideas. In his
speech on the occasion I describe, he piled thought
upon thought, laced sentence within sentence, mingled satire and philosophy, fact and argument, history
and anecdote, as if he had been a cornucopia, and

was anxious to disburden himself of its abundance. In all this there were several hard hits, and Canning evidently felt them. As he rose to reply, I took careful note of his appearance, for he was then, I imagine, the most conspicuous of the British statesmen. He was a handsome man, with a bald, shining pate, and a figure slightly stooping in the shoulders. His face was round, his eye large and full, his lips a little voluptuous—the whole bearing a lively and refined expression. In other respects his appearance was not remarkable. His voice was musical, and he spoke with more ease and fluency than most other orators of the House of Commons; yet even he hesitated, paused, and repeated his words, not only in the beginning, but sometimes in the very midst of his argument. He, however, riveted the attention of the members, and his keen observations frequently brought out the ejaculation of "hear, hear," from both sides of the house. Brougham and Mackintosh watched him with vigilant attention, now giving nods of assent, and now signs of disapprobation.

The difference between the manner of speaking in the British Parliament and the American Congress, has frequently been the subject of remark. There is certainly great heaviness, and a kind of habitual hesitation, in nearly all English public speakers, strikingly in contrast to the easy and rapid fluency, so common with us. I have heard not only the famous men just mentioned in the British Parliament, but Peel, Palmerston, O'Connell, and others, and all of them would have been considered dull speakers —so far as mere manner is concerned—here in the United States. I could never perceive in any of them an approach to the easy and melodious flow of Everett, the melting earnestness of Clay, or the majestic thunderings of Webster.

On the occasion I am describing, Sir Francis Burdett*—then a man of notoriety, but now almost wholly forgotten—made a short speech. He was a tall, slender person, with a singularly prominent forehead, the rest of his face being comparatively thin and insignificant. He was rather dandily dressed, and diddled from right to left as he was speaking, in a very curious fashion. His voice was small, but penetrating. His attacks upon the ministry were very direct, but he evidently excited no great attention. It

* The history of this individual is curious. He was born in 1770— and though the youngest son of a youngest son, by a series of calamitous deaths, he succeeded to the title and estates of his affluent and ancient family. His wealth was increased by his marrying, in 1793, the daughter of Coutts, the banker. In 1802, after a hot contest, he was returned to Parliament for Middlesex, but the House found the election void, and imprisoned the sheriffs. In 1807, while he was disabled by a duel, he was chosen for Westminster, and continued to represent that borough for nearly thirty years. He was of a turbulent disposition, and having quarreled with the House of Commons, resisted the speaker's warrant for his arrest, thus creating an excitement in which several lives were lost. When the sergeant-at-arms went to his house to arrest him, he found him affectedly teaching a young child the Magna Charta! He was for some time imprisoned in the Tower. The general impression is that, while professing democracy, he was a thorough aristocrat, at least in feeling. This opinion was confirmed in 1835, when he totally changed his politics, and vehemently supported the tory side. He died in 1844.

seemed to me astonishing that he should ever have
been a popular leader, for his whole appearance
was that of the affected and supercilious aristocrat.
The populace have very often been made the dupes
of men whose hearts were full of despotism, and
who, in flattering the masses, only sought the means
of gratifying their unprincipled love of power. Every careful observer has seen examples of this hollow
and base democracy, and one might easily suspect
Sir Francis Burdett to have been one of them.

Of course I visited the House of Lords—paying
two shillings and sixpence for admittance. The
bishops wore their surplices; a few of the lords had
stars upon the breast, but most of them were without
any badge whatever. The general aspect of the assembly was eminently grave and dignified. Eldon
was the chancellor—a large, heavy, iron-looking
man—the personification of bigoted conservatism.
He was so opposed to reforms, that he shed tears
when the punishment of death was abolished for
stealing five shillings in a dwelling-house! When
I saw him, his head was covered with the official
wig: his face sufficed, however, to satisfy any one
that his obstinacy of character was innate.

While I was here, a committee from the House of
Commons was announced; they had brought up a
message to the Lords. The chancellor, taking the
seals in his hands, approached the committee, bowing three times, and they doing the same. Then

they separated, each moving backward, and bowing. To persons used to such a ceremony, this might be sublime; to me, it was ludicrous—and all the more so on account of the ponderous starchness of the chief performer in the solemn farce. There was a somewhat animated debate while I was present, in which Lords Liverpool, Lauderdale, Harrowby, and Grey participated; yet nothing was said or done by either that would justify particular notice at this late day.

A great event happened in the musical world while I was in London—the appearance of Catalani at the Italian opera, after several years of absence. The play was *Le Nozze di Figaro*. I had never before seen an opera, and could not, even by the enchantments of music, have my habits of thought and my common sense so completely overturned and bewitched, as to see the whole business of life—intrigue, courtship, marriage, cursing, shaving, preaching, praying, loving, hating—done by singing instead of talking, and yet feel that it was all right and proper. It requires both a musical ear and early training, fully to appreciate and feel the opera—which aims at a union of all the arts of rhetoric, poetry, and music, enforced by scenic representations, and the intense enthusiasm of congregated and sympathetic masses. Even when educated to it, the English, as well as the Americans, have too practical a nature and are too much grooved with business habits, to give themselves up to it, as is done in Italy, and in some other parts of the continent.

Madame Catalani was a large, handsome woman, a little masculine, and past forty. She was not only a very clever actress, but was deemed to have every musical merit—volume, compass, clearness of tone, surpassing powers of execution. Her whole style was dramatic, bending even the music to the sentiments of the character and the song. Some of her displays were almost terrific, her voice drowning the whole soul in a flood of passion. I could appreciate, unlettered as I was in the arts of the opera, her amazing powers—though to say the truth, I was quite as much astonished as pleased. Pasta and Garcia—both of whom I afterwards heard—gave me infinitely greater pleasure, chiefly because their voices possessed that melody of tone which excites sympathy in every heart—even the most untutored. Madame Catalani gave the opera a sort of epic grandeur—an almost tragic vehemence of expression; Pasta and Garcia rendered it the interpretation of those soft and tender emotions which haunt the soul, and for the expression of which God seems to have given music to mankind. It was, no doubt, a great thing to hear the greatest cantatrice of the age, but my remembrance of Madame Catalani is that of a prodigy, rather than an enchantress. On the occasion I am describing, she sang, by request, Rule Britannia, between the acts, which drew forth immense applause, in which I heartily joined—not that I liked the words, but that I felt the music.

It was about this time that a great attraction was announced at one of the theatres—nothing less than the king and queen of the Sandwich Islands, who had graciously condescended to honor the performance with their presence. They had come to visit England, and pay their homage to George the Fourth; hence the government deemed it necessary to receive them with hospitality, and pay them such attentions as were due to their rank and royal blood. The king's name was Tamehamaha, but he had also the sub-title or surname of Rhio-Rhio—which, being interpreted, meant Dog of Dogs. Canning's wit got the better of his reverence, and so he profanely suggested that, if his majesty was Dog of Dogs, what must the queen be? However, there was an old man about the court who had acquired the title of Poodle, and he was selected as a fit person to attend upon their majesties. They had their lodgings at the Adelphi Hotel, and might be seen at all hours of the day, looking at the puppet-shows in the street with intense delight. Of all the institutions of Great Britain, Punch and Judy evidently made the strongest and most favorable impression upon the royal party.

They were, I believe, received at a private interview by the king at Windsor; every thing calculated to gratify them was done. I saw them at the theatre, dressed in a European costume, with the addition of some barbarous finery. The king was an enormous man—six feet, three or four inches; the queen was short, but otherwise of ample dimensions. Besides these persons, the party comprised five or six other members of the king's household. They had all large, round, flat faces, of a coarse, though good-humored expression. Their complexion was a ruddy brown, not very unlike that of the American Indians; their general aspect, however, was very different, and entirely destitute of that mysterious, ruminating air which characterizes our children of the forest. They looked with a kind of vacant wonder at the play, evidently not comprehending it; the farce, on the contrary, seemed greatly to delight them. It is sad to relate that this amiable couple never returned to their country; both died in England—victims either to the climate, or the change in their habits of living.*

---

* The chief whom I have here noticed was Tamehamaha II. His name is now generally spelled Kamehamaha, and his other title is written Liho-Liho. They sailed in the British ship L'Aigle, October, 1823, and arrived at Portsmouth, May, 1824. Of the twenty-five thousand dollars shipped in their chests, only ten thousand were found—twelve thousand having been robbed, and three thousand taken for pretended expenses. Kamamalu, the principal queen, and the two or three inferior wives of his majesty, exhibited themselves at first in loose trowsers and velveteen bed-gowns—but ere long their waists, for the first time, were subjected to corsets, and their forms to Parisian fashions. They wore native turbans, which became the rage in high circles. The king was dressed in the English style, with certain embellishments denoting his rank. They generally behaved with propriety, though one of the party seeing a mullet, resembling a species common in the Sandwich Islands, seized it and hurried home, where their majesties devoured it raw, probably finding it the sweetest morsel they had tasted since they left home. In June, 1824, the whole party were attacked by the measles, Manui, the steward, first, and the king next. On the evening of the 8th the queen died, having taken an affectionate leave of her husband. His heart seemed to be broken, and on the 14th he breathed his

One or two items more, and this chapter shall be
closed. Among the prominent objects of interest in
London at this period was Edward Irving, then
preaching at the Caledonian Chapel, Cross-street, Hat-
ton Gardens. He was now in the full flush of his
fame, and such was the eagerness to hear him that it
was difficult to get admission. People of all ranks,
literary men, philosophers, statesmen, noblemen, persons of the highest name and influence, with a full and
diversified representation of the fair sex, crowded to
his church. I was so fortunate as to get a seat in the
pew of a friend, a privilege which I appreciated all
the more, when I counted twenty coroneted coaches
standing at the door—some of those who came in
them, not being able to obtain even an entrance into
the building. The interior was crowded to excess;
the alleys were full, and even fine ladies seemed
happy to get seats upon the pulpit stairway. Persons
of the highest title were scattered here and there, and
cabinet ministers were squeezed in with the mass of
common humanity.

Mr. Irving's appearance was very remarkable. He
was over six feet in height, very broad-shouldered,
violently cross-eyed, with long black hair hanging in
heavy, twisted ringlets down upon his shoulders.
His complexion was pallid yet swarthy, the whole

last. The bodies of the royal pair were taken to their native islands,
and there interred with great pomp. The remainder of the party returned to their home, one of them, however, Kapihe, dying on the way,
at Valparaiso.

expression of his face—half sinister and half sanctified—creating in the mind of the beholder a painful
doubt whether he was a great saint or a great sinner.
He wore a black-silk gown, of rich material and ample, graceful folds. His hair was sedulously parted
so as to display one corner of his forehead, which a
white hand and a very pure linen handkerchief frequently wiped, yet so daintily as not to disturb the
love-locks that inclosed it.

There was a strange mixture of saintliness and
dandyism, in the whole appearance of this man. His
prayer was affected—strange, quaint, peculiar, in its
phraseology—yet solemn and striking. His reading
of the psalm was peculiar, and a fancy or feeling
crossed my mind that I had heard something like it,
but certainly not in a church. There was a vague mingling in my imagination of the theatre and the house
of worship : of foot-lights, a stage, a gorgeous throng of
spectators—an orchestra and a troop of players—and
side by side with these—there seemed to come a psalm
and a text and a preacher. I was in fact seeking to
trace out a resemblance between this strange parson
and some star of Drury Lane or Covent Garden. Suddenly I found the clew : Edward Irving in the pulpit
was imitating Edmund Kean upon the stage ! And he
succeeded admirably—his tall and commanding person giving him an immense advantage over the little,
insignificant, yet inspired actor. He had the tones of
the latter—his gestures, his looks even, as I had often

seen him in Richard the Third and Shylock. He had evidently taken lessons of the renowned tragedian, but whether in public or private, is not for me to say.

The text was Genesis iii. 17, 18. I will extract from my notes, for your entertainment, a rough sketch of the discourse.

" This malediction—'Cursed is the ground for thy sake ; in sorrow shalt thou eat of it all the days of thy life; thorns also and thistles shall it bring forth to thee: and thou shalt eat the herb of the field'— this was the charter under which man held his existence till the birth of Christ, when the benediction— ' Peace on earth and good-will to man,' was pronounced. Since that time, these two principles and powers—the malediction and the benediction—have been at strife. To trace some of the consequences of this conflict is our present business.

" Moses discriminates between the two natures of man, by first stating the creation of his body as the completion of one distinct part or portion of his nature, and then the Creator breathing into him a living soul, or more literally the spirit of lives, thus completing the other portion of his being.

" I can not but pause a moment to note the striking coincidence between the statement of Moses and the result of philosophic speculation, which now makes the same discrimination; the study of the structure of the body, or physiology, being one branch of science, and the study of the mind or spirit, called metaphysics, being another. The French school, some time since, blended the whole nature of man in one physical organization, and Helvetius found in the sensibility of the fingers, all the rudiments—the entire foundation—of the moral and intellectual faculties of man. This crept into English philosophy, until the immortal mind was degraded into a mere tool of the body : the crumbling, earthy tenement alone was regarded, while the godlike inhabitant was made its servant and its slave.

" Let us do justice to the truth ! The spirit consists of three parts : the understanding, which discourseth of sensible ideas and powers—the basis of what is called knowledge ; the reason, which discourseth of insensible objects and insensible ideas, and has relation to principles and abstract science ; and conscience, which discourseth of duty, and hath regard to the relations between man and man, and also between man and his Maker.

" Now the proper vocation of the body is to minister to the spirit in this threefold character.

" Yet, I grieve to say it—the conduct of mankind reverses this system: it is the faculties of the spirit, debased from their high mission, which are everywhere made subservient to the body. I am loth to pain and disgust you with pictures in evidence of this, but every speculation should be supported by fact. I beg you therefore to consider the state of things in this city—the Babylon around us. Divest yourselves of that magic influence which is exercised by the term—*people;* of that morbid fashion of seeing in low vice and humble misery, only matter for mirth and song; of that cruel taste which haunts the dark and dismal courts and lanes and labyrinths of labor, of want and wretchedness, for subjects for the pencil and the stage. Stand all aloof from the sad jollity with which unthinking men survey such scenes. Wrap the mantle of immortality about thee and go forth, and in the scales of eternity, weigh the things thou seest!

"In the gray of the morning, you hear beneath your casement the heavy tread of the laborer plodding to his toil. This gradually increases, till one pervading volume of sound shakes every part of the city. Go forth and study the scene—the producers of this mighty uproar—the wagoner plodding by the side of his heavy wain, the porter staggering beneath his burden, the scavenger picking and prowling among the offal—the hundreds, the thousands, pouring along in a tide, and bent on their various labors. Survey them as they pass, and how fearfully is the heart smitten with the fact that these are reversing the true order of human destiny: not one among them is subjecting the body to the mind—all are subjecting the mind to the body—all are submitting themselves to the Malediction of the outcasts of Eden, as if the Benediction of the gospel had never been pronounced. From the gray dawn to the deep night, these beings, to whom is offered the bread of immortal life, are occupied with the poor thought of gaining a few crusts to feed the mortal body!

"If we turn to the higher classes, the picture is equally dark, and perhaps even more discouraging. Whatever we may here find of spiritual culture or intellectual tastes, we still see that the cares, the passions, the desires of the body, though they may often be disguised and refined, still master the soul. The being, whose imagination is capable of reaching the stars, and whose power of faith might carry him to the throne of God and the companionship of angels and just men made perfect—those whose ample means raise them above the groveling necessities of life— still cling to this earthly footstool, still think only of the pleasures of this fleeting animal existence. Whatever there may be of soul, in their pursuits, is a subjugation of it to the senses. A subtle epicureanism pervades the whole atmosphere they breathe. Pleasure, ambition, pride, the desire of honor, of wealth, of name, fame—all hopes, all fears—center in the little narrow kingdom of these poor five senses. These which were given only as windows from which the soul might look out upon immortality, are used as doors and avenues by which the soul passes into its prison-house of earthly enjoyments. Thus the gifted, the rich, the exalted, the favorites of fortune —are, after all, forgetful of the bread of life, and while pampering the body with oil and wine, are

starving the soul with shriveled husks and unsatis-
fying straw.

"How hard, how disheartening is the steep ascent
of duty, which calls upon us to contend with a world
thus embattled against the truth. And yet, as soldiers of the cross, we may not ground our arms. If
we can not do all we would, let us at least accomplish
what we may. To-day, I ask you here to join me, not
in the impossible, but the possible. If the poor reject the bread of life, it is perhaps not altogether by
choice : the heavy sin of Dives, who, being rich and
able to choose, preferred a sensual life, is not laid
upon their souls—the groveling necessities of Lazarus
have subdued them, crushed them, mastered them. It
is through ignorance, through peculiar temptations,
through the cares and needs of life, that they thus go
astray. The mother, uncertain of bread, alike for herself and her offspring—the father, anxious lest he shall
not have a shelter for those whom God has given him
—how can these think of aught but the immediate
pressing cares of the body ? How can these slaves of
mortality put on immortality ? Let Christianity kneel,
mourning and penitent, at the throne of grace, and
confessing that these things are so, rouse itself, and
say they shall be so no longer. I see around me the
great, the powerful : let them speak, and the work is
done. Let us carry Comfort to the poor, and as that
enters one door, the Gospel with its glad tidings, will
come in at the other. Each may do something.

None are too high, none too humble, to assist in this glorious work. The rich, the proud, the strong, in the confidence of their strength, may reject even the bread of life; the poor will welcome it. Relieve the famished body from its suffering for the want of daily bread, and the soul, delivered from its humiliation, will ascend to the throne of grace, and God will bless it, and he will bless you also who have ministered to the good work."

This is a mere outline of the discourse, and only gives an idea of its general drift and argument. The phraseology—which was rich, flowing, redundant, and abounding in illustration, and seemed to me carefully modeled after that of Jeremy Taylor—I did not attempt to preserve. In spite of the evident affectation, the solemn dandyism, the dramatic artifices of the performer—for, after all, I could only consider the preacher as an actor—the sermon was very impressive. Some of the pictures presented to the imagination were startling, and once or twice it seemed as if the whole audience was heaving and swelling with intense emotion, like a sea rolling beneath the impulses of a tempest. The power of the thought, aided by the deep, sympathetic voice of the speaker, and still further enforced by his portentous figure and emphatic action, overrode all drawbacks, and carried the whole heart and imagination along upon its rushing tide. Considered as a display of oratorical art, it was certainly equal to any thing I have

ever heard from the pulpit; yet it did not appear
to me calculated to have any permanent effect in
enforcing Christian truth upon the conscience. The
preacher seemed too much a player, and too little an
apostle; the afterthought was, that the whole effect
was the result of stage trick, and not of sober truth.

The character and career of Edward Irving present
a strange series of incongruities. He was born in Scotland in 1792; he became a preacher, and acquired
speedy notoriety, as much by his peculiarities as his
merits. He attracted the attention of Dr. Chalmers,
and through his influence was for a time assistant
minister in the parish of St. John's, at Glasgow.
From this place he was called to the Caledonian
Chapel, where I heard him. His fame continued to
increase; and having published a volume of discourses, under the quaint title, "For the Oracles of
God, four Orations; for Judgment to come, an Argument in nine Parts"—three large editions of the
work were sold in the space of six months. Where-
ever he preached, crowds of eager listeners flocked to
hear him. His eccentricities increased with his fame.
He drew out his discourses to an enormous length,
and on several occasions protracted the services to
four hours! He soon became mystical, and took to
studying unfulfilled prophecy, as the true key to the
interpretation of the scriptures. From this extravagance, he passed to the doctrine that Christians, by
the power of faith, can attain to the working of mira-

cles and speaking with unknown tongues, as in the primitive ages. Such at last were his vagaries, that he was cut off from communion with the Scottish Church ; in consequence, he became the founder of a sect which continues to the present time in England, bearing the title of Irvingites. Worn out with anxiety and incessant labors, he died at Glasgow, while on a journey for his health, in 1834, at the early age of forty-two.

The history of this extraordinary man teaches us various important lessons. It shows us that genius, even though it be allied to sincerity, is easily led astray by flattery and personal vanity; that eccentricity naturally ends in extravagance; that fanaticism is not superior to the use of artifice and affectation, even when they invade the pulpit and assume the badge of the preacher of the gospel; in short, that a man of great gifts, if so be he is not controlled by common sense—if he do not conform his conduct to that every-day but safe regulator, called *propriety*—is very apt to become a misguiding and bewildering light to his fellow-men, just in proportion as his abilities may surpass those of other persons. A large observation of mankind has satisfied me that a great man, even though he be a preacher, if he despises the suggestions of good sense, decency, congruity, usually becomes a great curse. Nearly all the religious vagaries which have led the world astray, have originated with individuals of this character. A large portion of the infidelity of mankind has its origin in the foibles of those who are set up as the great lights of Christianity.

One more event I must notice—the arrival in London of the mortal remains of Lord Byron, and their lying in state previous to interment. His body had been preserved in spirits, and was thus brought from Greece, attended by five persons of his lordship's suite. Having been transferred to the coffin, it was exhibited at the house of Sir Edward Knatchball, No. 20 Great George-street, on Friday and Saturday, the 9th and 10th of July, 1824. It caused a profound sensation, and such were the crowds that rushed to behold the spectacle, that it was necessary to defend the coffin with a stout wooden railing. When I arrived at the place the lid was closed; I was told, however, that the countenance, though the finer lines had collapsed, was so little changed as to be easily recognized by his acquaintances. The general muscular form of the body was perfectly preserved.

The aspect of the scene, even as I witnessed it, was altogether very impressive. The coffin was covered with a pall, enriched by escutcheons wrought in gold. On the top was a lid, set round with black plumes. Upon it were these words—

"GEORGE GORDON NOEL BYRON.

Born in London, 22d January, 1788:

Died at Missolonghi, April 19th, 1824."

BYRON'S COFFIN.   Vol. 2, p. 250,

At the head of the coffin was an urn containing the ashes of his brain and heart—this being also covered with a rich pall, wrought with figures in gold. The windows were closed, and the darkened room was feebly illumined by numerous wax-tapers.

And this was all that remained of Byron! What a lesson upon the pride of genius, the vanity of rank, the fatuity of fame—all leveled in the dust, and despite the garnished pall and magnificent coffin, their possessor was bound to pass through the same process of corruption as the body of a common beggar. And the soul—the soul?

Ah, what questions rose in my mind as I stood beside that coffin! Where art thou, Byron? What art thou? I have never seen thee—I have never known thee, face to face: yet hast thou often spoken to me, and in words that can never die! Thou art not dead—that were impossible: speak to me, then! Tell me—for such as thou might break the seal of the grave—what art thou?—where art thou? Whisper in my ear the dread secret of the tomb! Thou art silent—even thou. How fearful, how terrible is that spell which holds lips like thine—Childe Harold, Manfred, Cain—in the bondage of perpetual stillness! This, indeed, is death!

LETTER XLV.

Return to America—Removal to Boston—Literary position of Boston—
Prominent literary characters—The Press—The Pulpit—the Bar—New
York now the literary metropolis—My publication of various works—
The Legendary—N. P. Willis—The era of Annuals—The Token—The
artists engaged in it—The authors—Its termination.

My dear C******

Having made a hurried trip to Paris and back
to London, I departed for Liverpool, and thence embarked for the United States, arriving there in October, 1824. I remained at Hartford till October, 1826,
as already stated, and then removed to Boston, with
the intention of publishing original works, and at the
same time of trying my hand at authorship—the latter
part of my plan, however, known only to myself.

At that time, Boston was notoriously the literary
metropolis of the Union—the admitted Athens of
America. Edward Everett had established the North
American Review,* and though he had now just left
the editorial chair, his spirit dwelt in it, and his fame
lingered around it. Rich'd H. Dana, Edw'd T. Channing, Jared Sparks, George Bancroft, and others, were
among the rising lights of the literary horizon. The

---

* The North American was founded in 1815, by William Tudor, who
had previously been one of the principal supporters of the Monthly
Anthology. Mr. Everett, however, may be said to have given perma-
nency to the publication by his masterly administration of the editorial
department

newspaper press presented the witty and caustic Galaxy, edited by Buckingham; the dignified and scholarly Daily Advertiser, conducted by Nathan Hale;* and the frank, sensible, manly Centinel, under the editorial patriarch—Benjamin Russell. Channing was in the pulpit and Webster at the forum. Society was strongly impressed with literary tastes; genius was respected and cherished: a man, in those days, who had achieved a literary fame, was at least equal to a president of a bank, or a treasurer of a manufacturing company. The pulpit shone bright and far, with the light of scholarship radiated from the names of Beecher, Greenwood, Pierpont, Lowell, Palfry, Doane, Stone, Frothingham, Gannett: the bar also reflected the glory of letters through H. G. Otis, Charles Jackson, William Prescott, Benjamin Gorham, Willard Philips, James T. Austin, among the older members, and Charles G. Loring, Charles P. Curtis, Richard Fletcher, Theophilus Parsons, Franklin Dexter, J. Quincy, jr., Edward G. Loring, Benj. R. Curtis, among the younger. The day had not yet come when it was glory enough for a college professor to marry a hundred thousand dollars of stocks, or when it was the chief end of a lawyer to become

---

* The Boston Daily Advertiser was founded in March, 1814, and Mr. Hale began his editorial career with it. It may be taken as the model of the highest class of newspapers in the United States—able, calm, sincere, wise, and gentlemanly. It would be difficult to name a single journal in any country which, in a union of these qualities, takes rank above it. In the United States there are some which emulate it, but few, if any, which surpass it.

the attorney of an insurance company, or a bank, or a manufacturing corporation. Corporations, without souls, had not yet become the masters and moulders of the soul of society. Books with a Boston imprint had a prestige equal to a certificate of good paper, good print, good binding, and good matter. And while such was the state of things at Boston, how was it at New York? Why, all this time the Harpers, who till recently had been mere printers in Dover-street, had scarcely entered upon their career as publishers,* and the Appletons,† Putnam, Derby, the Masons, and other shining lights in the trade of New York at the present time, were either unborn, or in the nursery, or at school.

What a revolution do these simple items suggest— wrought in the space of thirty years! The scepter has departed from Judah : New York is now the

---

* James Harper, the eldest of the four brothers now associated in the concern, served his time as apprentice to the trade of printing to Abm. Paul, of New York ; he and his brother John commenced as printers in Dover-street, 1817 ; in 1818, having removed to Fulton-street, they printed and published Locke's Essays, which was their first enterprise as publishers. For a long time their publications were almost exclusively foreign books : at the present time, three-fourths are American works. Their Magazine publishes about one hundred and seventy thousand numbers a month, and surpasses any other publication of the kind in its circulation. The publishing establishment of the Messrs. Harper, the legitimate result of industry, discretion, energy, and probity, is justly the pride of New York, and one of the reflected glories of our literature, probably surpassing every other establishment of the kind in the world in its extent and the perfectness of its organization.

† The present eminent publishing house of Appleton & Co., consisting of Mr. W. Appleton and his four brothers, was founded by their father, Daniel Appleton, who came from New England to New York about the year 1826. He died in 1849, aged fifty-eight.

acknowledged metropolis of American literature, as well as of art and commerce. Nevertheless, if we look at Boston literature at the present time, as reflected in the publishing lists of Messrs. Little, Brown & Co., Ticknor & Fields, Philips, Sampson & Co., Crocker & Brewster, Gould & Lincoln, we shall see that the light of other days has not degenerated. Is it not augmented, indeed—for since the period I speak of, Prescott, Longfellow, Hawthorne, Whipple, Holmes, Lowell, Hillard, have joined the Boston constellation of letters?

It can not be interesting to you to know in detail my business operations in Boston at this period. It will be sufficient to say, that among other works I published an edition of the novels of Charles Brockden Brown, with a life of the author, furnished by his widow, she having a share of the edition. I also published an edition of Hannah More's works, and also of Mrs. Opie's works—these being, I believe, the first complete collections of the writings of these several authors. In 1827 I published Sketches by N. P. Willis, his first adventure in responsible authorship. The next year I issued the Common-place Book of Prose, the first work of the now celebrated Dr. Cheever. This was speedily followed by the Common-place Book of Poetry and Studies in Poetry, by the same author.*

---

* Among my lesser publications were Beauties of the Souvenirs, History of the Kings and Queens of France, Beauties of the Waverley Nov-

In 1828, I published a first, and soon after a second, volume of the Legendary, designed as a periodical, and to consist of original pieces in prose and verse, principally illustrative of American history, scenery, and manners.* This was edited by N. P. Willis, and was, I believe, his first editorial engagement. Among

---

els, Blair's Outlines of Ancient History, Blair's Outlines of Chronology, Blair's History of England, C. A. Goodrich's Outlines of Modern Geography, the American Journal of Education, issued monthly, Poems by Mrs. Sigourney, Records of the Spanish Inquisition, translated from the original documents by S. Kettell, Comstock's Mineralogy, Child's Botany, Sad Tales and Glad Tales by G. Mellen, Mary's Journey, Memoirs of a New England Village Choir, Specimens of American Poetry, 3 vols., edited by S. Kettell, Universal History, illustrated, copied, with additions, from Straus, the Garland of Flora, Balbi's Geography, edited by T. G. Bradford, Historical Cyclopædia, edited by F. A. Durivage, and doubtless some others, which I have forgotten. These were mostly original works. After 1835, I ceased to be a publisher, except for my own works; since 1845, these have been entirely published by others.

* I give a few extracts from a criticism of this work upon its first appearance: these will serve to show the estimate put upon some of the productions of popular authors at that time, by a noted critic; they will also show a state of things strikingly in contrast with the habits of the present day—for the reviewer found time and patience to notice, seriatim, every article in the book, some thirty in number. This was the day of great things in criticism, and small things in the production of materials for criticism.

"REVIEW.—THE LEGENDARY.

"It would be a reproach to our country, if the proprietor of a work of this nature, got up under circumstances so favorable to the growth of our native literature—even if the Legendary were no better than the mob of books that one may see every day of the year pouring forth out of the shops of people who pay more for puffs than for copyrights—a reproach to our country, I vow, if he were to suffer by the enterprise. If we are to have a literature of our own, we must pay for it; and they who are the first to pay for it, deserve to be the first to be repaid for it —with usury. * * *

"The first of the tales, by the author of 'Hobomok,' is called the 'Church of the Wilderness.' Here we have the serene, bold, and beautiful style of writing which had to be found fault with in the review of

the contributors I find the names of Halleck, Crosby,
Lunt, W. G. Clark, H. Pickering, J. O. Rockwell,
Miss Sedgewick, Miss Francis, Mrs. Sigourney, Willis, Pierpont, Cutter, I. M'Lellan, Jr., J. W. Miller,
and other popular writers of that day. It was kindly treated by the press, which generously published

---

'Hobomok'—no, not of 'Hobomok,' of some other story by the same
author, the title of which I forget. What I said then, I say now.

"The second affair is a piece by a young man of this town—Wm.
Cutter—whom I never suspected before of poetry. It is called the
'Valley of Silence,' and of a truth will bear to be treated as poetry. *
* * But I do not believe that in a poem of forty lines, it would be fair
play for any author to repeat the same idea more than eighty times, or
that HUSHING and RUSHING are altogether where they should be in the
forty lines now before me. For example, we have a bird that '*hushed*
his breath,' and we have the hush of the slumbering air, and we have
echoes '*hushed* in their caves,' and a '*hush* that is grand, not awful,'
and a '*hushed* worship,' and '*hushed* voices,' and all those by-baby-
bunting epithets in one single poem! * * *

"'Unwritten Poetry,' by N. P. W., the editor of the Legendary.
There are touches of exquisite beauty in this paper, and not a little of
what, to speak reverently of a brother poet, I should call heavenly nonsense. * * *

"'Descriptive Sonnets,' by Mr. H. Pickering. I hate sonnets; I
never saw a good one, and never shall.

"'The Clouds:' Grenville Mellen. Would this were better—would
it were worthier of my young friend. Some of the ideas are beautiful,
and some powerful; but the abrupt termination of almost every stanza,
the truncated air of the finest passages—a line being a period by itself
—who that knows poetry, or knows what poetry should be, can forgive?

"'The Pampas of Buenos Ayres,' by I. M'Lellan, jr. Here we have a
poet; I do not mean to say that here we have poetry, or, properly speaking, much poetry—for some there certainly is in every paragraph; but
simply that the author has within him a sure, and I believe a deep well
of poetry. If he has, however, he will never know its depth, nor
what riches may lie there, till the waters have been troubled—by an
angel—if you like, for angels are mighty troublesome now, as well as of
yore, to the fountains of life and health.

"'The Haunted Grave:' E. P. Blount. Never heard of this writer
before. Who is he? He shows talent—strong, decided, peculiar talent.

"'Extract from a Journal,' &c. *Mellen*—hey? A mere scratch or

without charge, the best pieces in full, saving the
reading million the trouble of buying the book and
paying for the chaff, which was naturally found with
the wheat. Despite this courtesy, the work proved
a miserable failure. The time had not come for such
a publication : at the present day, with the present

---

two of a free pen. The author, if it is he, will make a better figure in
prose yet than he ever made in poetry. I do not speak of this paper,
but of others that I know to be his.

" ' Grave of an Unknown Genius :" Joseph H. Nichols. Good poetry
here, though not much. The best is—

> ' And worthy of their harps was he,
> Worthy to wake with them, the grand
> War-anthem, or the music free
> Of love, *with burning lip and hand.*'

" ' Mere Accident :' N. P. Willis. Rather too Tom Moorish. However, let that pass. For, do ye know, ye blue-eyed, fair-haired girls,
and ye of the dark, lamping eyes and a shadowy crown—do ye not
know that the old proverb about kissing and telling is not worth a fig?
I'll give you a better one : ' They that kiss never tell—and they that tell
never kiss.'

" ' The Nun,' by Emma C. Manly. High and pure and sensible
poetry. But who is Emma C. Manly? Is it not another name for
N. P. W. ?

" ' Romance in Real Life :' author of Redwood. This very sensible
and happy writer, if she had more courage, and were willing to tell the
very truth and nothing but the truth of our country manners, would be
more thought of a hundred years hence than she is now.

" ' Ascutney :' Mrs. A. M. Wells. Upon my word, it is very encouraging to see what a few of our Yankee women are about in the world of
literature. They only want fair play to shoot ahead of their teachers,
the hatted ones of our earth.

" ' Telling the Dream :' Willis. Heigho ! " Do dreams always prove
true, Ianthe ?" I say, brother Willis, you deserve to be whipped backward through your alphabet for the false quantity in that last line—the
very pith and marrow of the whole poem. Up with your fingers, and
count them ; out with your hand for the ferule, or shut your eyes and
open your mouth, like a good boy, and see what the ladies will send
you. And then—' Do dreams always prove true, Ianthe ?' * * *

" ' The Bruce's Heart,' by the author of ' Moral Pieces.' Very good
poetry, and very like what a ballad of our time should be—a ballad of

accessories, and the present public spirit, I doubt not that such an enterprise would be eminently successful.

I believe I have already alluded to the Age of Annuals*—the first work of the kind, entitled the Forget-me-not, having been issued by the Ackermans of London, in the winter of 1823, while I was in that city. It was successfully imitated by Carey & Lea, at Philadelphia, in a work entitled the Atlantic Souvenir, and which was sustained with great spirit for several years. In 1828 I commenced and published the first volume of the Token, and which I continued for fifteen years, editing it myself, with the exception of the volume for 1829, which came out under the auspices of Mr. Willis. In 1836 the Atlantic Souvenir ceased, and after that time, by arrangement with the publishers, its title was added to that of the Token.

---

the war, I mean. But—I have always a *but* in reserve, you know—why deal so with the Moors? * * *

" 'Columbus,' by J. W. Miller. This man must be capable of writing magnificent poetry. The proof:

'Stands he upon the narrow deck
    Of yon lone caravel,
Whose tall shape *as with princely beck*
    Bound to the heaving swell;
And when the conqueror o'er her side
Crossed meekly, *rose with living pride.*"
                        From the Yankee, June 28, 1828.

* We are doubtless indebted to the Germans for originating the race of Annuals, but Ackerman's Forget-me-not was the first attempt at producing them with all the luxurious embellishments of art, and which became, in fact, their distinctive characteristic. At first the literary department was held inferior to the mechanical, but at last, Scott, Rogers, Campbell, Mrs. Hemans, Moore, &c., in England, and Bryant, Irving, Halleck, in America, became contributors to these works; nay, Bryant, Sands, and Verplanck produced in New York an annual entitled the Talisman, and which was continued for three years.

The success of this species of publication, stimulated new enterprises of the kind, and a rage for them
spread over Europe and America. The efforts of the
first artists and the first writers were at length drawn
into them, and for nearly twenty years every autumn
produced an abundant harvest of Diadems, Bijous,
Pearls, Gems, Amethysts, Opals, Amaranths, Bou-
quets, Hyacinths, Amulets, Talismans, Forget-me-
nots, Remember-me's, &c.* Under these seductive
titles, they became messengers of love, tokens of
friendship, signs and symbols of affection, and luxury and refinement; and thus they stole alike into the
palace and the cottage, the library, the parlor, and the
boudoir. The public taste grew by feeding on these

* Besides these Annuals, there were, in England and the United
States, the following:

Gift, Keepsake, Souvenir, Literary Souvenir, Boudoir, Floral Offering,
Friendship's Offering, Iris, Laurel, Wreath, Jewel, Cabinet, Drawing-
room Annual, Pictorial Annual, Continental Annual, Picturesque Annual, Fancy Annual, Court Album, Anniversary, Pearls of the East,
Pearls of the West, The Favorite, The Rhododendron, The Waif, The
Gleaner, The Rose, and many others. Among the works which may be
considered as successors of the Annuals, being all splendidly illustrated, there were Tableaux of Prose and Poetry, Baronial Halls of England, Authors of England, Artist's Sketch Book, Book of Art, Book
of the Passions, Calendar of Nature, Continental Sketches, Etched
Thoughts, Finden's Tableaux, Wanderings of Pen and Pencil, Tales of
the Brave and the Fair, Poetry of the Year, British Ballads, Book of
Art, Book of the Passions, Gems of British Poetry, Lays of Ancient
Rome, and a multitude of others.

The effect of the circulation of such works as these, in creating and
extending a taste for the arts, and in their most exquisite forms, can only
be appreciated by those who have examined and reflected upon the subject. Even in the United States alone, four thousand volumes of one
of these works, at the price of twelve dollars each, have been sold in a
single season! Not five hundred would have been sold in the same
space of time, twenty years ago.

luscious gifts, and soon craved even more gorgeous works of the kind, whence came Heath's Book of Beauty, Lady Blessington's Flowers of Loveliness, Bulwer's Pilgrims of the Rhine, Butler's Leaflets of Memory, Christmas among the Poets, and many others of similar design and execution. Many of the engravings of these works cost five hundred dollars each, and many a piece of poetry, fifty dollars a page. In several of these works the generous public spent fifty thousand dollars a year!

At last the race of Annuals drew near the end of its career, yet not without having produced a certain revolution in the public taste. Their existence had sprung, at least in part, from steel-engraving, which had been discovered and introduced by our countryman, Jacob Perkins. This enabled the artist to produce works of more exquisite delicacy than had ever before been achieved; steel also gave the large number of impressions which the extensive sales of the Annuals demanded, and which could not have been obtained from copper. These charming works scattered the very gems of art far and wide, making the reading mass familiar with the finest specimens of engraving, and not only cultivating an appetite for this species of luxury, but in fact exalting the general standard of taste all over the civilized world.

And thus, though the Annuals, by name, have perished, they left a strong necessity in the public mind for books enriched by all the embellishments of art.

Hence we have such works as the Women of the
Bible, Women of the New Testament, the Republican
Court, by Dr. Griswold, together with rich illustrated
editions of Byron, Rogers, Thomson, Cowper, Campbell, and others, including our own poets—Bryant,
Halleck, Sigourney, Longfellow, Reed, &c. Wood-
engraving has, meanwhile, risen into a fine art, and
lent its potent aid in making books one of the chief
luxuries of society, from the nursery to the parlor.

In comparison with these splendid works, the Token was a very modest affair. The first year I offered
prizes for the best pieces in prose and poetry. The
highest for prose was awarded to the author of
"Some Passages in the Life of an Old Maid." A
mysterious man, in a mysterious way, presented himself for the money, and, giving due evidence of his
authority to receive it, it was paid to him, but who
the author really was, never transpired, though I had,
and still have, my confident guess upon the subject.* Even the subsequent volumes, though they
obtained favor in their day, did not approach the splendor of the modern works of a similar kind. Nevertheless, some of the embellishments, by John Cheney,†

---

* The prizes were one hundred dollars for the best piece in prose, and
the same for the best in verse. The judges—Charles Sprague, F. W.
P. Greenwood, and J. Pierpont—hesitated between two pieces for the
latter: The Soldier's Widow, by Willis, and Connecticut River, by Mrs.
Sigourney. They finally recommended that the prize be divided between them, which was accepted by the authors.

† John Cheney, who may be regarded as the first of American engravers in sweetness of expression and delicacy of execution, was a native of

Ellis, Smilie, Andrews, Hatch, Kelly, Danforth, Durand, and Jewett, engraved from the designs of Allston, Leslie, Newton, Cole, Inman, Fisher, Doughty, Chapman, Weir, Brown, Alexander, and Healey, were very clever, even compared with the finest works of art at the present day.

The literary contributions were, I believe, equal, on the whole, to any of the Annuals, American or European. Here were inserted some of the earliest productions of Willis, Hawthorne, Miss Francis, now Mrs. Child, Miss Sedgewick, Mrs. Hale, Pierpont, Greenwood, and Longfellow. Several of these first made acquaintance with the public through the pages of this work. It is a curious fact that the latter, Longfellow, wrote prose, and at that period had shown neither a strong bias nor a particular talent for poetry.

The Token was continued annually till 1842, when it finally ceased. The day of Annuals had, indeed, passed before this was given up, and the last

---

Manchester, eight miles east of Hartford, Conn. When I first met him, he was working at Hartford with Mr. Willard, a map engraver. I encouraged him to come to Boston, and for several years, during which time he visited London and Paris, he was wholly employed for the Token. His brother Seth, not less celebrated for his admirable portraits in crayon, was also induced to come to Boston by me, making my house at Jamaica Plain, his stopping place at the beginning. Both these admirable artists are wholly self-taught. They have six brothers, the youngest of whom made some valuable improvement in machinery which led to the establishment of a silk manufactory at their native place, which some of the rest have joined, and it has made all rich who are concerned in it.

two or three years, it had only lingered out a poor and fading existence. As a matter of business, it scarcely paid its expenses, and was a serious drawback upon my time and resources for fifteen years— a punishment no doubt fairly due to an obstinate pride which made me reluctant to allow a work to die in my hands, with which my name and feelings had become somewhat identified.

LETTER XLVI.

The Contributors to the Token—N. P. Willis—N. Hawthorne—Miss Francis —Mr. Greenwood—Mr. Pierpont—Charles Sprague—Mrs. Sigourney— Miss Sedgwick—Mrs. Osgood, and others— Quarrels between Authors and Publishers—Anecdotes—The Publishers' Festival.

MY DEAR C******

As to the contributors for the Token, you may expect me to say a few words more. The most prominent writer for it was N. P. Willis; his articles were the most read, the most admired, the most abused, and the most advantageous to the work. I published his first book, and his two first editorial engagements were with me; hence the early portion of his literary career fell under my special notice.

He had begun to write verses very early, and while in college, before he was eighteen, he had acquired an extended reputation, under the signature of Roy. In

1827, when he was just twenty years old, I published his volume entitled "Sketches." It brought out quite a shower of criticism, in which praise and blame were about equally dispensed: at the same time the work sold with a readiness quite unusual for a book of poetry at that period. It is not calculated to establish the infallibility of critics, to look over these notices at the present day: many of the pieces which were doubly damned have now taken their place among the acknowledged gems of our literature, and others, which excited praise at the time, have faded from the public remembrance.

One thing is certain—everybody thought Willis worth criticising.* He has been, I suspect, more writ-

---

* In 1831, there appeared in Boston a little book, of some fifty or sixty pages, entitled, "Truth: A New Year's Gift for Scribblers." It was written by Joseph Snelling, who had been, I believe, an under officer in the United States army, and stationed in the Northwest, perhaps at Prairie du Chien. He came to Boston, and acquired some notoriety as a nervous and daring writer—his chief desire seeming to be, notoriety. The work was little more than a string of abuse, without regard to justice; yet it was executed with point and vigor, and as it attacked everybody who had written verses, it caused a good deal of wincing. The following is the exordium:

"Moths, millers, gnats, and butterflies, I sing;
Far-darting Phœbus, lend my strain a sting;
Much-courted virgins, long-enduring Nine,
Screw tight the catgut of this lyre of mine:
If D-na, D-wes, and P-rp-nt ask your aid,
If W-ll-s takes to rhyming as a trade,
If L-nt and F-nn to Pindus' top aspire,
I too may blameless beg one spark of fire;
Not such as warmed the brains of Pope and Swift—
With less assistance I can make a shift:
To Gifford's bow and shafts I lay no claim—
He shot at hawks, but I at insects aim:
Yet grant, since I must war on little things,
Just flame enough to singe their puny wings;

ten about than any other literary man in our history. Some of the attacks upon him proceeded, no doubt, from a conviction that he was a man of extraordinary gifts, and yet of extraordinary affectations, and the lash was applied in kindness, as that of a schoolmaster to a loved pupil's back; some of them were dictated by envy, for we have had no other example of literary success so early, so general, and so flattering. That Mr. Willis made mistakes in literature and life—at the outset—may be admitted by his best

---

> A feather besom, too, to bring them down,
> And pins to stick them in my beaver's crown."
>
> * * * *

Here are specimens from the body of the work:

> "The wax still sticking to his fingers' ends,
> The upstart Wh-tt-r, for example, lends
> The world important aid to understand
> What's said, and sung, and printed in the land."
>
> * * * *

> "'Tis plain the county Cumberland, in Maine,
> Contains no hospital for folks insane:
> Though never there, the fact I nothing doubt,
> Since N-al and M-ll-n run at large about.
> When the moon waxes, plaintive M-ll-n howls;
> But Johnny, like a bull-dog, snaps and growls;
> Or strikes his brother poetasters mute
> With harsh vibrations on his three-stringed lute."
>
> * * * *

> "Dear Halleck, Nature's favorite and mine,
> Curst be the hand that plucks a hair of thine:
> Accept the tribute of a muse inclined
> To bow to nothing, save the power of mind.
> Bard of Bozzaris, shall thy native shore
> List to thy harp and mellow voice no more?
> Shall we, with skill like thine so nigh at hand,
> Import our music from a foreign land?
> While Mirror M-rr-s chants in whimpering note,
> And croaking D-na strains his screech-owl throat;
> While crazy N-al to meter shakes his chains,
> And fools are found to listen to his strains;
> While childish Natty P. the public diddles,
> And L-nt and R-ckw-ll scrape his second fiddles;

friends; for it must be remembered that before he was five-and-twenty, he was more read than any other American poet of his time; and besides, being possessed of an easy and captivating address, he became the pet of society, and especially of the fairer portion of it. Since that period, his life, on the whole, has been one of serious, useful, and successful labor. His reputation as a poet has hardly advanced, and probably the public generally regard some of his early verses as his best. As an essayist, however, he

> While Brooks, and Sands, and Smith, and either Clark,
> In chase of Phœbus, howl, and yelp, and bark—
> Wilt thou be silent? Wake, O Halleck, wake!
> Thine and thy country's honor are at stake!
> Wake, and redeem the pledge—thy vantage keep;
> 'Tis pity, one like thee so long should sleep!"
>
> * * * * *
>
> "One bard there is I almost fear to name,
> Much doubting whether to applaud or blame.
> In P-rc-v-l's productions, wheat and chaff
> Are mixed, like sailor's tipple, half and half;
> But, duly bolted through the critic's mill,
> I find the better part is wholesome still."

The following is a part of the amiable notice bestowed upon Willis:

> "Muse, shall we not a few brief lines afford
> To give poor Natty P. his meet reward?
> What has he done to be despised by all
> Within whose hands his harmless scribblings fall?
> Why, as in bandbox-trim he walks the streets,
> Turns up the nose of every man he meets,
> As if it scented carrion? Why, of late,
> Do all the critics claw his shallow pate?
> True, he's a fool;—if that's a hanging thing,
> Let Pr-nt-ce, Wh-tt-r, M-ll-n also swing."

Willis replied contemptuously, but effectively, in some half-dozen verses inserted in the Statesman, and addressed to *Smelling* Joseph. The lines stuck to poor Snelling for the remainder of his life, and I suspect, in fact, contributed to his downfall. As he had attacked everybody, everybody joined in the chuckle. He soon fell into habits of dissipation, which led from one degradation to another, till his miserable career was ended.

stands in the first rank, distinguished for a keen sagacity in analyzing society, a fine perception of the beauties of nature, an extraordinary talent for endowing trifles with interest and meaning. As a traveler, he is among the most entertaining, sagacious, and instructive. It is within my knowledge, that Mr. Webster was an admiring reader of his itinerary sketches.

His style is certainly peculiar—and is deemed affected, tending to an excess of refinement, and displaying an undue hankering for grace and melody—sometimes sacrificing sense to sound. This might once have been a just criticism, but the candid reader of his works now before the public, will deem it hypercritical. His style is suited to his thought; it is flexible, graceful, musical, and is adapted to the playful wit, the spicy sentiment, the dramatic tableaux, the artistic paintings of sea, earth, and sky, of which they are the vehicle. In the seeming exhaustlessness of his resources, in his prolonged freshness, in his constantly increasing strength, Mr. Willis has refuted all the early prophets who regarded him only as a precocity, destined to shine a few brief years, and fade away.

As to his personal character, I need only say that from the beginning, he has had a larger circle of steadfast friends than almost any man within my knowledge. There has been something in his works which has made the fair sex, generally, alike his lite-

rary and personal admirers. For so many favors, he
has given the world an ample return; for, with all
his imputed literary faults—some real and some imaginary—I regard him as having contributed more
to the amusement of society than almost any other
of our living authors.*

. It is not easy to conceive of a stronger contrast
than is presented by comparing Nathaniel Hawthorne
with N. P. Willis. The former was for a time one
of the principal writers for the Token, and his admirable sketches were published side by side with those
of the latter. Yet it is curious to remark that every
thing Willis wrote attracted immediate attention, and
excited ready praise, while the productions of Hawthorne were almost entirely unnoticed.

The personal appearance and demeanor of these
two gifted young men, at the early period of which I
speak, was also in striking contrast. Willis was
slender, his hair sunny and silken, his cheek ruddy,
his aspect cheerful and confident. He met society
with a ready and welcome hand, and was received
readily and with welcome. Hawthorne, on the contrary, was of a rather sturdy form, his hair dark and

---

* Mr. N. P. Willis was the son of Nathaniel Willis, of Boston, originally a printer, but for a long time an editor, and much respected for
his industry, his good sense, his devotion to whatever he deemed his
duty, and his useful services rendered to morals, religion, Christianity,
and philanthropy. His wife was a woman of uncommon mental endowments; her conversation was elegant, full of taste, reading, and refinement. The beautiful tributes which N. P. Willis has rendered to her
memory, are no more than was due from a gifted son to a gifted mother.

bushy, his eye steel-gray, his brow thick, his mouth sarcastic, his complexion stony, his whole aspect cold, moody, distrustful. He stood aloof, and surveyed the world from shy and sheltered positions.

There was a corresponding difference in the writings of these two persons. Willis was all sunshine and summer, the other chill, dark, and wintry; the one was full of love and hope, the other of doubt and distrust; the one sought the open daylight—sunshine, flowers, music, and found them everywhere—the other plunged into the dim caverns of the mind, and studied the grisly specters of jealousy, remorse, despair. It is, perhaps, neither a subject of surprise nor regret, that the larger portion of the world is so happily constituted as to have been more ready to flirt with the gay muse of the one, than to descend into the spiritual charnel-house, and assist at the psychological dissections of the other.

I had seen some anonymous publication which seemed to me to indicate extraordinary powers. I inquired of the publishers as to the writer, and through them a correspondence ensued between me and "N. Hawthorne." This name I considered a disguise, and it was not till after many letters had passed, that I met the author, and found it to be a true title, representing a very substantial personage. At this period he was unsettled as to his views; he had tried his hand in literature, and considered himself to have met with a fatal rebuff from the reading world. His mind vacillated between various projects, verging, I think, toward a mercantile profession. I combated his despondence, and assured him of triumph, if he would persevere in a literary career.

He wrote numerous articles, which appeared in the Token; occasionally an astute critic seemed to see through them, and to discover the soul that was in them; but in general they passed without notice. Such articles as Sights from a Steeple, Sketches beneath an Umbrella, the Wives of the Dead, the Prophetic Pictures, now universally acknowledged to be productions of extraordinary depth, meaning, and power, extorted hardly a word of either praise or blame, while columns were given to pieces since totally forgotten. I felt annoyed, almost angry indeed, at this. I wrote several articles in the papers, directing attention to these productions, and finding no echo of my views, I recollect to have asked John Pickering* to read some of them, and give me his opinion of them. He did as I requested; his answer was that they displayed a wonderful beauty of style, with a kind of double vision, a sort of second sight, which revealed, beyond the outward forms of life and being, a sort of spirit world, somewhat as a

---

* John Pickering, son of Timothy Pickering, Washington's Secretary of State, was a distinguished jurist and philologist, and a refined and amiable gentleman. A good notice of him is given in Messrs. Duyckinck's excellent Cyclopedia of American Literature, vol. i. page 625. To this, by the way, I have often been indebted for assistance in the preparation of this work.

lake reflects the earth around it and the sky above it : yet he deemed them too mystical to be popular. He was right, no doubt, at that period, but, ere long, a portion of mankind, a large portion of the reading world, obtained a new sense—how or where or whence, is not easily determined—which led them to study the mystical, to dive beneath and beyond the senses, and to discern, gather, and cherish gems and pearls of price in the hidden depths of the soul. Hawthorne was, in fact, a kind of Wordsworth in prose—less kindly, less genial toward mankind, but deeper and more philosophical. His fate was similar : at first he was neglected, at last he had worshipers.

In 1837, I recommended Mr. Hawthorne to publish a volume, comprising his various pieces, which had appeared in the Token and elsewhere. He consented, but as I had ceased to be a publisher, it was difficult to find any one who would undertake to bring out the work. I applied to the agent of the Stationers' Company,* but he refused, until at last I

---

* The Stationers' Company, organized in the autumn of 1836, was a joint-stock company, in which some of the leading lawyers and literary men of Boston engaged, with a view of publishing original American works of a high character, and in such a way as to render due compensation and encouragement to authors. One of the works which then sought a publisher, without success, was Prescott's Ferdinand and Isabella—it being at that day supposed to be absurd for Americans to presume to write general histories. This was in fact one of the first works issued by this concern. In 1838 the country was suffering under a state of general commercial panic and paralysis, and this company was precipitated into the gulf of bankruptcy, with thousands of others. Though

relinquished my copyrights on such of the tales as I had published, to Mr. Hawthorne, and joined a friend of his in a bond to indemnify them against loss ; and thus the work was published by the Stationers' Company, under the title of Twice Told Tales, and for the author's benefit. It was deemed a failure for more than a year, when a breeze seemed to rise and fill its sails, and with it the author was carried on to fame and fortune.

Among the most successful of the writers for the Token was Miss Francis, now Mrs. Child. I have not seen her for many years, but I have many pleasant remembrances of her lively conversation, her saucy wit, her strong good sense, and her most agreeable person and presence. To Rev. F. W. P. Greenwood—the author of "Niagara" and the "Sea"—articles which are still admired by all tasteful readers—I was indebted not only for some of the best contributions, but for excellent counsel and advice in my literary affairs. He was a man of fine genius, gentle manners, and apostolic dignity of life and character.

To Mr. Pierpont, I was indebted for encouragement and sympathy in my whole career, and for some of the best poems which appeared in the work I am noticing. I remember once to have met him, and to have

---

I was a hesitating and reluctant subscriber to the stock, and in fact was the last to join the association, I still shared largely—I may say fatally —in its misfortunes. It entailed upon me the loss of the little property I had accumulated, and embarrassments which have haunted me to the present day.

asked him to give me a contribution for the Token. He stopped and said, reflectingly, " I had a dream not long ago, which I have thought to put into verse. I will try, and if I am successful you shall have it." A few days after he gave me the lines, now in all the gem books, beginning—

> " Was it the chime of a tiny bell,
>> That came so sweet to my dreaming ear—
> Like the silvery tones of a fairy's shell,
>> That he winds on the beach so mellow and clear,
> When the winds and the waves lie together asleep,
> And the moon and the fairy are watching the deep—
> She dispensing her silvery light,
> And he his notes, as silvery quite,
> While the boatman listens and ships his oar,
> To catch the music that comes from the shore ?
>> Hark! the notes on my ear that play,.
>> Are set to words; as they float, they say,
>>> ' Passing away, passing away !' "

Charles Sprague wrote for me but little, yet that was of diamond worth. Next to Willis, Mrs. Sigourney was my most successful and liberal contributor; to her I am indebted for a large part of the success of my editorial labors in the matter now referred to. To Miss Sedgwick, also, the Token owes a large share of its credit with the public. Grenville Mellen —a true poet, and a most kind, gentle spirit, doomed early to " pass away"—was a favorite in my pages, and to me a devoted friend. To B. B. Thacher—also among the good and the departed; to Mrs. Osgood, gifted and gone; to John Neale, A. H. Everett, Bishop Doane, Mr. Longfellow, Caleb Cushing; to the two Sargents—Epes and John, though masked as Charles Sherry or the modest letter E.; to Miss Gould, Miss Leslie, H. T. Tuckerman, O. W. Holmes, Orville Dewey, J. T. Fields, T. S. Fay, G. C. Verplanck—to all these and to many others, I owe the kind remembrance which belongs to good deeds, kindly and graciously bestowed.

It is not to be supposed that in a long career, both as bookseller and editor, I should have escaped altogether the annoyances and vexations which naturally attach to these vocations. The relation of author and publisher is generally regarded as that of the cat and the dog, both greedy of the bone, and inherently jealous of each other. The authors have hitherto written the accounts of the wrangles between these two parties, and the publishers have been traditionally gibeted as a set of mean, mercenary wretches, coining the heart's blood of genius for their own selfish profits. Great minds, even in modern times, have not been above this historical prejudice. The poet Campbell is said to have been an admirer of Napoleon because he shot a bookseller.

Nevertheless, speaking from my own experience, I suspect, if the truth were told, that, even in cases where the world has been taught to bestow all its sympathy in behalf of the author, it would appear that while there were claws on one side there were

teeth on the other. My belief is, that where there
have been quarrels, there have generally been mutual
provocations. I know of nothing more vexatious,
more wearisome, more calculated to beget impatience, than the egotisms, the exactions, the unrea-
sonablenesses of authors, in cases I have witnessed.*

---

* I could give some curious instances of this. A schoolmaster came
to me once with a marvelously clever grammar : it was sure to overturn
all others. He had figured out his views in a neat hand, like copper-
plate. He estimated that there were always a million of children at
school who would need his grammar ; providing for books worn out,
and a supply for new-comers, half a million would be wanted every
year. At one cent a copy for the author—which he insisted was exceedingly moderate—this would produce to him five thousand dollars a
year, but if I would publish the work he would condescend to take half
that sum annually, during the extent of the copyright—twenty-eight
years ! I declined, and he seriously believed me a heartless block-
head. He obtained a publisher at last, but the work never reached a
second edition. Every publisher is laden with similar experiences.

I once employed a young man to block out some little books to be
published under the nominal authorship of Solomon Bell ; these I remodeled, and one or two volumes were issued. Some over-astute critic announced them as veritable Peter Parleys, and they had a sudden sale.
The young man who had assisted me, and who was under the most solemn obligations to keep the matter secret, thought he had an opportunity to make his fortune ; so he publicly claimed the authorship, and
accused me of duplicity ! The result was, that the books fell dead from
that hour ; the series was stopped, and his unprinted manuscripts, for
which I had paid him, became utterly worthless. A portion I burnt,
and a portion still remain amidst the rubbish of other days.

In other instances, I was attacked in the papers, editorially and personally, by individuals who were living upon the employment I gave
them. I was in daily intercourse with persons of this character,
who, while flattering me to my face, I knew to be hawking at me in
print. These I regarded and treated as trifles at the time ; they are less
than trifles now. One thing may be remarked, that, in general, such
difficulties come from poor and unsuccessful writers. They have been
taught that publishers and booksellers are vampires, and naturally feed
upon the vitals of genius ; assuming—honestly, no doubt—that they are
of this latter class, they feel no great scruple in taking vengeance upon
those whom they regard as their natural enemies.

That there may be examples of meanness, stupidity, and selfishness, in publishers, is indisputable. But in general, I am satisfied that an author who will do justice to a publisher, will have justice in return.

In judging of publishers, one thing should be considered, and that is, that two-thirds of the original works issued by them, are unprofitable. An eminent London publisher once told me that he calculated that out of ten publications, four involved a positive, and often a heavy, loss; three barely paid the cost of paper, print, and advertising; and three paid a profit. Nothing is more common than for a publisher to pay money to an author, every farthing of which is lost. Self-preservation, therefore, compels the publisher to look carefully to his operations. One thing is certain—he is generally the very best judge as to the value of a book, in a marketable point of view : if he rejects it, it is solely because he thinks it will not pay, not because he despises genius.

Happily, at the present day, the relations between these two parties—authors and publishers—are on a better footing than in former times : the late Festival*

My editorial experience also furnished me with some amusing anecdotes. An editor of a periodical once sent me an article for the Token, entitled *La Longue-vue ;* the pith of the story consisted in a romantic youth's falling in love with a young lady, two miles off, through a telescope ! I ventured to reject it, and the Token for that year was duly damned in the columns of the offended author.

And yet, while noticing these trifles, I am bound to say distinctly, that, on the whole, I have had generous and encouraging treatment from the press, and most kindly intercourse with authors.

* The Complimentary Fruit Festival of the New York Book Publish-

in New York, given by the publishers to the authors, was a happy testimonial to the prevailing feeling that both are partners in the fellowship of literature, and that mutual good offices will best contribute to mutual prosperity. Indeed, a great change has taken place in the relative positions of the two classes. Nothing is now more marketable than good writing—at least in this country—whatever may be its form—poetry or prose, fact or fiction, reason or romance. Starving, neglected, abused genius, is a myth of bygone times. If an author is poorly paid, it is because he writes poorly. I do not think, indeed, that authors are adequately paid, for authorship does not stand on a level with other professions as to pecuniary recompense, but it is certain that a clever, industrious, and judicious writer may make his talent the means of living.*

---

ers' Association to Authors and Booksellers, took place at the Crystal Palace, September 27, 1855, and was one of the most gratifying and suggestive occasions I ever witnessed. The opening address of the president, Mr. W. Appleton, the introductory statistical sketch, by Mr. G. P. Putnam, the genial toasts, the excellent letters of Charles Sumner, Edward Everett, and R. C. Winthrop; the admirable speech of W. C. Bryant, the eloquent addresses of Messrs. Milburn, Allen, Chapin, Osgood, Beecher, together with the witty and instructive poem by J. T. Fields—all together marked it as an era of prodigious interest in our literary annals.

* I am here speaking particularly of the state of things in America at the present day. No man has more cause to know and feel the disappointments, the wear and tear of health, the headaches, the heartaches, which attend authorship as a profession and a means of support, than myself. No one has more cause to feel and remember the illusiveness of literary ambition, perhaps I may say of even humble literary success. In most cases, these are only obtained at the expense of shattered nerves and broken constitutions, leaving small means of enjoying what has

LETTER XLVII.

*The First of the Parley Books—Its Reception—Various Publications—
Threatening Attack of Illness—Voyage to Europe—Consultation of Physicians at Paris—Sir Benj. Brodie, of London—Abercrombie, of Edinburgh—Return to America—Residence in the Country—Prosecution of
my Literary Labors—Footing up the Account—Annoyances of Authorship—Letter to the New York Daily Times.*

MY DEAR C******

Though I was busily engaged in publishing various works, I found time to make my long meditated
experiment in the writing of books for children. The
first attempt was made in 1827, and bore the title of
the Tales of Peter Parley about America. No persons but my wife and one of my sisters were admitted to the secret—for in the first place, I hesitated
to believe that I was qualified to appear before the
public as an author, and in the next place, nursery
literature had not then acquired the respect in the
eyes of the world it now enjoys. It is since that period, that persons of acknowledged genius—Scott,

---

been thus dearly won. Still it is quite true that if a man has talent, and
is wise and moderate, and if he feels and practises Agur's prayer, he
may live by authorship; if he aspires to easy independence, let him
rather drudge in almost any other employment. As an amusement to
a man of fortune, who is also a man of genius, authorship is a glorious
pastime ; to men of other and more active and profitable professions, it
is often an inspiring episode; but to one who has no resources but his
brains, it is too often the coining of his heart's blood to feed his family.
One thing should never be forgotten by those who are tempted to follow
a literary career, that not one author in a hundred attains success in
life by this profession alone.

Dickens, Lamartine, Mary Howitt, in Europe, and Abbott, Todd, Gallaudet, Miss Sedgwick, Mrs. Child, and others, in America, have stooped to the composition of books for children and youth.

I published my little book, and let it make its way. It came before the world untrumpeted, and for some months seemed not to attract the slightest attention. Suddenly I began to see notices of it in the papers, all over the country, and in a year from the date of its publication, it had become a favorite. In 1828, I published the Tales of Peter Parley about Europe; in 1829, Parley's Winter Evening Tales; in 1830, Parley's Juvenile Tales, and Parley's Asia, Africa, Sun, Moon, and Stars. About this time the public guessed my secret—it being first discovered and divulged by a woman—Mrs. Sarah J. Hale, to whom, by the way, I am indebted for many kind offices in my literary career — yet I could have wished she had not done me this questionable favor. Though the authorship of the Parley books has been to me a source of some gratification, you will see, in the sequel, that it has also subjected me to endless vexations.

I shall not weary you with a detail of my proceedings at this busy and absorbed period of my life. I had now obtained a humble position in literature, and was successful in such unambitious works as I attempted. I gave myself up almost wholly for about four years—that is, from 1828 to 1832—to author-

ship, generally writing fourteen hours a day. A
part of the time I was entirely unable to read, and
could write but little, on account of the weakness
of my eyes. In my larger publications, I employed
persons to block out work for me ; this was read to
me, and then I put it into style, generally writing by
dictation, my wife being my amanuensis. Thus embarrassed, I still, by dint of incessant toil, produced
five or six volumes a year, mostly small, but some of
larger compass.

In the midst of these labors—that is, in the spring
of 1832—I was suddenly attacked with symptoms,
which seemed to indicate a disease of the heart, rapidly advancing to a fatal termination. In the course
of a fortnight I was so reduced as not to be able to
mount a pair of stairs without help, and a short walk
produced palpitations of the heart, which in several
instances almost deprived me of consciousness. There
seemed no hope but in turning my back upon my
business, and seeking a total change of scene and climate. In May I embarked for England, and after a
few weeks reached Paris. I here applied to Baron
Larroque, who, assisted by L'Herminier—both eminent
specialists in diseases of the heart—subjected me to
various experiments, but without the slightest advantage. At this period I was obliged to be carried up
stairs, and never ventured to walk or ride alone,
being constantly subject to nervous spasms, which
often brought me to the verge of suffocation.

Despairing of relief here, I returned to London, and was carefully examined by Sir B. C. Brodie.* He declared that I had no organic disease, that my difficulty was nervous irritability, and that whereas the French physicians had interdicted wine and required me to live on a light vegetable diet, I must feed well upon good roast beef, and take two generous glasses of port with my dinner! Thus encouraged, I passed on to Edinburgh, where I consulted Abercrombie,† then at the height of his fame. He confirmed the views of Dr. Brodie, in the main, and regarding the irregularities of my vital organs as merely functional, still told me that, without shortening my life, they would probably never be wholly removed. He told me of an instance in which a patient of his, who, having been called upon to testify before the committee of the House of Commons, in the trial of Warren Hast-

---

* Sir Benjamin C. Brodie was at this time one of the most eminent surgeons in London. His reputation has since even been enhanced; his various publications—Clinical Lectures in Surgery, Pathological and Surgical Observations on Diseases of the Joints, Lectures on Diseases of the Urinary Organs, and Surgical Works—all of which have been published in this country—have given him a world-wide fame. It was not a little remarkable to me, to find a man of his eminence thus positively and authoritatively reversing the recommendations of French practitioners, of hardly inferior fame. Of one thing I am convinced, that for us Anglo-Saxons an Anglo-Saxon practitioner is much better than a Gallic one. I shall have a few words more to say on this subject.

† Dr. John Abercrombie held the highest rank in his profession at this period. He was still more distinguished as a writer, his Inquiries concerning the Intellectual Powers being published in 1830, and his Philosophy of the Moral Feelings in 1833. He was a man of refined personal appearance, and most gentle manners. He died in 1844, aged 63.

ings — from mere embarrassment—had been seized with palpitation of the heart, which, however, continued till his death, many years after. Even this somber view of my case was then a relief. Four and twenty years have passed since that period, and thus far my experience has verified Dr. Abercrombie's prediction. These nervous attacks pursue me to this day, yet I have become familiar with them, and regarding them only as troublesome visitors, I receive them patiently and bow them out as gently as I can.*

After an absence of six months I returned to Boston, and by the advice of my physician took up my residence in the country. I built a house at Jamaica Plain, four miles from the city, and here I continued for more than twenty years. My health was partially restored, and I resumed my literary labors. It would

---

* I make this statement chiefly because I think it may be useful to persons, who, like myself, have abused their constitutions by sedentary habits and excessive mental labor, and who consequently are afflicted with nervous attacks, putting on the semblance of organic diseases of the heart. Not long since, I met with an old friend, a physician, who had abandoned his profession for authorship : with a dejected countenance he told me he was sinking under a disease of the heart ! I inquired his symptoms, which corresponded with my own. I related to him my experience. A few days after I met him, and saw in his cheerful face that I had cured him. I give this prescription gratis to all my literary friends : let them beware of overtasking the brain; but if they do make this mistake, let them not lay the consequent irregularities of the vital organs to the heart. In nine cases out of ten they belong to the head—to the nervous system—which centers in the brain. Get that right by bodily exercise, by cheerful intercourse with friends, by a conscience void of offense, by generous living, by early rising and early going to bed, and by considering that the body will always take vengeance upon the mind, if the latter is permitted to abuse the former.

be tedious and unprofitable to you, were I even to enumerate my various works—produced from the beginning, as I have described it—to the present time. I may sum up the whole in a single sentence: I am the author and editor of about one hundred and seventy volumes, and of these seven millions have been sold! If you have the curiosity to trace my literary history more in detail, you can consult the catalogue which I herewith inclose.*

I have said that however the authorship of Parley's Tales has made me many friends, it has also subjected me to many annoyances. Some of these are noticed in a letter I addressed to the editor of the New York Times in December, 1855, a portion of which I here copy, with slight modifications, as the easiest method of making you comprehend my meaning.

Sir:—Some days since I learned, through a friend, that the editor of the Boston Courier, in noticing the death of the late Samuel Kettell,† had said or intimated that he was the author of Peter Parley's Tales. I therefore wrote to the said editor on the subject, and he has this day furnished me with the paper alluded to—December 10th—in which I find the following statement:

---

* For a list of my various works, see p. 537 of this volume.

† Mr. Samuel Kettell was a native of Newburyport, Mass., and born A. D. 1800. He was for the most part self-educated, and without being a critical scholar, was a man of large acquirements, the master, I believe, of more than a dozen languages. In 1832 he visited Europe, and wrote some clever essays in the British magazines. In 1848 he assumed the editorship of the Boston Courier, and so continued till his death in 1855, though his active labors were suspended for some months before by his protracted illness.

"Mr. S. G. Goodrich also found work for him—Mr. Kettell—and many of those historical compendiums which came out under the name of Peter Parley, were in fact the work of Mr. Kettell. He is the veritable Peter Parley," &c.

Now, Mr. Editor, it happens that for nearly thirty years, I have appeared before the public as the author of Peter Parley's Tales. It would seem, therefore, if this statement were true, that I have been for this length of time arrayed in borrowed plumes, thus imposing upon the public, and now wronging the dead. It was no doubt the amiable purpose of the writer of the article in question to place me in this position. I am, however, pretty well used to this sort of thing, and I should not take the trouble to notice this new instance of impertinence, were it not that I have a batch on hand, and may as well put them all in and make one baking of them.

To begin. There is a man by the name of Martin, in London, and who takes the name of Peter Parley Martin. He writes books boldly under the name of Peter Parley, and they are palmed off as genuine works by the London publishers. These, and other forgeries of a similar kind by other writers, have been going on for fifteen years or more, until there are thirty or forty volumes of them in circulation in England.

Among these London counterfeiters, there was formerly a bookseller by the name of Lacey. He was what is called a Remainder Man—that is, he bought the unsold and unsalable ends of editions, put them in gaudy bindings, and thus disposed of them. When he got possession of a defunct juvenile work, he galvanized it into life by putting Parley's name to it—as "Grandfather's Tales, by Peter Parley," &c. This proved a thrifty trade, and the man, as I have been told, has lately retired upon a fortune.

It is indeed notorious, that handsome sums have been realized in London by authors and publishers there, in republishing the genuine Parley books, and also by publishing counterfeit ones. This matter has gone to such lengths, and has become so mis-

chievous to me as well as to the public, that I have brought an
action against Darton & Co.,* one of the principal London houses
concerned in this fraud, and I hope to have it decided that an
author who gives value to a name—even though it be fictitious
—may be protected in its use and profit, as well as the Amos-
keag Manufacturing Company for their trade-mark, "A No. 1,"
put upon their cottons, and which the courts have decided to be
their property.

In general, my rights in regard to the use of the name of
Parley, have been respected in the United States; but it appears
that about two years ago, when I was in Europe, a New York
bookseller—under the inspiration of a man who writes *Reverend*
before his name—undertook to follow in the footsteps of these
English counterfeiters; so he put forth two volumes, naming
the one Parley's Pictorial, and the other Parley's Household
Library, &c. I understand that these are made up of old plates
from Parley's Magazine, with slight alterations so as to disguise
the real nature and origin of the works. In order more completely to deceive the public, he attached the above titles, which
imply that these works are by me, and are issued, in their present
form, by my sanction.

Thus the innocent public is duped. In point of fact, there is
not, I think, a page of my writing in these volumes, excepting
passages taken from my works, in violation of my copyrights.
The credit of originating these productions belongs, I believe, to
the reverend gentleman above alluded to, and not to the publisher—though the latter, knowing the character of the works,
aids and abets their circulation.

A still more recent instance of this borrowed use of Peter
Parley's name has been brought to my notice. A few days
since a man named . . . . . ? who, it is said, has been a government employé abroad, and has lately got leave to return, was
introduced to one of the public schools in this city as the veritable author of Peter Parley's Tales. To certify his identity, it

* See pages 296–306.

was further added by the teacher that he was the father of "Dick Tinto!" This man, who was not your humble servant, nor, I am happy to say, a relative, nor an acquaintance of his, still received these honors as his due—and perhaps I shall ere long be obliged to defend myself against a claim that he is I, and that I am not myself!

To pass over these and other similar instances, I come now to the latest, if not the last—the declaration of the editor of the Boston Courier, that Mr. Kettell was the real author of Parley's Tales. If Mr. Kettell were living, he would even more readily contradict this assertion than myself, for he would have felt alike the ridicule and the wrong that it would attach to his name. Were it my purpose to write a biographical notice of this gentleman, I should have nothing unpleasant to say of him. He was a man of large acquirements, a good deal of humor, and some wit, with great simplicity, truth, and honor of character. He was not, however, thrifty in the ways of the world. Among all his writings there is not, I believe, a book of which he was the designer, or, strictly speaking, the author. But he was still a ready writer when he had his task set before him. So much is due as a passing notice to the memory of a man with whom I had relations for twenty years, always amicable, and I believe mutually satisfactory, if not mutually beneficial.

But as to the statements of the editor of the Boston Courier above alluded to, as well as some others in his obituary of Mr. Kettell, there is great inaccuracy. Let me lay the axe at the root of the main statement at once, by declaring, that of the thirty or forty volumes of Parley's Tales, Mr. Kettell never wrote a line or sentence of any of them, nor, so far as I now recollect, did any other person except myself. The Parley series was begun and in the full tide of success before I ever saw Mr. Kettell.

It is quite true, that in my larger geographical and historical works—some of them extending to over one thousand royal octavo pages—I had assistants, as is usual, nay, indispensable, in such cases, Mr. Kettell among others. Some of these were young men, who have since risen to fame in both hemispheres. If all who assisted me were now to come forward and claim to be original Peter Parleys, there would be a very pretty family of us!

The writer of the Courier article in question intimates that Mr. Kettell was ill paid, and by a Latin quotation suggests that I made use of him to my own advantage, while he, the real author of books which I published, was robbed of his due! This is a serious charge, and it may be well to give it a pointed answer.

As to the statement that Mr. Kettell was ill paid—let me ask the reason, if such were the fact? In general, things will bring their value—literature as well as any other commodity. Why was it, then, that he accepted this insufficient pay? If I did not compensate him adequately, why did he serve me? The world is wide, the market free; Mr. Kettell was familiarly acquainted with every publisher in Boston: if he wrote for me, the inference is that I paid him better than anybody else would have done. Nay, if the editor of the Boston Courier does not know, there are others who do, that I was for years his only reliance and resource. He went to Europe without a dollar in his pocket except what I gave him for his writings. While at Paris, being in a state of absolute destitution, he wrote home to his friend, S. P. Holbrook, for help. This was furnished by the contributions of his friends, myself among the number.

The editor, in enumerating Mr. Kettell's literary labors, gives him high credit as the editor of the three volumes of Specimens of American Poetry, which I published. This is no doubt one of the instances, according to this writer, in which I sponged the brains of another to his wrong and my advantage. Let us see the facts:

I projected the aforesaid work, and employed Mr. F. S. Hill as editor. He began it, collected materials, and wrote the first part of it. At his instance, I had purchased nearly one hundred scarce books for the enterprise. The work, thus begun, the plan indicated, the materials to a great extent at command, with numerous articles actually written, passed into Mr. Kettell's hands. I think, with the editor of the Courier, that considering the extent of the undertaking, and that it was then a new enterprise, compelling the editor to grope in the mazes of a new and unexplored wilderness, that Mr. Kettell displayed a tolerable degree of patience and research, and a fair share of critical sagacity. But nevertheless, the work was a most disastrous failure, involving me not only in a pecuniary loss of fifteen hundred dollars, but the mortification of having the work pass into a kind of proverb of misfortune or misjudgment. More than once I have heard it spoken of as " Goodrich's *Kettle* of Poetry !" This arose, no doubt, partly from the idea then encouraged by the critics, that it was the height of folly for us, Americans, to pretend to have any literature. To include the writings of Timothy Dwight, Joel Barlow, and Phillis Wheatley in a book called Poetry, was then deemed a great offense at the bar of criticism. It is true that these notions have passed away, and Dr. Griswold and Messrs. Duyckinck have found in the mine wrought so abortively by Mr. Kettell, both gold and glory. There were, however, other reasons for his failure, and among them an unfortunate slip as to the authorship of " Hail Columbia," which stood thus:

" J. HOPKINSON :

" We have no knowledge of this author. The popular national ode which follows, appeared first, we believe, in Philadelphia."

Such ignorance and such carelessness were deemed offensive by the friends of Judge Hopkinson, son of the well-known author of the " Battle of the Kegs," and other popular effusions, and himself a somewhat noted poet. Mr. Walsh made this, and other blunders, the occasion of a stinging castigation in his National Gazette. The result was injurious to Mr. Kettell in many ways: it injured his rising literary reputation, and so shattered his nerves that for some years he lost courage as well as encouragement, except what I continued to give him, despite this failure. It was subsequent to this that I supplied him with the means of going to Europe, and thus furnished him with the opportunity of taking a new start in the world. And yet I sponged this man's brains, and stole his fair fame—according to this Boston writer!

I suppose, Mr. Editor, that this is enough for the present; and yet I am disposed to crave a little more of your patience and your space, to state more precisely my relations with Mr. Kettell, and thus remove him from the disadvantageous light in which he is placed by the ill-judged pretenses of his too earnest friend.

During a space of twelve or fifteen years, and that the most active and engrossed portion of my life, I suffered greatly from a disease in my eyes, which threatened blindness : sometimes for weeks together I was confined to a dark room. At that period I wrote almost wholly by dictation, my wife being my amanuensis. I wrote several of the Parley books, she sitting on one side of a green curtain in the light, and I on the other side, confined to the darkness. Several volumes of the Token were mostly edited in this way.

It is quite obvious that in such a condition, and being at the time busily engaged in writing, as well as publishing books, I must have needed assistance. At this time, Mr. Kettell was useful to me, especially as he was familiar with libraries, and had a remarkable tact in finding facts. And yet it is equally true that Mr. Kettell never wrote a page for me at his own suggestion, nor by his own planning. He wrote on subjects prescribed by me, and in the manner prescribed by me—even to the length of paragraphs, verses, and chapters. Moreover, what he had thus blocked out, was laboriously remodeled to suit my own taste, to clothe it in my own style, and to bring it into conformity with my own plan. Often this process was infinitely more laborious to me than would have been the outright and entire compilation, if I could have used my eyes. In this way, however, and under these circumstances, Mr. Kettell aided me; he was also, sometimes, my amanuensis; but he was not, nor did he ever claim to be, in any proper sense of the word, the author of a single page of a book which was published under my own name, or that of Peter Parley. In the large geographical work already alluded to, in which I had the assistance of Mr. Kettell, as well as of two other persons of great ability and reputation, this assistance was duly acknowledged in the preface.*

Now, while I thus correct the misrepresentations of this Boston editor, I desire to leave no unpleasant impressions upon the name and memory of Mr. Kettell. He is, indeed, beyond the reach of praise or blame; but still truth has its requisitions, and it would be a violation of these, were I to cast upon him any reproach. He certainly was deficient in the art of devising serious and extended works; he had not the steady, penetrating judgment necessary to such performances. Still, he possessed certain faculties in high perfection—a marvelous capacity for the acquisition of languages, a taste for antiquarian lore, a large stock of historical anecdote, a genial humor, a playful though grotesque wit, and, withal, a kind, gentle, truthful heart. He was so much a man of genius, that his fame could not be benefited by the reputation of the humble authorship of Parley's Tales. Certainly his honest nature would have revolted at the pretense now set up that he was in any manner or degree, entitled to it.†

---

* See preface to Universal Geography, published in 1832.

† This letter led to a lengthened controversy, the result of which is stated in the Appendix to this volume, page 543.

LETTER XLVIII.

Republication of Parley's Tales in London—Mr. Tegg's operations—Imitated by other publishers—Peter Parley Martin—Letter to Mr. Darton—An edition of the false Parleys in America—The consequences.

MY DEAR C******

When I was in London, in 1832, I learned that Mr. Tegg, then a prominent publisher there, had commenced the republication of Parley's Tales. I called upon him, and found that he had one of them actually in press. The result of our interview was a contract,* in which I engaged to prepare several

---

* As my claim to the authorship of the Parley Tales has been disputed in London, by interested publishers, I may as well copy the contract made with Mr. Tegg, which is now before me. It is, I believe, universally admitted that the works published by him, were the first that introduced the name of Peter Parley to the public there, and as the contract explicitly refers them to me, it seems there should be no further doubt on the subject.

"MEMORANDUM OF AGREEMENT, between Thomas Tegg, publisher, of London, and S. G. Goodrich, of Boston, United States of America:

"The said S. G. Goodrich having written and compiled several works, as Peter Parley's Tales of Animals, Peter Parley's Tales of America, of Europe, of Asia, of Africa, of the Sea, of the Islands in the Pacific Ocean, of the Sun, Moon, and Stars, &c., &c.

"Now said Goodrich is to revise said works, and carefully prepare them for publication, and said Tegg is to get copyrights for and publish the same, with cuts, maps, &c., as may be required, and said Tegg is to supply the market, and push the sales, and take all due measures to promote the success of said works.

"And in consideration of the premises, said Tegg agrees to pay said Goodrich, ten pounds sterling on every thousand copies printed of Parley's Tales of Animals, after the first edition (which consists of four thousand copies, and is nearly printed); and for each of the other works he agrees to pay said Goodrich five pounds on the delivery of the revised copy for the same, and five pounds for every thousand copies printed

of these works, which he agreed to publish, giving me a small consideration therefor. Four of these works I prepared on the spot, and after my return to America, prepared and forwarded ten others. Some time after, I learned that the books, or at least a portion of them, had been published in London, and were very successful. I wrote to Mr. Tegg several letters on the subject, but could get no reply.

Ten years passed away, and being in pressing need of all that I might fairly claim as my due, I went to London, and asked Mr. Tegg to render me an account of his proceedings, under the contract. I had previously learned, on inquiry, that he had indeed published four or five of the works as we had agreed, but taking advantage of these, which passed readily into extensive circulation, he proceeded to set aside the contract, and to get up a series of publications upon the model of those I had prepared for him, giving them, in the title-pages, the name of Parley, and passing them off upon the public, by every artifice in his power, as the genuine works of that

after the first edition, and also a premium or bonus of five pounds on each work (in addition to the above stipulations), when four thousand copies are sold or disposed of, of the same.

"And when said Goodrich is out of the country, said Tegg is to furnish certificates of sales, &c., as may be required by said Goodrich or his agent. Said Tegg, it is understood, is not bound to publish any of these works which he deems unsuited to the country; but said Goodrich is at liberty to dispose of, to any other publisher, any work which said Tegg, on application, declines publishing.

"THOMAS TEGG,
"S. G. GOODRICH."

"London, June 30, 1832."

author. He had thus published over a dozen volumes, which he was circulating as "Peter Parley's
Library." The speculation, as I was told, had succeeded admirably, and I was assured that many thousand pounds of profit had been realized thereby.

To my request for an account of his stewardship,
Mr. Tegg replied, in general terms, that I was misin-
formed as to the success of the works in question;
that, in fact, they had been a very indifferent speculation; that he found the original works were not
adapted to his purpose, and he had consequently got
up others; that he had created, by advertising and
other means, an interest in these works, and had thus
greatly benefited the name and fame of Parley, and,
all things considered, he thought he had done more
for me than I had for him; therefore, in his view,
if we considered the account balanced, we should not
be very far from a fair adjustment.

To this cool answer I made a suitable reply, but
without obtaining the slightest satisfaction. The
contract I had made was a hasty memorandum, and
judicially, perhaps, of no binding effect on him. And
besides, I had no money to expend in litigation. A
little reflection satisfied me that I was totally at
Tegg's mercy—a fact of which his calm and collected
manner assured me he was even more conscious than
myself. The discussion was not prolonged. At the
second interview he cut the whole matter short, by
saying—"Sir, I do not owe you a farthing; neither

justice nor law require me to pay you any thing. Still, I am an old man, and have seen a good deal of life, and have learned to consider the feelings of others as well as my own. I will pay you four hundred pounds, and we will be quits! If we can not do this, we can do nothing." In view of the whole case, this was as much as I expected, and so I accepted the proposition. I earnestly remonstrated with Mr. Tegg against the enormity of making me responsible for works I never wrote, but as to all actual claims on the ground of the contract, I gave him a receipt in full, and we parted.

Some years after this Mr. Tegg died, but his establishment passed into the hands of one of his sons, with another person, by whom it is still continued; the false "Parley's Library" having been recently enlarged by the addition of other counterfeits.* An example so tempting and so successful as that I have described, was sure to be followed by others, and ere long many of the first publishers of juvenile works in London, had employed persons to write books under the name of Peter Parley—every thing being done in the title-pages, prefaces, advertisements, &c., to make the public receive them as genuine works. The extent to which this business was carried, and the position in which it placed me, may be gathered from a letter I addressed to a publishing house in London some two years since, and which was substantially as follows:

* For a list of some of these works see p. 551 ; see also, p. 553.

ST. PAUL'S COFFEE-HOUSE, LONDON,
October 18, 1854.

MR. DARTON, BOOKSELLER,
  HOLBORN HILL, LONDON.

SIR,—Happening to be in this city, I called two days since at your counting-room, and while waiting there for an answer to inquiries I had made, I was attracted by a volume, glowing in red and gold, lying upon the table. I took it up, and read in the title-page—

PETER PARLEY'S ANNUAL:
A Christmas and New-Year's Present for Young People.
NEW YORK: EVANS AND DICKINSON, ETC.

I was informed that this was one of your publications, designed for the coming winter sales, and I had no difficulty in discovering that there was to be, not only an edition for England, but one for the United States.

Now I have long known that among the various books that had been got up in London, under the pretended authorship of Peter Parley, you have issued an annual volume, with the above, or a similar title. Some dozen years ago, I remonstrated with you upon this, and threatened that I would show you up in the London Times. You replied, "I will give you fifty pounds to do it." "How so?" said I. "Because you will sell my books without the trouble of my advertising them," was your answer. "But it will ruin your character," I added. "Poh!" said you; "London is too big for that."

So the matter passed, and might still have passed, had it not been for the above-named New-York imprint. This has forced me to a reconsideration of the whole subject of these London impostures, and I have come to the conclusion, that duty to myself, as well as to the public on both sides of the water, makes it indispensable that I should attempt to put an end to this great wrong. The course I propose to pursue is, immediately on my return to the United States, if I find your edition has been on sale there, to bring an action against the venders of it, and I have no doubt it will be suppressed. It is a counterfeit, injurious to me, and fraudulent towards the public. Our courts have decided that it is unlawful for a man in the United States to counterfeit even British labels or trademarks upon British manufactures, these being deemed private property, which the law holds sacred. If they will thus protect a foreigner, I think they will of course protect an American citizen in a case involving the same or similar principles.

If I fail in an attempt at legal remedy, I shall appeal to the American public, and I cannot doubt that any vender of these fraudulent publications will be so rebuked as to put an end to such practices, there. On a former occasion, it was proposed to issue a work at New York, under the name of Peter Parley. I simply published the fact, that this was without my concurrence, and a hurricane of denunciation from the press, all over the country, silenced the project forever.

So far my course is clear: as to the British public, I propose to publish the facts, and make an appeal to their sense of justice. In respect to the past, there is perhaps no remedy. No doubt I have too long neglected this matter, and perhaps my silence may be urged by interested and unscrupulous parties as having sanctioned the fraud which has consequently grown into a system. Nevertheless, the fact certainly is, that it has always been known and admitted, in England as elsewhere, that I am the original author of Peter Parley's Tales, and am entitled to the merit, or demerit, of having given currency to that name. You have had intercourse with me for the last fifteen years, and you have always known and admitted my claims. You have vindicated your publication of this false Annual to me, on no higher grounds than that it was begun by other parties, and would be carried on by others if you abandoned it.

I have had applications, as the author of Peter Parley's Tales, from various publishers in England, and interviews with still others, but never, in a single instance, have I known these claims to be questioned. I have seen my name circulating, for the last dozen years, in the London papers, as the author of Parley's Tales. All over Europe I have met with English people, who recognized me as such.

I am aware that there is in London a man by the name of Martin, who has written many of these counterfeit Parley books, and is familiarly known there as "Peter Parley Martin." I believe he is the editor of your Annual. Now we know it to be proverbial, that a man may tell a falsehood so often as to believe it; and hence it is quite possible that this Martin thinks himself the real Peter. Still, if it be so, he is only one self-duped monomaniac: neither you nor any other publisher in London is deceived by it. How honorable men can have intercourse with such a creature, and even become accessory to his impostures, passes my comprehension.

It is plain then, that if I have thus delayed to rectify this wrong, the real facts of the case are not obscured. The British public know that I am the author of the veritable works of Peter Parley. They may not, they cannot always distinguish between the true and the false, and therefore buy

both, indiscriminately.   Still, though thus accessory to the
fraud, it is ignorantly and unwittingly done, and they are not
chargeable with wrong, at least toward me.   The publishers
and authors of these counterfeits are the guilty parties.   I
may complain of these, but not of the people of England, until
I have first stated to them, authoritatively, the facts, and
pointed out the true and the false publications.   When I have
done this, if they still encourage the perpetrators of this
wrong, they will become its participators.   If I understand the
tone and sentiment of the English people, they will be quite
as ready to rebuke this system of piracy as were the people of
the United States on the occasion to which I have referred.

Another thing is plain, that neither the authors nor publishers concerned in this system of deception and plunder,
pursue it in doubt or ignorance of the facts.   You will not
pretend this for yourself.   Other cases are equally clear.
Some dozen years ago, being in London, and in pressing need
of the avails of my literary labor and reputation, I was introduced to Mr. T..., then in active business, and taking the
lead in juvenile publications.   I proposed to him to publish
some of mine, which I had just revised and emended.   After
a week's examination, he returned them, saying that they were
clever enough in their way, but they would not do for him.
They were tainted with Americanisms, republicanisms, latitu-
dinarianisms, in church and state.   He could only publish
books, orthodox according to British ideas.   If I could remodel them, or allow them to be remodeled, so as to conform
to this standard, we could do a good business together.

This I did not accede to, and we parted.   Yet within about
a twelvemonth, this same Mr. T... published a book entitled

" *Peter Parley's Lives of the Apostles, etc.*" It was written in a pious strain; it was thoroughly orthodox, according to the British platform. It was, moreover, beautifully bound, printed, and illustrated. No doubt it was a capital speculation, for besides its artistic and mechanical recommendations, it was suited to the public taste, and of course the innocent public were ignorant of its illegitimate parentage. Not so the scrupulous Mr. T...—not so the pious author: they knew that each page was contaminated with falsehood, and all the more base, because from the beginning to the end, there was a sedulous and, I might add, a skillful effort to make it appear that the book was written by me. Would the British people buy even such embellished orthodoxy, if they knew that the "trail of the serpent was over it all?"

I recite this, not because it is the worst case, but rather because it is a fair example of the conduct of British authors and British publishers in this matter. Examples of practices more mean, if not more wicked, might be cited. At the period above-mentioned, there was a bookseller in London, whose sign was "Books for the Million"—a "remainder" man, who bought unsold sheet-stock of publishers, put it in gaudy binding, and sold it at a cheap rate. As I ascertained, he was accustomed to tear out the original and true titles of these defunct publications, and put in new and false ones, such as " *Grandfather's Tales, by Peter Parley*," or something of that kind. Peter Parley thus fathered quite a library—and thus, galvanized into new life, this man sold his works *by the million*, according to his sign. Recently, I am told, he has retired upon a handsome fortune.

I think, therefore, that the plea of ignorance, on the part of the British authors and publishers in this system of counter-feits, will not avail, even if it be made. And what other ex-cuse can they offer? If by way of palliative, rather than de-fense, they say one has done it, and another has done it, and therefore I did it, and it has hitherto passed with impunity—though I cannot believe this will satisfy either the consciences of the wrong-doers, or British public opinion; still, I feel dis-posed to let it pass as a sort of excuse for the past. But as to the future, is it not my manifest duty to deprive them of this plea? Is it right, supposing I had no personal interest or feeling in the matter, to let this go on? *You must be aware that a new and material fact is introduced into the question: you have begun, or are beginning, this system of fraud in America, in New York, at the threshold of my domicile. You carry the war into Africa. An example thus set, if not resisted, will be soon followed, and my name will be as cheap in the United States as in the Three Kingdoms.* Can I be held innocent, if I remain silent, and permit the American public to be abused and debauched by the introduction of this system there?   .

It appears to me there can be but one answer. And even supposing I could waive these considerations, may I not, must I not, as a man having some self-respect, and being besides de-pendent upon my literary exertions and reputation, resist this inroad upon my rights, and endeavor to throw off this grow-ing incubus upon my name and fame? Such a burden in one hemisphere is enough: must I bear it in both?

It is difficult to reflect on such a subject as this without ir-ritation. Nevertheless I endeavor to school myself into a cer-tain degree of calmness. As to my course in America, the

first step is clear, as I have indicated. But how shall I begin
in England? Shall I expose the facts, refer to names, point
out the counterfeits and the counterfeiters, and appeal to the
moral sense of the people there? This is undoubtedly my
right, and a natural indignation suggests that it is my duty.
Yet I shrink from such a proceeding. I know that I may
bring upon myself many an envenomed shaft; for there may
be a powerful interest aroused into activity against me. We
all know that in London, as elsewhere, there are mercenary
presses, which can be hired to defend a bad cause, and such a
defense generally consists in vengeful recrimination.

Now I may not—nay, I do not—fear the result. I will not
suspect for a moment, that in so plain a case, the verdict of
public opinion in England could be otherwise than favorable
to me. Nevertheless, I am a peace-loving man, and do not
court the process. I have been often attacked—sometimes
very unjustly; yet I have seldom made a reply.

Many years ago, I presided at a convention in Boston,
which passed resolutions against International Copyright.
As president I signed the proceedings, and thus became the
target of many a bitter shaft, hurled at me personally, by the
London press, which was then somewhat rabid in its attempts
to force us into the proposed literary partnership. The late
Mr. Hood stuck me all over with epithets of ridicule. His
books are still published, and are in the popular libraries of
the United States, with these passages in full. I have often
read them myself, and laughed at them, too, notwithstanding
their intrinsic malevolence. Yet, though I had and have an
answer to make, and I believe an effective one, I have never
thought it worth while to give it to the public. Being in

London, in 1842 I saw Mr. Hood, and suggested to him that there was another side to this question, and he offered me the pages of his magazine for the publication of my views. Yet I did not accept of this ; my conviction was that the venom of his attack would die out, and I should be spared the irritation and annoyance of a controversy, necessarily in some degree personal, inasmuch as I had been personally assailed. Events have shown that I judged rightly. I may add, too, that I am constitutionally anti-pugnacious, and instinctively recoil at the idea of a personal and public discussion. I have no doubt indulged this to the extent of weakness, in respect to the matter in hand, and hence the evil has assumed its present enormity.

And, in addition to this, I dislike to disturb the amicable relations which have long subsisted between you and me ; I dislike exceedingly to arraign you before the world, as one of the very leaders—in point of fact, the head and front offender —in what I consider a great public and personal wrong. What I desire is, if possible, to conduct this affair so as to avoid any direct notice of yourself in the appeal to the British public, if I conclude to make it. What I have to propose is, that you now enter into an engagement, henceforth to issue no volume and sell no volume whatever, with Parley's name, of which I am not the acknowledged author ; and furthermore, that you make such indemnity to me, and such explanations to the public, as may be deemed right and reasonable by arbitrators between us. If you must publish an annual, put Mr. Martin's name to it, or any other name you choose, only not mine. I am told that you have thriven in business, and that " *Parley's* Annual " has largely contributed to your success. Your purse, then, and I hope your feelings, will make this suggestion easy.

If you cannot be persuaded to adopt this line of conduct by the argument against injustice and fraud; if you pay no regard to the influence which a public declaration of the facts may have on your reputation, still, reflect on my position. Many of these counterfeit Parley books are to me nauseous in style, matter, and purpose. According to my taste, they are full of vulgarisms, degrading phrases, and coarse ideas. In some cases they advocate principles which are not mine, and manners and customs I disapprove. This very volume of yours, for 1854, in spite of its gold edges, colored engravings, and embossed binding, is mainly written in a low, bald, and vulgar style; and withal is ridiculous from its affected Parleyisms. Rich outside, it is within smitten with poverty. Yet I am obliged to bear all this. Is it fair, is it neighborly, to treat any one thus?

Remember, I am not speaking hypothetically. My reputation has been attacked, my literary rank degraded, by being made responsible for works I never wrote. The Westminster Review, some years ago, criticised the Parley Books, as sullied by coarse phrases and vulgar Americanisms. Extracts were made to verify this criticism, and yet every extract was from a false book, or a false passage foisted into a true one. Not one line of the damnatory examples did I ever write. Precisely this process of degradation must have been going on against me, for the last dozen years, in the public mind of England, through the influence of your counterfeits.

Is this fair? Will this do? Will you stand by it here and hereafter? Remember, this is a totally different question from that of International Copyright. I have never complained that you or any other foreign publisher has reprinted my books as I wrote them. Do this, as much as you please; so long as the law remains as it is, such a course is inevitable, on both sides of the water. Alter my books, if you please, and publish them, only stating distinctly what you have done. This is lawful, and I shall not complain of it. In point of fact, you have published at least one book—for that I chanced to see—made up nearly, if not quite, of extracts from my works, yet a man by the name of Greene figured in the title-page as the author. I have also seen whole pages of my writings, in your other various publications, the same, by the manner of insertion, appearing as being original there. Of all this, however I might disapprove it, I have never uttered a word of complaint. But what I do complain of, is this: *that you take my name, to which I have given currency, in order to sell books I never wrote. You say to the world, Mr. Goodrich, the author of Peter Parley's Tales, wrote this: the world buy it, and judge me accordingly.* And thus I am robbed of what to me is property, and at the same time I suffer that other and greater calamity, the loss or damage of a good name. That is my complaint.

If upon this appeal, you assent to my proposition—though I must carry on the proposed prosecution in the United States, if the edition referred to has been sent there—I shall feel that I can afford, so far as the British public are concerned, to make a general and not a particular and specific declaration of the facts herein alluded to. I shall not then need to direct attention personally to you, or to anybody. If, on the contrary, you do not enter into this or some satisfactory arrangement, I shall feel that you have been fairly warned, and that you can not hold me responsible for any annoyance you may suffer from the consequences. I shall, moreover, consider myself at liberty, should I deem it best, to give publicity to this letter. However hastily written, it embodies the substance of my views, and though further publications would doubtless become necessary, this might serve as one link in the chain of my statement.

I am yours truly,

S. G. GOODRICH.

This letter was forwarded from Paris, where I was then residing, some weeks after it was written. Receiving no reply, I addressed a reminder to Mr. Darton, but that also was unanswered. In July, 1855, I returned to New York, and on inquiry, found that *sixteen hundred copies of the Parley's Annual, referred to in the preceding letter, had been sent there, and were actually in the Custom-house!** I could not but con-

---

* These sixteen hundred copies, being enjoined, and remaining in the Custom-house beyond the time allowed by law, were consequently sold at auction in June, 1856, and were thus thrown into the New York market. The following are extracts from this work :

" The Americans equal Mr. Jesse for story-telling. They are not particularly nice as to data. Some of their stories are so preposterously absurd, as to puzzle us exceedingly." * * * *

"Peter Parley loves our good Queen, and delights to follow her in her various progresses," &c. * * * *

" It was delightful for old Peter to behold the Queen and the Prince, and not less so to see the young Prince of Wales emulating the British Tar, and looking like an embryo Nelson, and his heart beat with ardor at the cheers of the sailors and the roaring of the guns." * * * *

"He (old Peter) loves the sea-breeze, and he would sing with his poor old voice, like a shattered clarionet, ' Rule, Britannia,' and thank God that he has lived to see the day when England exhibits to the world that she is still able to ' rule the waves.' " * * * *

sider this as a defiance on the part of Mr. Darton, and accordingly I commenced an action against him, as I had told him I should do.

The case is still undecided. It is, perhaps, a question, whether a New York court has jurisdiction in the case, the defendant being a foreigner, but if it has, I trust it will be settled by our courts that an author is entitled to protection in the use and behoof of a name—however it may be fictitious—with which he has become identified in the public mind, and to which he has given a commercial value. This principle has been fully established in this country as well as in England, in application to manufacturers and merchants, and it is not to be supposed that an author shall be denied the same protection.

Now, you can not suppose, from the facts here stated, that these things do not give me great annoyance. But one thing I am bound to say, which is, that I feel no personal hostility to Mr. Darton. He is a most amiable man, and I believe would be the last person in the world to do an intentional wrong. In the present case, he has probably yielded to the guidance of other parties, implicated like himself, and is rather fighting their battles than his own.

I have great respect for the Queen of England, for I consider her virtuous example, in her high station, as beneficial, not to her own boundless realms alone, but to the whole world; I have no objection to Englishmen singing " Rule Britannia"—but it is not pleasant to find these things in a book, issued in the name of Peter Parley, the preface of which is signed Peter Parley, and which is all written so as to make the world believe it is the work of an American.

LETTER XLIX.

Objections to the Parley Books—My theory as to books for children—
Attempt in England to revive the old nursery books—Mr. Felix Summerly
—Hallowell's Nursery Rhymes of England—Dialogue between Timothy
and his mother—Mother Goose—The Toad's Story—Books of instruction.

My dear C*******

It is not to be supposed that the annoyances
arising from the falsification of the name of Parley,
which I have just pointed out, have been the only
obstacles which have roughened the current of my
literary life. Not only the faults and imperfections of
execution in my juvenile works—and no one knows
them so well as myself—have been urged against
them, but the whole theory on which they are founded has been often and elaborately impugned.

It is quite true that when I wrote the first half-
dozen of Parley's Tales, I had formed no philosophy
upon the subject. I simply used my experience with
children in addressing them. I followed no models,
I put on no harness of the schools, I pored over no
learned examples. I imagined myself on the floor
with a group of boys and girls, and I wrote to them as
I would have spoken to them. At a later period I had
reflected on the subject, and embodied in a few simple
lines the leading principle of what seemed to me the
true art of teaching children—and that is, to consider
that their first ideas are simple and single, and formed

of images of things palpable to the senses; and hence
that these images are to form the staple of lessons to
be communicated to them.

THE TEACHER'S LESSON.

I saw a child, some four years old,
    Along a meadow stray;
Alone she went, uncheck'd, untold,
    Her home not far away.

She gazed around on earth and sky,
    Now paused and now proceeded;
Hill, valley, wood, she passed them by
    Unmarked, perchance unheeded.

And now gay groups of roses bright
    In circling thickets bound her—
Yet on she went with footsteps light,
    Still gazing all around her.

And now she paused and now she stooped,
    And plucked a little flower;
A simple daisy 'twas, that drooped
    Within a rosy bower.

The child did kiss the little gem,
    And to her bosom press'd it,
And there she placed the fragile stem,
    And with soft words caressed it.

I love to read a lesson true
    From nature's open book—
And oft I learn a lesson new
    From childhood's careless look.

Children are simple, loving, true—
    'Tis God that made them so;
And would you teach them ?—be so, too,
    And stoop to what they know.

Begin with simple lessons, things
  On which they love to look;
Flowers, pebbles, insects, birds on wings—
  These are God's spelling-book!

And children know his A B C,
  As bees where flowers are set:
Wouldst thou a skillful teacher be?
  Learn then this alphabet.

From leaf to leaf, from page to page,
  Guide thou thy pupil's look;
And when he says, with aspect sage—
  "Who made this wondrous book?"

Point thou with reverend gaze to heaven,
  And kneel in earnest prayer—
That lessons thou hast humbly given
  May lead thy pupil there!

From this initial point I proceeded to others, and
came to the conclusion that in feeding the mind of
children with facts, with truth, and with objective
truth, we follow the evident philosophy of nature and
providence, inasmuch as these had created all children to be ardent lovers of things they could see and
hear and feel and know. Thus I sought to teach
them history and biography and geography, and all
in the way in which nature would teach them—that
is, by a large use of the senses, and especially by the
eye—the master organ of the body as well as the
soul. I selected as subjects for my books, things capable of sensible representation, such as familiar animals, birds, trees, and of these I gave pictures, as a

" FLOWERS, PEBBLES, INSECTS, BIRDS ON WINGS—
THESE ARE GOD'S SPELLING BOOK "

starting point.   The first line I wrote was, " Here I am ; my name is Peter Parley," and before I went further, gave an engraving representing my hero, as I wished him to be conceived by my pupils.   Before I began to talk of a lion, I gave a picture of a lion —my object being, as you will perceive, to have the child start with a distinct image of what I was about to give an account of.   Thus I secured his interest in the subject, and thus I was able to lead his under-standing forward in the path of knowledge.

These views of course led me in a direction ex-actly opposite to the old theories in respect to nursery books, in two respects.   In the first place, it was thought that education should, at the very threshold, seek to spiritualize the mind, and lift it above sensi-ble ideas, and to teach it to live in the world of im-agination.   A cow was very well to give milk, but when she got into a book, she must jump over the moon ; a little girl going to see her grandmother, was well enough as a matter of fact, but to be suited to the purposes of instruction, she must end her ca-reer in being eaten up by a wolf.   My plan was, in short, deemed too utilitarian, too materialistic, and hence it was condemned by many persons, and among them the larger portion of those who had formed their tastes upon the old classics, from Homer down to Mother Goose !

This was one objection ; another was, that I aimed at making education easy — thus bringing up the

child in habits of receiving knowledge only as made
into pap, and of course putting it out of his power to
relish and digest the stronger meat, even when his
constitution demanded it.   The use of engravings in
books for instruction, was deemed a fatal facility,
tending to exercise the child in a mere play of the
senses, while the understanding was left to indolence
and emaciation.

On these grounds, and still others, my little books
met with opposition, sometimes even in grave Quar-
terlies and often in those sanctified publications, entitled Journals of Education.   In England, at the period that the name of Parley was most current—both
in the genuine as well as the false editions—the feeling against my juvenile works was so strong among
the conservatives, that a formal attempt was made to
put them down by reviving the old nursery books.
In order to do this, a publisher in London reproduced
these works, employing the best artists to illustrate
them, and bringing them out in all the captivating luxuries of modern typography. A quaint, quiet, scholarly old gentleman, called Mr. Felix Summerly—a dear
lover of children—was invented to preside over the
enterprise, to rap the knuckles of Peter Parley, and
to woo back the erring generation of children to the
good old orthodox rhymes and jingles of England.

I need hardly say that this attempt failed of success : after two bankruptcies, the bookseller who conducted the enterprise finally abandoned it.   Yet such

was the reverence at the time for the old favorites of the nursery, that a man by the name of Hallowell* expended a vast amount of patient research and antiquarian lore, in hunting up and setting before the world, the history of these performances, from Hey diddle diddle to

> " A farmer went trotting upon his gray mare—
> Bumpety, bumpety, bump !"

To all this I made no direct reply ; I ventured, however, to suggest my views in the following article inserted in Merry's Museum for August, 1846.

DIALOGUE BETWEEN TIMOTHY AND HIS MOTHER.

Timothy. Mother ! mother ! do stop a minute, and hear me say my poetry !

Mother. Your poetry, my son ? Who told you how to make poetry ?

T. Oh, I don't know ; but hear what I have made up.

M. Well, go on.

T. Now don't you laugh ; it's all mine. I didn't get a bit of it out of a book. Here it is !

> " Higglety, pigglety, pop !
> The dog has eat the mop ;
>   The pig's in a hurry,
>   The cat's in a flurry—
> Higglety, pigglety—pop !"

M. Well, go on.

T. Why, that's all. Don't you think it pretty good ?

M. Really, my son, I don't see much sense in it.

T. *Sense ?* Who ever thought of *sense*, in poetry ? Why,

---

* Nursery Rhymes of England, &c., Collected and Edited by James Orchard Hallowell.

mother, you gave me a book the other day, and it was all poetry, and I don't think there was a bit of sense in the whole of it. Hear me read. [*Reads.*]

> " Hub a dub !
>   Three men in a tub—
> And how do you think they got there ?
>   The butcher,
>   The baker,
>   The candlestick-maker,
> They all jumped out of a rotten potato :
> 'Twas enough to make a man stare."

And here's another.

> " A cat came fiddling out of a barn,
>   With a pair of bagpipes under her arm ;
>   She could sing nothing but fiddle cum fee—
>   The mouse has married the humblebee—
>   Pipe, cat—dance, mouse—
>   We'll have a wedding at our good house !".

And here's another.

> " Hey, diddle, diddle,
>   The cat and the fiddle,
>   The cow jumped over the moon—
>   The little dog laughed
>   To see the craft,
> And the dish ran after the spoon."

Now, mother, the book is full of such things as these, and I don't see any meaning in them.

M. Well, my son, I think as you do: they are really very absurd.

T. Absurd ? Why, then, do you give me such things to read ?

M. Let me ask you a question. Do you not love to read these rhymes, even though they are silly ?

T. Yes, dearly.

M. Well, you have just learned to read, and I thought these jingles, silly as they are, might induce you to study your book, and make you familiar with reading.

T. I don't understand you, mother ; but no matter.

> " Higglety, pigglety, pop !
>   The dog has eat the mop ;
>   The pig's in a hurry—"

M. Stop, stop, my son. I choose you should understand me.

T. But, mother, what's the use of understanding you?

> "Higglety, pigglety, pop!"

M. Timothy!

T. Ma'am?

M. Listen to me, or you will have cause to repent it. Listen to what I say! I gave you the book to amuse you, and improve you in reading, not to form your taste in poetry.

T. Well, mother, pray forgive me. I did not mean to offend you. But I really do love poetry, because it is so silly!

> "Higglety, pigglety, pop!"

M. Don't say that again, Timothy!

T. Well, I won't; but I'll say something out of this pretty book you gave me.

> " Doodledy, doodledy, dan!
> I'll have a piper to be my good man—
> And if I get less meat, I shall get game—
> Doodledy, doodledy, dan!"

M. That's enough, my son.

T. But, dear mother, do hear me read another.

> " We're all in the dumps,
> For diamonds are trumps—
> The kittens are gone to St. Paul's—
> The babies are bit,
> The moon's in a fit—
> And the houses are built without walls."

M. I do not wish to hear any more.

T. One more; one more, dear mother!

> " Round about—round about—
> Maggoty pie—
> My father loves good ale,
> And so do I."

Don't you like that, mother?

M. No; it is too coarse, and unfit to be read or spoken.

T. But it is here in this pretty book you gave me, and I like it very much, mother. And here is a poem, which I think very fine.

> " One-ery, two-ery,
> Ziccary zan,
> Hollow bone, crack a bone—
> Ninery ten:
> Spittery spat,
> It must be done,
> Twiddledum, tweddledum,
> Twenty-one,
> Hink, spink, the puddings stink—"

M. Stop, stop, my son. Are you not ashamed to say such things ?

T. Ashamed? No, mother. Why should I be? It's all printed here as plain as day. Ought I to be ashamed to say any thing that I find in a pretty book you have given me? Just hear the rest of this.

> " Hink, spink, the puddings—"

M. Give me the book, Timothy. I see that I have made a mistake ; it is not a proper book for you.

T. Well, you may take the book ; but I can say the rhymes, for I have learned them all by heart.

> " Hink, spink, the puddings—"

M. Timothy, how dare you!

T. Well, mother, I won't say it, if you don't wish me to. But mayn't I say—

> "Higglety, pigglety, pop!"

M. I had rather you would not.

T. And " Doodledy, doodledy, dan"—mayn't I say that ?

M. No.

T. Nor " Hey, diddle, diddle?"

M. I do not wish you to say any of those silly things.

T. Dear me, what shall I do ?

M. I had rather you would learn some good, sensible things.

T. Such as what?

M. Watts's Hymns, and Original Hymns.

T. Do you call them sensible things? I hate 'em.

> " Doodledy, doodledy, dan !"

M. [*Aside.*] Dear, dear, what shall I do? The boy has got his head turned with these silly rhymes. It was really a very unwise thing to put a book into his hands, so full of nonsense and vulgarity. These foolish rhymes stick like burs in his mind, and the coarsest and vilest seem to be best remembered. I must remedy this mistake; but I see it will take all my wit to do it. [*Aloud.*] Timothy, you must give me up this book, and I will get you another.

T. Well, mother, I am sorry to part with it; but I don't care so much about it, as I know all the best of it by heart.

> " Hink, spink, the puddings stink"—

M. Timothy, you'll have a box on the ear, if you repeat that !

T. Well, I suppose I can say,

> " Round about—round about—
>   Maggoty pie—"

M. You go to bed !

T. Well, if I must, I must.   Good-night, mother !

> " Higglety, pigglety, pop !
>   The dog has eat the mop ;
>   The cat's in a flurry,
>   The cow's in a hurry,
>   Higglety, pigglety, pop !"

Good-night, mother !

I trust, my friend, you will not gather from this that I condemn rhymes for children. I know that there is a certain music in them that delights the ear of childhood. Nor am I insensible to the fact that in Mother Goose's Melodies, there is frequently a sort of humor in the odd jingle of sound and sense. There is, furthermore, in many of them, an historical significance, which may please the profound student who puzzles it out; but what I affirm is, that many of these pieces are coarse, vulgar, offensive, and it is precisely these portions that are apt to stick to the minds of children. And besides, if, as is common, such a book is the first that a child becomes acquainted with, it is likely to give him a low idea of the purpose and meaning of books, and to beget a taste for mere jingles.

With these views, I sought to prepare lessons which combined the various elements suited to children—a few of them even including frequent, repetitious rhymes—yet at the same time presenting rational ideas and gentle kindly sentiments. Will you excuse me for giving you one example—my design being to show you how this may be done, and how even a very unpromising subject is capable of being thus made attractive to children.

THE TOAD'S STORY.

Oh, gentle stranger, stop,
And hear poor little Hop
Just sing a simple song,
Which is not very long—
　　Hip, hip, hop.

I am an honest toad,
Living here by the road;
Beneath a stone I dwell,
In a snug little cell,
　　Hip, hip, hop.

It may seem a sad lot
To live in such a spot—

But what I say is true—
I have fun as well as you !
    Hip, hip, hop.

Just listen to my song—
I sleep all winter long,
But in spring I peep out,
And then I jump about—
    Hip, hip, hop.

When the rain patters down,
I let it wash my crown,
And now and then I sip
A drop with my lip :
    Hip, hip, hop.

When the bright sun is set,
And the grass with dew is wet,
I sally from my cot,
To see what's to be got,
    Hip, hip, hop.

And now I wink my eye,
And now I catch a fly,
And now I take a peep,
And now and then I sleep :
    Hip, hip, hop.

And this is all I do—
And yet they say it's true,
That the toady's face is sad,
And his bite is very bad !
    Hip, hip, hop.

Oh, naughty folks they be,
That tell such tales of me,
For I'm an honest toad,
Just living by the road :
    Hip, hip, hop !

These were my ideas in regard to first books—toy books—those which are put into the hands of children, to teach them the art of reading. As to books of amusement and instruction, to follow these, I gave them Parley's tales of travels, of history, of nature, and art, together with works designed to cultivate a love of truth, charity, piety, and virtue, and I sought to make these so attractive as to displace the bad books, to which I have already alluded—the old monstrosities, Puss in Boots, Jack the Giant-killer, and others of that class.* A principal part

---

* For what I have said upon these subjects, I refer the reader to vol. i. page 166. In a recent edition of Jack the Giant-killer, I find his exploits summed up as follows, on the last page: " At his wedding he went over all the tricks he had played upon the giants; he showed the company how one had tumbled into a pit and had his head cut off; how he had throttled two others with a rope; how another, the double-headed Welch monster, had ripped himself open to let the hasty-pudding out; and how he had brought another on his knees by a chop with his sword of sharpness, and spitted another like a fat fowl," &c. On the cover of this very book, which, by the way, is one of a series in the same vein, called HOUSEHOLD STORIES FOR LITTLE FOLKS, I find the argument in behalf of this class of books for children, thus set forth:

" The extravagance of the stories, the attractive manner of telling them, the picturesque scenery described, the marvelous deeds related, the reward of virtue and punishment of vice, upon principles strictly in accordance with ethical laws, as applied to the formation of character, render them peculiarly adapted to induce children to acquire a love for reading, and to aid them to cultivate the affections, sympathies, fancy, and imagination."

If it had been said that these tales were calculated to familiarize the mind with things shocking and monstrous; to cultivate a taste for tales of bloodshed and violence; to teach the young to use coarse language, and cherish vulgar ideas; to erase from the young heart tender and gentle feelings, and substitute for them fierce and bloody thoughts and sentiments; to turn the youthful mind from the contemplation of the real loveliness of nature, and to fill it with the horrors of a debased and debauched fancy; to turn the youthful mind from the gentle pleasures

of my machinery was the character of Peter Parley—
a kind-hearted old man, who had seen much of the
world—and not presuming to undertake to instruct
older people, loved to sit down and tell his stories
to children. Beyond these juvenile works, I prepared a graduated series upon the same general plan,
reaching up to books for the adult library ; and thus
I attained one hundred and seventy volumes.

It is true that occasionally I wrote and published
a book, aside from this, my true vocation ; thus I edited the Token, and published two or three volumes of
poetry. But out of all my works, about a hundred
and twenty are professedly juvenile ; and forty are
for my early readers, advanced to maturity. It is
true that I have written openly, avowedly, to attract
and to please children ; yet it has been my design at
the same time to enlarge the circle of knowledge,
to invigorate the understanding, to strengthen the
moral nerve, to purify and exalt the imagination.
Such have been my aims ; how far I have succeeded,
I must leave to the judgment of others. One thing
I may perhaps claim, and that is, my example and
my success have led others—of higher gifts than
my own—to enter the ample and noble field of juve-

---

of home, of love and friendship at the fireside, at the school, in the
playground, and to stretch it upon the rack of horrible dreams of giants,
grinding the bones of children between their teeth, and satisfying their
horrible thirst upon the blood of innocent men and women and infants ;
in short, had it been said that these books were calculated to make crim-
inals of a large part of the children who read them, I think the truth
would have been much more fairly stated than in the preceding notice.

14*

nile instruction by means of books ; many of them
have no doubt surpassed me, and others will still
follow, surpassing them.   I look upon the art of writing for children and youth, advanced as it has been
of late years, still as but just begun.

LETTER L.

Journey to the South—Anecdotes—Reception at New Orleans.

My dear C*******

If thus I met with opposition, I had also my
success, nay, I must say, my triumphs.   My first pa-
trons were the children themselves, then the mothers,
and then, of course, the fathers.   In the early part of
the year 1846, I made a trip from Boston to the South,
returning by the way of the Mississippi and the Ohio.
I received many a kind welcome under the name of
the fictitious hero whom I had made to tell my stories.
Sometimes, it is true, I underwent rather sharp cross-
questioning, and frequently was made to feel that I
held my honors by a rather questionable title.   I, who
had undertaken to teach truth, was forced to confess
that fiction lay at the foundation of my scheme !   My
innocent young readers, however, did not suspect me :
they had taken all I had said as positively true, and
I was of course Peter Parley himself.

"Did you really write that book about Africa?"

said a black-eyed, dark-haired girl of some eight years old, at Mobile.

I replied in the affirmative.

" And did you really get into prison, there ?"

" No; I was never in Africa."

" Never in Africa ?"

" Never."

" Well, then, why did you say you had been there ?"

On another occasion, I think at Savannah, a gentleman called upon me, introducing his two grandchildren, who were anxious to see Peter Parley. The girl rushed up to me, and gave me a ringing kiss at once. We were immediately the best friends in the world. The boy, on the contrary, held himself aloof, and ran his eye over me, up and down, from top to toe. He then walked around, surveying me with the most scrutinizing gaze. After this, he sat down, and during the interview, took no further notice of me. At parting, he gave me a keen look, but said not a word. The next day the gentleman called and told me that his grandson, as they were on their way home, said to him—

" Grandfather, I wouldn't have any thing to do with that man : he ain't Peter Parley."

" How do you know that ?" said the grandfather.

" Because," said the boy, " he hasn't got his foot bound up, and he don't walk with a crutch !"*

---

* The little book entitled " *Parley's Method of Telling about Geography to Children*," had a picture, drawn by Tisdale, representing Parley

On my arrival at New Orleans I was kindly received, and had the honors of a public welcome. The proceedings were published in the papers at the time, and I here inclose you a copy of them, which I take from the Boston Courier of March 21st, 1846. You will readily perceive the egotism implied in placing before you such a record as this; but if I chronicle my failures and my trials, must I not, as a faithful scribe, tell you also of my success? If you reply that I might do it in a more modest way than thus to spread the whole proceedings before you, I answer, that in sending you this document, I by no means require you to read it. If you do read it, you will have a right to laugh at my vanity: if not, I trust you will hold your peace.

S. G. GOODRICH AT NEW ORLEANS.

As it may gratify many of our readers, and especially the friends of Peter Parley, we give in full the proceedings at New Orleans, which took place on the 28th of February last. The following is the report as published in the New Orleans Commercial Times of March 2d:

COMPLIMENT TO MR. GOODRICH, *the author of Parley's Tales.*—Our fellow-citizens are already aware that soon after Mr. Goodrich's arrival in our city, a large subscription, by our leading gentlemen, was filled, with a view to give him the compliment of a public dinner. But Mr. Goodrich's stay being too short

---

sitting in a chair, with his lame foot bound up, and a crutch at his side, while he is saying to the boys around—"Take care, don't touch my gouty toe; if you do, I won't tell you any more stories!" Of this work two millions were sold, and of course Parley and his crutch were pretty generally associated together, in the minds of children.

to allow of completing these arrangements, advantage was taken of the polite offer of Alfred Hennen, Esq., to give him a public reception at his house, under the auspices of the officers of the People's Lyceum, and some of our most prominent citizens. Accordingly, the ceremony took place on Saturday the 28th, between twelve and three o'clock. During this period there was assembled an immense crowd of children, mothers, teachers, and friends of education, eager to give the author of Parley's Tales a hearty welcome. Among the throng we noticed Mr. Clay, the Governor and Lieutenant-governor, Mayor, Recorder, Speaker of the House, and several members of the legislature. The scene was one of the most cheerful and agreeable we ever witnessed. While the leading visitors were present, the following address, in substance, was made by M. M. Cohen, Esq., President of the People's Lyceum:

"Mr. Goodrich, or, as we all love to call you, Peter Parley—The too kind partiality of indulgent friends of yours, has induced them to select me as their organ to address you on the present occasion. Their request was this morning conveyed to me on my way to the Commercial Court, where I have been engaged in a very dull, dry law case. The judge of that court has been pleased to allow me a few minutes to run up here and to say something to you, though what that something is, I have not yet any very clear perception. I can only hope, sir, that you have a much more assured knowledge of the reply which you are about to make to such remarks as I may offer, than I have at present of what my remarks may be. Yet, though I am wholly unprepared for the occasion, I should pity the heart that could remain so cold and callous to every noble emotion, as not to gather warmth and inspiration from the beaming eyes of beautiful mothers and the glad faces of happy children, smiling around us. But, sir, I am here as the representative of others, and will say to you what I presume they would say, if all were to speak at once.

"Permit me, then, in behalf of these friends and fellow-citizens, and what is more, and much better and brighter—in behalf of 'our better halves'—the ladies, God bless 'em!—to express the pleasure they derive from your visit to New Orleans, to welcome you to this hospitable mansion of our enlightened host, Mr. Hennen, on this the last day of your sojourn in our city. Let me assure you how glad and grateful they all are of this opportunity, which enables them—as is the expression in some parts of our country—to 'put your face to your name,' and to say to your face what they have so often said behind your back—that they regard you as a blessed benefactor to the youth of the rising generation, as one who has emphatically earned the proud and endearing appellation of '*l'Ami des Enfans.*'

"For, sir, who knows into how many thousand habitations in the United States Peter Parley's works have found their way, and made the hearts of the inmates glad, and kept them pure? Who can tell how oft, in the humble cottage of the poor, sorrow has been soothed and labor lightened, as the fond mother read to her listening child Peter Parley's Tales, while tears of pity started in their glistening eyes, or pleasure shook their infant frames?

"I have just alluded, sir, to the genial influence of your works in the United States. The immortal bard of Avon has said—

> "'How far that little candle throws his beams !
> So shines a good deed in a naughty world.'

But your name has crossed the Atlantic; and, in the hope of instilling into the minds of the youth now present a salutary proof how far good works will travel, permit me to read to them the following note, which has just been handed to me :

"NEW ORLEANS, February 28th, 1846.

"DEAR SIR: Having, with much pleasure, this moment understood that you, as the President of the People's Lyceum, have been requested to say something to-day to the universal friend of Children, Peter Parley, perhaps it would be interesting to you that I should state one or two anecdotes in reference to the name and fame of that distinguished character.

"When in London, I rarely ever passed a place where notices are allowed to be pasted up, without having my eyes gladdened with the sight of the name of Peter Parley. These announcements were made to carry gladness to the hearts of children. On such occasions, I often amused myself by stopping to witness the effect upon the children as they passed along in the streets. Such as the following scene was of frequent occurrence. When they cast their eyes upon these announcements it really appeared as though they had been touched by an electric spark which filled their hearts with joy. They would jump and frisk about, clap their hands, dance and stamp in front of these big handbills, and sing out in the perfect fullness of delight, begging their mothers or nurses to go away to the bookstore and get them the 'new Peter Parley.' Sometimes I have heard them thus answered : 'Oh no, you can not have Peter Parley, because you have been a bad little child, and none but good children are allowed to read Peter Parley.' The child, with tears glistening in its eyes, would reply : 'Oh, indeed, indeed, ma, if you will only get me Peter Parley this time, I will never be bad again.' I concluded, from what I saw, that all children in that country were taught to feel that it was a privilege and luxury to read Peter Parley.

"On more than one occasion, when spending a few days among the delightful cottages of 'our fatherland,' have I witnessed the congregation of children called from the nursery to the drawing-room, when they would come bounding and shaking their locks, singing out—'Oh, mamma, why did you send for us so soon ? we were reading such a pretty story from Peter Parley !' A new work from Peter Parley was always welcomed as a species of carnival among children. I thought, here is a grateful answer to the question once bitterly and tauntingly asked— 'What *man* in England ever reads an American book ?' Availing myself of the prerogative of my countrymen, I answer by asking—' What *child* is there in England so unfortunate as *not* to have read Peter Parley ?'

"A short time after his return from England, Mr. Webster said to me —' These are the American names which are better and more universally known and admired in England than all other American names put together,' and he asked me if I was Yankee enough to 'guess' who they were. I answered, Washington, and Chief-justice Marshall. 'No,' said he, 'I mean living persons—and they are Judge Story, and Peter Parley; for while the former is known to every lawyer in England, and generally among the educated classes, the latter has the entire possession of the young hearts of old England.' He added that whenever he went into an English family, and the children were brought in and presented to him as Mr. Webster, an American gentleman—they would be sure, with scarcely a single exception, to approach him, and looking him in the face, with the utmost curiosity, would say—' Do you know Peter Parley ?'

"Such facts as these were always delightful to an American when abroad. It made me feel proud of my country. And while I looked upon scenes which must be ever interesting to every right-thinking American, and acknowledged with gratitude my obligations to the land of Shakspeare and Milton, of Burke and Junius, I felt that we were fast compensating that debt by worthy productions from the pure and classic pens of Irving, Prescott, Bancroft, and Peter Parley.

"Respectfully yours,

"GREER B. DUNCAN.

"M. M. COHEN, Pres. People's Lyceum."

"To this note I will only add that, not a moment ago, a gentleman from Greece assured me that your works were well known in his country, and one from England has just declared that although he learned to-day, for the first time, that Peter Parley was an American, yet that his books were known and admired all over Great Britain.

"You came, sir, to New Orleans unheralded, unannounced— nor military guards, nor glittering arms, nor streaming banners, nor artillery, accompanied your steps. Neither trumpets' clangor, nor cannon's roar, nor ear-piercing fife, nor spirit-stirring drum gave token of your arrival. A plain citizen you had been in your beautiful brown cottage near Boston— at once the cradle of liberty and of literature—in slippers and night-cap, carving out with the pen a better immortality than military chieftains achieve with the sword! There, at Jamaica Plain, you were writing for young misses and masters little Peter Parley stories, and you all the while little dreaming of what a great man you were becoming—

"'Great, not like Cæsar, stained with blood—
But only great as you are good.'

"Farewell, sir, and when you leave us, be sure that when ' the curfew tolls the knell of parting day'—or in plainer words, Mr. Parley, when little boys and girls have had their bread and milk and are going to bed, and when church-bells ring to Sunday-school—then will

"'Infant hands be raised in prayer,
That God may bless you and may spare.'

"Once more, farewell! May you live long years of happiness,

as you must of honor; and when you die, may your 'works,' in one sense, not 'follow after' you, but remain on earth, to profit and delight, and be, like your fame, immortal!"

To which Mr. Goodrich replied as follows:

"Mr. President—It would be idle affectation in me to pretend that this cheerful spectacle, your kind and flattering words, the welcome in these faces around, are not a source of the liveliest gratification to myself personally. Yet, if I were to regard this occasion as designed merely to bestow upon me a passing compliment, on my first visit to the Crescent City, I should feel a degree of humiliation—for it would force me to consider how little I have achieved, compared with what remains to be done, and how disproportioned are these manifestations of regard to any merits which I can presume to claim. From the moment I set my foot in New Orleans, I have been greeted by a succession of agreeable surprises; and nothing has interested me more than the enlightened state of public opinion which I find to exist here in respect to *popular education*. I am at no loss to discover, in the hospitality with which I have been greeted, a lively appreciation of the great subject to which my humble labors in life have been directed; and it adds to my gratification to find this deeper meaning in the present scene.

"Considering the position of New Orleans, I have looked with peculiar satisfaction upon your public schools. Some of them would be deemed excellent in any part of New England—nay, in Boston itself. Nor is this all; these institutions, as I learn, are mainly supported by the popular vote—by self-taxation. This marks a great advance in civilization, and insures, from this time forward, a constant progress toward perfection. There is always a sharp contest between light and darkness, between ignorance and knowledge, before the mass of society will come up to the work, and support public instruction at the public expense. That battle has been fought here, and it has resulted in the triumph of truth and humanity. There is, if I may be permitted the allusion, a closer association between Plymouth

Rock and New Orleans than I had imagined. You have here both *faith* and *works*. Your schools declare that the wise and philanthropic social principles of the Pilgrims have taken root in the midst of a city signalized over the world by the extent and activity of its commerce.

"Nor is this subject only to be viewed as it respects New Orleans itself. If I rightly judge, you have a mission to perform even beyond this. The Crescent City is indeed the favorite daughter of the great Father of Waters, into whose lap he pours his unmeasured harvests. It is the commercial emporium of the finest valley on the globe, receiving a tribute which no one can estimate who has not looked upon your wondrous levee. Yet it is and is to be, perhaps for centuries to come, even something more—the metropolis of opinion, of fashion—giving social law to the millions of to-day, and the millions which are to follow in the boundless West. If we consider the ascendency which New Orleans has already acquired, especially in comparison with the infancy of many of our southwestern settlements, it is surely not extravagant to regard her influence and example, in many things, as likely to be little less than decisive. We may, therefore, consider the Mississippi under the image of a mighty tree, whose foot is on the verge of the tropics, while its tops are playing with the snows of the icy north. New Orleans stands at the root, and must furnish the sap, at least to some extent, which circulates through branches that spread over a surface equal to one-half the extent of Europe, and thus giving character, for good or ill, to the fruit that may follow. In this view, your position becomes intensely interesting, and it may serve to give added impulse to that patriotism and philanthropy which are at work among you.

"As I see around me some of your public functionaries—the master-minds of the State—and as, moreover, the subject of *public instruction* is occupying the attention of the legislature, assembled under your new constitution, I may be excused for saying a few words, of a general nature, upon this topic. It might sound trite and common-place, if I were to say that education is the only ladder by which mankind can ascend from barbarism to civilization, from ignorance to knowledge, from darkness to light, from earth to heaven. Yet, if this be true, can public men—rulers and lawgivers—be excused, if they seek not to furnish this ladder to every individual in the State? And let them bear in mind that the controlling lessons of life are given in childhood. Men are hard, and repel instruction. Youth is plastic, and readily takes the impress of the die that is set upon it. If a giant should undertake to give symmetry of form to the aged oak, he might momentarily subdue its gnarled and jagged branches to his will; but if they fly not back and strike him in the face, ere to-morrow's sun every limb and fiber will have returned to its wonted position. Thus it is that, in dealing with grown-up, obdurate *men*, the highest talent exerted for their good is often baffled, and perhaps repaid by ingratitude or reproach. On the other hand, how different is it with youth! Like saplings in the nursery, they readily take the form or character which a kindly hand may bestow. The humble gardener, only able to carry a watering-pot in one hand and a pruning-knife in the other, may rear up a whole forest of trees, beautiful in form, and productive of the choicest fruits. What field so wide, so promising, in every point of view so inviting, so worthy the attention of the patriot and statesman, as the *national nursery*, budding by millions into life and immortality?

"I should not be excused, were I to omit saying a few words to the mothers here present. From the moment that a woman becomes a mother, we all know that dearer interests than houses or lands are henceforth invested in the offspring. How hopeful, how fearful, are her duties now! Washington and Napoleon, Howard and Robespierre, were children once, and each upon a mother's knee. What mighty issues for good or ill are before the mother, in the possible consequences of the education she may give her child! Yet I would not lay upon her heart a responsibility which might seem too great to bear. The best of books, as well as universal experience, are full of encouragement to the faithful mother. If she performs her duty, God and nature take her part. She is the first divinity before which the budding spirit worships. The lessons which are gathered then, are likely to exert a controlling influence upon its after destiny. The child may be compared to a stream, and the parent to the mother earth over which it flows. She may not, can not stop its progress, but she may guide its course. She may trace out a channel in which it will be prone to flow, and after having fertilized and blessed its borders, it will find its way in peace to the great reservoir of waters. If, on the contrary, the mother neglect or misguide her offspring, it may, like a torrent, rush on, and after spreading desolation on every side, disappear in some sandy desert, or lose itself amid dreary and pestilent marshes.

"And now, one word to my juvenile friends—those who have received me with such winning smiles—one word to them. I dare not begin to tell them stories in the character of their old friend Peter Parley, for I should not know where to leave off. But let me repeat what I said to those whom I met the other day—on the celebration of Washington's birthday—*come and see me when you visit Boston!* You will find me in a brown house, some four miles out of town, in a pleasant village called Jamaica Plain. Come one and come all, and be assured of a hearty welcome. And that you may bring some sign that we have met before, please remember these lines—

> " Ne'er till to-morrow's light delay
> What may as well be done to-day—
> Ne'er do the thing you'd wish undone,
> Viewed by to-morrow's rising sun.

"If you will practise according to these verses, you will not only gratify your old friend who addresses you, but you will win the world's favor. Farewell!"

LETTER LI.

Retrospection—Confessions—The mice among my papers—A reckoning with the past.

My dear C******

In the three preceding letters I have spoken chiefly of the books I have written for children, and the true design of which was as much to amuse as to instruct them. These comprise the entire series called Parley's Tales, with many others, bearing Parley's name. As to works for education—school-books, including readers, histories, geographies, &c., books for popular reading, and a wilderness of prose and poetry, admitting of no classification—I have only to refer you to the catalogue already mentioned. Let me cheer you with the statement that this is the closing chapter of my literary history. I have little indeed to say, and that is a confession.

In looking at the long list of my publications, in reflecting upon the large numbers that have been sold, I feel far more of humiliation than of triumph. If I have sometimes taken to heart the soothing flatteries of the public, it has ever been speedily succeeded by the conviction that my life has been, on the whole, a series of mistakes, and especially in that portion of it which has been devoted to authorship. I have written too much, and have done nothing really

well. You need not whisper it to the public, at least
until I am gone; but I know, better than any one
can tell me, that there is nothing in this long catalogue that will give me a permanent place in literature. A few things may struggle upon the surface
for a time, but—like the last leaves of a tree in autumn, forced at last to quit their hold, and cast into
the stream—even these will disappear, and my name
and all I have done will be forgotten.

A recent event, half ludicrous and half melancholy, has led me into this train of reflection. On
going to Europe in 1851, I sent my books and papers
to a friend, to be kept till my return. Among them
was a large box of business documents—letters, accounts, receipts, bills paid, notes liquidated—comprising the transactions of several years, long since passed
away. Shortly after my return to New York—some
three months ago—in preparing to establish myself
and family here, I caused these things to be sent to
me. On opening the particular box just mentioned,
I found it a complete mass of shavings, shreds, fragments. My friend had put it carefully away in the
upper loft of his barn, and there it became converted
into a universal mouse-nest! The history of whole
generations of the mischievous little rogues was still
visible; beds, galleries, play-grounds, birth-places,
and even graves, were in a state of excellent preservation. Several wasted and shriveled forms of various sizes—the limbs curled up, the eyes extinct, the

teeth disclosed, the long, slender tails straight and stiffened—testified to the joys and sorrows of the races that had flourished here.

On exploring this mass of ruins, I discovered here and there a file of letters eaten through, the hollow cavity evidently having been the happy and innocent cradle of childhood, to these destroyers.   Sometimes I found a bed lined with paid bills, and sometimes the pathway of a gallery paved with liquidated accounts.   What a mass of thoughts, of feelings, cares, anxieties, were thus made the plunder of these thoughtless creatures!   In examining the papers, I found, for instance, letters from N. P. Willis, written five and twenty years ago, with only "Dear Sir" at the beginning and "Yours truly" at the end.   I found epistles of nearly equal antiquity signed N. Hawthorne, Catharine M. Sedgwick, Maria L. Child, Lydia H. Sigourney, Willis Gaylord Clark, Grenville Mellen, William L. Stone, J. G. C. Brainard—sometimes only the heart eaten out, and sometimes the whole body gone.

For all purposes of record, these papers were destroyed.   I was alone, for my family had not yet returned from Europe; it was the beginning of November, and I began to light my fire with these relics. For two whole days I pored over them, buried in the reflections which the reading of the fragments suggested.   Absorbed in this dreary occupation, I forgot the world without, and was only conscious of

bygone scenes which came up in review before me.
It was as if I had been in the tomb, and was reckoning with the past. How little was there in all that I
was thus called to remember—save of care, and struggle, and anxiety; and how were all the thoughts,
and feelings, and experiences, which seemed mountains in their day, leveled down to the merest grains
of dust! A note of hand—perchance of a thousand
dollars—what a history rose up in recollection as I
looked over its scarcely legible fragments: what
clouds of anxiety had its approaching day of maturity
cast over my mind! How had I been with a trembling heart to some bank-president*—he a god, and
I a craven worshiper—making my offering of some
other note for a discount, which might deliver me
from the wrath to come! With what anxiety have
I watched the lips of the oracle—for my fate was in
his hands! A simple monosyllable—yes or no—
might save or ruin me. What a history was in that
bit of paper—and yet it was destined only to serve
as stuffing for the beds of vermin! Such are the agonies, the hopes, and fears of the human heart, put
into the crucible of time!

---

* Let no one say that I speak irreverently of bank-presidents. One
of my best friends during many years of trial was Franklin Haven, president of the Merchants' Bank at Boston—who found it in his heart,
while administering his office with signal ability and success, to collect
a library, cultivate letters, learn languages, and cherish a respect for
literary men. It must be one among other sources of gratification,
arising from his liberal tastes, that he long enjoyed the confidence and
friendship of Daniel Webster.

I ought, no doubt, to have smiled at all this—but I confess it made me serious. Nor was it the most humiliating part of my reflections. I have been too familiar with care, conflict, disappointment, to mourn over them very deeply, now that they were passed; the seeming fatuity of such a mass of labors as these papers indicated, compared with their poor results— however it might humble, it could not distress me. But there were many things suggested by these letters, all in rags as they were, that caused positive humiliation. They revived in my mind the vexations, misunderstandings, controversies of other days; and now, reviewed in the calm light of time, I could discover the mistakes of judgment, of temper, of policy, that I had made. I turned back to my letter-book; I reviewed my correspondence—and I came to the conclusion that in almost every difficulty which had arisen in my path, even if others were wrong, I was not altogether right: in most cases, prudence, conciliation, condescension, might have averted these evils. Thus the thorns which had wounded me and others too, as it seemed, had generally sprung up from the seeds I had sown, or had thriven upon the culture my own hands had unwisely, perhaps unwittingly bestowed.

At first I felt disturbed at the ruin which had been wrought in these files of papers. Hesitating and doubtful, I consigned them one by one to the flames. At last the work was complete; all had perished, and the feathery ashes had leaped up in the strong draft of the chimney and disappeared forever. I felt a relief at last; I smiled at what had happened; I warmed my chill fingers over the embers; I felt that a load was off my shoulders. "At least"—said I in my heart—"these things are now past; my reckoning is completed, the account is balanced, the responsibilities of those bygone days are liquidated. Let me burden my bosom with them no more!" Alas, how fallacious my calculation! A few months only had passed, when I was called to contend with a formidable claim which came up from the midst of transactions, to which these extinct papers referred, and against which they constituted my defence. As it chanced, I was able to meet and repel it by documents which survived, but the event caused me deep reflection. I could not but remark that, however we may seek to cover our lives with forgetfulness, their records still exist, and these may come up against us when we have no vouchers to meet the charges which are thus presented. Who then will be our helper? "I will think of that—I will think of that!"

LETTER LII.

Speech at St. Albans—Lecture upon Ireland and the Irish—The Broad-street Riot—Burning the Charlestown Convent—My Political Career—A. H. Everett—The Fifteen Gallon Jug—The Harrison Campaign of 1840—Hard Cider and Log Cabins—Universal Bankruptcy—Election of Harrison—His Death—Consequences—Anecdotes—The Small Tail Movement—A Model Candidate—William Opp, or Shingling a Barn.

MY DEAR C******

The first public speech I ever made was at St. Albans, England, in June, 1832, at a grand celebration of the passage of the Reform Bill,* having accompanied thither Sir Francis Vincent, the represen-

---

* The Reform Bill was a popular measure, which swept away the rotten boroughs, and greatly extended the suffrage. After a long and violent struggle, it passed the House of Lords on the 4th of June, 1832, and received the royal sanction on the 7th. That day I arrived in Liverpool, amid a general feeling of joy and exhilaration. The Duke of Wellington had protested against the bill, though the king, William IV., and the ministry had favored it; in consequence, he was insulted by a mob, while passing on horseback through one of the streets of London, June 18th, the anniversary of the battle of Waterloo. A few days after this, there was a military review in Hyde Park, and King William being present, a large concource of people assembled; among them was the Duke of Wellington. After the review was over, he was encircled by an immense mass of persons, indignant at the insult he had received, and desirous of testifying their respect and affection. Most of them condemned his opposition to the reform bill, but this could not extinguish or diminish their sense of his great merit. I was present, and moved on at the side of the old veteran, mounted on horseback and dressed as a citizen—his hat off, and testifying by his looks, his sensibility to these spontaneous marks of regard. He was conducted to the gate of the park, near his residence—Apsley House, and there he bade adieu to his shouting escort.

On this occasion, as well as on others, I saw King William IV., a large,

tative in Parliament of that ancient borough. More than three thousand people, men, women, and children, gathered from the town and the vicinity, were feasted at a long table, set out in the principal street of the place. After this feast there were various sports, such as donkey races, climbing a greased pole, and the like. At six o'clock, about one hundred and fifty of the gentry and leading tradesmen and mechanics, sat down to a dinner, Sir Francis presiding. The President of the United States was toasted, and I was called upon to respond. Entirely taken by surprise, for not a word had been said to me upon the subject, I made a speech. I could never recall what I said: all I remember is a whirl of thoughts and emotions as I rose, occasional cries of " hear ! hear !" as I went on, and a generous clapping of hands as

---

red-faced man, with an amiable, though not very intellectual expression. He was, however, very popular, and in contrast to George IV., who was exceedingly disliked during the latter part of his reign, he was a favorite with the people, who gave him the title of the "patriot king."

As I shall have no other opportunity, I may as well complete my gallery of British sovereigns, by a brief notice of Queen Victoria, whom I have often seen. Of her character I have already spoken ; as to her personal appearance, all the world have a general idea of it, from the portraits in the shop-windows ; but truth compels me to declare that all the personal beauty in these representations, is ideal. Her majesty is really a very ordinary and rather coarse-looking woman—especially to one whose standard is founded upon the delicate and graceful type of American female beauty. When I say she is as good as she is homely, and is loved and cherished by her people according to her merits, I give strong testimony to her virtues. Prince Albert is a very handsome man, and it must be said that the large family of princes and princesses not only resemble him, strikingly, but share in his personal good looks. I have seen few more gratifying sights in England than this royal family —deserving and receiving the affection of the people.

I wound off. Whether this last was because I really made a good hit, or from another principle—

" The best of Graham's speeches was *his last*"—

I am totally unable to say.

My next public appearance was in a lecture at the Tremont Temple, in Boston—my subject being Ireland and the Irish. Although my discourse was written, and pretty well committed to memory, yet for several days before the time appointed for its delivery arrived—when I thought of my engagement, my heart rolled over with a heavy and sinking sensation. When the hour came, I went to the door of the room, but on seeing the throng of persons collected, I felt that my senses were deserting me : turning on my heel, I went out, and going to Smith, the apothecary —fortified myself with some peppermint lozenges. When I got back, the house was waiting with impatience. I was immediately introduced to the audience by Dr. Walter Channing, and stepping upon the platform, began. After the first sentence, I was perfectly at my ease. I need only add that I repeated the same lecture more than forty times.*

---

* About this time there was a strong popular excitement in Boston and the vicinity against the Irish, and especially the Roman Catholic religion. It manifested itself in what was called the "Broad-street Riot"—June 11, 1839—in which the Irish, who gathered in that quarter, were attacked, their houses rifled, their beds ripped open, and the furniture destroyed to the amount of two thousand dollars ; and also in burning down the Catholic Female Seminary—a species of Convent, where it was said there were evil doings—in the adjacent town of Charlestown. My purpose was to allay this excitement by presenting

In the autumn of 1836 there was a large evening party at Jamaica Plain, at the house of Mrs. G . . . ., the lady patroness of the village. . Among the notables present was Daniel Webster, whom I had frequently seen, but to whom I was now introduced for the first time. He spoke to me of many things, and at last of politics, suggesting that the impending presidential election involved most important questions, and he deemed it the duty of every man to reflect upon the subject, and to exert his influence as his conscience might dictate.

Since my residence in Massachusetts, a period of nearly eight years, I had been engrossed in my business, and had never even cast a vote. Just at this time I was appointed, without any suggestion of my own, one of the delegates to the whig convention to nominate a person to represent us—the Ninth Congressional District—in Congress. This was to take place at Medway, at the upper end of the district. I went accordingly, and on the first ballot, was the highest candidate, save one—Mr. Hastings, of Mendon. I declined of course, and he was unanimously nominated.

The canvass that ensued was a very animated one,

---

the history of the Irish people, with the adversities they had suffered, and the many amiable and agreeable traits that had survived, amid all the causes which had operated to degrade them. I believe that my efforts were not wholly fruitless : the lecture was encouraged, and when printed, received a commendatory notice even from the North American Review—written by T. C. Grattan, himself an Irishman.

Mr. Van Buren being the democratic candidate for the presidency. He was considered as the heir-apparent of the policy of Gen. Jackson, and had indeed promised, if elected, to walk in the footsteps of his illustrious predecessor. Without the personal popularity of that remarkable man, he became the target for all the hostility which his measures had excited. He was, however, elected, but to be overwhelmed with a whirlwind of discontent and opposition four years after.

The candidate for Congress in our district in opposition to Mr. Hastings, was Alexander H. Everett, who had been hitherto a conspicuous whig, and who had signalized himself by the ability and the bitterness of his attacks on Gen. Jackson and his administration. He had singled out Mr. Van Buren for especial vehemence of reproach, because, being Secretary of State at the time, Mr. Everett was superseded as Minister to Spain without the customary courtesy of an official note advising him of the appointment of his successor. To the amazement of the public in general and his friends in particular, on the 8th January, 1836, Mr. Everett delivered an oration before the democracy of Salem, in which—ignoring the most prominent portion of his political life—he came out with the warmest eulogies upon Gen. Jackson and his administration! About the first of May, the precise period when it was necessary, in order to render him eligible to Congress in the Ninth District, he took up his residence within its precincts, and, as was easily foreseen, was the democratic candidate for Congress.

The whig district committee, of which I was one, and Charles Bowen, Mr. Everett's publisher, another — issued a pamphlet, collating and contrasting Mr. Everett's two opinions of General Jackson's policy, and especially of Mr. Van Buren—the one flatly contradicting the other, and, in point of date, being but two or three years apart. This was circulated over the towns of the district. It was a terrible document, and Mr. Everett felt its force. One of them was left at his own door in the general distribution. This he took as a personal insult, and meeting Bowen, knocked him over the head with his umbrella. Bowen clutched him by the throat, and would have strangled him but for the timely interference of a bystander.

I had been among Mr. Everett's personal friends, but he now made me the object of special attack. A paper, then conducted by B. F. H . . . ., circulated a good deal in the district, and here, under the name of Peter Parley, I was severely lashed, not because I was a candidate for office, but because I was chairman of the whig district committee. I recollect that one day some rather scandalous thing came out against me in the editorial columns of this journal, and feeling very indignant, I went to see the editor. I did not know him personally, but from occasionally reading his paper, I had got the idea that he was a very monster of violence and vandalism. He was not at the office, but such was my irritation and impatience that I went to his house. I rang, and a beautiful black-eyed girl, some eight years old, came to the door. I asked if Mr. H. was in? "Mother," said the child, in a voice of silver, "is father at home?" At this moment another child, and still younger—its bullet-pate all over curls—came to the door. Then a mild and handsome woman came, and to my inquiry she said that her husband was out, but would return in a few moments.

My rage was quelled in an instant. "So," said I to myself, "these children call that man father, and this woman calls him husband. After all, he can not be such a monster as I have conceived him—with such a home." I turned on my heel and went away, my ill-humor having totally subsided. Some two years after, I told this anecdote to Mr. H., and we had a good-humored laugh over it. Both of us had learned to discriminate between political controversy and personal animosity.

The attacks made upon me during this canvass had an effect different from what was intended. I was compelled to take an active part in the election, and deeming the success of my party essential to my own defense, I naturally made more vigorous efforts for that object. Mr. Everett was largely defeated, and the whig candidate as largely triumphed. At the same time I was chosen a member of the legislature for Roxbury

—Jamaica Plain, where I resided, being a parish of that town. The next year I was a candidate for the senate, in competition with Mr. Everett,* and was elected. In this manner I was forced into politics, and was indebted mainly to opposition for my success.

During the ensuing session of the legislature, the winter of 1837–8, the famous "Fifteen Gallon Law" was passed—that is, a law prohibiting the sale of intoxicating liquors in less quantities than fifteen gallons. The county I represented was largely in favor of the measure, and I voted for it, though I was by no means insensible to the agitation it was certain to produce. I had determined not to be a candidate for

* Alexander H. Everett was a native of Massachusetts, and a younger brother of Edward Everett, born in 1790. He studied law in the office of John Quincy Adams at Boston, and in 1809 he accompanied him as attaché in his mission to Russia. Mr. Everett's political career clearly displays the influence of this early connection with Mr. Adams. Having remained at St. Petersburg two years, he returned to the United States by way of England, where he spent some months. He now took part with the democrats, and wrote against the Hartford Convention and in favor of the war. Soon after the peace he was appointed secretary of legation to Governor Eustis, in his mission to the Netherlands. Here he continued several years, the latter part of the time as chargé. On visiting Brussels in 1824, I called upon him, and was agreeably impressed by his fine person and dignified, though cold and distant, manners. In 1825, he was appointed by his former patron, then President of the United States, Minister to Spain, where he remained till he was dismissed by Gen. Jackson. Mr. Everett, having failed of success in his attempts to obtain office from the people of Massachusetts, was employed by the general government, first as Commissioner to Cuba, and afterward to China. He died a few months subsequent to his arrival at Canton—that is, in June, 1847. In literature, he held a respectable position, having written several works of learning and ability, and some essays of great elegance. In politics, unfortunately, he followed the example of Mr. Adams, in a sudden and startling change of his party, under circumstances which injured his character and impaired his usefulness.

re-election, and therefore considered myself free to engage in the discussion which preceded the next election, and which, of course, mainly turned upon this law. Among other things, I wrote a little pamphlet, entitled " Five Letters to my Neighbor Smith, touching the Fifteen Gallon Jug"—the main design of which was to persuade the people of Massachusetts to make the experiment, and see whether such a restraint upon the sale of intoxicating drinks would not be beneficial. This was published anonymously, and my intention was to have the authorship remain unknown. It, however, had an enormous sale—a hundred thousand copies—in the course of a few months, and curiosity soon guessed me out.

Now in the village of Jamaica Plain, I had a neighbor, though not by the name of Smith—a rich liquor dealer, who did his business in Boston—a very respectable man, but a vehement opposer of the Fifteen Gallon Law. As the election approached, the citizens of the State were drawn out in two camps, the men of Israel—those in favor of prohibition—on one side, and the Philistines—the men in favor of free liquor—on the other. My neighbor was rather the Goliath of his party—six cubits and a span, and all helmeted in brass—by which I mean that he was the wealthiest, the most respectable, and the most valiant of all the soldiers of the Philistine camp! He insisted that by "My Neighbor Smith," I meant him, and though I had said nothing disagreeable of that personage, but, on the contrary, had drawn his portrait in very amiable colors, he held that it was a malicious personal attack. In vain did I deny the charge, and point to the fact that the residence, character, qualities of my fictitious hero, were inapplicable to him. Anxious, like Mawworm, to be persecuted, he insisted upon it that he was persecuted.

At the county convention, which took place some two months prior to this election, I declined being a candidate. The members present, however, clearly discerning the gathering storm, refused to release me, and I was forced to accept the nomination. The election was to take place on Monday, in November. On the Saturday previous, there was issued in Boston a pamphlet, entitled the "Cracked Jug," a personal and political attack upon me, written with great malice and some ability. It was scattered like snow-flakes all over the county, and was, I suspect, the Sunday reading of all the tipplers and taverners of the county. The bar-room critics esteemed it superior to any thing which had appeared since the letters of Junius, and of course considered me as annihilated.

On Monday, election-day, my family were insulted in the streets of Jamaica Plain, and as I went into the town-hall to cast my vote, I heard abundance of gibes cast at me from beneath lowering beavers. The result was that there was no choice of senators in the county. The election, when the people had thus failed to fill their places, fell upon the legislature, and

I was chosen. The storm gradually passed away. The fifteen gallon law was repealed, but it nearly overturned the whig party in the State, which, being in the majority, was made responsible for it.* I deemed it necessary to reply to my Neighbor Smith's Cracked Jug, and he rejoined. What seemed at the time a deadly personal struggle, was ere long forgotten—neither party, I believe, carrying, in his character or his feelings, any of the scars inflicted during the battle. Both had in some sort triumphed—both

---

* In this election, Edward Everett, who had been governor of the State since 1835, and had administered the government with great success, was defeated by a single vote, Marcus Morton, a judge of the Supreme Court, and who had been the standing democratic candidate for many years without any seeming prospect of success, being chosen in his place. It is an interesting fact that such is the respect for the ballot, that among a hundred thousand votes, a majority of one was submitted to without question or opposition. A good anecdote is connected with this incident. Governor Morton with his party had opposed the encouragement of railroads by the use of the State credit. Nevertheless, while he was governor, the branch railroad, running through his own town, Taunton, to the thriving and enterprising town of New Bedford, was completed. This event was to be celebrated by a jubilee at the latter place, and the governor was invited to be present. The ceremonies were to commence at twelve o'clock, but at that hour his excellency had not arrived. The whole proceedings were delayed and embarrassed, until just as the clock was striking one, the governor appeared. J. H. Clifford, the witty and eloquent State's attorney, so universally known for his admirable management of the trial of Dr. Webster, the murderer of Parkman, and afterward himself governor of the State, immediately rose and offered the following sentiment—

Governor Morton, who always gets in by one!

It is needless to say that the sentiment, as well as the governor, was hailed with acclamation; and it may be stated incidentally, that, inasmuch as a railroad had passed through the governor's own town, he, and I may add his party, thenceforward were advocates of railroads. The next year (1840), in the whirlwind of the Harrison campaign, Governor Morton gave place to "honest John Davis," a name known and honored throughout the whole United States.

in some sort been beaten—both could, therefore, afford to return to the amicable relations of village neighborhood.

The presidential canvass of 1840 presented the most remarkable political spectacle which has ever been witnessed in the United States. Gen. Jackson's measures in regard to the currency and the tariff resulted in a tempest, which was precipitated upon the administration of his successor—Mr. Van Buren. Bankruptcy* and ruin had swept over the country, involving alike the rich and the poor, in their avalanche of miseries. In the autumn of this year, the whigs nominated William Henry Harrison, as the candidate for the presidency, in opposition to Mr. Van Buren. He

---

* The bankruptcies that took place in Boston from November 1, 1836, to May 12, 1837, were one hundred and sixty-eight—some of very large amount. About the same time, the crash in New York was terrific, bearing down many of the oldest and wealthiest houses in the city. In New Orleans, in May, 1837, the failures in two days, amounted to twenty-seven millions of dollars. A committee of New York, addressing the President, stated that the depreciation of real estate in that city was forty millions of dollars in six months! They also stated that two hundred and fifty failures took place in the space of two months; that the depreciation of local stocks was twenty millions, and the fall of merchandise thirty per cent. within the same period. Twenty thousand persons, dependent upon their labor, were said to be thrown out of employment, at the same time. The committee added, "the error of our rulers has produced a wider desolation than the pestilence which depopulated our streets, or the conflagration which laid them in ashes." Similar ruin visited every part of the Union—the people, corporations, States, being reduced to bankruptcy. It was estimated that half a million of persons were made bankrupt by reason of the various measures of the Jackson and Van Buren administrations. Hundreds and thousands of persons, destitute of employment, and almost destitute of bread, found relief in swelling the Harrison processions and gatherings, in singing patriotic songs, and shouting for reform.

had held various civil and military trusts, in which he had displayed courage, wisdom, and patriotism. His personal character was eminently winning to the people, being marked with benevolence and simplicity. He had long retired from public life, and for several years had lived as a farmer on the "North Bend" of the Ohio, near Cincinnati. The democrats ridiculed him as drinking hard cider and living in a log cabin. The masses, resenting this as coming from those who—having the government spoils—were rioting in the White House on champagne, took these gibes, and displayed them as their mottoes and symbols upon their banners. They gathered in barns, as was meet for the friends of the farmer of North Bend, using songs and speeches as flails, threshing his enemies with a will. The spirit spread over mountain and valley, and in every part of the country, men were seen leaving their customary employments to assemble in multitudinous conventions. Many of these gatherings numbered twenty thousand persons.

During this animated canvass, I was not a candidate for office, yet I took part in the great movement, and made about a hundred speeches in Massachusetts and Connecticut. Everybody, then, could make a speech,* and everybody could sing a song. Orators

---

* A speechmaker, in the western part of the State of Virginia during the canvass, has given us the following anecdote. He was holding forth upon the merits of Gen. Harrison, and especially upon his courage, tact, and success as a military commander. While in the midst of his discourse, a tall, gaunt man—who was probably a schoolmaster in

sprang up like mushrooms, and the gift of tongues was not more universal than the gift of music. Towns, cities, and villages, were enlivened with torch-light processions and with long, bannered phalanxes, shouting for the hero of Tippecanoe! The result of the election was such as might have been anticipated—a most emphatic rebuke by the people of that policy which had spread disaster and ruin over the country—by the election of Harrison, giving him two hundred and thirty-four votes, leaving only sixty for Van Buren! The death of Harrison, however, which took place thirty days after he had en-

---

those parts—arose from the crowd, and said, in a voice which penetrated the whole assembly—

"Mister—Mister! I want to ax you a question." To this the orator assented, and the man went on as follows:

"We are told, fellow-citizens, that Gineral Harrison is a mighty great gineral; but I say he's one of the very meanest sort of ginerals. We are told here to-night, that he defended himself bravely at Fort Meigs; but I tell you that on that occasion he was guilty of the *Small Tail Movement*, and I challenge the orator here present to deny it!"

The speaker declared his utter ignorance of what the intruder meant by "Small Tail Movement."

"I'll tell you," said the man; "I've got it here in black and white. Here is Grimshaw's History of the United States"—holding up the book —"and I'll read what it says: 'At this critical moment, Gen. Harrison executed a *novel* movement!' Does the gentleman deny that?"

"No : go on."

"Well, he executed a *novel* movement. Now, here's Johnson's dictionary"—taking the book out of his pocket and holding it up—"and here it says : 'NOVEL—*a small tale!*' And this was the kind of movement Gen. Harrison was guilty of. Now, I'm no soger, and don't know much of milentary tictacks—but this I do say : a man who, in the face of an enemy, is guilty of a *Small Tail Movement*, is not fit to be President of the United States, and he shan't have my vote!"

The relator of the anecdote says that it was quite impossible for him to overcome the effect of this speech, and we are left to conclude that the vote of that vicinity was given to Van Buren.

tered upon the duties of his office, with consequent divisions among the leading members of the whig party at Washington, deprived the country of nearly the whole benefit due to a change so emphatically pronounced by the voice of the people.

From this period, I have taken no active part in politics. In reviewing the past—while duly appreciating the honor conferred by the confidence bestowed upon me by the citizens who gave me their suffrages, I still regard my political career as an unprofitable, nay, an unhappy episode, alien to my literary position and pursuits, and every way injurious to my interests and my peace of mind. It gave me painful glimpses into the littleness, the selfishness, the utter charlatanism* of a large portion of those politicians who lead, or seem to lead, the van of parties; and who, pretending to be guided by patriotism, are

---

* For example : while I was in the Senate, and the Fifteen Gallon prohibitory law was under discussion, many people came into the lobby to listen to the debates, which excited great interest. Among these was a very respectable man from my own county of Norfolk. He asked me how I was going to vote. I replied that I had hardly made up my mind, and asked his opinion as to what I ought to do. He strongly enjoined it upon me to vote for the measure, saying that the public mind generally was prepared for it, and that in our county, especially, the sentiment in favor of it was overwhelming. And yet, at the next election this very man was a candidate against me, *on the ground that he was in favor of the repeal of the law.* He insisted that it was an extreme measure ; and although he was a temperance man—God forbid that he should be any thing else—he still thought it would do harm to the good cause ! Therefore he contended for its repeal, and the substitution of some milder course ! This man was a type of a very numerous class, whose principles fluctuate with the tide of public opinion, and the chances which arise in riding into office.

usually only riding issues, principles, platforms, as ser-
vile hobbies which may carry them into office. As
some compensation for this, it has also led me to a
conviction that the great mass of the people are governed by patriotic motives—though even with these
I often noted curious instances in which the public
interests were forgotten in a desire to achieve some
selfish or sinister end.*

---

* About these days, in a certain town not far from Boston, there was
a large family, of several generations, by the name of Cpp. At one of
the elections for members to represent the place in the General Court, it
appeared that among the votes distributed at the polls were a large
number for William Cpp, and the whole family were present, like
swarming bees, actively engaged in promoting his election. One of
them came up to the person who told me the story, and asked him to
vote for William. He naturally desired to know the reason for such a
measure, and the more particularly as he had never heard of any peculiar claims or qualifications, for the office in question, which the said
William possessed. "Well," said the Cpp, "I'll tell you how 'tis.
William's got a little behindhand, and wants to shingle his barn. This
will cost about a hundred dollars. Now, if he can go to the General
Court one session, he'll save a hundred dollars, and so, you see, he can
shingle his barn!" I have seen a good deal of this barn-shingling, even
in New England.

LETTER LIII.

International copyright—Mr. Dickens's Mission—His failure and his revenge—The Boston Convention—Inquiry into the basis of copyright—Founded in absolute justice—What is property?—Grounds upon which government protects property—History of copyright—Present state of copyright law—Policy the basis of local copyright law—International Copyright demanded by justice—Scheme for International Copyright with Great Britain—Reasons for it.

MY DEAR C******

In the winter of 1842, Mr. Charles Dickens arrived in Boston, where he was received with open arms. A complimentary dinner* was got up for him, and fine speeches were made by many of the first citizens, all in a strain of welcome to the distinguished stranger. The ball thus set in motion rolled over the country, and wherever Mr. Dickens went, he was received in a similar manner—that is, with welcome, with feasting, with compliments. I remember

---

* This dinner took place on the 1st of February, 1842. It was deemed a matter of sufficient importance to have the whole proceedings—speeches, letters, and toasts—reported, and published in a book. In the light of the present day, many of these—though sparkling with wit and good feeling—are rather calculated to make us regret the whole occasion. The strain of compliment was excessive; it set an example which, in this respect, was copied elsewhere—and the object of all this blunt adulation, as we now know, laughed at it in his sleeve at the time, and openly afterward, when he had got safe back to England. This should be a lesson to us for all future time. Foreigners will judge us somewhat according to their own standard. They regard all excessive demonstrations of the kind here alluded to as proceeding either from snobbery, or a desire to exhibit themselves, on the part of the leaders. They are, therefore, rather disgusted than conciliated by these overdone attentions.

to have seen him at one of the President's levees at Washington, there being many distinguished guests present—Washington Irving, the Earl of Carlisle, &c. These were totally neglected, while a crowd of curious and admiring followers, forming a gorgeous train of fair women and brave men, glittered behind Mr. and Mrs. Dickens. They were, in truth, the observed of all observers.

It appeared in the sequel, that the author of Pickwick had crossed the Atlantic for a double purpose— to write a book, and to obtain international copyright. In the first he succeeded, in the latter he failed. Since that time, however, the subject of international copyright has been a theme of animated discussion in this country, and has even been made a matter of diplomatic conference between Great Britain and the United States. A treaty has been, I believe, actually agreed upon between the agents of the two governments, for the purpose of establishing international copyright, but it has never been consummated; the subject was referred to the Senate, and there it has remained in suspense for the last two years.

You will, no doubt, expect me, in giving my recollections, to say something upon this subject. I cou l, indeed, hardly pass it over. I beg, however, instead of writing a new essay upon the subject, to copy what I wrote about three years ago, at the request of a senator in Congress, but which was never forwarded. With slight modifications, it was as follows:

INTERNATIONAL COPYRIGHT is altogether a modern idea. The conception appears to have been formed, or at least matured, about twenty years ago, when the subject of a revision of the law of copyright was before the British Parliament.* At that

---

* The first English parliamentary statute in regard to copyright, is that of Queen Anne, A. D. 1710, giving copyright to the author for twenty-one years, and if he be living at the expiration of this time, for the residue of his life. By subsequent acts, this period was extended to twenty-eight years. The movement above alluded to, which commenced in 1837, and in which Talfourd took a leading part, aimed at extending the protection to forty-two years, which, after about two years of consideration, became and remains the law of Great Britain on this subject. If the author shall have died before the expiration of the forty-two years, the heirs may have an extension of the time for seven years from the date of his death.

During the discussion which ensued, the subject of copyright was viewed in every possible light. A large number of petitions was presented to Parliament in behalf of increased protection; among them was one from Thomas Hood, in which the following passages occur:

"That your petitioner is the proprietor of certain copyrights, which the law treats as copyhold, but which in justice and equity should be his freehold. He cannot conceive how 'Hood's Own,' without a change in the title-deed as well as the title, can become 'Everybody's Own' hereafter.

"That cheap bread is as desirable and necessary as cheap books, but it hath not yet been thought just or expedient to ordain that after a certain number of crops, all cornfields shall become public property.

"That as a man's *hairs* belong to his head, so his head should belong to his *heirs;* whereas, on the contrary, your petitioner hath ascertained, by a nice calculation, that one of his principal copyrights will expire on the same day that his only son should come of age. The very law of nature protests against an unnatural law, which compels an author to write for everybody's posterity except his own."

Among these petitions is one from John Smith, bookseller of Glasgow, who says that about the year 1820, he wrote an essay in behalf of perpetual copyright, as demanded by justice and equity. I have seen no assertion of this principle prior to this date.

The earliest direct advocacy of international copyright that I have met with, is by John Neal, in the "Yankee," 1828.

period, the leading authors of Great Britain combined to obtain
an extension of the privileges of authorship. In the course of
the discussion, it was suggested that authors had an absolute
right to the use and behoof of the products of their labor—and,
consequently that British authors might claim copyright, not
only in Great Britain, but in all other countries. Having observed that the American market absorbed a very large amount
of popular English literature, an eager desire sprang up among
the principal British writers to annex the United States to Great
Britain in this matter of copyright. Accordingly, a general act
was passed by Parliament, to the effect that the privileges of the
copyright laws in the Three Kingdoms should be granted to all
countries which should extend to Great Britain the privileges of
their copyright laws. In this state of things, Mr. Dickens came
to America to consummate an international arrangement on
this subject. His writings being exceedingly popular here, it
was deemed that we could hardly resist a demand, regarded as
reasonable in itself, and urged by a universal favorite, who might
add to the requisitions of justice the argument and the feeling of
personal gratitude to himself.

As you are aware, Mr. Dickens's mission proved abortive, and
he took his revenge upon us by his Notes on America, in which
he plucked out the feathers of the American Eagle, and then
called it a very unclean bird. It is quite as easy to explain his
failure as his anger. The demand of International Copyright
was suddenly made and rudely enforced. Mr. Dickens brought
with him letters and petitions to individuals, to Congress, and to
the American people—from eminent British authors, some of
them couched in offensive terms, and demanding copyright on
the principle of absolute justice. In order to carry the point at a
blow, the whole British press burst upon us with the cry of thief,
robber, pirate, because we did precisely what was then and had
been done everywhere—we reprinted books not protected by
copyright! We resemble our ancestors, and do not like to be
bullied. The first effect, therefore, of this demand thus urged,

was resentment;* to this, reflection added apprehension. About this time there was a Convention in Boston of persons interested in the production of books : booksellers, printers, paper-makers, type-founders, book-binders, and others connected with the book manufacture. Their chief object was to petition Congress for a modification of the tariff—a reconstruction of the entire tariff system being then under consideration—so as to afford additional protection to their various interests ; but, alarmed at the demand of the British authors, they took the occasion to remonstrate, earnestly, against this proposed international compact.

Discussion of course followed, and has been continued to the present time. Authors in the United States have generally favored the measure; booksellers and publishers resisted it for a time, but many of them now favor it. The manufacturing interests connected with the book-trade have generally opposed it.

---

* Various circumstances conspired to aggravate this feeling. Mr. Carlyle compared our reprinting British books, without copyright, to Rob Roy's cattle-stealing; while at the same time British publishers had done and continued to do the same thing in respect to American books. The British government had indeed offered to go into a mutual interchange of copyright law, but in the mean time their publishers went on reprinting American works, without compensation, as before. Their position, therefore, was only this : *they would stop thieving when we would ; and the condition of their giving up what they held to be piracy, was a bargain in which they would get a thousand pounds, where we should obtain perhaps a hundred !* And still again : one of the last acts of Mr. Dickens, before he left England on his mission, was the reproduction in his " Pic-nic Papers" of the Charcoal Sketches of Joseph C. Neale, of Philadelphia, not only without copyright, but concealing the name of the author, and merely saying that " it was from an American source" —leaving the impression that it was originally written for his book ! In addition to all this, reflecting men saw that this claim of international copyright was chiefly based on principles of absolute and universal right, which were repudiated, not only by the local copyright law of Great Britain, but that of all other civilized countries. These were hindrances to the immediate passage of any international copyright in this country, because they created a prejudice against it as well as fear of its consequences. But these difficulties are now past, and it is time to consider the subject in a calmer and wiser spirit.

So far as the people at large are concerned, I believe that a great majority also take an unfavorable view of the scheme.

Now, where is the right of this question? What ought we to do? What ought our government to do?

If, as has been and is asserted, the abstract right of the author to the fruit of his labor is absolute, and if governments recognize the obligation to protect all abstract rights, then the question is settled: justice, morality, conscience, and usage require us to give what is asked. In this state of the case, we have no right to consider what is convenient or expedient; we must yield, whatever may be the consequence, to a claim which rests upon such foundations.

Let us then inquire, first, is this abstract claim of absolute right, on the part of authors, well founded; and, second, do governments recognize the obligation to protect and enforce all such abstract rights?

It is indisputable that the author has just as good, and in fact the same right, to the use and behoof of the fruit of his labor, as the farmer and the mechanic. In general, it may be said, that what a man makes is his, and that if it is valuable to him and useful to the community, he is entitled to protection in the possession of it. The farmer produces corn, the cabinet-maker a chair, the wheelwright a cart. The right of the producers of these things to use them, sell them, to control them, absolutely, according to their will and pleasure, is so familiar to the mind as to seem self-evident.

The author asks to be put upon the same footing. He writes a book; in its first stage it is in manuscript. To this his claim is undeniable; but it is a barren right, for in this condition it is unproductive of value. It consists of material signs— letters, words, sentences—conveying ideas. It is susceptible of being copied and multiplied by print, and these copies can be sold, and a reward for the author's labor may be thus realized. The value of the author's work, therefore—that is, the means of obtaining compensation for his labor—lies in selling copies of it;

and what he claims is the right, and the exclusive right, thus to copy his book—or, in other words, *copyright*. The commodity of the author, as well as the method of recompense, are different from those of the farmer, but his claim to the fruit of his labor rests on the same principle. The farmer's commodity is his corn, and he claims the right to control it; the author's commodity is copyright, and he claims the right to control it. The farmer's property is corporeal, the author's, incorporeal; but the right to the one is the same as that to the other. No ingenuity has been able to show any distinction whatever between the principle on which the author's copyright is founded, and that on which the farmer's right to his crop is founded.*

---

* Various suggestions have been urged against this; it has been said that the author's right consists of two things—his manuscript and his ideas; the one material, the other incorporeal. His claim to the first is valid, and remains with him, but he parts with the other by publication. This objection is fully answered by a suggestion already made, that it is only by the power to control the copying of his work, that an author can obtain compensation for his labor.

Another suggestion has been made by Mr. H. C. Carey, to this effect, that a book consists of two parts—facts and ideas, which he calls the body, and the language, which he considers the clothing. Now, he says, facts and ideas are old, and have become common property; they are like a public fountain—common to all—and for this portion of his work the author can claim no reward: all he can ask compensation for is the language in which he has clothed these facts and ideas.

Now there are two objections to this: one is as to the fact on which this theory is founded, and the other in respect to the inferences drawn from it. Mr. Carey has written some clever works on Political Economy; he may say that there is nothing new in these, and that his only merit lies in having put old ideas into new language, but the public will not agree with him in this. The public will not agree that there is nothing new in the facts and ideas of the histories of Prescott, Bancroft, and Macaulay; in the romances of Cooper and Scott; in the poetry of Wordsworth and Byron; in the delightful travels of Bayard Taylor, and the inspired song of Hiawatha. Indeed, there has probably been no age of the world, in which literature has been so highly original, in its facts and ideas, as during this particular portion of time, which Mr. Carey considers as wholly barren and unproductive of thought.

His inferences seem as illogical as his premises are unsound. If a man makes salt from the sea, which is a common reservoir, is that a reason

This is clear, but now comes the other question, does government hold itself bound to secure every abstract right? In general, it may be said that civilized governments protect property: to do this is in fact one of the chief functions of government What, then, is property?

In looking at learned authorities, we find two distinct definitions: one regards property as a certain inherent, abstract right; the other—the legal interpretation—a possession secured by law. This is, in fact, the general notion of property: it is ownership —the right to possess, enjoy, and control a thing, according to law. It has been asserted that property, even in this sense, rests upon an abstract right, and that the principle of this is, that what a man produces is his own. And yet, when we come to look at property, as it is distributed around us, we shall see that by far the larger portion of it, throughout the world, is not in the hands of the producers.* The present distribution of land, 'in all countries, has been made to a great extent by violence, by conquest, usurpation, robbery. The foundations of the great estates throughout Europe, is that of might and not of right. And hence it is impossible to base the idea of property, which government actually does protect, on abstract right. Indeed, in looking at the great authorities on this subject—Cicero, Seneca, Grotius, Montesquieu, Blackstone—the idea is traceable through them all, that *property is a possession according to law.* They all admit that there is such a thing as abstract right, natural right, and insist upon it, and upon this they base what is called

---

why he shall not have complete control of the product of his labor? A man has a right to the fruit of his toil; the public may and will fix a price upon his products, according to the amount of labor, skill, and capital bestowed, but they may not deny his right to them, or confiscate them or any portion of them. If a man uses old ideas, the public will reward him accordingly, but it is no argument in behalf of denying him the right to sell what he has produced, for what he can get.

* There are other modes of acquisition, as discovery, hunting, fishing, which carry the same right of possession, an actual production by manual labor.

common law; but yet no one lays down the principle that abstract right or natural right is either a complete and perfect right, in itself, or that it is essential to the idea of property.

Such is authority, as we find it, with the conservatives; there is a new school which denies this individual right, and claims every thing for society. Bentham lends some countenance to this: he denies altogether the doctrine of abstract right as the foundation of property, and insists that in its principle it is the gift of law. What the law gives a man is his: nothing else. Proudhon goes further, and declares that "property is robbery" —in other words, not only is the present distribution of property the result of artifice, fraud, violence, but, in the nature of things, property belongs to the community, and not to individuals. According to him, a man who appropriates a thing to his own use and behoof, robs society of what belongs to them.*

---

* Nothing is more opposed to man's instincts than the negation of his individuality, implied by Communisn. A man feels that he is a being, in himself; that he has the right to act and think independently, and of and for himself. It is this individuality, this independence, which gives value, meaning, responsibility, to his conduct. Communism overturns this idea: this regards mankind as grouped into societies, each society being like a tree, of which the individual person is but a leaf; or like the madrepores—a myriad of little insects living in the fibres of a sort of animal-plant rooted to a rock — all breathing, all nourished, all acting, with one nervous system, one consciousness, one sensorium. This is phalansterianism; here is the root of Proudhon's apothegm—as every thing belongs to society, it is robbery for an individual to appropriate any thing to himself. Nevertheless, in looking at civilized society, in all ages, we find something of this communism; that is to say, we find that mankind, living together in communities, give up at least a portion of their abstract rights, and agree to be governed by laws which take into view the highest good of all. Thus society is a compromise, in which both the principle of individual rights, according to Blackstone, and communal rights, according to Proudhon, are recognized. The rule was laid down nearly two thousand years ago— *Do to another as you would have another do to you,* and we are not likely to get a better. That regards man as a being of intellect, conscience, and responsibility, and bound to seek his own happiness by promoting the happiness of others. That is Christianity, which is above Communism — though the latter has certainly taught us, in some respects,

Thus vague, confused, and contradictory are the ideas which attach to the principle of property, even among the learned. The fact certainly is, that in its distribution very little respect has been paid to abstract rights. Nearly all laws, by all governments, from the Romans downward, have been based upon considerations of policy, or what they call the public good. Some deference has no doubt been paid to the common instincts of men, and as justice is one of these, the theory of abstract rights has been recognized; but yet how rarely have kings, and princes, and potentates molded their laws or their acts in obedience to the rights of man.*

---

better how to carry out the aims of Christianity. As a system, it is fallacious; as having developed instructive facts, it has contributed largely to civilization.

* The idea, so familiar now, that a man has a right to the fruit of his labor, is after all of rather modern date. So long as governments could compel men to plow, sow, reap, and thus feed society—by holding them in slavery—so long this was practiced all over Europe. A fundamental idea of the feudal system was, that the land-workers were *villains*, and belonged either to the soil or to the lord of the manor, and were transferred, in purchase and sale, as such. In England, in 1360, "the Statute of Laborers" punished workmen who left their usual abodes, by being branded in the foreheads with the letter F.; it required persons not worth forty shillings to dress in the coarsest russet cloth, and to be served once a day "with meat, fish, or the offal of other victuals." In 1461, the king of France ordained that "the good fat meat should be sold only to the rich, and the poor should be confined to the buying of lean and stinking meat."

During these periods, laborers who removed from place to place must have letters-patent granting them this privilege, or be put in the stocks. In 1406, children of poor parents must be brought up in the trade or calling of their parents. These absurd and iniquitous laws did not cease till the time of Charles II.; indeed, so late as 1775, the colliers of Scotland were considered as belonging to the collieries in which they had been accustomed to work!

The source of this system was a desire on the part of the capitalists to compel the laborers to work for them as slaves; it was the conspiracy of capital against free labor; nor was it abandoned until it was discovered by the governments that this system of compulsory or slave labor was unprofitable. Policy, necessity indeed, dictated the protection of labor, and it is in pursuance of this policy for some two hun-

If we look at the history of copyright, we shall see that authors have been, from the beginning, treated according to these principles of government—which shape all things with a primary and controlling regard to policy or the public good. Knowledge is power, and this was as well understood by the despotisms of the middle ages as it is by those of the present day. They sought therefore to keep it in their own hands. When the art of printing was discovered, some four centuries ago, and threatened to diffuse knowledge among the masses of mankind, the governments became alarmed, and immediately subjected it to supervision and restraint.

Hitherto the right of copy had been worthless to the author; his works could only be reproduced by the pen, and writing for publication was never practiced. Now a mighty change in his position had taken place: the press multiplied his works as by magic. A new idea, a new interest, was thus created. Mankind had already learned to prize books: a copy of the Bible would command the price of a farm. The power to multiply and vend copies of books, was seen at once to be a mighty power. This was naturally claimed by the printer as to old works, and as to new ones, by the author. Thus arose the notion of copyright—the direct result of the discovery of the art of printing. Yet it does not appear that this natural, abstract, absolute right of authors was at all regarded. They were, in fact, looked upon with suspicion; the press was deemed by governments as well as the people, a device of the devil. Kings, princes, and potentates, therefore, immediately seized upon it, not as a thing to be encouraged, but to be dreaded, watched, restrained. They suppressed whatever was offensive, and licensed only what was approved. This license was a grant of the sovereign, and it was the first form of actual copyright. It was founded on privilege alone. The licenses granted were during the lifetime of the author, or in perpetuity, according to the

---

dred years that the right of a man to the fruit of his labor has come to be regarded as an axiom in all truly civilized countries.

good pleasure of the king. These were deemed property, and were bought and sold as such. Thus copyright, in its origin, was the gift of government, or in other words, of the law.

This was the practice of all civilized governments. In France, the ordinance of Moulins, in 1566, a decree of Charles IX., in 1571, and a patent of Henry III., constituted the ancient law on this subject. The king always egarded himself as at liberty to grant or refuse the license, and to impose such conditions and restrictions as he pleased. Generally the right of the author was perpetual, unless he assigned it to a bookseller, in which case it was thrown open to the public at his death.

The early history of copyright was similar to this, in England. It was illegal to print a book without the government imprimatur. This continued to be the law until the time of Queen Anne, when a general law—1710—was passed, giving the author an interest of twenty-one years in his work.

Thus it appears that for nearly three hundred years after the origin of printing, copyright rested upon privilege granted by the crown. During the latter part of this period it had become familiar to the mind that the farmer and the mechanic were entitled to the use and behoof of the fruits of their labor. These held their right at common law ; but no such right was accorded to the author, nor was he permitted to print and sell his book, but by license, by privilege. Even so late as 1774, and long after the passage of a general act on this subject, the House of Lords, upon solemn adjudication, decided that the right of an author to his copy was the gift of the statute, and not one flowing from principles of justice. This doctrine has been substantially affirmed by the recent decision in England—that of the House of Lords reversing Lord Campbell's opinion.

And one thing more is to be regarded, that when more liberal ideas had begun to prevail—when the author was emancipated from the censorship, and his claims were based on a general law, and not on privilege—the perpetual right of copy was taken away, and it was limited to twenty-one years ! Since that time the number of authors has increased, and the press has risen into a mighty interest, and yet, to this day, in no country on the face of the globe, is the author placed on the footing of the farmer and the mechanic : these enjoy, by the common law, and the acknowledged principles of justice, the absolute right to their products, while the author has only a limited protection, dependent entirely upon the statute. The present copyright laws of all civilized governments are nearly the same; except in Great Britain, the United States, and a few other countries, the press is under a censorship, the governments suppressing what they choose : the protection given is generally for about forty-two years, after which time, the works of authors are thrown open to the public.

It is thus obvious that from the beginning to the present time, the fundamental idea of copyright in all countries has been and is, that protection in the enjoyment of it is the gift of statute law—of an enactment of government. Nowhere does it rest on abstract right ; in no country is the doctrine recognized that an author has the same right to the fruit of his labor, as has the farmer or the mechanic to the fruit of his. Material property everywhere is protected by common law : everywhere is literary property the gift of statute law.

And yet, International Copyright is urged by its advocates, upon principles of abstract justice, principles of common law, principles rejected in the practice of every civilized government on the face of the globe !

It is, I think, one of the great misfortunes of this question, that it has been thus placed on a false basis, and for this obvious reason, that where a claim rests on principles of justice, the denial of it implies moral obliquity. In such a case, hard names, harsh epithets, bitter feelings, are likely to be engendered : irritation rather than conviction is the result. Whatever may be the abstract right of the matter, the fact is, that all governments have hitherto founded local copyright on policy alone. When, therefore, the people of Great Britain ask us to enter into a partnership of international copyright, we very nat-urally test the question by the principles which govern them, as well as other civilized nations, in dealing with local copyright. If they call us pirates, because we reprint books not secured by copyright, it is inevitable that we retort by saying that they do the same. If they say, we are holier than thou, because we offer you international copyright, we are tempted to reply, that in the mean time your attitude is no better than this: you say to us——" We will stop stealing when you do, and not before!" If they insist that we are robbers in not giving copyright to Mr. Dickens, because no law protects him at the distance of three thousand miles——we reply that you are robbers, because you give no copyright to the heirs of Dryden, or Pope, or Swift, or Scott, or Chalmers, *nor do you give copyright to anybody after a lapse of about forty-two years.*

All this we have said, and with some show of reason, and yet I think, if the subject be fairly considered, it still leaves us in a false position. Though, it may be, and no doubt is, true that all governments have denied the claim of the author to an ab-solute and perpetual right of copy, still no civilized government has assumed that he has no claim. *All such governments have in fact given him a limited protection, and this has been gradual-ly extended with the increase of light and justice among mankind.*

If we scrutinize the motives of governments in the more recent legislation on this subject, we are at no loss to discover that these consist of two considerations: one is, that the au-thor, like every other laborer, is worthy of his hire; as he contributes to the public amusement and instruction, he is en-titled to compensation ; and the other is, that it is for the pub-lic good to encourage those who thus promote the happiness of society. Here, then, the right of the author to the fruit of his toil, is at least partially recognized; society admits it, but in un-dertaking to protect him in this right, society assumes the liberty of prescribing certain conditions in view of the public good. As it might tend to limit the beneficent influence of genius, and to restrain the full light of literature in after-times, to entail upon the author and upon his heirs, forever, the exclusive control of his works, it has been deemed best to limit that control to a period of about forty-two years.

This is, I think, the theory of local copyright law, among the most enlightened nations of the present day. Now, let us Americans consider our position in relation to living British authors. Their books come among us; they are published and circulated among us. You and I and everybody read them, and profit by them. And do we pay the author any thing for all this? Not a farthing; nay, when he asks us for compensation, we say to him, you live three thousand miles off, and the laws of honesty and morality do not extend so far!

Now, is that an honorable position? Is it an extenuation to say that other people do this? Does it not enhance the unfairness of our conduct to consider that the British government stands ready to remedy this wrong?

Let us suppose that two farmers live on opposite banks of a river; and it occasionally happens that their flocks and herds cross this stream, and stray into the neighboring grounds. What is the true principle of conduct between these two parties: is it that each shall confiscate to his own use the property that thus strays into his premises? That certainly is a barbarous practice. But suppose one says to the other, "I am satisfied this is wrong—let us come to an understanding: if you will restore to me such of my flocks and herds as stray into your grounds, I will do the same to you, and thus peace and justice will be established between us." And let us suppose that the other refuses this reasonable proposition, and says, "No; we have both been accustomed to this kind of stealing, and I am determined to continue it." Is not this farmer in the wrong?

And in our refusal to make British authors any compensation, are we not in the precise attitude of this ungenerous farmer?

The truth undoubtedly is, that in refusing International Copyright altogether, we are wrong: we cannot vindicate ourselves

16*

by saying that we follow the example of governments in their local copyright law, for although, as I have shown, *these do not recognize the absolute and perpetual claim of authors to the right of copy, yet all allow that they have a right to some compensation for their works.* Our wrong lies in this, that we deny all compensation. This, if it is voluntary, is not very far from robbery.

Now I do not believe the people of the United States are to be charged with this willful wrong: I am persuaded that the subject has not been well understood. It has appeared to them that a questionable right has been urged, as the means of forcing us into an unreasonable bargain. The general idea of the proposed international copyright, has been a mutual extension of the local copyright laws to the authors of the two countries; that is to say, the British author shall avail himself of our copyright law, and the American author shall avail himself of the British copyright law. In this sense, the two countries would be thrown into one market, available on the same terms to the authors, publishers, and booksellers of each.

For myself, it seems hardly worth while seriously to discuss such a scheme as this, and for the plain reason that it never can be enacted by our government, or if enacted, it would speedily be repealed by the people. This claim to international copyright, as I have said, has been urged in such a spirit by British writers, that the public mind here has been prejudiced against it. It may be remarked, that the discussion of the subject, by its advocates on this side of the water, has added to this feeling of aversion, a very extended conviction that sound policy forbids such a measure.

The grounds of objection to the scheme thus presented are various, but the most formidable one is this: *if the two countries thus become one market, it will be mainly to the advantage of the British publishers.* The British are a nation of sellers, not buyers. They preach free trade to all the world, but when a market is open, they rush in and engross it. It is free trade, but only to them. If we enter into the proposed partnership, they will buy few of our copyrights—those only of our first authors, and few books beyond samples. We may perhaps be permitted to purchase some copyrights of them, and publish the works here; but the general course of things will be this: the London publishers, having the control of British copyrights, will send their agents to New York, Boston, and Philadelphia, or they will here form branch establishments. *Through these we shall be supplied with Britsh books from British type, on British paper, and with British binding.*

This is the great objection, and if we are permitted to settle the question by a regard to the interests of the country, it is fatal to the scheme. Yet if we examine the case more closely we shall see that *the difficulty is not with British authors, but with British publishers; it is not against foreign copyright, but foreign booksellers.* We have an immense interest involved in the diversified industries employed in the manufacture of books, embracing thousands of families and millions of dollars. This naturally revolts at a scheme which threatens to paralyze, possibly to ruin it, in many of its branches. *But no difficulty of this nature could arise from an arrangement giving copyright to British authors, provided their works be published by American citizens, and be manufactured in the United States.* Nay, I think it is easy to suggest a plan of this nature, which would be beneficial to all the interests concerned—those of American authors as well as American book producers.

The scheme I propose is this:

1. An author, being a citizen of Great Britain, shall have copyright in the United States for a period not exceeding fourteen years, on the following conditions:

2. He shall give due notice, in the United States,* of his inten-

---

* This notice should be recorded in some one office, say in a register, kept for that purpose, at the Smithsonian Institute, so that by reference to this, any person may know if copyright of a work which is announced, is to be copyrighted, and also may see whether this requisition of the law has been complied with.

tion to secure his copyright in this country, three months before the publication of his book; and this shall be issued in the United States within thirty days after its publication in Great Britain.

3. His work shall be published by an American citizen, who shall lodge a certificate in the office of the clerk of the court of the district where he resides, stating in whose behalf the copyright is taken, and this shall be printed on the back of the titlepage.

4. The work shall be printed on American paper,* and the binding shall be wholly executed in the United States.

5. This privilege shall extend only to books, and not to periodicals.

6. The arrangement thus made in behalf of the British authors in America, to be extended to the American authors in Great Britain, and upon similar conditions.

This is a mere outline of the general principles of the scheme, by no means pretending to be complete in its details, or in the technical form of an enactment. To such a plan I can conceive no serious objections; not only the authors of this country, but the publishers would favor it. I am confident it would meet the feelings, views, and wishes of the country at large. My reasons for these views are briefly as follows:

1. This plan gives us the pledge of one of our own citizens, living among us, and responsible in his person, character, and position, for a faithful conformity to the law. Without meaning to cast invidious reflections, it may be said that it would be a strong temptation to any foreigner, under the circumstances— having various inducements and many facilities for imposing upon

---

* I had entertained the idea that it would be proper to prescribe the condition that the books should be from American type, and American engravings, but several eminent publishers think it will be for the advantage of all concerned, to permit the use of foreign stereotype plates, inasmuch as there will often be great economy in this. We shall soon send as many of these to England as we shall take from thence. On the whole, it is believed that the true interest of engravers and type-founders even, will be best consulted by letting the arrangement be made as here proposed.

us books manufactured at home—to commit this wrong; it is wise, therefore, to make provision against it. And besides, this plan, securing the publication in the hands of American citizens, will prevent the encouragement of British agencies and branch establishments, so much apprehended among us.

2. A still more important point is this—that, inasmuch as the books will be issued by American publishers, they are likely to conform to American ideas in respect to price. One of the apprehensions of international copyright, as heretofore proposed, has been that, inasmuch as British books would be to a great extent supplied to us by British publishers—either directly from London or through their agents here—that they would be in expensive and unsuitable forms, and at all events would come to us at exaggerated prices. The plan proposed evidently removes all reasonable grounds for these apprehensions.

3. It is true that British works, thus copyrighted and published in this country, would be somewhat dearer than they are now, without copyright. But how much? The common rate of copyright for an author, in the United States, is ten per cent. on the retail price. Let us double this, and we have twenty per cent. as the increased cost of the English book to the retail purchaser. Thus, instead of paying one dollar for a work by Dickens or Bulwer or Macaulay, we shall pay one dollar and twenty cents—half of this addition going to the author, and half to the publisher.*

4. Will the American reader object to this? Let him consider the reasons for it. In the first place, it is not pleasant, even though it be lawful, to read Mr. Dickens's book, and refuse to make him any return for the pleasure he has given us. In the absence of any arrangement by which we can render to him this compensation, we may lawfully peruse his works; but when a

---

* In many, and probably most cases, the increased cost of books would not be more than ten per cent., and for this reason, that we should import English stereotype plates, thus making a great saving in the outlay of capital. This would certainly be the case in works embellished with engravings.

plan is proposed to us, and that a reasonable plan, and compatible with the best interests of the country--then such refusal becomes voluntary and designed on our part, and is a willful taking without liberty, which is a plain definition of a very disreputable act.   No American can be gratified by such a state of things; on the contrary, I believe that every truly American heart would rejoice to make ample compensation to British authors, for the privilege of perusing their works.   The English language being our mother-tongue, we claim, as our birthright, free access to the great fountain of British literature, that has become the common property of the Anglo-Saxon race; *but we will not seek to rob the living author of the fruit of his genius or his toil.*

5. Besides, we Americans should remember two other things: first, that in consideration of the proposed arrangement in behalf of Mr. Dickens and his brethren of the British quill, our Irvings, Prescotts, Longfellows—the brotherhood of the American quill —would receive a corresponding compensation on the other side of the water.   This would be something.   Would it not be agreeable to every American thus to certify his gratitude to those of his countrymen who not only bestow upon him his most exalted sources of pleasure and improvement, but eminently contribute to the best interests of society?

But, in the second place, there are considerations infinitely higher than those of a personal nature.   Literature is at once a nation's glory and defence.*   Without its poets, orators, histo-

---

* "But are we to have—ought we have—a literature of our own?   I say yes—we not only are to have, but we ought to have such a thing. It would do more for us in a time of peace, than our battles on the sea or our battles on the land in a time of war.   In fact, authors are the militia of a country on the peace establishment; it is they that are to defend us and our firesides, the character of our country, our institutions, our hope and our faith, when they are assailed by the pen-militia of Europe.   And though—as I have had occasion to say before—it may be cheaper to buy our literature ready-made; cheaper, so far as the money goes, for the present age 'to import it in bales and hogsheads,' than to make it for ourselves, yet in the long run it would be sure to turn out otherwise.   It would be cheaper to buy soldiers ready-made,

rians—the liberty, the arts, the genius of Greece would have perished ages ago. These, being recorded and reflected by its literature, she became immortal—surviving even conquest and oppression and the lapse of time. Would you that our national glory should be exalted—that our liberty should be vindicated, extended, perpetuated? Would you that arts should arise and flourish among us: that a noble and lofty pitch be given to the national mind, and that a noble and lofty destiny achieved, at last be recorded, reflected, and carried down to after-times? Whoever has these aspirations, thereby pleads for a national literature.

To such I present the consideration that this, like every thing else, must live by encouragement. That literature is encouraged in this country, and, in some respects, as it is encouraged nowhere else, I admit. That we surpass all other nations in our periodical press, in our books for primary education, in the literature of the people, in manuals for the various arts and professions, is undeniable. Nor are we wholly delinquent in the higher forms of literature—science, history, romance, poetry, eloquence. In these things we have made a good beginning, but yet we are only at the threshold of what we can do and should do. In pro-

---

the mercenaries of Europe to defend us in time of war, than it would be to make soldiers of our fathers and brothers and sons—cheaper in the outset, perhaps; and yet, who would leave his country to the care of a military stranger—to the good faith of hired legions? Where would be the economy, after a few years? Even if it were cheaper to import our defenders, therefore, it would be safer and wiser to manufacture defenders; and if in a time of war, why not in a time of peace?

"But granting a native literature to be essential to our character—and who is there to deny it?—for books travel the earth over; books are read everywhere; and every great writer, every renowned author confers a dignity upon his native country, of more worth and of more durability than the warrior does—granting it, I say, to be so important for the character and safety of a people in time of peace, how are we to have it? By paying for it. By making it worth the while of our young men to give up a portion of their time to the study of writing, not as a boyish pastime—no, nor even as a trade, but as an art—a science."— *John Neal.*

portion as we love and honor our native land ; in proportion as we feel desirous that our country should be honored by the world—just in that proportion, by every logical consideration, should we feel bound to protect and encourage its literature.

And yet, our actual position is opposed to this. We allow untaxed British authorship to come into this country to the detriment, the discouragement of our own. American authors, in competition with British authors, are in the position that our manufacturers would be, if British merchandise were gratuitously distributed in our markets. The scheme herein proposed reme- dies these evils ; it taxes British literature, and thus—withhold- ing the encouragement it receives from being freely given away —prevents it from being a fatal and discouraging competitor of our own literature.

For these reasons, as well as others which need not be sug- gested, I believe the proposed scheme, or something resembling it, would be acceptable to the country. If the arrangement is made by treaty, it may be stipulated that it is to be terminated after five years, at the pleasure of either party. In its nature, therefore, it will be provisional and experimental, and may be terminated or modified, as time and experience may dictate. If it be said, either in this country or in Great Britain, that this is not all that may be desired, let us consider whether, as a prac- tical question, it is not as much as it is now possible to obtain. It is to be considered that International Copyright is a modern idea ; and it is not altogether unreasonable that in dealing with it—especially in this country, where so many and so important interests are at stake—we should follow the cautious steps of the mother country in granting copyright to her own citizens, which at first was limited to twenty-one years.

Such are the views I had formed three years ago. I was then in Europe ; since my return, I am con- firmed in them by various considerations, and especially by finding that some enlightened publishers, who have hitherto doubted the expediency of international copyright, in view of some such arrangement as is here suggested, are now earnestly in favor of it. Why, then, should we not try it?

One thing is certain—the subject will never rest, until International Copyright is adopted, in some form or other. It is based on the same abstract but still manifest right, by which every laborer claims the use and behoof of the fruits of his toil; admitting that governments may regulate and modify these rights, according to the public good, still they may not altogether annihilate them. I have taken the ground that governments, in local copyright laws, deny the absolute and perpetual claim; they refuse to base their protection on common law; but still one thing is to be considered, and that is, that *local copyright everywhere does in fact make some compensation to the author*, and thus substantially admits his claim. We, who refuse international copyright, must reflect that so far as we are concerned, *we deny all compensation to the foreign author*, and thus are manifestly in the wrong.* We may pretend, indeed, that local copy-

---

* In France, copyright was regulated by royal decrees, till 1789, when a general law was passed, establishing the old practice, which gave the author copyright in perpetuity, except that in case of sale to a publisher, it terminated at his death. At present, by acts of 1793 and 1810, the author has copyright during his life, and then his children twenty years after. If there are no children, the actual heirs enjoy it for ten years.

The copyright law of England is stated elsewhere.

In Holland and Belgium, the copyright laws of France are adopted.

right affords all needful encouragement; but is it fair
for us, refusing ourselves to contribute to this, to take
to our use and behoof the articles for which we thus
refuse to pay—and that against the protest of those
whose toil has produced them? Is that honorable—
is it fair play?

The law is similar in Prussia, and also in the Zollverein, the heirs enjoying the right, however, for thirty instead of twenty years, after the
author's decease.

In Russia, the law gives copyright during the lifetime of the author,
and twenty-five years after. An additional period of ten years is granted, if an edition is published within five years before the expiration of
the copyright.

Sardinia adopted the French law in 1846.

In Portugal the law is similar to that of Prussia.

Spain formerly gave unlimited copyright, but often to religious communities, and not to the author. At present, the author has copyright
during his lifetime, and his heirs fifty years after his death.

Prussia was the first nation to pass a general act, offering International
Copyright to all countries that would reciprocate the same. This was
incorporated into her copyright law of 1837. England followed this
example in 1838.

Treaties for International Copyright have been entered into between
Austria, Sardinia, and Tessin, 1840; Prussia and England, 1846; France,
Sardinia, Hanover, England, and Portugal, in 1846, 1850, and 1851.

France has added a law prohibiting the counterfeiting of foreign books
and works of art, without requiring reciprocal stipulations from other
countries.

It is to be remarked, that International Copyright between these European States, generally having different languages, and trifling interests
at stake, is very easy and natural; it is practically a very different matter
between England and the United States, which have the same language,
and immense industrial arts, trades, and professions, directly connected
with the subject. There may, indeed, be as good a reason why such an
agreement should exist between Great Britain and the United States as
between Great Britain and France, but still, as it involves infinitely
greater consequences, it is reasonable to treat the subject with more
mature and careful consideration.

LETTER LIV.

Statistics of the Book Trade—Its Extension—The Relative Increase of American Literature, as compared with British Literature.

My dear C*******

In my last letter I presented to you some suggestions respecting International Copyright. In doing this I have naturally gathered up my recollections of the book trade in the United States for the last forty years, and compared the past with the present. I am so impressed with certain prominent and remarkable results and inferences, that I deem it proper to present them to you. These may be grouped under two general heads :

1. The great extension of the book production in the United States.

2. The large and increasing relative proportion of American works.

Unfortunately we have no official resources for exact statistics upon this subject. The general fact of a vast development in all the branches of industry connected with the press, is palpable to all persons having any knowledge on the subject ; but the details upon which this is founded, and the precise degree of increase, are to a considerable extent matters of conjecture. Nevertheless, there are some facts within our reach, and by the grouping of these, we may approach the results we seek, with a sufficient degree of certainty, for all practical purposes.

I. *As to the extension of the book manufacture.*

THE BOOK PRODUCTION OR MANUFACTURE IN 1820.

Let us go back to the year 1820, and endeavor to estimate the gross amount of this trade in the United States at that period. The following statement, it is supposed, may approach the truth:

Amount of books manufactured and sold in the United States in 1820.

School books	$750,000
Classical books	250,000
Theological books	150,000
Law books	200,000
Medical books	150,000
All others	1,000,000
Gross amount	$2,500,000

☞ The space between 1820 and 1830 may be considered as the period in which our national literature was founded; it was the age in which Irving, Cooper, Bryant, Halleck, Paulding, J. R. Drake, John Neal, Brainard, Percival, Hillhouse, and others, redeemed the country from the sneer that nobody read American books. During this period we began to have confidence in American genius, and to dream of literary ambition. The North American Review, already established, kept on its steady way, and other attempts were made in behalf of periodical literature, but with little success.

THE BOOK MANUFACTURE IN 1830.

If we take 1830 as a period for estimating the product of the book manufacture, we suppose it may stand thus:

School books	$1,100,000
Classical books	350,000
Theological books	250,000
Law books	300,000
Medical books	200,000
All others	1,300,000
Gross amount	$3,500,000

☞ This shows an increase of production of forty per cent. in ten years.

From 1830 to 1840 was an era of great and positive development, and the foundation of a still more active era of progress and expansion in the book trade. It may be considered as the point at which our literature became established in our own confidence, and to some degree, in the respect of the world. During this period, the following names either first appeared or became eminently conspicuous :

In History—Prescott, Sparks, Bancroft, Irving.

In Mathematics—Day, Farrar, and the self-taught Bowditch, whose translation of the Méchanique Celeste of Laplace, is admitted to be superior to the original, by reason of its happy illustrations and added discoveries.

In Philology—Webster, whose quarto Dictionary is now admitted by high British authority to take precedence of all others.

In Theology—Bush, Barnes, Norton, Stuart, Woods, Jenks, Robinson, Spring, A. Alexander, Durbin, Hodge, Bangs, Olin, L. Beecher, Tyng, Thornwell.

In Political Economy, Philosophy, &c.—H. C. Carey, Colton, Lieber, Wayland, Upham, Tucker.

In General Science, Natural History, &c.—Silliman, Henry, Morton, Rogers, Redfield, Espy, Audubon, Olmsted, Dana, Gray, Nuttall, Burritt.

In Jurisprudence, International Law, &c.—Kent, Story, Wheaton, Duer, Cowen.

In Medicine and Surgery—Dunglison, N. Smith, N. R. Smith, Bigelow, Dewees, Beck, Doane, Wood, Mott, Eberle.

In Travels, Geography, &c.—Schoolcraft, Ruschenberger, Stephens, Farnham.

In Essay and Criticism—Channing, the two Everetts, Emerson.

In Fiction—Cooper, Ware, Simms, Bird, Kennedy, Poe, Miss Sedgwick, Mrs. Child, Miss Leslie, Fay, Hoffman.

In Poetry—Bryant, Sprague, Pierpont, Dana, Willis, Longfellow, Whittier, Mrs. Sigourney, Mellen, Morris, McLellan, Prentice, Benjamin.

In Educational and Church Music—Lowell Mason, probably the most successful author in the United States.

☞ This period is to be noted for the effective labors of W. C. Woodbridge, James G. Carter, Horace Mann, Henry Barnard, and others, in behalf of common-school education, and an immense improvement in school-books, both in literary and mechanical execution, by means of which geography, grammar, and history, very extensively became common school studies. During the same period, history, chemistry, natural philosophy, moral philosophy, rhetoric, geology, were all popularized, and introduced into the public high-schools. The change in school-books during this period amounted to a revolution, and resulted in that amazing expansion in their use and distribution, which now marks the subject of education in the United States. This also was the era of Annuals, which added largely to the amount of the book-trade.

This is the era of the establishment of the Penny Press, which is at once a sign and instrument of progress. Its home is in the midst of business, education, literature—in the very breathing and heart-beating of life and action; and it gives impulse and vigor to all these interests. So powerful an instrument must sometimes seem to produce evil, but on the whole it must be regarded as a great civilizer. We may advert to a single illustration of its expanding influences : the three principal penny papers of New York, at the present day, 1856—the Herald, Tribune, and Times—each of them is a political paper, with political opinions, yet each treats politics as a matter of general information, and publishes the principal doings and documents of all parties. This is not so in any country where the penny press does not exist.

This is also the era in which monthly and semi-mothly Magazines began to live and thrive among us. Among the most noted, are the Knickerbocker, Merchants' Magazine, Graham's, Southern Literary Messenger, all continued to the present time, with others which have ceased to exist.

THE BOOK MANUFACTURE IN 1840.

The book production for 1840 may be estimated as follows :*

School books	$2,000,000
Classical books	550,000
Theological books	800,000
Law books	400,000
Medical books	250,000
All others	2,000,000
Gross amount	$5,500,000

☞ This calculation shows an increase of about sixty per cent. for ten years.

From 1840 to 1850 was a period of general prosperity in the country, and the full impulse of the preceding period continued through this.

American authorship was more appreciated at home and abroad—a circumstance greatly due to the enlightened and patriotic labors of Dr. Griswold, who may be considered as among the first and most influential of our authors in cultivating a respect for our own literature. New American publications became very numerous during this period; the style of book manufacture was greatly improved; numerous magazines were

---

* The following is a table of estimates of the various Industrial Interests connected with the press, presented to Congress in behalf of the Convention which met at Boston in 1842. Mr. Tileston, of Dorchester, and myself were the committee appointed to proceed to Washington to enforce the wishes of the petitioners, founded upon this exhibition. Mr. Fillmore, the chairman of the Committee of Ways and Means, then

founded; the penny press was diffused, and became more elevated in its character and more enlarged in its scope—several of the editors connected with it marking the age by their sagacity, vigor, and largeness of view.

This era is also marked by the production of numerous works richly illustrated by steel and wood engravings. The Harpers entered upon the publication of handsome editions of books in all departments of literature, many of them embellished by fine wood engravings; the Appletons of New York, Butler of Philadelphia, and others, gave to the public those luxurious volumes, successors of the annuals, already alluded to. The success of these rich and costly works signalizes the advance of public taste. Putnam gives us Washington Irving's works in a guise suited to their excellence, and a little later, the Homes of American Authors, also in a style suited to the subject. About the same time the writers for the Knickerbocker present its veteran editor with a Memorial —an exquisite volume—as much a sign of the public appreciation as their own.

The immense development of the school-book trade is a feature of this era; we now see editions of five, ten, twenty thousand copies of geographies, grammars, spelling-books, readers. Spelling-books count by millions, and geographies by hundreds of thousands. The mechanical character of these works is changed; they have cast their brown-paper slough, and appear in the costly dress of fine paper, fine illustrations, and good binding. Twenty thousand dollars are paid for the getting up of a school geography!

---

charged with framing the Tariff bill which soon after passed into a law, gave us a patient hearing, and the views of the petitioners were duly considered and acceded to.

EMPLOYMENTS, &c.	No. of persons employed.	Amount of business annually.	No. of books, &c., annually produced.	Capital invested.
Publishing and Bookselling.	4,000	$7,000,000	12,000,000 vols	4,000,000
Periodicals, exclusive of Newspapers	....	500,000	3,000,000 Nos.	200,000
Bookbinders	3,060	1,646,000	....	800,000
Type & Stereotype Founders	700	426,000	. ...	400,000
Engraving, Wood, Steel, & Copper, includ. Designs	500	250,000		
Plate Printing	500	400,000	{ 300,000,000 sheets ann'y.	2,200,000
Newspapers	....	6,000,000		
Printing, including Newspapers	25,088	7,126,912	....	3,000,000
Paper of all kinds used for printing	8,000	5,000,000	....	5,000,000

☞ At the present time, 1856, it will be safe to double most of these estimates, to represent the present state of the same interests.

Most of the authors which we have named as belonging to the preceding era, shed their luster upon this. Among those who now first entered the lists, we may name—

In History—Hildreth, Ingersoll, Eliot, Hawks, T. Irving, Frost, Headley, Abbott, Brodhead, Mrs. Willard, Lossing, C. A. Goodrich, and soon after, Motley, who, at the very outset, has attained a high reputation. In political history—Young, Benton.

In Jurisprudence—Greenleaf, George T. Curtis, W. W. Story, and soon after, B. R. Curtis, T. Parsons, Edwards, Dayton, Dean, E. F. Smith, Dunlap, Waterman, Willard.

Mathematics—Pierce, Davies, Courtenay, Millington, Hackley, Loomis.

Philology—Prof. C. A. Goodrich, editor of Webster's Dictionary; Worcester, Pickering.

Political Economy, Philosophy, &c.—E. P. Smith, Mahan, Tappan, Hickok.

Theology—Bushnell, Hawes, Cheever, Wainwright, Wines, Huntington, Spring, Wisner, J. A. Alexander, Taylor, McClintock, E. Beecher, Williams, Stevens, Fisk, Dowling, Cross, Conant, Choules.

Medicine and Surgery—J. C. Warren, Greene, Parker, Bartlett, Clymer, Drake, Pancoast, H. H. Smith, Harris, Carson; and since 1850, Bedford, Watson, Gross, Flint, Lee, Blackman.

General Science, Natural History, Geography, &c.—Agassiz and Guyot—whom we now claim as citizens; with Bartlett, Squiers, Maury, Mitchell, J. D. Dana, Baird, Hall, Emmons, Mahan, D. A. Wells, Wood, St. John, Wilkes—the latter giving us a new continent by discovery; Lynch, who has furnished the best account of the Dead Sea and its environs; and, we may add, Com. Perry, who introduces us to Japan.

In Classical Literature—Leverett, Anthon, Andrews, Gould, Brooks, McClintock, Owen, Kendrick, Sophocles, Johnson, Thacher.

Essay and Criticism—Prescott, Chapin, Giles, Sprague, Hague, Charles Sumner, Whipple, Palfrey, Winthrop, Beecher, Cheever, Milburn.

Travels, Geography, &c.—Catlin, Stephens, Curtis, Bayard Taylor, Bartlett, Willis, Southgate, Robinson, Olin, Kendall, Fremont, Kidder, Parkman, Coggshall, Colton.

In light, racy writing, full of life-pictures and luscious fancies—Curtis, Cozzens, Mitchell, Bayard Taylor, Willis, Matthews, Baldwin.

In Miscellaneous Literature—Ticknor, Tuckerman, Longfellow, Griswold, Mrs. Child, Hall, Headley, Mrs. Kirkland, Grace Greenwood, Mrs. Ellet, Mrs. Hale, Seba Smith; and in 1856, E. A. and G. L. Duyckinck.

In Fiction—Melville, Kimball, Mayo, Mrs. Stowe, Miss Mackintosh, Alice Carey, Elizabeth Warner, Mrs. Southworth, Miss Wormley, Mrs. Oakes Smith, Minnie Myrtle.

In Poetry—Holmes, Lowell, Buchanan Read, Bayard Taylor, Saxe, Epes Sargent, W. R. Wallace, T. W. Parsons, Cranch, Fields.

Books of Practical Utility—Miss Catharine Beecher, Miss Leslie, Fanny Fern, G. P. Putnam, J. L. Blake, Downing, Haven, and many others.

It is not possible to give all the names of those who have distinguished themselves in Educational Manuals; among them, however, are the following: Mitchell, Olney, Smith, Morse, Willard, Monteith, McNally, Fitch, Miss Cornell, Mrs. Willard, in School Geographies; in Readers and Spellers, Emerson, Parker, Town, Saunders, Swan, Sargent, Tower, McGuffie, Cobb, Lovell; in Grammars, Kirkham, Clark, Brown, R. C. Smith, Weld, Wells, Dalton, Greene, Pineo; in Arithmetics, Emerson, Davies, Greenleaf, Thomson, Stoddard, R. C. Smith, Adams; in various other works, Hooker, Gallaudet, Comstock, Burritt, Mrs. Phelps, Page, Mansfield, H. N. Day, Boyd, Miss Dwight, Darley, Gillespie; in Maps and Atlases, Mitchell, J. H. Colton. The latter has in progress, and nearly completed, the best General Atlas ever published in any country.

THE BOOK MANUFACTURE IN 1850.

The era of 1850 affords the following estimates:

School books	$5,500,000
Classical books	1,000,000
Theological books	500,000
Law books	700,000
Medical books	400,000
All other books	4,400,000
Gross amount	$12,500,000

This shows an advance of one hundred and twenty-five per cent. in ten years.

From 1850 to 1856, the momentum of preceding periods was reinforced by the quickening impulse of a host of female writers, whose success presents a marked phenomenon in the history of our literature at this time.

To this era belongs Mrs. Stowe, who, so far as the sale of her works is concerned, may be considered the most successful woman-writer ever known; Miss Warner, Fanny Fern, Mrs. Stephens, Miss Cummings, Marion Harland (Miss Hawes), and others, produce books of which twenty, thirty, forty, fifty thousand are sold in a year.

About this time is the successful era of monthly magazines, as Harpers', Putnam's, &c. The former outstrips all other works of the kind yet published, issuing one hundred and seventy thousand numbers a month!

The last ten years have been noted for the production of local, state, town, and city histories, as well as genealogical histories. Many of these are of great interest, going back to the lights and shadows of colonial periods. Here are the future resources of historic poetry and romance, of painting and sculpture.

During this period there have also been produced numerous valuable and costly works by the General Government, relating to navigation, geography, &c., and also local, State surveys, under State patronage, of great interest and utility.

During this period, pictorial-sheet literature is brought to a climax in every form, up to the blanket-folio. This is the age of vigorous advertising, by means of which "fifty thousand copies are sold before a book is printed."

This is also the millennial era of Spiritual Literature, which has now its periodicals, its presses, and its libraries.

It is also the climax of the Thrilling, Agonizing Literature, and which, by the way, is thus rather wickedly mocked by the poet of the "Fruit Festival" already alluded to:

> "This is the new 'Sensation' Book—
> A work of so much force
> The first edition all blew up,
> And smashed a cart and horse!
> A friend who read the manuscript
> Without sufficient care,
> Was torn to rags, although he had
> Six cables round his hair!
>
> "'The Eggs of Thought' I'll recommend
> As very thrilling lays;
> Some poets poach—but here is one
> That all the papers praise.
> The school commissioners out West
> Have ordered seventy tons,
> That widely they may be dispersed
> Among their setting suns!
>
> "And here's a most Astounding Tale—
> A volume full of fire;
> The author's name is known to fame—
> Stupendous Stubbs, Esquire!
> And here's 'The Howling Ditch of Crime,'
> By A. Sapphira Stress:
> Two hundred men fell dead last night
> A working at the press!"

THE BOOK MANUFACTURE IN 1856.

The amount of the production of our American book-trade at this time—that is, for the year 1856—may be estimated at about sixteen millions of dollars; and the annual increase of this interest at about a million of dollars a year.

This sum may be distributed as follows:

Produced in New York city in the year 1856.............. $6,000,000
In other parts of the State—Albany, Schenectady, Utica, Syracuse, Cazenovia, Ithaca, Rochester, Auburn, Buffalo, &c.   600,000
In Boston.. 2,500,000
In other New England towns—New Haven, Hartford, Providence, Springfield, Northampton, Salem, Newburyport, Portland, Keene, &c....................................   600,000
In Philadelphia............... 3,400,000

[The operations of the book-trade in this city are enormous, but a large amount of the books distributed from this point are manufactured elsewhere. The house of Lippincott, Grambo & Co. does a larger book business than any other in the world. They are very extensive publishers, but they often order whole editions of other houses.]

In Cincinnati.. 1,300,000

[This city is less than a century old, from its first log-cabin; yet an excellent authority says: "In 1850 this western city, with a population of 116,000, has twelve publishing houses, which give employment to seven hundred people. The value of books and periodicals published here is $1,250,000 a year. I consider that there is more reading of books in Ohio than in Germany. The chief works in demand are religious and educational."*]

In the Northwestern States—Detroit, Chicago, Milwaukee...   100,000
In the District of Columbia—by the Government..........   750,000
The Southern and Southwestern States consume a considerable amount of books, though small in comparison to the rest of the United States. Their production of books and of literature is still less in proportion. Baltimore, Richmond, Charleston, Columbus, Savannah, Macon, Mobile, New Orleans, St. Louis, and Louisville, are considerable markets for the sale of books, and a few works are published in some of these places. In Baltimore and Louisville, the publishing interest is extensive. We may estimate the whole book production in this section at   750,000

Total in the United States............................$16,000,000

You will bear in mind that this estimate, throughout, regards only books manufactured in the United States; the amount of books imported is probably about a million of dollars a year. If so, the whole consumption of books in this country is probably not far from seventeen millions of dollars annually!

---

* See the "Bibliographical Guide to American Literature" of Messrs. Trübner & Co., London—an interesting work, abounding in curious and startling yet gratifying facts, in respect to the literature of the United States.

Now, my dear C...., you must remember that the details of these estimates are not founded upon precise official statistics, but are only inferences from general facts tolerably well established. Considering these as estimates merely, they may still be such probable approximations to the truth as to give us a general view of the amount and movement of the book production of the United States. This, of course, leaves out the newspaper and periodical press, which circulates annually six millions of copies, and five hundred millions of separate numbers! I do not dilate upon the fact that we have two hundred colleges, a hundred thousand elementary schools, fifty theological seminaries, twenty law schools, forty medical schools, and that our public and school libraries number five millions of volumes;* yet these are to be taken in connection with the tabular views I have given. Then, I ask, have we not a literature?

I now invite your attention to another topic:

II. *The large and increasing proportion of American productions—that is, productions of American mind—in the books published in the United States.*

Taking, as before, certain prominent facts as the basis of calculation, we arrive at the following conclusions:

In 1820, the book manufacture of the United States was based upon works of which thirty per cent. was the production of American authors, and seventy per cent. of British authors.

---

* See Trübner's Bibliographical Guide, before quoted, page xxvii. It is there estimated that in 1860 the public libraries will amount to ten millions of volumes.

☞ From 1820 to 1830, as we have seen, a considerable impulse was given to American literature, which now began sensibly to diminish the relative proportion of British works among us.

In 1830, the book production of the United States embraced forty per cent. of American works, and sixty per cent. of British works.

☞ From 1830 to 1840, still greater activity prevailed in American authorship, and school-books were extensively multiplied ; we shall see, therefore, during this period, a corresponding relative increase of American works.

In 1840, we estimate the proportion of American works to be fifty-five per cent., and that of British works forty-five per cent.

☞ From 1840 to 1850 has been the most thriving era of American literature, and during this ten years we find that the balance has turned largely in favor of American works.

In 1850, we estimate the proportion of American works to be seventy per cent. and of British works to be thirty per cent.

In 1856, it is probable that the proportion of American works is eighty per cent. and that of British books twenty per cent.

☞ It will be understood that we here speak of all new editions of every kind: of the works of living British authors, the proportion is much less than twenty per-cent.

Some general observations should be made by way of explanation.

1. School-books constitute a very large proportion of the book product of the United States ; probably thirty to forty per cent. of the whole. Sixty years ago we used English readers, spelling-books, and arithmetics ; forty years ago we used English books adapted to our wants. Now our school-books are superior to those of all other countries, and are wholly by American authors. More than a million of Webster's Spelling-books are published every year. We produce annually more school-books than the whole continent of Europe !

2. The classical works in use, formerly altogether British, are now seven-eighths American.

3. The elementary treatises on law, medicine, theology, and science, are mostly American.

4. The dictionaries in general use are American.

5. The popular reading of the masses is three-fourths American.

6. Three-fourths of the new novels and romances are American.

7. The new foreign literature, reproduced among us, consists mainly of works of science, philosophy, jurisprudence, medicine and surgery, divinity, criticism, and general literature. Thirty per cent. of the works of

these classes—constituting the higher walks of literature generally—
are of foreign origin.—*See Note II., p.* 552, *vol. ii.*

Now, not insisting upon the precise accuracy of
these estimates, but still regarding them as approaches
to the truth, we have the basis for some interesting
observations.

Though, as an independent nation, we are less than
a century old, and though we have been busily engaged in exploring wildernesses, in felling forests,
founding States, building cities, opening roads ; in
laying down railways, in teaching steamboats to
traverse the waters before only known to the Indian
canoe ; in converting lakes and rivers—the largest in
the world—into familiar pathways of commerce, and
as a consummation of our progress, in netting half a
continent with lines of telegraph—still, we have found
time, and courage, and heart, to outstrip all that the
world has before seen, in the diffusion of knowledge,
by means of the periodical press ; in the number and
excellence of our common schools ; in the number,
cheapness, and excellence of our books for elementary education.

Though not claiming comparison with the Old
World in the multitude of new works of the highest
class in literature and science, we have still made a
good beginning, and have many readers in the other
hemisphere, under the eaves of universities and colleges, which have been founded for centuries.

In the midst of the haste and hurry of life, induced

by the vast fields of enterprise around us and beckoning us on to the chase—we still find a larger portion of our people devoted to education, and reading, and meditation, and reflection, than is to be met with in any other land; as a corollary of this, we find, relatively, more hands, more purses, more heads and hearts, devoted to the support of literature and the dissemination of knowledge, than in any other country of equal population.

It is also to be observed that, after all that has been said and surmised as to the dependence of American literature upon the British press, that the element of British mind, in the production of American publications, is really but about twenty per cent., and this proportion is rapidly diminishing. Of the new books annually produced in the United States, not more than one-fifth part are either directly or indirectly of foreign origin.

It is, however, to be at the same time admitted and reflected upon, that our deficiency and our dependence lie chiefly in the higher efforts of mind and genius—those which crown a nation's work, and which confirm a nation's glory; and it is precisely here that we are now called upon, by every legitimate stimulus, to rouse the emulation, the ambition, the patriotism of our country.* It is, as tributary to such

* "In order that America may take its due rank in the commonwealth of nations, a literature is needed which shall be the exponent of its higher life. We live in times of turbulence and change. There is a general dissatisfaction, manifesting itself often in rude contests and ruder

a consummation, that I would earnestly urge upon
our people, and those whom they have placed in authority, to adopt the modified but still desirable
measure of International Copyright, already suggested.   Just at present this would be a little against us,
that is to say, we should buy more copyrights of the
British than they of us ; but, at the rate of progress
hitherto attained by American literature, before twenty years—probably before ten years—are past, the

---

speech, with the gulf which separates principles from actions. Men are
struggling to realize dim ideals of right and truth, and each failure adds
to the desperate earnestness of their efforts. Beneath all the shrewdness and selfishness of the American character, there is a smouldering
enthusiasm which flames out at the first touch of fire—sometimes at the
hot and hasty words of party, and sometimes at the bidding of great
thoughts and unselfish principles. The heart of the nation is easily
stirred to its depths ; but those who rouse its fiery impulses into action
are often men compounded of ignorance and wickedness, and wholly
unfitted to guide the passions which they are able to excite. There is
no country in the world which has nobler ideas embodied in more worthless shapes. All our factions, fanaticisms, reforms, parties, creeds, ridiculous or dangerous though they often appear, are founded on some
aspiration or reality which deserves a better form and expression. There
is a mighty power in great speech. If the sources of what we call our
fooleries and faults were rightly addressed, they would echo more majestic and kindling truths. We want a poetry which shall speak in
clear, loud tones to the people ; a poetry which shall make us more in
love with our native land, by converting its ennobling scenery into the
images of lofty thoughts ; which shall give visible form and life to the
abstract ideas of our written constitutions ; which shall confer upon
virtue all the strength of principle and all the energy of passion ; which
shall disentangle freedom from cant and senseless hyperbole, and render it a thing of such loveliness and grandeur as to justify all self-sacri-
fice ; which shall make us love man by the new consecrations it sheds
on his life and destiny ; which shall force through the thin partitions of
conventionalism and expediency ; vindicate the majesty of reason ; give
new power to the voice of conscience, and new vitality to human affection ; soften and elevate passion ; guide enthusiasm in a right direction ; and speak out in the high language of men to a nation of men."
                                                            E. P. Whipple.

scales will be turned in our favor, and they will buy more copyrights of us than we shall of them. At all events, an immediate and powerful stimulus would be added to authorship, and to some of the trades and professions connected with the production of books in this country, if we could have the British market opened to us on some such plan as is herein proposed. Nearly every new work would be stereotyped, and a set of plates sent to England; and these, in view of the increased sale, and the high and improving standard of taste, abroad, would be got up in a superior manner, in all respects. Let us think well of these things!

LETTER LV.

Recollections of Washington—The House of Representatives—Missouri Compromise—Clay, Randolph, and Lowndes—The Senate—Rufus King—William Pinkney—Mr. Macon—Judge Marshall—Election of J. Q. Adams—President Monroe—Meeting of Adams and Jackson—Jackson's Administration—Clay—Calhoun—Webster—Anecdotes.

MY DEAR C ******

In the autumn of 1846, I went with my family to Paris, partly for literary purposes, and partly also to give my children advantages of education, which, in consequence of my absorbing cares for a series of years, they had been denied. Here they remained for nearly two years, while I returned home to attend to my affairs, spending the winters, however,

17*

with them. Leaving my observations upon Paris to be grouped in one general view, I pass on with my narrative.

Toward the close of 1849 I removed to New York, to execute certain literary engagements. These completed, I went, in December, 1850, to Washington, taking my family with me. Here we remained for three months, when, having received the appointment of United States Consul to Paris, I returned to New York, and after due preparation, sailed on the 5th of April, 1851, to enter upon the official duties which thus devolved upon me.

I invite you to return with me to Washington. I had often been there, and had of course seen and observed many of the remarkable men who had figured in the great arena of politics, through a space of thirty years. I shall now gather up and present to you a few reminiscences connected with this, our national metropolis, which still linger in my mind. Avoiding political matters, however, which are duly chronicled in the books, I shall only give sketches of persons and things, less likely to have fallen under your observation.

My first visit to Washington was in the winter of 1819–20. Monroe was then President, and D. D. Tompkins, Vice-president; Marshall was at the head of the Supreme Court; Clay, Speaker of the House of Representatives. In the latter body, the two most noted members, exclusive of the speaker, were William Lowndes of South Carolina, and John Randolph of Virginia.

At the period of my visit, the clouds were mustering in the horizon for that tempest which not only agitated Congress, but the whole country, in consequence of the application of Missouri for admission into the Union. A few weeks later, the "Compromise of 36° 30'," was passed by both houses, but the actual admission of the State did not take place till the ensuing session. I was at Washington but one day, and of course could only take a hurried view of the principal objects of interest. I was in the House of Representatives but a single hour. While I was present, there was no direct discussion of the agitating subject which already filled everybody's mind, but still the excitement flared out occasionally in incidental allusions to it, like puffs of smoke and jets of flame which issue from a house that is on fire within. I recollect that Clay descended from the speaker's chair, and made a brief speech, thrilling the House by a single passage, in which he spoke of "poor, unheard Missouri"—she being then without a representative in Congress. His tall, tossing form, his long, sweeping gestures, and above all, his musical, yet thrilling tones, made an impression upon me which I can never forget. Some time after, in the course of the debate, a tall man, with a little head and a small, oval countenance like that of a boy prematurely grown old, arose and addressed the chair. He paused a moment, and I had time to study his appearance. His hair was jet black, and clubbed in a queue; his eye was black, small, and painfully penetrating. His complexion was a yellowish-brown, bespeaking Indian blood. I knew at once that it must be John Randolph. As he uttered the words, "Mr. Speaker!"—every member turned in his seat, and facing him, gazed as if some portent had suddenly appeared before them. "Mr. Speaker"—said he, in a shrill voice, which, however, pierced every nook and corner of the hall—"I have but one word to say; one word, sir, and that is to state a fact. The measure to which the gentleman has just alluded, originated in a dirty trick!" These were his precise words. The subject to which he referred I did not gather, but the coolness and impudence of the speaker were admirable in their way. I never saw better acting, even in Kean. His look, his manner, his long arm, his elvish fore-finger—like an exclamation-point, punctuating his bitter thought—showed the skill of a master. The effect of the whole was to startle everybody, as if a pistol-shot had rung through the hall.*

---

* A remarkable instance of the license which Mr. Randolph allowed to himself, occurred in the Senate, of which he was then a member, soon after Mr. Adams's accession to the presidency. In a discussion which took place upon the "Panama Mission," Randolph closed a very intemperate speech with the following words, on their face referring to events which had occurred at a recent race-course, but, in fact, plainly meaning the alliance between Mr. Adams and Mr. Clay :

"I was defeated, horse, foot, and dragoons—cut up, clean broke down

Soon after Lowndes arose, and there was a general movement of the members from the remote parts of the room, toward him. His appearance was remarkable. He was six feet two inches high—slender, bent, emaciated, and evidently of feeble frame. His complexion was sallow and dead, and his face almost without expression. His voice, too, was low and whispering. And yet he was, all things considered, the strong man of the House; strong in his various knowledge, his comprehensive understanding, his pure heart, his upright intentions, and above all, in the confidence these qualities had inspired. Every thing he said was listened to as the words of wisdom. It was he who gave utterance to the sentiment that the "office of president was neither to be solicited nor refused." I was unable to hear what he said, but the stillness around—the intent listening of the entire assembly—

by the coalition of Blifil and Black George—*by the combination, unheard of till then, of the Puritan with the Black-leg!*"

The "Coalition," so much talked of at the time, charged Mr. Clay with giving Mr. Adams his influence in the election to the presidency, in consideration that he was to be Secretary of State. This was urged with great vehemence and effect, both against Mr. Adams's administration and Mr. Clay, personally. Randolph's endorsement of the charge, at this time, fiendish as the manner of it was, seemed a staggering blow, and Mr. Clay thought it necessary to call him to account for it. The duel took place on the banks of the Potomac, but Randolph fired in the air, and the difficulty was appeased.

No man in our history has been more discussed than John Randolph. He was undoubtedly a man of genius, but, on the whole, both in public and private, was an exceedingly dangerous example. He said some good things, and sometimes seemed almost inspired, but his mind and heart were soured and narrowed by inherent physical defects, which at last led to occasional lunacy. He died at Philadelphia in 1833, aged 60.

bore testimony to the estimation in which he was held. I never saw him afterward. About two years later, he died on a voyage to England for the benefit of his health, and thus, in the language of an eminent member of Congress, "were extinguished the brightest hopes of the country, which, by a general movement, were looking to him as the future chief-magistrate of the nation."

These sketches, I know, are trifles; but as this was my first look at either branch of Congress, and as, moreover, I had a glance at three remarkable men, you will perhaps excuse me for recording my impressions.

In the Senate, the persons who most attracted my attention were Rufus King, of New York, then holding the highest rank in that body for able statesmanship, combined with acknowledged probity and great dignity of person, manner, and character; Harrison Gray Otis, whom I have already described; William Hunter, of Rhode Island, noted for his agreeable presence and his great conversational powers; William Pinkney,* of Maryland, the most dis-

---

* William Pinkney was a native of Annapolis, born 1764. He was appointed to various European missions by the United States government, and held other eminent public stations. His greatest celebrity, however, was attained at the bar, where he was distinguished alike for learning and eloquence. He was a great student, and prepared himself with the utmost care, though he affected to rely chiefly on his native powers. A member of Monroe's Cabinet once told me that he heard Pinkney, about five o'clock of a winter morning, reciting and committing to memory, in his room, the peroration of a plea which he heard delivered the same day before the Supreme Court!

tinguished lawyer of that era—a large, handsome man, and remarkable for his somewhat foppish dress —wearing, when I saw him, a white waistcoat, and white-top boots; and Mr. Macon, of North Carolina, a solid, farmer-like man, but greatly esteemed for combining a sound patriotism with a consistent political career. On the whole, the general aspect of the Senate was that of high dignity, sobriety, and refinement. There were more persons of that body who had the marks of well-bred gentlemen, in their air, dress, and demeanor, than at the present day. In manners, the Senate has unquestionably degenerated.

During the half hour in which I was present, there was no debate. I went to the hall of the Supreme Court, but the proceedings were without special interest. Among the judges were Marshall and Story, both of whom riveted my attention. The former was now sixty-four years old, and still in the full vigor of his career. He was tall and thin, with a small face, expressive of acuteness and amiability. His personal manner was eminently dignified, yet his brow did not seem to me to indicate the full force of his

---

His senatorial displays are said to have been often more florid than profound. Soon after first taking his seat in the House of Representatives he made a speech, which was very brilliant, but rather pretentious and dictatorial. John Randolph gave him a hint of this. He said: " Mr. Speaker, the gentleman from Maryland"—then pausing, and looking toward Pinkney, added—"I believe the gentleman is from Maryland?" As Pinkney had been ambassador to several courts in Europe, and was the most conspicuous lawyer at the bar of the Supreme Court, he felt this sarcasm keenly. When I saw him, he had just taken his seat in the Senate; two years afterward he died, aged fifty-seven.

great abilities and lofty moral qualities. I saw him many times afterward, and learned to look with reverence upon him, as being the best representative of the era and spirit of Washington, which lingered among us.

I pass over several visits which I made at different periods to the capital, and come to the winter of 1825, when J. Q. Adams was elected President by the House of Representatives. I was in the gallery of that body at the time the vote was declared. The result produced no great excitement, for it had been foreseen for some days. The popular sentiment of the country, however, was no doubt overruled by electing to the chief-magistracy the second* of the three candidates eligible to the office, and this was severely avenged four years afterward at the polls. Mr. Adams, with all the patronage of the government, was displaced by his rival, Gen. Jackson, in 1828, by an electoral vote of one hundred and seventy-eight to eighty-three.

But it is not my purpose to load these light letters with the weightier matters of politics. I only give an

---

* The electoral vote stood thus: for Gen. Jackson, ninety-nine; Mr. Adams, eighty-four; Mr. Crawford, forty-one; Mr. Clay, thirty-seven. It was perfectly constitutional to elect Mr. Adams, but the event showed the difficulty of sustaining a President who has less than one-third of the popular vote in his favor.

The vote in the House of Representatives was first declared by Daniel Webster, and then by John Randolph. At the announcement that Adams was elected, there was some clapping of hands and there were some hisses, whereupon the galleries were cleared.

outline of public events, which may serve as frames to the personal tableaux which I wish to present to your view. Let me take you, then, to the President's levee, the evening of the 2d of February, 1825—in the afternoon of which Adams had triumphed and Jackson had been defeated.

The apartments at the White House were thronged to repletion—for not only did all the world desire to meet and gossip over the events of the day, but this was one of the very last gatherings which would take place under the presidency of Monroe, and which had now continued for eight years. It was the first time that I had been present at a presidential levee, and it was therefore, to me, an event of no ordinary excitement.

The President I had seen before at Hartford, as I have told you; here, in the midst of his court, he seemed to me even more dull, sleepy, and insignificant in personal appearance, than on that occasion. He was under size, his dress plain black, and a little rusty; his neckcloth small, ropy, and carelessly tied; his frill matted; his countenance, wilted with age and study and care. He was almost destitute of forehead, and what he had, was deeply furrowed in two distinct arches over his eyes, which were small, gray, glimmering, and deeply set in large sockets. Altogether, his personal appearance was owlish and ordinary—without dignity, either of form or expression; indeed, I could scarce get over the idea that

there was a certain look of meanness in his countenance. The lowness of his brow was so remarkable
that a person in the room said to me, in looking at
him—" He hasn't got brains enough to hold his hat
on !" His manners, however, which were assiduously
courteous, with a sort of habitual diplomatic smile
upon his face, in some degree redeemed the natural
indifference of his form and features. I gazed with
eager curiosity at this individual—seeking, and yet
in vain, to discover in his appearance the explanation of the fact that his presidency had been considered as the era of a millennial truce between the great
parties whose strife had agitated the country to its
foundations ; and also of another fact—that he had,
like Washington, been elected to the presidency a
second time, almost without opposition. I could,
however, find no solution of these events in the
plain, homely, undemonstrative presence before me.
History has indeed given the interpretation—for we
know that, despite these traits in his personal appearance, Mr. Monroe possessed a quiet energy of
character, combined with a sound and penetrating
judgment, great experience, and strong sense, which
rendered his administration in some respects eminently successful.

Mrs. Monroe appeared much younger, and was of
very agreeable manners and person. During the
eight years of her presidency over the sociabilities of
the White House, she exercised a genial influence in

infusing elegance and dignity into the intercourse of the society which came under her sway.

I shall pass over other individuals present, only noting an incident which respects the two persons in the assembly who, most of all others, engrossed the thoughts of the visitors—Mr. Adams the elect, Gen. Jackson the defeated. It chanced in the course of the evening that these two persons, involved in the throng, approached each other from opposite directions, yet without knowing it. Suddenly, as they were almost together, the persons around, seeing what was to happen, by a sort of instinct stepped aside and left them face to face. Mr. Adams was by himself; Gen. Jackson had a large, handsome lady on his arm. They looked at each other for a moment, and then Gen. Jackson moved forward, and reaching out his long arm, said—"How do you do, Mr. Adams? I give you my left hand, for the right, as you see, is devoted to the fair: I hope you are very well, sir." All this was gallantly and heartily said and done. Mr. Adams took the general's hand, and said, with chilling coldness—"Very well, sir: I hope Gen. Jackson is well!" It was curious to see the western planter, the Indian fighter, the stern soldier who had written his country's glory in the blood of the enemy at New Orleans—genial and gracious in the midst of a court, while the old courtier and diplomat was stiff, rigid, cold as a statue! It was all the more remarkable from the fact that, four hours before, the former had been defeated, and the latter was the victor, in a struggle for one of the highest objects of human ambition. The personal character of these two individuals was in fact well expressed in that chance meeting: the gallantry, the frankness, and the heartiness of the one, which captivated all; the coldness, the distance, the self-concentration of the other, which repelled all.*

---

* A somewhat severe but still acute analyst of Mr. Adams's character says : " Undoubtedly, one great reason of his unpopularity was his cold, antipathetic manner, and the suspicion of selfishness it suggested, or at least aided greatly to confirm. None approached Mr. Adams, but to recede. He never succeeded, he never tried to conciliate."

I recollect an anecdote somewhat illustrative of this. When he was candidate for the Presidency, his political friends thought it advisable that he should attend a cattle-show at Worcester, Mass., so as to conciliate the numbers of influential men who might be present. Accordingly he went, and while there many persons were introduced to him, and among the rest a farmer of the vicinity—a man of substance and great respectability. On being presented, he said—

" Mr. Adams, I am very glad to see you. My wife, when she was a gal, lived in your father's family ; you were then a little boy, and she has told me a great deal about you. She has very often combed your head."

" Well," said Mr. Adams, in his harsh way—" I suppose she combs yours now !" The poor farmer slunk back like a lashed hound, feeling the smart, but utterly unconscious of the provocation.

Mr. Adams's course in the House of Representatives—to which he was elected for a series of years, after he had been President—was liable to great and serious exception. His age, the high positions he had held, his vast experience and unbounded stores of knowledge, might have made him the arbiter of that body. Such, however, was his love of gladiatorial displays, that he did more to promote scenes of collision, strife, and violence, in words and deeds, than any other member. I remember one day to have been on the floor of the House, when he attacked Mr. Wise with great personality and bitterness. In allusion to the Cilley duel, with which he was connected, he spoke of him as coming into that assembly, " his hands dripping with blood !" There was a terrible yarring tone in his voice, which gave added effect to the denunciation. Every person present seemed to be thrilled with a sort

I pass over several years, and come to the period when Jackson was President, at which time I was often at Washington. It was a marked epoch, for Webster, Calhoun, and Clay were then in the Senate. It is seldom that three such men appear upon the theater of action at the same time. They were each distinct from the other in person, manners, heart, constitution; they were from different sections of the country, and to some extent reflected the manners, habits, and opinions of these diverse regions. They were all of remarkable personal appearance: Webster of massive form, dark complexion, and thoughtful, solemn countenance; Clay, tall, of rather slight frame, but keen, flexible features, and singular ease and freedom in his attitudes, his walk, and his gestures. Calhoun was also tall, but erect, and rigid in his form—his eye grayish blue, and flashing from beneath a brow at once imperious and scornful. All these men were great actors, not through art, but nature, and gave to the effect of their high intellectual endowments, the added power of commanding personal presence and singularly expressive countenances. They have passed from the stage, and all

---

of horror, rather toward Mr. Adams than the object of his reproaches. In speaking of this scene to me afterward, an eminent member of Congress said, that "Mr. Adams's greatest delight was to be the hero of a row." There is no doubt that the rude personal passages which often occur in the House of Representatives, derived countenance from Mr. Adams's example. It is melancholy to reflect how a great intellect, and, on the whole, a great life, were marred and dwarfed by inherent personal defects.

that survives of them belongs to the domain of history. Many of the speeches, now recorded in their books, I heard and remember, with their lofty images still painted in my eye and their thrilling tones still echoing in my ear. Those who never heard them, never saw them, will hereafter read and ponder and admire the glowing words, the mighty thoughts they have left behind; but they can never compass the conceptions which linger in the minds of those who beheld them in the full exercise of their faculties, and playing their several parts on their great theater of life and action—the Senate of the United States.

Calhoun was educated in Connecticut, first graduating at Yale College, and then at the Litchfield law school. I have often heard his classmates speak of him as manifesting great abilities and great ambition, from the beginning. He was particularly noted for his conversational powers, and a cordiality of manners which won the hearts of all. He was deemed frank, hearty, sympathetic. One of his intimates at Yale, told me that about the year 1812 he was elected to Congress. Mr. Calhoun was then a member, and one of the greatest pleasures his classmate anticipated, was in meeting his college friend. He was kindly received, but in the first interview, he discovered that the heart of the now rising politician was gone. He had already given up to ambition what was meant for mankind.

Mr. Calhoun had, however, many friends in New

England, partly from the favorable impression he made while residing there, and partly also from his conduct during the earlier portion of his public career. He had, indeed, promoted the war of 1812, but in many of his opinions—especially in the support of a navy—he coincided with the North. His administration of the war department from 1817, during the long period of seven years, was singularly successful, and everywhere increased his reputation as a practical statesman. It is a curious circumstance, explained by the facts I have just mentioned, that in the election of 1824, while Jackson was defeated for the presidency, Calhoun was still chosen vice-president, and mainly by northern votes.* Thus far his measures, his policy, had been national; but he soon changed, and frequently shifting his position, lost the confidence of his own party and of the country. For the last fifteen years of his life, " he was like a strong man struggling in a morass : every effort to extricate himself only sinking him deeper and deeper." He has passed away, leaving abundant evidences of his abilities, but with the sad distinction of having successfully devoted the last years of his life to the establishment of the doctrine in his own State and among many of his admirers, that domestic Slavery is a good and beneficent institution—compatible with the Constitution of the United States, and entitled to pro-

---

* Mr. Calhoun had one hundred and fourteen votes from the non-slaveholding States, and sixty-eight only from the others.

tection and perpetuity beneath its banner! What a departure is this from the views and opinions of the founders of our National Independence and the Federal Union — Washington, Franklin, Jefferson, and Madison!

Mr. Clay was also a supporter of the war of 1812, and probably was, more than any other individual, responsible for it. During its progress, he was the eloquent defender of the administration, through its struggles and disasters, and was hence the special object of New England hostility. He, however, joined Mr. Adams, in 1825, and having contributed, by his commanding influence, to his election, became his Secretary of State. His policy upon the tariff afterward brought him into harmony with the North, and he was long the favorite candidate of the whigs for the presidency. But he, too, like Calhoun, was a man of "positions," and with all his abilities—with all his struggles—he slipped between them, and fell, without realizing the great object of his eager ambition—the presidency.*

---

* There seems to have been a singular fatuity in Mr. Clay's great measures—if we may be permitted to test them by time and their result. He promoted the war, but was himself one of the negotiators of a peace with the enemy, without a single stipulation in regard to the causes of the war, and this too after an expenditure of thirty thousand lives and a hundred millions of dollars on our side, and probably an equal expenditure on the other. The Missouri Compromise of 1820, which he so far favored as to gain the credit of it, has been recently expunged, leaving national discord and local civil war in its place. The Compromise of 1833 was regarded by many of the eminent men in the country, as one of the most disastrous political movements that could

The first time I ever saw Mr. Webster was on the 17th of June, 1825, at the laying of the corner-stone of the Bunker Hill Monument. I shall never forget his appearance as he strode across the open area, encircled by some fifty thousand persons — men and women—waiting for the "Orator of the Day," nor the shout that simultaneously burst forth, as he was recognized, carrying up to the skies the name of "Webster!" "Webster!" "Webster!"

It was one of those lovely days in June, when the

---

have been devised, and by its inconsistency with his previous doctrines, lost him forever the confidence of his best friends, especially at the North. Mr. J. Q. Adams once told me that he considered this as a fatal mistake on Mr. Clay's part, as he saved Mr. Calhoun without conciliating him, at the same time alienating many leading men throughout the country who had before been devoted to him. The Compromise of 1850, in which Mr. Clay was the chief, has already lost its force, and is likely hereafter to be rather a source of agitation than of peace. His grand and comprehensive system, to which he gave the name of "American," and which proposed to build up a mighty nation through a National Bank, giving us a currency—Internal Improvements, promoting commerce and binding the States in the bonds of union—the Tariff, to render us independent of foreign nations in peace and in war—and the Panama Mission, placing us at the head of the powers of this continent,—all these have been trampled under foot by Jackson, and Van Buren, and Polk, and Pierce, and the People. They have been erased from our policy, and their history is chiefly memorable for the ability with which their great originator promoted them, and yet only to insure the defeat of his own ambition. After a few brief years, Henry Clay will be only known to the student of history, who looks beyond existing monuments for testimonials of the giants of bygone generations. Even his speeches, stirring as they were on those who heard them—having no eminence in literature, no body and soul of general truth, reflection, and philosophy, and little connection with current politics—will soon be, among the traditions of the past. The fallacy of Mr. Clay's career lay in this—he created issues, founded schemes, planned systems. as the ladders of ambition; the truer plan, even for ambition, is to make truth and duty and principle the polar star of life and action.

sun is bright, the air clear, and the breath of nature so sweet and pure as to fill every bosom with a grateful joy in the mere consciousness of existence. There were present long files of soldiers in their holiday attire; there were many associations, with their mottoed banners; there were lodges and grand lodges, in white aprons and blue scarfs; there were miles of citizens from the towns and the country round about; there were two hundred gray-haired men, remnants of the days of the Revolution; there was among them a stranger, of great mildness and dignity of appearance, on whom all eyes rested, and when his name was known, the air echoed with the cry—" Welcome, welcome, Lafayette!"* Around all this scene, was a

---

* I was at this time Master of the Lodge at Hartford, St. John's No. 4, and attended this celebration officially as a deputy from the Grand Lodge of Connecticut. I recollect that when the lodges assembled at Boston, Gen. Lafayette was among them. I had seen him before in Paris, at a dinner on Washington's birthday, A. D. 1824, when he first announced his intention of coming to America. I afterward saw him, both at Washington and Paris. I may mention a single anecdote, illustrative of his tenderness of heart. While he was at Washington, Mr. Morse—since so universally known as the inventor of the electric telegraph—was employed to paint his portrait for the City Hall of New York. One day, when the people were collecting in the hall of the hotel for dinner, I saw Mr. Morse apart, in the corner of the room, reading a letter. I noticed, in a moment, that he was greatly agitated. I went to him, and asked him the cause. He could not speak; he put the letter into my hand, and staggered out of the room. I looked over the epistle, and saw that it contained the fatal intelligence of the death of his wife, at New Haven, whom he had left there, in health, a few days before. He felt it necessary to leave Washington immediately, and go to his friends, and I agreed to accompany him. It was necessary that this should be communicated to Lafayette. I went to him and told him the story. He was very much affected, and went with me to see Mr. Morse. He took him in his arms and kissed him, and wept over him,

rainbow of beauty such as New England alone can furnish.

I have seen many public festivities and ceremonials, but never one, taken all together, of more general interest than this. Every thing was fortunate : all were gratified ; but the address was that which seemed uppermost in all minds and hearts. Mr. Webster was in the very zenith of his fame and of his powers. I have looked on many mighty men— King George, the "first gentleman in England;" Sir Astley Cooper, the Apollo of his generation; Peele, O'Connell, Palmerston, Lyndhurst—all nature's noblemen ; I have seen Cuvier, Guizot, Arago, Lamartine—marked in their persons by the genius which have carried their names over the world ; I have seen Clay, and Calhoun, and Pinkney, and King, and Dwight, and Daggett, who stand as high examples of personal endowment, in our annals, and yet not one of these approached Mr. Webster in the commanding power of their personal presence. There

---

as if he had been his own child. Nothing could be more soothing than this affectionate sympathy.

In Mr. Webster's discourse, which I have been noticing, there was a passage addressed to Lafayette, which, I believe, is slightly altered in the present printed copy. It was told as an anecdote, some years ago, that he composed the discourse while fishing for cod off Nantasket Beach. It would seem that as he came to the point of addressing Lafayette, he had a vigorous bite, and from habit, more than attention to the business in hand, began to haul in. Just as the fish emerged from the water, Mr. Webster went on thus—"Fortunate man ! the representative of two hemispheres—welcome to these shores !"—whereupon the huge fish was safely jerked into the boat. I can not vouch for the authenticity of the story, but I tell it as too good to be lost.

was a grandeur in his form, an intelligence in his deep dark eye, a loftiness in his expansive brow, a significance in his arched lip, altogether beyond those of any other human being I ever saw. And these, on the occasion to which I allude, had their full expression and interpretation.

In general, the oration was serious, full of weighty thought and deep reflection. Occasionally there were flashes of fine imagination, and several passages of deep, overwhelming emotion.* I was near the speaker, and not only heard every word, but I saw every movement of his countenance. When he came to address the few scarred and time-worn veterans— some forty in number—who had shared in the bloody scene which all had now gathered to commemorate, he paused a moment, and, as he uttered the words "Venerable men," his voice trembled, and I could see a cloud pass over the sea of faces that turned upon the speaker. When at last, alluding to the death of Warren, he said—

---

* One incident, which occurred on this occasion, is worth mentioning. I sat near two old men, farmers I should judge, who remained with their mouths open from the beginning to the end of the oration. Not a sentence escaped them. I could see reflected in their countenances the whole march of the discourse. When it was over, they rose up, and having drawn a long breath, one said to the other—"Well, that was good; *every word seemed to weigh a pound!*" While Mr. Webster was in Europe in 1839, I wrote a series of anecdotical sketches of him, published in the National Intelligencer, and among other things, recited this incident. It found its way to England, and the London Times, in describing Mr. Webster's manner in the speech he made at the Oxford Cattle Show, repeated this anecdote as particularly descriptive of his massive and weighty eloquence.

" But ah, Him!—the first great martyr of this
great cause. Him, the patriotic victim of his own
self-devoting heart. Him, cut off by Providence in
the hour of overwhelming anxiety and thick gloom:
falling ere he saw the star of his country rise—how
shall I struggle with the emotions that stifle the utterance of thy name!" Here the eyes of the veterans around, little accustomed to tears, were filled
to the brim, and some of them "sobbed aloud in their
fullness of heart." The orator went on:

" Our poor work may perish, but thine shall endure: this monument may molder away, the solid
ground it rests upon may sink down to the level of
the sea; but thy memory shall not fail. Wherever
among men a heart shall be found that beats to the
transports of patriotism and liberty, its aspirations
shall claim kindred with thy spirit!"

I have never seen such an effect, from a single passage: a moment before, every bosom bent, every
brow was clouded, every eye was dim. Lifted as
by inspiration, every breast seemed now to expand,
every gaze to turn above, every face to beam with a
holy yet exulting enthusiasm. It was the omnipotence of eloquence, which, like the agitated sea, carries a host upon its waves, sinking and swelling with
its irresistible undulations.

It was some years subsequent to this that I became personally acquainted with Mr. Webster. From
1836, to the time of his death, I saw him frequently,

sometimes in public and sometimes in private. I
have heard some of his great speeches, as well at
Washington as elsewhere, but I must say that his
conversation impressed me quite as strongly as his
public addresses. I once traveled with him from
Washington to Baltimore. During a ride of two
hours, he spoke of a great variety of subjects—agriculture, horticulture, physical geography, geology—
with a perfectness of knowledge, from the minutest
details to the highest philosophy, which amazed me.
One thing I particularly remarked, he had no half
conceptions, no uncertain knowledge. What he knew,
he was sure of. His recollection seemed absolutely
perfect. His mind grasped the smallest as well as
the greatest things. He spoke of experiments he
had made at Marshfield in protecting trees, recently
planted, by interposing boards between them and the
prevailing winds, observing that these grew nearly
twice as rapidly as those which were exposed to the
full sweep of the blasts. He spoke of the recent
discoveries of geology — which had converted the
rocky lamina of the earth, hidden from the beginning, into leaves of a book, in which we could trace
the footprints of the Creator — with perfect knowledge of the subject, and a full appreciation of the
sublimity of its revelations.

At Baltimore, while sitting at table after tea, the
conversation continued, taking in a great variety of
subjects. One of the ladies of our company asked

Mr. Webster if he chose Marshfield for a residence because it was near the sea.

"Yes, madam," was the reply.

"And do you love the seashore?"

"Yes, I love it, yet not perhaps as others do. I can not pick up shells and pebbles along the shore. I can never forget the presence of the sea. It seems to speak to me, and beckon to me. When I see the surf come rolling in, like a horse foaming from the battle, I can not stoop down and pick up pebbles. The sea unquestionably presents more grand and exciting pictures and conceptions to the mind, than any other portion of the earth, partly because it is always new to us, and partly, too, because of the majestic movement of its great mass of waters. The mystery of its depths, the history of its devastations, crowd the mind with lofty images.

> " ' The armaments which thunderstrike the walls
>   Of rock-built cities, bidding nations quake,
>   And monarchs tremble in their capitals—
>   The oak leviathans, whose huge ribs make
>   Their clay creator the vain title take
>   Of lord of thee and arbiter of war:
>   These are thy toys, and as the snowy flake,
>   They melt into the yeast of waves, which mar
> Alike the Armada's pride or spoils of Trafalgar.

> " ' Thou glorious mirror, where the Almighty's form
>   Glasses itself in tempests : in all time,
>   Calm or convulsed—in breeze or gale or storm,
>   Icing the pole, or in the torrid clime,

Dark-heaving : boundless, endless, and sublime—
The image of Eternity—the throne
Of the Invisible ; even from out thy slime
The monsters of the deep are made : each zone
  Obeys thee : thou goest forth dread, fathomless, alone !'

I know of few descriptions of nature equal in sublimity to that."

It is impossible to give any impression of the effect of this passage, recited in low, solemn tones like the bass of an organ, the brow of the speaker seeming to reflect the very scenes it described.

Yet Mr. Webster was not always serious. In the circle of intimate friends he was generally cheerful and sometimes playful, not only relishing wit and repartee, but contributing to it his proper share. I have heard of one occasion in which he kept a full table in a roar for half an hour with his sallies. Many years ago there was a contested election in Mississippi—the seats of two sitting members being claimed by a Mr. Word and the famous orator, S. S. Prentiss.* The two claimants came to Washington,

---

* S. S. Prentiss was a native of Maine, but removed to Mississippi, where he soon distinguished himself as a brilliant orator. In the Harrison Campaign of 1840, " he took the stump," and made a series of most effective speeches, crowds gathering from many miles around, to hear him. One day he met with a caravan of wild beasts, and it was suggested that he should speak from the top of one of the wagons. He mounted that of the hyenas, and as he was lame, and carried a strong cane, occasionally he poked this through a hole in the top and stirred up the hyenas within. Prentiss had scathing powers of denunciation, and he was unsparing in his sarcasms upon the administration of Jackson and his successor Van Buren, which, as he insisted, had caused the ruin then

and argued their case before the House, but it was dismissed, and they were sent back for a new election. Prentiss, however, had sustained himself with so much ability, that before his departure a few of his whig friends concluded to give him a dinner. This was private, though some thirty persons were present. Late in the evening, when all were warmed with the cheer, Preston, of South Carolina, rose and proposed this sentiment :

" Daniel Webster—a Northern man with Southern principles !"

Mr. Webster, after a moment's hesitation, said : " Mr. Chairman, I rise in obedience to the flattering call of my good friend from South Carolina : *Daniel Webster—a Northern man with Southern principles !* Well, sir, I was born in New Hampshire, and therefore I am a northern man. There is no doubt of that. And if what the people say of us be true, it is equally certain that I am a man of southern principles. Sir, do I ever leave a heel-tap in my glass ? Do I ever pay my debts ? Don't I always prefer

---

desolating the country ; but when to his blasting sentences were added the howlings of the hyenas, judiciously put in at the climaxes, it was something more than words—it was " action, action, action !"

I remember once to have heard this famous orator, the same season, at a whig meeting in Faneuil Hall, Edward Everett presiding. I hardly knew which most to admire—the polished elegance, spiced with graceful and pertinent wit, of Everett, or the dashing splendor of Prentiss. The one seemed like the fountain of Velino playing amid Grecian sculpture ; the other, a cataract of the Far West, fed from inexhaustible fountains, and lighting whole forests with its crystals and its foam.

Mr. Prentiss died in 1850, greatly lamented, at the early age of forty.

challenging a man who won't fight?" And thus he
went on in a manner more suitable to the occasion
than to these pages—until at last, amid roars of laughter and shouts of applause, he sat down.

The countenance of Mr. Webster was generally
solemn, and even severe, especially when he was absorbed in thought : yet when relaxed with agreeable
emotions, it was irresistibly winning. I have heard
an anecdote which furnishes a pleasing illustration of
this. At the time Mr. Wirt was Attorney-general,
Mr. Webster, having some business with him, went
to his office. Mr. Wirt was engaged for a few moments at his desk, and asked Mr. Webster to sit down
a short time, when he would come to him. Mr. Webster did as requested, and for some moments sat looking moodily into the fire. At length one of Mr.
Wirt's children—a girl of six or eight years old—
came in, and thinking it was her father, went to Mr.
Webster, and putting her elbows on his knee, looked
up in his face. In an instant she started back,
shocked at her mistake, and appalled by the dark,
moody countenance before her. At the same moment Mr. Webster became aware of her presence.
His whole face changed in an instant : a smile came
over his face ; he put out his hand, and all was so
winning, that the child, after hesitating a moment,
also smiled, and went back and resumed her confiding
position, as if it had indeed been her father.

That Mr. Webster had his faults, we all know ;

but the general soundness of his heart and character, as well as the soundness of his intellect, are demonstrated by his works.   These are an indestructible monument, attesting alike his greatness and his goodness.   Among all these volumes, so full of thought, so pregnant with instruction, so abounding in knowledge, there is not an impure suggestion, not a mean sentiment, not a malicious sentence.   All is patriotic, virtuous, ennobling.   And the truths he thus uttered —how are they beautified, adorned, and commended by the purity of the style and the elegance of the diction!   In this respect there is a remarkable difference between him and his great rivals, Clay and Calhoun. Mr. Webster's works abound in passages which convey beautiful sentiments in beautiful language*—gems of

---

* It would be easy to fill volumes with passages of this sort: the following, taken at random from Mr. Webster's published works, will illustrate what I have said :

"Justice, sir, is the great interest of man on earth.   It is the ligament which holds civilized beings and civilized nations together.   Where her temple stands, and so long as it is duly honored, there is a foundation for social security, general happiness, and the improvement and progress of our race."

"One may live as a conqueror, a king, or a magistrate, but he must die as a man.   The bed of death brings every human being to his pure individuality ; to the intense contemplation of that deepest and most solemn of all relations, the relation between the Creator and the created."

"Real goodness does not attach itself merely to this life ; it points to another world."

"Religion is the tie that connects man with his Creator, and holds him to his throne.   If that tie be all sundered, all broken, he floats away, a worthless atom in the universe—its proper attractions all gone, its destiny thwarted, and its whole future nothing but darkness, desolation, and death."

Speaking at Valley Forge of the sufferings of the American army

thought set in golden sentences, fitting them to become the adornments of gifted and tasteful minds,
for all future time. With these other orators it is
not so : there is an earnest, direct, vigorous logic in
Calhoun, which, however, can spare not a sentence
to any subsidiary thought ; there is a warm, glowing,
hearty current of persuasion in Clay, yet he is too
ardent in the pursuit of his main design, to pause for

---

there, under Washington, in the winter of 1777–8, he described them
as " destitute of clothing, destitute of provisions, destitute of every
thing but their faith in God and their immortal leader."

" The slightest glance must convince us that mechanical power and
mechanical skill, as they are now exhibited in Europe and America,
mark an epoch in human history worthy of all admiration. Machinery
is made to perform what has formerly been the toil of human hands,
to an extent that astonishes the most sanguine, with a degree of power
to which no number of human arms is equal, and with such precision
and exactness as almost to suggest the notion of reason and intelligence
in the machines themselves. Every natural agent is put unrelentingly
to the task. The winds work, the waters work, the elasticity of metals
works ; gravity is solicited into a thousand new forms of action ; levers
are multiplied upon levers ; wheels revolve on the peripheries of other
wheels ; the saw and the plane are tortured into an accommodation to
new uses, and last of all, with inimitable power, and ' with whirlwind
sound,' comes the potent agency of steam."

" Steam is found in triumphant operation on the seas ; and under the
influence of its strong propulsion, the gallant ship,

> ' Against the wind, against the tide,
> Still *steadies* with an upright keel.'

It is on the rivers, and the boatman may repose on his oars ; it is on
highways, and begins to exert itself along the courses of land conveyance ; it is at the bottom of mines, a thousand feet below the earth's
surface ; it is in the mill, and in the workshops of the trades. It rows,
it pumps, it excavates, it carries, it draws, it lifts, it hammers, it spins,
it weaves, it prints."

" Whether it be consciousness, or the result of his reasoning faculties, man soon learns that he must die. And of all sentient beings, he
alone, as far as we can judge, attains to this knowledge. His Maker
has made him capable of learning this. Before he knows his origin

a moment to gather or scatter flowers by the wayside. In all the works of these two great men, it is not easy to select a page which may challenge admiration on account of its artistic beauty, or because it enshrines general truth and philosophy, so happily expressed as to enforce them upon the worship of the heart.

Of Mr. Webster's magnanimity, there are abundant

---

and destiny, he knows that he is to die. Then comes that most urgent and solemn demand for light that ever proceeded, or can proceed, from the profound and anxious broodings of the human soul. It is stated, with wonderful force and beauty, in that incomparable composition, the book of Job : 'For there is hope of a tree, if it be cut down, that it will sprout again, and that the tender branch thereof will not cease ; that, through the scent of water, it will bud, and bring forth boughs like a plant. *But if a man die, shall he live again ?*' And that question nothing but God, and the religion of God, can solve. Religion does solve it, and teaches every man that he is to live again, and that the duties of this life have reference to the life which is to come. And hence, since the introduction of Christianity, it has been the duty, as it has been the effort, of the great and the good, to sanctify human knowledge, to bring it to the fount, and to baptize learning into Christianity ; to gather up all its productions, its earliest and its latest, its blossoms and its fruits, and lay them all upon the altar of religion and virtue."

"I shall enter on no encomium upon Massachusetts ; she needs none. There she is. Behold her, and judge for yourselves. There is her history ; the world knows it by heart. The past, at least, is secure. There is Boston, and Concord, and Lexington, and Bunker Hill ; and there they will remain forever. The bones of her sons, falling in the great struggle for Independence, now lie mingled with the soil of every State, from New England to Georgia ; and there they will lie forever. And, sir, where American Liberty raised its first voice, and where its youth was nurtured and sustained, there it still lives, in the strength of its manhood and full of its original spirit. If discord and disunion shall wound it, if party strife and blind ambition shall hawk at and tear it, if folly and madness, if uneasiness under salutary and necessary restraint, shall succeed in separating it from that Union by which alone its existence is made sure, it will stand, in the end, by the side of that cradle in which its infancy was rocked ; it will stretch forth its arm, with whatever of vigor it may still retain, over the friends who gather round

evidences. His whole course in the House as well as in the Senate evinced it. He never displayed, because he never felt that littleness of soul, which signalizes itself in envy, and malice, and uncharitableness. Nothing can be finer than the uniform dignity of his conduct through a congressional period of more than twenty years. But there are two instances of his greatness of soul, which have appeared to me remarkable, and especially worthy of being recorded, because they refer to those individuals, Clay and Calhoun, who of all others he might have been supposed to regard with feelings of aversion, if not of hostility.

It is well remembered by all those who are conversant with the history of the times, that Mr. Webster, then acting as Secretary of State in the Tyler Cabinet, thought fit to continue in his place, when the

---

it ; and it will fall at last, if fall it must, amid the proudest monuments of its own glory, and on the very spot of its origin."

It is known that some of these fine passages were suddenly struck out in the heat of debate ; others no doubt were polished and perfected with care. On a certain occasion, Mr. Webster startled the Senate by a beautiful and striking remark in relation to the extent of the British empire, as follows : " She has dotted the surface of the whole globe with her possessions and military posts, whose morning drum-beat, following the sun and keeping company with the hours, circle the earth daily with one continuous and unbroken strain of the martial airs of England."

On going out of the Senate, one of the members complimented Mr. Webster upon this, saying that he was all the more struck with it as it was evidently impromptu. " You are mistaken," said Mr. Webster ; "the idea occurred to me when I was on the ramparts of Quebec, some months since. I wrote it down, and re-wrote it, and after several trials, got it to suit me, and laid it by for use. The time came to-day, and so I put it in."

other members resigned. This conduct drew upon him attacks from various quarters, and especially from those who were known to take counsel of Mr. Clay. It was manifest, as well from the bitterness as the persistence of the onslaught, that the purpose was to effect Mr. Webster's destruction as a public man. This object was not accomplished, for it soon appeared to the world that he had been governed by the highest motives of patriotism, in the course he had adopted, and that he had indeed made it the means of accomplishing a great national benefit—the settling of the irritating and threatening question of the " Maine boundary." In fact, Mr. Webster rather gained than lost in the confidence of men whose opinions are of value, in spite of this conspiracy which sought to overwhelm him.

In the spring of 1844, Mr. Clay, having been on a trip to the South, came to Washington. He was already indicated by public opinion as the whig candidate for the presidency, and it seemed highly probable that the time had now come for the realization of his known and cherished aspirations, in respect to that high position. He was himself sanguine of success. On the 1st of May he was nominated at Baltimore, by a whig convention, for the office in question, and the next day there was to be a grand rally of young men, to ratify the nomination. It was suggested to Mr. Clay that it was eminently desirable that Mr. Webster should add his influence in behalf

of the nomination ; but he is said to have felt that
he neither needed nor desired it. His friends, however,
thought otherwise, and a message was dispatched to
Mr. Webster, begging him to come on to the convention, already gathering at Baltimore. This reached
him while he was dining at the Astor House, in New
York. He immediately left the table, and after a
brief communion with himself, departed, and arrived
in time to join his voice in a powerful speech, to the
enthusiasm of the occasion.

A very short period after this, the clouds began
to thicken in the political horizon. Mr. Polk had
been nominated, and the important State of Pennsylvania was seen to be in danger of giving him her
vote. In this emergency, Mr. Webster was besought
to go there and address the people at Philadelphia,
and in the mining districts, where large masses were
congregated. Perfectly well knowing Mr. Clay's
sentiments and conduct toward him, he still went,
and made a series of addresses, among the most eloquent that he ever uttered. In the course of these,
he had occasion to speak of Mr. Clay. It was a
delicate task, therefore, to do justice to his position,
as an advocate of Mr. Clay's candidacy, while at the
same time Mr. Clay's treatment of him was fresh in
the public mind. Yet with a tact, which does infinite credit to his good taste, and a magnanimity which
equally honors his heart, he spoke of Mr. Clay in the
following words :

" There are two candidates in the field, Mr. Clay of Kentucky, and Mr. Polk of Tennessee. I shall speak of them both with the respect to which their character and position entitle them ; and at the same time with that freedom and candor which ought to be observed in discussing the merits of public men, especially those who are candidates for the highest office in the gift of the people.

" Mr. Clay has been before the country for a long period, nearly forty years. Over thirty years he has taken a leading and highly important part in the public affairs of this country. He is acknowledged to be a man of singular and almost universal talent. He has had great experience in the administration of our public affairs in various departments. He has served for many years with wonderful judgment and ability, in both houses of Congress, of one of which he performed the arduous and difficult duties of its presiding officer, with unexampled skill and success. He has rendered most important services to his country of a diplomatic character, as the representative of this government in Europe, at one of the most trying periods of our history, and ably assisted to conduct to a satisfactory conclusion a very delicate and important negotiation. He has performed the duties of the department of State with ability and fidelity. He is a man of frankness and honor, of unquestioned talent and ability, and of a noble and generous bearing.

" Mr. Polk is a much younger man than Mr. Clay. He is a very respectable gentleman in private life; he has been in Congress ; was once Speaker of the House of Representatives of the United States, and once Governor of the State of Tennessee."

We may not only refer to this passage as evidence of Mr. Webster's magnanimity of soul, but as a high example of gentlemanly dignity—in the very heat of an animated party discussion, not forgetting to render justice even to an adversary.

In respect to Mr. Calhoun, Mr. Webster displayed similar elevation of mind. It is matter of history that, in the earlier periods of their congressional life, these two men were drawn together by mutual admiration. But party exigences have no respect for private feelings, and accordingly Mr. Calhoun joined the conspiracy, which, in 1832, was formed to crush Mr. Webster; a measure which it was hoped to accomplish through the eloquence of Mr. Hayne, assisted by the united talent of the democratic party, at that time powerfully represented in the Senate. That he escaped, was owing to his own matchless abilities*— for there is hardly an instance on record in which a man, single-handed, has withstood and baffled and punished so formidable a combination. For several years immediately following, Mr. Webster was called into an almost perpetual conflict with Mr. Calhoun— from this point his stern, unflinching adversary. By general consent, others stood aloof, almost in awe of the conflict between these two champions. The struggle furnishes some of the most remarkable passages in our political history. But an event at last

---

* The "great debate" here alluded to, took place in the Senate, in January, 1830. Colonel Hayne had attacked Mr. Webster with great power, fortified as he was by facts, arguments, and suggestions, furnished by democratic members from all parts of the Union, and going over Mr. Webster's whole political life. The reply was triumphant and overwhelming, and is justly considered the greatest forensic effort which our history supplies. There is, indeed, so far as I know, no speech which equals it, if we regard the variety of its topics, the vast scope of its leading considerations, the beauty and felicity of many of its passages, and its completeness as a whole.

arrived which was to put an end to the strife. Mr. Calhoun, who had gradually been sinking under a decay of health and constitution, expired at Washington on the 31st of March, 1850. It was then that Mr. Webster rose in the Senate and pronounced upon him a eulogium, in which all his merits were beautifully set forth, without one of the many shadows which truth might have furnished.

"Sir," said Mr. Webster, "the eloquence of Mr. Calhoun, or the manner of his exhibition of his sentiments in public bodies, was part of his intellectual character. It grew out of the qualities of his mind. It was plain, strong, terse, condensed, concise; sometimes impassioned, still always severe. Rejecting ornament, not often seeking far for illustration, his power consisted in the plainness of his propositions, in the closeness of his logic, and in the earnestness and energy of his manner. These are the qualities, as I think, which have enabled him through such a long course of years to speak often, and yet always command attention. His demeanor as a Senator is known to us all—is appreciated, venerated by us all. No man was more respectful to others; no man carried himself with greater decorum, no man with superior dignity.

"Sir, I have not in public or in private life known a more assiduous person in the discharge of his appropriate duties. He seemed to have no recreation but the pleasure of conversation with his friends. Out of the chambers of Congress, he was either devoting himself to the acquisition of knowledge pertaining to the immediate subject of the duty before him, or else he was indulging in some social interviews in which he so much delighted. His colloquial talents were certainly singular and eminent. There was a charm in his conversation not often found. He delighted especially in conversation and intercourse with young men. I suppose that there has been no man among us who had more winning manners, in such an intercourse and such conversation, with men comparatively young, than Mr. Calhoun. I believe one great power of his character, in general, was his conversational talent. I believe it is that, as well as a consciousness of his high integrity, and the greatest reverence for his talents and ability, that has made him so endeared an object to the people of the State to which he belonged.

"Mr. President, he had the basis, the indispensable basis, of all high character—and that was, unspotted integrity, unimpeached honor and character. If he had aspirations, they were high, and honorable, and noble. There was nothing groveling, or low, or meanly selfish, that came near the head or the heart of Mr. Calhoun. Firm in his purpose, perfectly patriotic and honest, as I am sure he was, in the principles that he espoused and in the measures that he defended, aside from that large regard for that species of distinction that conducted him to eminent stations for the benefit of the Republic, I do not believe he had a selfish motive or selfish feeling. However, sir, he may have differed from others of us in his political opinions or his political principles, those principles and those opinions will now descend to posterity under the sanction of a great name. He has lived long enough, he has done enough, and he has done it so well, so successfully, so honorably, as to connect himself for all time with the records of his country. He is now an historical character. Those of us who have known him here will find that he has left upon our minds and our hearts a strong and lasting impression of his person, his character, and his public performances, which while we live will never be obliterated. We shall hereafter, I am sure, indulge in it as a grateful recollection, that we have lived in his age, that we have been his contemporaries, that we have seen him, and heard him, and known him. We shall delight to speak of him to those who are rising up to fill our places. And, when the time shall come that we ourselves shall go, one after another, to our graves, we shall carry with us a deep sense of his genius and character, his honor and integrity, his amiable deportment in private life, and the purity of his exalted patriotism."

Was there not something grand and at the same time affecting in a scene like this—a great man—all selfish thought rebuked, all passed bitterness forgot —uttering words like these, over the now prostrate competitor with whom it had been his lot to wrestle through long years of the bitterest party conflict?

But I must draw this chapter to a close; yet my memory is, indeed, full of the images of other men of mark whom I have seen upon the great stage of action at Washington. Among them was William Wirt, an able lawyer, an elegant writer, an accomplished gentleman—and, at the time I knew him, Attorney-general of the United States; Mr. Forsyth, Gen. Jackson's accomplished Secretary of State, at whose house I remember once to have dined when Mr. Benton, Isaac Hill, John M. Niles,* and others

---

* John M. Niles was a native of Windsor, Connecticut. He studied law, and settled at Hartford, devoting himself, however, to politics. He was of small, awkward, and insignificant personal appearance, and for this reason, probably, was for many years treated and regarded with some degree of contempt, especially by the federalists, to whom he was politically opposed. I knew him well, and early learned to appreciate the logical force of his understanding. He was associated in the Times newspaper, and was probably, more than any other single person, the instrument of overturning the federal party in the State, in 1817. He now rose to various eminent public stations, at last becoming a Senator of the United States, and for a short time Postmaster-general under Mr. Polk. He had strong common sense, and close reasoning powers, which operated with the precision of cog-wheels. Mr. Webster regarded his speech upon the tariff, while he was in the Senate, as one of the very ablest ever delivered upon that subject.

I must give a sketch of a scene in Mr. Forsyth's parlor, on the occasion

were present; "John Taylor of Caroline," an able Virginian statesman, and the very personification of old-fashioned dignity and courtesy; Albert Gallatin, a dark, swarthy man, with an eye that seemed to penetrate the souls of all who approached him; Henry R. Storrs,* a native of Connecticut, but a representative from New York—one of the ablest debaters of his day; Hayne of South Carolina, the gallant but unsuccessful jouster with Mr. Webster; Burgess of Rhode

---

above alluded to, as it presents a tableaux of three marked men. The dinner had been finished for some time, but several of the gentlemen lingered at the table. The ladies had retired, and made a considerable semicircle around the fire in the parlor. Mr. Forsyth was in the middle of this room, receiving the gentlemen as they came from the dining-hall, and who, after a little conversation with him, bowed to the ladies and took their leave.

At last Messrs. Benton, Hill, and Niles came from the dining-room together, and stopped to converse with Mr. Forsyth. Mr. Hill, who was very lame, said good-night to his host and went straight to the door, without taking the slightest notice of the bright circle around the fire-side. Benton came next; but he is an old courtier, and therefore paid his addresses to the ladies, beginning with Mrs. Meigs—Mrs. Forsyth's mother—and bowing gracefully to each, was about to take his leave. Niles came next. His first idea evidently was to follow the example of Isaac Hill, but as Benton was actually performing his courtesies, he felt it impossible wholly to disregard such a pattern. Setting out first for the door, he soon diverged toward the fireside; when near the ladies, he was suddenly seized with panic, and pulling out a red bandanna handkerchief from his pocket, gave a loud blast upon his nose, shot out of the door, and thus safely effected his retreat.

Mr. Niles died at Hartford in 1856, aged sixty-nine.

* Mr. Storrs was a native of Middletown, Connecticut, and brother of the present Judge Storrs of that State. He was educated at Yale, and was there considered a dull scholar, yet he early became eminent as a lawyer and a statesman. He first settled at Utica, but afterward removed to the city of New York, where he died in 1837, aged forty-nine. He was distinguished for various acquirements, great powers of discrimination, remarkable logical exactness, and a ready and powerful elocution.

Island—a man of prodigious powers of sarcasm, and who made even John Randolph quail; Silas Wright of New York, ever courteous, ever smiling—a giant in strength, conquering his antagonists with such an air of good-humor as to reconcile them to defeat: these, and still others among the departed, live in my memory, and were there time and occasion, would furnish interesting themes of description and comment. Of those among the living—Crittenden, noted for his close argument and polished sarcasm; Benton of Missouri, who has fought his way through many prejudices, till he has attained the reputation of unrivaled industry, vast acquisitions, and an enlarged statesmanship; Bell of Tennessee, always dignified and commanding respect—these linger in my memory as connected with the senate-chamber, where indeed their chief laurels have been won. In the other house, I have often seen and heard Winthrop, Cushing, Wise, T. Marshall—all brilliant orators, and accustomed to "bring down the House," when the spirit moved.

In the White House, I have seen Monroe and Adams, and Jackson and Van Buren, and Harrison and Tyler, and Taylor and Fillmore. How many memories rise up at the mention of these names—associated as they are in my mind with the brilliant throngs I have seen at their levees, or with the public events connected with their names, or the whirlpools of party strife which I have seen fretting and foaming at the periods of their election!

But I must forbear. A single domestic event claims to be recorded here, and I shall then take leave of Washington. I have told you that I had come hither with my family. Among them was one to whom existence had hitherto been only a bright, unbroken spring. Gifted, beautiful, healthful, happy —loving all and loved by all—he never suggested by his appearance, an idea but of life, and enjoyment, and success, and prosperity. Yet he was suddenly taken from us. We mourned, though remembrances were mingled with our grief which softened, if they could not wholly remove it. His simple virtues, faintly recorded in the following stanzas, are still more indelibly written on our hearts:

A MEMORIAL.

Oh, tell me not that Eden's fall
Has left alike its blight on all—
For one I knew from very birth,
Who scarcely bore the stains of earth.
No wondrous bump of skull had he—
No mark of startling prodigy;
His ways were gentle, tranquil, mild—
Such as befit a happy child—
With thoughtful face, though bland and fair—
Of hazel eye and auburn hair.

When with his mates in mirthful glee—
A simple, joyous boy was he,
Whose harmless wit, or gentle joke,
A laughing echo often woke.

THE STUDENT.

"Oft have I seen him in the wood,
Wrapt in a meditative mood."   Vol. 2, p. 433.

He gaily joined the ardent chase,
And often won the bantering race.
His sled, endowed with seeming skill,
Flew swiftest down the snowy hill;
And o'er the lake his gliding skates
Left far behind his panting mates.
Yet 'mid the strife the gentle boy
Caught only bliss, and no alloy.
The vulgar oath—th' offensive word—
The lie, the jeer, the scoff, he heard—
Yet none of these e'er soiled his tongue,
Or o'er his breast their shadow flung;
No hidden vice, no lurking sin,
Told on his brow a curse within;
And still, as years flew lightly o'er,
The stamp of truth and peace he bore.

If thus he loved the sportive mood,
Still more he loved alone to brood
Along the winding river's brim,
Through arching forests hoar and dim;
Beside the ocean's shelly shore,
And where the surly cataracts pour.
Yet not an idle dreamer he,
Who wasted life in reverie;
For ocean, forest, fall, and brook—
Each was to him a speaking book:
And thus, untaught, he gained a store
Of curious art and wondrous lore.
I oft have seen him in the wood,
Wrapt in a meditative mood—
Now gazing at the forest high,
Now searching flowers with heedful eye,
Now watching with inquiring view,
Each feathered craftsman as he flew—

Now studying deep the spider's thread,
With wondrous cunning twined and spread—
Now tracing out the beetle's den,
Where sturdy insects work like men;
Now on his knees o'er ant-hill bent,
Upon the bustling town intent;
Now snatching with a skillful swoop,
From out the brook, a wriggling troop
Of tadpole, frog, and nameless wight,
O'er which he pored in strange delight.
And thus, all nature's varied lore
He loved to ponder o'er and o'er—
To watch alike, with studious gaze,
The insects and their wondrous ways;
The forest, with its flush of flowers—
The landscape, with its bloom of bowers—
The river, winding far away—
The ocean, in its ceaseless play—
The trembling stars, that seem to trace
God's footsteps o'er the depths of space!

And as in years he older grew,
Still sterner science won his view:
From books he gathered hidden lore,
Though none saw how he gained his store.
Yet most he loved to break the seal
Of nature's secrets, and reveal
The wondrous springs that hidden lie
Within her deep philosophy—
In pulley, axle, wedge, and beam—
In trembling air and flowing stream.
His mind, with shrewd invention fraught,
His hand, with ready practice wrought—
Constructing engines, sped by steam,
That flew o'er mimic rail and stream:

Meanwhile his room a shop became,
With lathe and bellows, forge and flame;
And in the midst, as each could see,
Mechanic—chemist—all was he.

And thus with knowledge he was fraught,
Not by an instinct, but by thought—
Patient and tranquil—bent with care—
O'er many a book—a student rare.
And while he thus the useful knew,
He still was just and truthful too:
He loved the good, the dutiful—
The tasteful, and the beautiful;
Still modest—simple—was his air;
Still found he pleasure everywhere;
Still found he friends on every hand:
The humble loved, for he was bland;
The high admired, for all refined,
His look and manner matched his mind.
No envy broke his bosom's rest—
No pride disturbed his tranquil breast—
No praise he heeded, for he knew
To judge himself by standards true;
And words to him were vain and waste,
If still unsatisfied his taste.

With rapid hand his pencil drew
Light sketches of the scenes he knew,
Which told how well his studious eye
Had traced the hues of earth and sky—
The playful change of light and shade
O'er rippling wave or spreading glade.
And music from his fingers swept
So sweet—so deep—the listener wept.
The tutored and untutored round,
In trembling trance, alike were bound;

For not alone with hand and heart,
He mastered all the gems of art,
But bade the soft piano's key
Reveal unwritten melody—
A flowing fount of playful feeling,
O'er which a plaintive tone was stealing—
As twilight oft is seen to throw
Its saddening shade o'er sunset's glow.
'Tis said, alas! that those who love
Sad melodies, go soon above;
And that fair youth—that gentle boy—
So full of light, and love, and joy—
Sixteen bright summers o'er his head—
He sleeps, companion of the dead!

How vain are tears! but memory's art,
While yet it wrings, still soothes the heart;
For if it bring the lost to sight,
He comes in some fond robe of light.
Of all his sports in life's fair day,
He loved the best down yonder bay
To speed his boat with shivering sail,
Or glide before the whispering gale;
For in the presence of the sea
He found a quiet ecstasy,
As if it came with mystic lore,
And beckoned to some happier shore.
And when his last sad hour was nigh,
And clouds were gathering o'er his eye,
His mother asked, "How now, my boy?"
He answered, with a beam of joy—
"I'm in my boat!" and thus he passed—
These simple, meaning words—his last!

LETTER LVI.

London and Paris compared—Paris thirty years ago—Louis XVIII.—
The Parisians—Garden of the Tuileries—Washington Irving—Mr.
Warden, the American Consul—Société Philomatique—Baron Larrey
—Geoffroy St. Hilaire—The Institute—Arago—Lamarck—Gay-Lussac
—Cuvier— Lacroix — Laplace — Laennec—Dupuytren—Talma—Made-
moiselle Mars.

My DEAR C******

About the middle of April, 1851, I arrived in
Paris, and soon after took charge of the Consulate
there. As you know, I have frequently been in this
gay city, and I now propose to gather up my recollections of it, and select therefrom a few items which
may fill up the blank that yet remains in my story,
and in some degree contribute to your amusement.

I first visited Paris in January, 1824, as I have told
you. I had spent a month in London, which is always
a rather gloomy place to a stranger, and in winter is
peculiarly depressing. The people who have houses
there, burrow into them, and lighting their coal fires,
make themselves happy ; but the wanderer from his
country, shut out from these cheerful scenes, and
forced into the streets, grimed with dirt and drizzle
below and incumbered with bituminous fogs above,
feels that he is in a dreary wilderness, where man
and nature conspire to make him miserable and
melancholy. In most great cities, there is something

to cheer the new-comer : it is precisely the reverse with London, and particularly at this dismal season. Its finest streets, its most sumptuous squares, even its noble monuments, which are not few, have always a rather dull aspect, and in the pitchy atmosphere of winter, they seem to be in mourning, and communicate their gloom to all around. St. Paul's, incrusted with soot and dripping with an inky deposit from the persistent fogs ; Nelson's monument, black with coal-smoke, and clammy with the chill death-damp of the season,—all these things—the very ornaments and glories of the city — are positively depressing, and especially to an American, accustomed to the transparent skies, the white snow-drifts, the bracing, cheering atmosphere of his own winter climate.

Paris is the very opposite of London. The latter is an ordinary city, impressed by no distinctive characteristics, except its gloom and its vast extent. It is little more than twenty Liverpools, crowded together, and forming the most populous city in the world. Paris, on the contrary, is marked with prominent and peculiar traits, noticed at once by the most careless observer. On entering the streets, you are struck with the air of ornament and decoration which belongs to the architecture, the effect of which is heightened by the light color of the freestone, the universal building material. The sky is bright, and the people seem to reflect its cheerfulness. The public gar-

dens and squares, surrounded with monuments of art
and teeming with men, women, and children, including abundance of rosy nurses aad plump babies, all
apparently bent on pleasure, and this, too, in mid-
winter—are peculiar and striking features of this gay
metropolis.   To an American who has just left London, his heart heavy with hypochondria, Paris is indeed delightful, and soon restores him to his wonted
cheerfulness.

At the time I first arrived here, this city was, however, very different from what it now is.   Louis
XVIII. was upon the throne, and had occupied it for
nine years.   During this period he had done almost
nothing to repair the state of waste and dilapidation
in which the allies had left it.   These had taken down
the statue of Napoleon on the column of the Place
Vendôme, and left its pedestal vacant; the king had
followed up the reform and erased the offensive name
of the exiled emperor from the public monuments,
and put his own, Louis XVIII., in their place; he had
caused a few churches to be repaired, and some pictures of the Virgin to be painted and placed in their
niches.   But ghastly mounds of rubbish—the wrecks
of demolished edifices—scattered heaps of stones at
the foot of half-built walls of buildings, destined
never to be completed,—these and other unsightly
objects were visible on every hand, marking the recent history of Napoleon, overthrown in the midst
of his mighty projects, and leaving his name and his

works to be desecrated alike by a foreign foe and a
more bitter domestic adversary.

The king, Louis XVIII., was a man of good sense
and liberal mind, for one of his race; but he was
wholly unfit to administer the government. He was
a sort of monster of obesity, and, at the time I speak
of, having lost the use of his lower limbs, he could
not walk, and was trundled about the palace of the
Tuileries in a cripple's go-cart. I have often seen
him let down in this, through the arch in the south-
eastern angle of the palace, into his coach, and returning from his ride, again taken up, and all this
more like a helpless barrel of beef than a sovereign.
Had the allies intended to make legitimacy at once
odious and ridiculous, they could not better have
contrived it than by squatting down this obese, imbecile extinguisher upon the throne of France, as the
successor of Napoleon!

The Parisians are, however, a philosophic race: as
they could not help themselves, they did not spend
their lives like children, in profitless poutings. They
had their jokes, and among these, they were accustomed to call Louis Dix-huit, *Louis des huîtres*—a tolerable pun, which was equivalent to giving him the
familiar title of Old Oyster Louis. Deeming it their
birthright to have three or four hours of pleasure
every day—whoever may be in power—they still fre-
quented the promenades, the Boulevards, and the
theaters. When, therefore, I first visited the gardens

of the Tuileries of a bright Sunday afternoon, and immediately after quitting the "dull fuliginous abyss"
of London, the scene seemed to me like enchantment. I find my impressions thus chronicled in my
notes:

"Weather fine, bright, and mild; some shrubs still
green, and many flowers yet in bloom; jets of fountains playing in the sunshine; too early in the day for
a great throng, yet a great many people here; all have
a quiet, sauntering look; hundreds of tidy nurses,
with bare arms and neat caps on their heads, the
children they carry about being richly dressed, their
little rosy cheeks imbedded in lace; the ladies tastefully attired, and walking with a peculiar air of grace
—very sentimental and modest in their countenances
—never look at you, as they do in London; very
provoking. There is no Sunday air in the scene,
but rather that of a calm pleasure-day; children are
rolling hoops; one boy making a dirt pie; two dogs,
which have probably been shut up for a week, having a glorious scamper; wild-pigeons cooing above in
the tree-tops; sparrows hopping about on the green
sod at the foot of the statues of Flora and Diana,
and picking up crumbs of bread thrown to them by
the children; a number of old men in the sunshine,
sheltered by a northern wall, reading newspapers;
several nurses there, sunning their babies; palace of
the Tuileries of an architecture never seen in America,
but still imposing; the Rue de Rivoli on the north,

superb; the Place Louis Quinze,* fine; the mint and other edifices along the opposite bank of the Seine, beautiful. Wonderful place, this Paris; different from any thing I have seen. It seems devised, in its sky, its edifices, its decorations, its ornaments, for a tasteful and pleasure-loving people. Even I, a wanderer, feel no sense of solitude, of isolation, here. London is repulsive, and seems continually to frown upon the stranger as an outcast; Paris smiles upon him and welcomes him, and makes him feel at home. The genial spirit of the French nation speaks in this, its capital: just as the temper and spirit of John Bull seem to be built into the brick and mortar of the streets of London."

I can not, perhaps, do better than to give you a few more passages from the hasty jottings I made at the time.

"February 6—Washington Irving returned our call. Strikingly mild and amiable; dress—claret coat, rather more pigeon-tailed than the fashion at New York; light waistcoat; tights; ribbed, flesh-colored silk stockings; shoes, polished very bright. This a fashionable dress here. He spoke of many

---

* This is now the Place de la Concorde, and is one of the most beautiful squares in the world. In the center is the famous obelisk of Luxor: from this point four superb works of architecture are seen at the four cardinal points—to the west, through the avenue of the Champs Elisées, is the Arc de Triomphe de l'Etoile; to the north, the Church of the Madeleine; to the east, the Palace of the Tuileries; to the south, the Chamber of Deputies.

things, all in a quiet manner, evidently with a fund of feeling beneath.

" February 14—Went with Mr. Warden* to a meeting of the 'Société Philomatique,' composed of members of the Institute ; saw Fourier, the famous geometrician and physician ; he accompanied Napoleon to Egypt ; wears a great brown wig ; a dull, clumsy speaker : Thénard, a famous chemist, associated with Gay-Lussac ; looks about forty : Larrey ; has long black hair parted on the forehead, with an air of gravity and solidity, mingled with simplicity ; spoke slowly, but with great clearness. Bonaparte said he was the most honest man he ever knew. He accompanied the expedition to Egypt ; is still a distinguished surgeon, and in full practice. Poisson, one of the first mathematicians in Europe ; he has a very fine head and splendid eye—seems about forty-eight : Geoffroy St. Hilaire, a zoologist, second only to Cuvier ; a bustling, smiling man, of very demonstrative manner ; he had two huge fish-bones, which he used for the purpose of illustrating his observations. He was also in the Egyptian expedition, and contributed largely to its scientific results. He seemed about forty-eight, and was listened to with great

---

* Mr. David Bailie Warden, who had been Secretary of Legation when Gen. Armstrong was Minister to Holland, was at this time Consul of the United States at Paris. He was a native of Ireland, but had become an American citizen. He was a corresponding member of the Institute, and was a man of considerable scientific and literary acquirements. He wrote a clever History of the United States. He died at Paris in 1845, aged 67.

attention. Bosc, a celebrated agriculturist, botanist, &c., old, respectable, gentlemanly.

"The proceedings were conducted with order and simplicity, forming a striking contrast to the pompous declamation I heard in London, in the Academy of Arts, upon hatching eggs.

"February 16—Went with Mr. Warden to a meeting of the Institute, held in the Hotel Mazarin : one hundred and fifty members present. Arago, president ; he is tall, broad-shouldered, and imposing in appearance, with a dark, swarthy complexion, and a black, piercing eye. Lamarck, the famous writer on natural history—old, infirm, blind—was led in by another member—a distinguished entomologist, whose name I have forgotten ; Fontaine, the architect—tall, homely, and aged : Gay-Lussac, a renowned chemist, under forty, active, fiery in debate : Cuvier, rather a large man, red face, eyes small, very near-sighted ; eyes near together and oddly appearing and disappearing ; features acute, hair gray, long, and careless ; he spoke several times, and with great pertinency and effect : Lacroix, the mathematician, old, and looks like a '76er : Laplace, the most famous living astronomer, tall, thin, and sharp-featured—reminded me of the portraits of Voltaire ; he is about seventy-five, feeble, yet has all his mental faculties.

"The principal discussion related to gasometers, the police of Paris having asked the opinion of the Institute as to the safety of certain new kinds, lately introduced. The subject excited great interest, and the debate was quite animated. Thénard, Gay-Lussac, Girard, Laplace, Cuvier, and others, engaged in the debate. Nearly all expressed themselves with great ease and even volubility. They were occasionally vehement, and when excited, several spoke at once, and the president was obliged often to ring his bell to preserve order.

" It was strange and striking to see so many old men, just on the borders of the grave, still retaining such ardor for science as to appear at a club like this, and enter with passion into all the questions that came up. Such a spectacle is not to be seen elsewhere, on the earth. The charms of science generally fade to the eye of threescore and ten ; few passions except piety and avarice survive threescore. It is evident, in studying this association, that the highest and most ardent exercises of the mind are here stimulated by the desire of glory, which is the reward of success. One thing struck me forcibly in this assembly, and that was the utter absence of all French foppery in dress, among the members. Their attire was plain black, and generally as simple as that of so many New England clergymen.

" In the evening, went to the Théâtre Français, to see Talma in the celebrated tragedy of Sylla, by Jouy. Did not well understand the French, but could see that the acting was very masterly. Had expected a great deal of rant, but was agreeably disappointed. In the more passionate parts there was a display of vigor, but at other times the performance was quiet and natural—without any of the stage-exaggeration I am accustomed to. Most of the scenes were such as might actually take place, under the circumstances indicated in the play. Talma is said to resemble Napoleon in person; he certainly looked very much like his portraits. His hair was evidently arranged to favor the idea of resemblance to the emperor. He is a very handsome man, and comes up to my idea of a great actor.

"February 20th—Went to see a new comedy by Casimir Delavigne, "L'Ecole des Vieillards." Talma and Mademoiselle Mars played the two principal parts. The piece consisted of a succession of rather long dialogues, without any change of scenery. The whole theater had somewhat the quiet elegance of a parlor. There were no noisy disturbers; there was no vulgarity—no boisterous applause. The actors appeared like groups of genteel people, conversing, as we see them in actual life. There was nothing very exciting in the situations, nothing highly romantic in the plot or denouement. The interest of the play consisted in playful wit, sparkling repartee, and light satire upon life and society—represented by the most beautiful acting I have ever seen. Talma is inimitable in the character of a refined but somewhat imbecile man, who has passed the prime of life; and Mademoiselle Mars is, beyond comparison, the most graceful and

pleasing of actresses. I am struck with the strict
propriety, the refinement even of the manners of the
audience. The whole entertainment seems, indeed,
to be founded upon a very different idea from that of
the English stage, which is largely adapted to delight
the coarse tastes of the pit. Here the pit—called the
parterre—is filled with people of refinement.

"February 21st—Went to the Hospital of La Cha-
rité. Saw Laennec, with his pupils, visiting the patients. He makes great use of the stethoscope, which
is a wooden tube applied to the body, and put to the
ear: by the sound, the state of the lungs and the vital
organs is ascertained. It is like a telescope, by which
the interior of the body is perceived, only that the ear
is used instead of the eye. It is deemed a great improvement. Laennec is the inventor, and has high
reputation in the treatment of diseases of the chest.
He has learned to ascertain the condition of the lungs
by thumping on the breast and back of the patient,
and putting the ear to the body at the same time.
He is a little man, five feet three inches high, and
thin as a shadow. However, he has acute features,
and a manner which bespeaks energy and consciousness of power.

"The whole hospital was neat and clean; bed-
steads of iron. French medical practice very light;
few medicines given; nursing is a great part of the
treatment. Laennec's pupils followed him from patient to patient. He conversed with them in Latin.

One of the patients was a handsome, black-eyed girl,
not very sick. All the young men must apply the
stethoscope to her chest; she smiled, and seemed to
think it all right.

"Same day, went to the Hotel Dieu, a medical and
surgical hospital. Saw Dupuytren and his pupils,
visiting the patients. He is a rather large man, of a
fine Bonapartean head, but sour, contumelious looks.
He holds the very first rank as a surgeon. His operations are surprisingly bold and skillful. Edward
C . . . ., of Philadelphia, who is here studying medicine,
told me a good anecdote of him. He has a notion that
he can instantly detect hydrocephalus in a patient,
from the manner in which he carries his head. One
day, while he was in the midst of his scholars at the
hospital, he saw a common sort of man standing at a
distance, among several persons who had come for
medical advice. Dupuytren's eye fell upon him, and
he said to his pupils—'Do you see yonder, that fellow
that has his hand to his face, and carries his head almost on his shoulder? Now, take notice: that man
has hydrocephalus. Come here, my good fellow!'

"The man thus called, came up. 'Well,' said Dupuytren—'I know what ails you; but come, tell us
about it yourself. What is the matter with you?'

" 'I've got the toothache!' was the reply.

" 'Take that'—said Dupuytren, giving him a box
on the ear—'and go to the proper department and
have it pulled out!' "

LETTER LVII.

Death of Louis XVIII.—Charles X.—The "Three Glorious Days"—Louis
Philippe—The Revolution of February, 1848.

My dear C******

I was again in Paris in the summer of 1832. Great changes had taken place since 1824 : Louis XVIII. was dead ; Charles X. had succeeded, and after a brief reign had been driven away by the revolution of the "Three Glorious Days." Louis Philippe was now on the throne. On the 29th of July, and the two following days, we saw the celebration of the event which had thus changed the dynasty of France. It consisted of a grand fête, in the Champs Elysées, closed by a most imposing military spectacle, in which eighty thousand troops, extending from the Arc de Triomphe to the Place Vendôme, marched before the admiring throng. Louis Philippe was himself on horseback as commander-in-chief, and such was his popularity among the masses that, in many instances, I saw men in blouses rush up and grasp his hand, and insist upon shaking it. Sixteen years after, I saw him hustled into a cab, and flying from the mob for his life—his family scattered, and he but too happy to get safe to England in the disguise of a sailor !

As I have told you, I established my family in

Paris in 1846; that winter and the following I was also there. I remember that on a certain Monday in February, 1848, I went up to see our countrywoman, the Marchioness Lavalette, to arrange with her about an introduction she had promised me to Guizot. She was not at home, but as I was coming down the hill from the Place St. George, I met her in her carriage. She asked me to walk back to her house, and I did so. I observed that she was much agitated, and asked her the cause. "We are going to have trouble!" said she. "I have just been to the Chambers: the ministry have determined to stop the meeting of the liberals to-morrow; the proclamation is already being printed."

"Well, and what then?" said I.

"Another 'Three Glorious Days!'"

To this I replied that I conceived her fears groundless; that Louis Philippe appeared to me strong in the confidence of the people; that he was noted for his prudence and sagacity; that Guizot, his prime minister, was a man of great ability; that the whole cabinet, indeed, were distinguished for their judgment and capacity. The lady shook her head, and rejoined—

"I know Paris better than you do. We are on the eve of an earthquake!"

Soon after this I took my leave. What speedily ensued, may best be told in a letter I addressed to a friend in Boston, and which was as follows:

PARIS, March 14th, 1848.

As it has been my fortune to be in Paris, and an observer of many of the most stirring and striking occurrences during the late revolution, I propose to give you a brief consecutive narrative of what I saw and heard, embracing a sketch of other leading events. My purpose will be to take you with me, and make you a participator, as far as possible, in the scenes witnessed and emotions experienced by one who was on the spot.

Before I begin, it may be well to state a few particulars as to the political condition of France at the moment of the revolt. It is well known that Louis Philippe accepted the crown at the hands of Lafayette, after the struggle of July, 1830, the latter saying, as he presented the king and charter to the people— "We give you the best of monarchies—the best of republics!" The circumstances, all considered, pledged Louis Philippe to a liberal government, in which the good of the people should be the supreme object, and the popular will the predominating element.

He commenced his career under fair auspices, and for a time every thing promised a happy fulfillment of what seemed his duty and his destiny. But by degrees a great change came over the monarch; the possession of power seduced his heart, and turned his head; and forgetting his pledges, and blind to his true interest, he set himself to building up a dynasty that should hand down his name and fame to posterity.

It seemed, at a superficial glance, that he might realize his dream. He had acquired the reputation of being the most sagacious monarch of his time. He had improved and embellished the capital; on all sides his "image and superscription" were seen in connection with statues, fountains, edifices, and works of beauty and utility. France was happier than the adjacent countries. The famine and the pestilence, that had recently desolated neighboring states, had trod more lightly here. The king was blessed with a large family. These had all reached maturity, and were allied to kings and queens, princes and princesses. The upholders of the crown in the parliament, were men whose names alone were a tower of strength. Peace reigned at home, and the army abroad had just succeeded in achieving a signal triumph over an enemy that had baffled them for seventeen years.*

Such was the outward seeming of affairs; but there were threatening fires within, which might at any moment produce a conflagration. Many thinking people were profoundly disgusted with the retrograde tendency of the government, with the corruption of its officers, the gradual subsidizing of the legislature by the crown, and the concentration of all the powers of the state in the hands of one man, who was now using them for family aggrandizement. Although the march of despotism had been cautious and stealthy, the plainest mind could see, and indeed the people generally began to feel, many galling evidences of the tyranny to which they had become actually subjected.

Among these grievances, were the constant increase of the national debt, and consequent increase of taxation, with the restraints put upon the liberty of the press and of speech. By a law of some years' standing, the people were prohibited from holding stated meetings of more than twenty persons, without license; and *reform banquets*, or meetings for the discussion of public affairs—of which about seventy had been held, in different parts of the kingdom, within the last year—were now pronounced illegal by the ministry. Finally, a determination to suppress one of them, about to be held in the twelfth ward of Paris, was solemnly announced by them in the Chamber of Deputies.

It is material to bear in mind, that there are always in this metropolis at least one hundred thousand workmen, who live from day to day upon their labor, and who, upon the slightest check to trade, are plunged into poverty, if not starvation. At the moment of which we are speaking, this immense body of

---

* Abd-el-Kadir, who had been the indomitable leader of the Arabs of the Desert, against the French, who had conquered Algiers, surrendered to Gen. Lamoricière, December 22d, 1847.

men, with their families, were suffering sorely from the stagnation of business in the capital. There were not less than two
hundred thousand persons who, for the space of three months,
had hardly been able to obtain sufficient food to appease the
cravings of hunger. How easy to stir up these people to rebellion!—how natural for them to turn their indignation against
the king and his government! The opposition members seized
the occasion now afforded them, to excite these discontented
masses against the ministry; and it may be added that the
latter, by their rashness, did more than their enemies to prepare
the mine and set the match to the train.

The crisis was now at hand. The opposition deputies declared
their intention to attend the proposed meeting; and in spite of
the threats of the ministry, the preparations for the banquet
went vigorously on. A place was selected in the Champs Elysées, and a building was in progress of erection for the celebration. The programme of the same was announced, the toast for
the occasion was published, the orator, O. Barrot, selected. The
day was fixed—an ominous day for tyranny—an auspicious one
for human freedom. It was the 22d of February, the birthday
of Washington! Whether it has received a new title to its place
in the calendar of liberty, must be left for the decision of time.

The evening of the 21st came, and then proclamations were
issued by the co-operation of the ministry and the police, prohibiting the banquet. This act, though it had been threatened, still
fell like a thunderbolt upon the people. It was known that an
immense military force had been quietly assembled in Paris and
the vicinity—eighty thousand troops, with artillery and ample
munitions—and that the garrisons around the Tuileries had
been victualed as if for a siege. But it had not been believed
that an attempt to stifle the voice of the people, so bold as this,
would really be made. Yet such was the fact. The leaders of
the opposition receded from their ground, and it was announced,
in the papers of the 22d, that the banquet, being forbidden by
the government, would not take place!

The morning of this day was dark and drizzly. I had antici-pated some manifestation of uneasiness, and at half-past nine o'clock went forth. Groups of people were reading the procla-mations posted up at the corners of the streets, but all was tranquil. I walked along the Boulevards for a mile, yet saw no symptoms of the coming storm.

The designated place of meeting for the banquet was the square of the Madeleine. This is at the western extremity of the Boulevards, and near the great central square, called the Place de la Concorde—a point communicating directly with the Chamber of Deputies, the Champs Elysées, the gardens of the Tuileries, &c. At eleven o'clock, A. M., a dark mass was seen moving along the Boulevards, toward the proposed place of meeting. This consisted of thousands of workmen from the faubourgs. In a few moments the entire square of the Madeleine was filled with these persons, dressed almost exclusively in their characteristic costume, which consists of a blue tunic, called *blouse*—a garment which is made very much in the fashion of our farmers' frocks.

The opening scene of the drama had now begun. The mass rushed and eddied around the Madeleine, which, by the way, is the finest church and the finest edifice in Paris. Such was the threatening aspect of the scene, that the shops were all sud-denly shut, and the people around began to supply themselves with bread and other food, for "three days." In a few moments, the avalanche took its course down the Rue Royale, swept across the Place de la Concorde, traversed the bridge over the Seine, and collected in swelling and heaving masses in the Place, or square, before the Chamber of Deputies. This building is defended in front by a high iron railing. The gate of this was soon forced, and some hundreds of the people rushed up the long flight of steps, and pausing beneath the portico, struck up the song of the Marseillaise—a song, by the way, interdicted by law on account of its exciting character. The crowd here rapidly increased; shouts, songs, cries, filled the air. East and west, along the quays, and through the streets behind the Chamber, came long lines of students from the various schools. Standing upon one of the pillars of the bridge, I commanded a view of the whole scene. It was one to fill the heart with the liveliest emotions. A hundred thousand people were now collected, seeming like an agitated sea, and sending forth a murmur resembling the voice of many waters. From the southern gate of the Tuileries now issued two bodies of troops—one, on horseback, coming along the northern quay. These were the Municipal Guard, a magnificent corps, richly caparisoned, and nobly mounted. Being picked men, and well paid, they were the chief reliance of the government, and for that very reason were hated by the people. The other body of troops were infantry of the line, and crossing the Pont Royal, came along the southern bank of the river. Both detachments approached the multitude, and crowding upon them with a slow advance, succeeded at last in clearing the space before the Chamber.

The greater part of the throng recrossed the bridge, and spread themselves over the Place de la Concorde. This square, perhaps the most beautiful in the world, is about five acres in extent. In the center is the far-famed obelisk of Luxor; on either side of this is a splendid fountain, which was in full action during the scenes we describe. To the east is the garden of the Tuileries; to the west are the Champs Elysées. This vast area, so associated with art, and luxury, and beauty, was now crowded with an excited populace, mainly of the working classes. Their number constantly augmented, and bodies of troops, foot and horse, arrived from various quarters, till the square was literally covered. The number of persons here collected in one mass was over one hundred thousand.

At the commencement, the mob amused themselves with songs, shouts, and pasquinades; but in clearing the space before the Chamber, and driving the people across the bridge, the guards had displayed great rudeness. They pressed upon the masses, and one woman was crushed to death beneath the hoofs of the horses. Pebbles now began to be hurled at the troops from the square. Dashing in among the people, sword in hand, the cavalry drove them away; but as they cleared one spot, another was immediately filled. The effect of this was to chafe and irritate the mob, who now began to seize sticks and stones and hurl them in good earnest at their assailants.

While this petty war was going on, some thousands of the rioters dispersed themselves through the Champs Elysées, and began to build barricades across the main avenue. The chairs, amounting to many hundreds, were immediately disposed in three lines across the street. Benches, trellises, boxes, fences— every movable thing within reach—were soon added to these barricades. An omnibus passing by was captured, detached from the horses, and tumbled into one of the lines. The flag was taken from the Panorama near by, and a vast procession paraded through the grounds, singing the Marseillaise, the Parisienne, and other patriotic airs.

Meanwhile, a small detachment of footguards advanced to the scene of action; but they were pelted with stones, and took shelter in their guard-house. This was assailed with a shower of missiles, which rattled like hail upon its roof. The windows were dashed in, and a heap of brush near by was laid to the wall and set on fire. A body of horse-guards soon arrived and dispersed the rioters; but the latter crossed to the northern side of the Champs Elysées, attacked another guard-house, and set it on fire. A company of the line came to the spot, but the mob cheered them, and they remained inactive. The revel proceeded, and, in the face of the soldiers, the people fed the fire with fuel from the surrounding trees and fences, sang their songs, cracked their jokes, and cried, "Down with Guizot!"—"Vive la Reforme!" &c. In these scenes the boys took the lead—performing the most desperate feats, and inspiring the rest by their intrepidity. A remarkable air of fun and frolic characterized the mob—wit flew as freely on all sides as stones and sticks; every missile seemed winged with a joke.

Such was the course of events the first day, so far as they fell under my own observation. It appears from the papers that similar proceedings, though in some cases of a more serious character, took place elsewhere. Great masses of people gathered at various points. They made hostile demonstrations before the office of Foreign Affairs, crying out, "Down with Guizot!" Some person called for the minister. "He is not here," said one; "he is with the Countess Lieven"—a remark which the habitués of Paris will understand as conveying a keen satire. At other points, a spirit of insubordination was manifested. Bakers' shops were broken open, armories forced, and barricades begun. Everywhere the hymn of the Marseillaise, and Dumas' touching death-song of the Girondins, were sung—often by hundreds of voices, and with thrilling effect. The rappel, for calling out the National Guard, was beaten in several quarters. As night closed in, heavy masses of soldiery, horse and foot, with trains of artillery, were seen at various points. The Place du Carrousel was full of troops, and at evening they were there reviewed by the king, and the Dukes of Nemours and Montpensier. Six thousand soldiers were disposed along the Boulevards, from the Madeleine to the Porte St. Martin. Patrols were seen in different quarters during the whole night. About twelve, tranquillity reigned over the city, disturbed only in a few remote and obscure places by the building of barricades, the arrest of rioters, and one or two combats, in which several persons were killed. Such was the first day's work—the prelude to the mighty drama about to follow.

Wednesday, the 23d, was fair, with dashes of rain at intervals, as in our April. I was early abroad, and soon noticed that companies of National Guards were on duty. Only regular troops had been called out the day before—a fact which showed the distrust entertained by the king of the National Guards. This was remarked by the latter, and was doubtless one of the causes which hastened the destruction of the government.

At nine o'clock, I passed up the Boulevards. Most of the

shops were shut, and an air of uneasiness prevailed among the people. At the Porte St. Denis, there was a great throng, and a considerable mass of troops. Barricades were soon after erected in the streets of St. Denis, Clery, St. Eustache, Cadran, &c. Several fusilades took place between the people at these points and the soldiers, and a number of persons were killed.

Some contests occurred in other quarters during the morning. At two o'clock, the Boulevards, the Rues St. Denis, St. Martin, Montmartre, St. Honoré—in short, all the great thoroughfares —were literally crammed with people. Bodies of horse and foot, either stationary or patrolling, were everywhere to be seen. It was about this time that some officers of the National Guard ordered their men to fire, but they refused. In one instance, four hundred National Guards were seen marching, in uniform, but without arms. It became evident that the soldiers generally were taking part with the people. This news was carried to the Palace, and Count Molé was called in to form a new ministry. He undertook the task, and orders were immediately given to spread the intelligence of this through the city.

Meanwhile the riot and revel went on in various quarters. The police were active, and hundreds of persons were arrested and lodged in prison. Skirmishes took place, here and there, between the soldiers and the people; long processions were seen, attended by persons who sang choruses, and shouted, "Down with Guizot!"—"Vive la reforme!"

About four o'clock, the news of the downfall of the Guizot ministry was spread along the Boulevards. The joyful intelligence ran over the city with the speed of light. It was everywhere received with acclamations. The people and the troops, a short time before looking at each other in deadly hostility, were seen shaking hands, and expressing congratulations. An immense population—men, women, and children—poured into the Boulevards, to share in the jubilation. Large parties of the National Guard paraded the streets, the officers and men shouting, "Vive la reforme!" and the crowd cheering loudly. Bands of five hundred to fifteen hundred men and boys went about making noisy demonstrations of joy. On being met by the troops, they divided to let them pass, and immediately resumed their cries and their songs.

Toward half-past six o'clock in the evening, an illumination was spoken of, and many persons lighted up spontaneously. The illumination soon became more general, and the populace, in large numbers, went through the streets, calling, " Light up!" Numerous bands, alone, or following detachments of the National Guards, went about, shouting, " Vive le roi!"—" Vive la reforme!" and singing the Marseillaise. At many points, where barricades had been erected, and the people were resisting the troops, they ceased when they heard the news of the resignations, and the troops retired. " It is all over!" was the general cry, and a feeling of relief seemed to pervade every bosom.

There can be no doubt that, but for a fatal occurrence which soon after took place, the further progress of the revolt might have been stayed. Many wise people now say, indeed, that the revolution was all planned beforehand; they had foreseen and predicted it; and from the beginning of the outbreak every thing tended to this point. The fact is unquestionably otherwise. The " Opposition," with their various clubs and societies distributed through all classes in Paris, and holding constant communication with the workmen, or blousemen, no doubt stood ready to take advantage of any violence on the part of the government which might justify resistance; but they had not anticipated such a contingency on the present occasion. It is not probable that the Molé ministry, had it been consummated, would have satisfied the people; but the king had yielded; Guizot, the special object of hatred, had fallen, and it was supposed that further concessions would be made, as concession had been begun. But accident, which often rules the fate of empires and dynasties, now stepped in to govern the course of events, and give them a character which should astonish the world.

In the course of the evening, a large mass of people had collected on the Boulevard, in the region of Guizot's office—the Hôtel des Affaires Etrangères. The troops here had unfortunately threatened the people, by rushing at them with fixed bayonets, after the announcement of the resignation of the ministry, and when a good feeling prevailed among all classes. This irritated the mob, and was partly, no doubt, the occasion of the large gathering in this quarter. For some reason, not well explained, a great many troops had also assembled here and in the vicinity. At ten o'clock, the street from the Madeleine to the Rue de la Paix, was thronged with soldiers and people. There was, however, no riot, and no symptom of disorder.

At this moment, a collection of persons, mostly young men, about sixty in number, came along the Boulevard, on the side opposite to the soldiers and the Foreign Office. It is said that the colonel anticipated some attack, though nothing of the kind was threatened. It appears that the soldiers stood ready to fire, when one of their muskets went off,* and wounded the commander's horse in the leg. He mistook this for a shot from the crowd, and gave instant orders to fire. A fusilade immediately followed. Twenty persons fell dead, and forty were wounded. The scene which ensued baffles description. The immense masses dispersed in terror, and carried panic in all directions. The groans of the dying and the screams of the wounded filled the air. Shops and houses around were turned into hospitals. "We are betrayed! we are betrayed!"—"Revenge! revenge!" was the cry of the masses.

From this moment the doom of the monarchy was sealed. The leaders of the clubs, no doubt, took their measures for revolution. An immense wagon was soon brought to the scene of the massacre; the dead bodies were laid on it, and flaring torches were lighted over it. The ghastly spectacle was para-

---

* It has since been said, and is generally believed, that a revolutionist by the name of Lagrange fired this shot with a pistol, having expected and designed the events which immediately followed.

ded through the streets, and the mute lips of the corpses doubt-less spoke more effectively than those of the living. Large masses of people, pale with excitement, and uttering execra-tions upon the murderers, followed in the train of the wagon, as it passed through the more populous streets of the city, and especially in those quarters inhabited by the lower classes. The effect was such as might have been anticipated. At midnight, the barricades were begun, and at sunrise, the streets of Paris displayed a net-work of fortifications from the place St. George to the church of Notre Dame, which set the troops at defiance. More than a thousand barricades, some of them ten feet in height, were thrown up during that memorable night; yet such were the suddenness and silence of the o' erations, that most of the inhabitants of the city slept in s' curity, fondly dreaming that the tempest had passed, and that the morning would greet them in peace.

On Thursday, the decisive day, the weather was still mild, and without rain, though the sky was dimmed with clouds. At eleven in the morning, I sallied forth. I can not express my astonishment at the scene. The whole Boulevard was a spec-tacle of desolation. From the Rue de la Paix to the Rue Mont-martre—the finest part of Paris, the glory of the city—every tree was cut down, all the public monuments reduced to heaps of ruins, the pavements torn up, and the entire wreck tumbled into a succession of barricades. Every street leading into this portion of the Boulevard was strongly barricaded. Such giant operations seemed like the work of enchantment.

But my wonder had only begun. At the point where the Rue Montmartre crosses the Boulevard, the entire pavement was torn up, and something like a square breastwork was form-ed, in which a cannon was planted. The whole space around was crowded with the populace. As I stood for a moment, surveying the scene, a young man, about twenty, passed through the crowd, and stepping upon the carriage of the cannon, cried out, "Down with Louis Philippe!" The energy with which this was spoken sent a thrill through every bosom; and the remarkable appearance of the youth gave additional effect to his words. He seemed the very demon of revolution. He was short, broad-shouldered, and full-chested. His face was pale, his cheek spotted with blood, and his head, without hat or cap, was bound with a handkerchief. His features were keen, and his deep-set eye was lit with a spark that seemed borrowed from a tiger. As he left the throng, he came near me, and I said, inquiringly, "Down with Louis Philippe?" "Yes!" was his reply. "And what then?" said I. "A republic!" was his answer; and he passed on, giving the watchword of "Down with Louis Philippe!" to the masses he encountered. This was the first instance in which I heard the overthrow of the king, and the adoption of a republic proposed.

In pursuing my walk, I noticed that the population were now abundantly supplied with weapons. On the two first days they were unarmed; but after the slaughter at the Foreign Office, they went to all the houses and demanded weapons. These were given, for refusal would have been vain. An evidence of the consideration of the populace, even in their hour of wrath, is furnished by the fact, that in all cases where the arms had been surrendered, they wrote on the doors in chalk, "*Armes données*"—arms given up—so as to prevent the annoyance of a second call.

It might seem a fearful thing to behold a mob, such as that of Paris, brandishing guns, fowling-pieces, swords, cutlasses, hatchets, and axes; but I must say that I felt not the slightest fear in passing among their thickest masses. Some of them, who had doubtless never handled arms before, seemed a little jaunty and jubilant. The *Gamins*, a peculiar race of enterprising, daring, desperate boys—the leaders in riots, rows, and rebellions—were swarming on all sides, and seemed to feel a head taller in the possession of their weapons. I saw several of these unwashed imps strutting about with red sashes around the waist, supporting pistols, dirks, cutlasses, &c.; yet I must state that over the whole scene there was an air of good-breeding, which seemed a guaranty against insult or violence. I may also remark here, that during the whole three days, I did not observe a scuffle or wrangle among the people; I did not hear an insulting word, nor did I see a menace offered—save in conflicts between the soldiers and the populace. I can add, that I did not see a drunken person during the whole period, with the single exception which I shall hereafter mention.

I took a wide circuit in the region of the Rue Montmartre, the Bourse, the Rue Vivienne, St. Honoré, and the Palais Royal. Everywhere there were enormous barricades and crowds of armed people. Soon after—that is, about twelve o'clock— I passed the southern quadrangle of the Palais Royal, which —lately the residence of the brother of the King of Naples— was now attacked and taken by the populace. The beautiful suit of rooms were richly furnished, and decorated with costly pictures, statues, bronzes, and other specimens of art. These were unsparingly tumbled into the square and the street, and consigned to the flames.* At the distance of one hundred and fifty feet from the front of the Palais Royal, was the Château d'Eau, a massive stone building occupied as a barrack, and at this moment garrisoned by one hundred and eighty municipal guards. In most parts of the city, seeing that the troops fraternized with the people, the government had given them orders not to fire. These guards, however, attacked the insurgents in and about the Palais Royal. Their fire was returned, and a desperate conflict ensued. The battle lasted for more than an hour, the people rushing in the very face of the

---

* Many occurrences, during the revolution, served to display, on the part of the people, commonly, but injuriously, called the *mob*, sentiments not inferior in beauty and elevation to those handed down for centuries in the histories of ancient Greece and Rome. During the sacking of the Palais Royal, the insurgents found an ivory crucifix. In the very heat of their fury against tyranny, they reverently paused, and taking the sacred emblem of their faith, bore it to the old church of St. Roch, where it was safely deposited.

muskets of the guard, as they blazed from the grated windows. At last the barrack was set on fire, and the guard yielded, though not till many of their number had fallen, and the rest were nearly dead with suffocation. The Château d'Eau is now a mere ruin, its mottled walls giving evidence of the shower of bullets that had been poured upon it.*

No sooner had the Château d'Eau surrendered, than the flushed victors took their course toward the Tuileries, which was near at hand ; shouting, singing, roaring, they came like a surge, bearing all before them. The Place du Carrousel was filled with troops, but not a sword was unsheathed—not a bayonet pointed—not a musket or a cannon fired. There stood, idle and motionless, the mighty armament which the king had appointed for his defense. How vain had his calculations proved ! for, alas ! they were founded in a radical error ! The soldiers would not massacre their brethren, to sustain a throne which they now despised !

But we must now enter the Tuileries. For several days previous to the events we have described, some anxiety had been entertained by persons in and about the palace. The king, however, had no fears. He appeared in unusual spirits, and if any intimation of danger was given, he turned it aside with a sneer or a joke. Even so late as Wednesday, after he had called upon Count Molé to form a new ministry, he remarked, that he was so "firmly seated in the saddle, that nothing could throw him off."

Molé soon found it impossible, with the materials at hand, to construct a ministry. Thiers was then called in, and after a long course of higgling and chaffering on the part of the king, it was agreed that he and Barrot should undertake to carry on

---

* In the recent improvements in Paris, the ruins of the Chateau d'Eau have been removed, and a square has been opened upon their site from the Palais Royal to the new portions of the Louvre. These and other alterations have rendered this one of the most beautiful quarters of the city. The Louvre and the Tuileries have been united, and now form one of the most magnificent palaces in Europe.

the government. This was announced by them in person, as they rode through the streets on Thursday morning. These concessions, however, came too late. The cry for a republic was bursting from the lips of the million. The abdication of the king was decreed, and a raging multitude were demanding this at the very gates of the palace. Overborne by the crisis, the king agreed to abdicate in favor of the Duke de Nemours. Some better tidings were brought him, and he retracted what he had just done. A moment after, it became certain that the insurgents would shortly burst into the palace. In great trepidation, the king agreed to resign the crown in favor of his grandson, the young Count de Paris—yet, still clinging to hope, he shuffled and hesitated before he would put his name to the act of abdication. This, however, was at last done, and the king and queen, dressed in black, and accompanied by a few individuals who remained faithful in this trying moment, passed from the Tuileries to the Place de la Concorde, through the subterranean passage constructed many years previously for the walks of the infant king of Rome. They here entered a small one-horse vehicle, and after a rapid and successful flight, landed safely at Dover, in England.*

Meanwhile, the mob had seized the royal carriages, fourteen in number, and made a bonfire of them, near the celebrated arch in the Place du Carrousel. Soon after, they forced the railing at several points, and came rushing across the square toward the palace. Scarcely had the various members of the royal family time to escape on one side of the building, when the mob broke in at the other.

I have not time to follow the adventures of these several individuals. We can not but sympathize with them in their misfortunes; but we may remark, that the fall of the Orleans dy-

---

* The various members of the royal family, having escaped to England, established themselves at Claremont, near London, where they have continued till this time. Louis Philippe died there the 22d of August, 1850.

nasty was not broken by a single act of courage or dignity on the part of any one of the family. Their flight seemed a vulgar scramble for mere life. Even the king was reduced to the most common-place disguises — the shaving of his whiskers, the change of his dress, the adopting an " alias!" I may add here, that they have all escaped ; and while everybody seems glad of this, there is no one behind who mourns their loss. None are more loud in denouncing the besotted confidence of the king, than his two hundred and twenty-five purchased deputies, who were so loyal in the days of prosperity.

We must now turn our attention toward another scene—the Chamber of Deputies. This body met on Tuesday, at the usual hour—twelve o'clock. While the riotous scenes we have described were transpiring during that day, in full view of the place where they had assembled, the deputies, as if in mockery of the agitation without, were occupied in a languid discussion upon the affairs of a broken country bank. Toward the close of the sitting, Odillon Barrot read from the tribune a solemn act of impeachment of the ministers. The next day, Wednesday, the Chamber again met, and Guizot in the afternoon announced that Count Molé was attempting to form a new ministry. It does not appear that Guizot or his colleagues were afterward seen in the Chamber. It is said that they met at the house of Duchatel on Thursday morning, and after consultation adopted the significant motto of Napoleon after the battle of Waterloo—" *Sauve qui peut !*"—Save himself who can. I am happy to add that the fugitives seem to have made good their retreat. It is said that Soult, disdaining to fly, remains at his house. I need not say that he will not be molested, for there is no sanguinary feeling toward any one, and Napoleon's old favorite, the victor in so many battles, would more readily find a Parisian populace to protect than injure him.

A short time after the king and queen had passed the Place de la Concorde, I chanced to be there. In a few moments Odillon Barrot appeared from the gate of the Tuileries, and, followed by a long train of persons, proceeded to the Chamber of Deputies. It was now understood that the king had abdicated, and that Thiers and Barrot were to propose the Count de Paris as king, under the regency of his mother, the Duchess of Orleans. The most profound emotion seemed to occupy the immense multitude. All were hushed into silence by the rapid succession of astonishing events. After a short space, the Duchess of Orleans, with her two sons, the Count de Paris and the Duke de Chartres, were seen on foot coming toward the Chamber, encircled by a strong escort. She was dressed in deep mourning, her face bent to the ground. She moved across the bridge, and passing to the rear of the building, entered it through the gardens. Shortly after this, the Duke de Nemours, attended by several gentlemen on horseback, rode up, and also entered the building.

The scene that ensued within, is said to have presented an extraordinary mixture of the solemn and the ludicrous. The duchess being present, O. Barrot proceeded to state the abdication of the king, and to propose the regency. It was then that Lamartine seemed to shake off the poet and philosopher, and suddenly to become a man of action. Seizing the critical moment, he declared his conviction that the days of monarchy were numbered, that the proposed regency was not suited to the crisis, and that a republic alone would meet the emergency and the wishes of France. These opinions, happily expressed and strenuously enforced, became decisive in their effect.

Several other speeches were made, and a scene of great confusion followed. A considerable number of the mob had broken into the room, and occupied the galleries and the floor. One of them brought his firelock to his shoulder, and took aim at M. Sauzet, the president. Entirely losing his self-possession, he abdicated with great speed, and disappeared. In the midst of the hubbub, a provisional government was announced, and the leading members were named. Some of the more obnoxious deputies were aimed at by the muskets of the mob, and skulking behind benches and pillars, they oozed out at back doors and windows. A blouseman came up to the Duke de Nemours, who drew his sword. The man took it from him, broke it over his knee, and counseled his highness to depart. This he did forthwith, having borrowed a coat and hat for the purpose of disguise. A call was made for the members of the provisional government to proceed to the Hotel de Ville. The assembly broke up, and the curtain fell upon the last sitting of the Chamber of Deputies—the closing scene of Louis Philippe's government.

It was about three o'clock in the afternoon, that I retraced my steps toward the Tuileries. The Place de la Concorde was crowded with soldiers, and fifty cannon were ranged in front of the gardens. Yet this mighty force seemed struck with paralysis. Long lines of infantry stood mute and motionless, and heavy masses of cavalry seemed converted into so many statues. Immediately before the eyes of these soldiers was the palace of the Tuileries in full possession of the mob, but not a muscle moved for their expulsion!

Passing into the gardens, I noticed that thousands of persons were spread over their surface, and a rattling discharge of fire-arms was heard on all sides. Looking about for the cause of this, I perceived that hundreds of men and boys were amusing themselves with shooting sparrows and pigeons, which had hitherto found a secure resting-place in this favorite resort of leisure and luxury. Others were discharging their muskets for the mere fun of making a noise. Proceeding through the gardens, I came at last to the palace. It had now been, for more than an hour, in full possession of the insurgents. All description fails to depict a scene like this. The whole front of the Tuileries, one-eighth of a mile in length, seemed gushing at doors, windows, balconies, and galleries, with living multitudes —a mighty beehive of men, in the very act of swarming. A confused hubbub filled the air and bewildered the senses with its chaotic sounds.

At the moment I arrived, the throne of the king was borne away by a jubilant band of revelers; and after being paraded through the streets, was burned at the Place de la Bastille—a significant episode in this tale of wonders. The colossal statue of Spartacus, which faces the main door of the palace, toward the gardens, was now decorated with a piece of gilt cloth torn from the throne and wreathed like a turban around his head. In his hand was a gorgeous bouquet of artificial flowers. It seemed as if the frowning gladiator had suddenly caught the spirit of the revel, and was about to descend from his pedestal and mingle in the masquerade.

I entered the palace, and passed through the long suites of apartments devoted to occasions of ceremony. A year before, I had seen these gorgeous halls filled with the flush and the fair, kings, princes, and nobles, gathered to this focal point of luxury, refinement, and taste, from every quarter of the world. How little did Louis Philippe, at that moment, dream of "coming events!" How little did the stately queen—a proud obelisk of silk, and lace, and diamonds—foresee the change that was at hand! I recollected well the effect of this scene upon my own mind, and felt the full force of the contrast which the present moment offered. In the very room where I had seen the pensive and pensile Princess de Joinville and the Duchess de Montpensier—the latter then fresh from the hymeneal altar, her raven hair studded with diamonds like evening stars—whirling in the mazy dance, I now beheld a band of creatures like Calibans, gamboling to the song of the Marseillaise!

On every side my eye fell upon scenes of destruction. Passing to the other end of the palace, I beheld a mob in the chambers of the princesses. Some rolled themselves in the luscious beds, others anointed their shaggy heads with choice pomatum, exclaiming, "Dieu! how sweet it smells!" One of the gamins, grimed with gunpowder, blood, and dirt, seized a tooth-brush, and placing himself before a mirror, seemed delighted at the manifest improvement which he produced upon his ivory.

On leaving the palace, I saw numbers of the men drinking wine from bottles taken from the well-stocked cellars. None of them were positively drunk. To use the words of Tam O'Shanter, "They were na fou, but just had plenty"—perhaps a little more. They flourished their guns and pistols, brandished their swords, and performed various antics, but they offered no insult to any one. They seemed in excellent humor, and made more than an ordinary display of French politesse. They complimented the women, of whom there was no lack, and one of them, resembling a figure of Pan, seized a maiden by the waist, and both rigadooned merrily over the floor.

Leaving this scene of wreck, confusion, and uproar, I proceeded toward the gate of the gardens leading into the Rue de Rivoli. I was surprised to find here a couple of ruthless-looking blousemen, armed with pistols, keeping guard. On inquiry, I found that the mob themselves had instituted a sort of government. One fellow, in the midst of the devastation in the palace, seeing a man put something into his pocket, wrote on the wall, "Death to the thief!" The Draconian code was immediately adopted by the people, and became the law of Paris. Five persons, taken in acts of robbery, were shot down by the people, and their bodies exposed in the streets, with the label of "Thieves" on their breast. Thus order and law seemed to spring up from the instincts of society, in the midst of uproar and confusion, as crystals are seen shooting from the chaos of the elements.

Three days had now passed, and the revolution was accomplished. The people soon returned to their wonted habits—the provisional government proceeded in its duties—the barricades disappeared, and in a single week the more obtrusive traces of the storm that had passed had vanished from the streets and squares of Paris. A mighty shock has, however, been given to society, which still swells and undulates like the sea after a storm. The adjacent countries seem to feel the movement, and all Europe is in a state of agitation. What must be the final result, can not now be foreseen; but I fear that, ere the sky be cleared, still further tempests must sweep over France and the surrounding nations. The day of reckoning for long years of tyranny and corruption has come, and the sun of liberty can hardly be expected to shine full on the scene, till a night of fear, and agitation, and tears has been passed.

———◆———

LETTER LVIII.

Events which immediately followed the Revolution—Scenes in the streets of Paris—Anxiety of Strangers—Proceedings of the Americans—Address to the Provisional Government—Reply of M. Arago—Procession in the streets—Inauguration of the Republic—Funeral of the Victims—Presentation of Flags—Conspiracy of the 15th of May—Insurrection of June —Adoption of the Constitution—Louis Napoleon President.

MY DEAR C******

It is quite impossible to give you any adequate idea of the state of things in Paris, immediately after the revolution described in my preceding letter. The Provisional Government, at the Hotel de Ville, consisting of persons who had seized the reins of authority which had suddenly fallen from the hands of the now prostrate monarchy, was as yet without real power. Every thing was in a state of paralysis, or disorganization. There was no effective police, no visible authority, no actual government; every man did what seemed good in his own eyes. Boys and blackguards paraded the streets with swords at their side, muskets in their hands, and sashes around their waists. Enormous processions of men, sometimes mingled with women, moved along the thorough-fares, singing the Marseillaise and "Mourir pour la Patrie." It was a general jubilee—and, strange to say, without riot, without violence, without fear. I walked freely abroad in the streets, taking my wife and children with me; we were constantly saluted by men and women offering us tricolored rosettes, which they pinned upon our breasts with the utmost good-humor, expecting, of course, a few sous in return. This state of things continued for some weeks—the people being a law unto themselves, and refraining alike from turbulence, from outrage, and from pil-lage. It is probable that in no other great city of the world could the masses be let loose from the restraints of government and law, and yet keep them-selves within the bounds of order and propriety, as did the Parisians during this remarkable era.

Of course, there was a general feeling of anxiety among all reflecting people in Paris, and especially those whose minds reverted to the first French revo-lution. This disquietude extended particularly to all foreigners, and they naturally cast about for the means of safety. It was difficult to leave Paris, for some of the railroads were broken up, and all the modes of conveyance were deranged. It was almost impossible to get money for the purposes of travel, and even if one could escape from Paris, more danger-ous agitation might exist in the country. The leading Americans took counsel together on this subject, and finally concluded to proceed, in procession, to the Provisional Government, and congratulate them upon the revolution.* A message was sent to inquire if this would be acceptable; the answer was favorable, and, indeed, they were desired to hasten the proceeding, as it was thought such a demonstration might contribute to give support to the trembling authority of the self-elected rulers.

In the preliminary meeting for bringing about the proposed address, I was chosen to preside, and was also selected as chairman of the committee to draw up the address itself. I had some curious counsel given me by my countrymen, while I was preparing this document. The Americans looked upon the revolution, not only as the overthrow of monarchy, but as the birth of that liberty which we are taught to cherish as one of the greatest boons of existence. The example of Paris extended like an electric shock to the adjacent countries. Italy, Austria, Prussia, seemed on the point of emancipating themselves from the yoke which had bound them for ages. With a generous sympathy, our countrymen wished success to these efforts. The formation of a republican government seems to us so easy, so obvious a work, that

---

* Mr. Rush, who was then our ambassador to France, proceeded in his official capacity to the Hotel de Ville, three or four days after the completion of the revolution, and recognized the government, congratulating them upon a change which had resulted in the establishment of a republic.

we suppose every nation which undertakes the task, will of course accomplish it. It was natural, therefore, for an American in Paris to believe that the good time had actually come, and that the people had only to inaugurate and establish it. I had several plans of addresses sent to me founded upon this idea ; one a declaration of principles, of seven foolscap pages, drawn up pretty much after the manner of our Declaration of Independence. Conceiving it, however, no time to be magniloquent, I prepared the following brief address, which was adopted :

"Gentlemen, members of the Provisional Government of the French People—As citizens of the United States of America, and spectators of recent events in Paris, we come to offer you our congratulations. A grateful recollection of the past, and the ties of amity which have existed between your country and ours, prompt us to be among the first to testify to you, and to the people of France, the sympathy, the respect, and the admiration which those events inspire. Acknowledging the right of every nation to form its own government, we may still be permitted to felicitate France upon the choice of a system which recognizes as its basis the great principles of rational liberty and political equality.

"In the progress of the recent struggle here, we have admired the magnanimity of the French people, their self-command in the hour of triumph, and their speedy return to order and law, after the tumult and confusion of revolution. We see in these circumstances, happy omens of good to France and to mankind—assurances that what has been so nobly begun will be consummated in the permanent establishment of a just and liberal government, and the consequent enjoyment of liberty, peace, and prosperity, among the citizens of this great country. Accept this testimonial of the sentiments which fill our hearts at the present moment, and be assured that the news of the revolution which you have just achieved, will be hailed by our countrymen on the other side of the Atlantic, with no other emotions than those of hope and joy for France and for the world."

All things being duly prepared, the Americans, about two hundred and fifty in number, marched in procession to the Hotel de Ville, the striped bunting and the tricolor waving together in harmony over our heads. The citizens of Paris looked upon us with welcome, and frequently the cry arose—" Vive la République Américaine !"*

The Hotel de Ville is one of the most sumptuous palaces in Europe; and here, in the magnificent apartment called the Hall of Reception, we were received by the Provisional Government—all dressed in their uniform of blue, ornamented with gold lace, and rich sashes around the waist. Lamartine was ill, and was not present; Arago presided. I began to read the address, in English, when a tipsy Frenchman, who had squeezed into the hall with the pro-

---

* The committee on the address, besides myself, were Messrs. Corbin, of Virginia, Shimmin, of Boston, and the late Henry Coleman, well known for his agricultural writings, as well as his travels in England and France.

The president on the occasion was Hon. G. W. Erving, formerly minister of the United States to Madrid.

The chief marshal was Wright Hawkes, Esq., of New York, assisted by Robert Wickliffe, Jr., of Kentucky, E. C. Cowden, of Boston, &c.

It is a curious fact, that the Americans in the procession were several inches taller than the average of Frenchmen—a circumstance which attracted general attention in Paris at the time.

cession, came forward and insisted that it should be read in French. He was pacified by being told that it would be read in that language after I had concluded. When the address was finished, M. Arago replied on behalf of the government, in appropriate terms. M. Poussin* then seized the two flags, and waving them together, pronounced an animated discourse, in which he acknowledged with gratitude the sympathy of the Americans in the recent revolution, and expressed the hope that France had now entered upon the long-hoped-for millennial era of equality, fraternity, and liberty.

It is not my design to give you a detailed history of the revolution, but I may sketch a few of the prominent events which followed. For this purpose, I make an extract from an account I have elsewhere given:

For several weeks and months, Paris was a scene of extraordinary excitement. The Provisional Government had announced that they would provide the people with labor. Consequently, deputations of tailors, hatters, engravers, musicians, paviors, cabinet-makers, seamstresses, and a multitude of other trades

---

* M. Guillaume Tell Poussin came to the United States many years ago, and was employed here as an engineer for a long time. After his return to France, he wrote an able statistical work on this country, in which he highly praised our institutions. When the French Republic was organized, he was sent as minister to Washington. Mr. Clayton, Secretary of State under Gen. Taylor, took exception to certain expressions used by M. Poussin in his correspondence with the department, and accordingly he ceased to represent his country here. M. Poussin is, however, a sincere republican, and a great admirer of the United States; and though his principles are well known, such is the respect entertained for him, that the suspicion of the French government, even under the empire, has never subjected him to constraint or annoyance.

and vocations, flocked in long lines to the Hotel de Ville, to solicit the favor of the government. Vast crowds of people perpetually haunted this place, and, in one instance, a raging multitude came thundering at the doors, demanding that the blood-red flag of the former revolution should be the banner of the new republic! It was on this occasion that Lamartine addressed the people, and with such eloquence as to allay the storm which threatened again to deluge France in blood. The members of the government were so besieged and pressed by business, that for several weeks they slept in the Hotel de Ville. They proceeded with a bold hand to announce and establish the republic. In order to make a favorable impression upon the people, they decreed a gorgeous ceremony at the foot of the column of July, on Sunday, February 27th, by which they solemnly inaugurated the new republic. All the members of the Provisional Government were present on horseback; there were sixty thousand troops and two hundred thousand people to witness the spectacle.

Another still more imposing celebration took place on the 4th of March. This was called the "Funeral of the Victims." After religious ceremonies at the Madeleine, the members of the government, with a long train of public officers, and an immense cortege of military, proceeded to the July column, conducting a superb funeral-car drawn by eight cream-colored horses. This contained most of the bodies of those slain in the revolution—about two hundred and fifty. These were deposited in the vault of the column, with the victims of the revolution of 1830.

Nothing can adequately portray this spectacle. A tricolored flag was stretched on each side of the Boulevards, from the Madeleine to the July column—a distance of three miles. As this consisted of three strips of cloth, the length of the whole was eighteen miles! The solemn movement of the funeral procession, the dirge-like music, the march of nearly a hundred thousand soldiers, and the sympathizing presence of three hundred thousand souls, rendered it a scene never surpassed and rarely equaled, either by the magnificence of the panorama, or the solemn and touching sentiments excited.

Still other spectacles succeeded, and in the summer four hundred thousand people assembled in the Champs Elysées to witness the Presentation of Flags to the assembled National Guards —eighty thousand being present. Such scenes can only be witnessed in Paris.

Events proceeded with strange rapidity. A Constituent Assembly was called by the Provisional Government, to form a constitution. The members were elected by ballot, the suffrage being universal—that is, open to all Frenchmen over twenty-one. The election took place in April, and on the 4th of May the first session was held, being officially announced to the assembled people from the steps of the Chamber of Deputies. On the 15th of May a conspiracy was disclosed, the leaders of which were Raspail, Barbès, Sobrier, Caussidière, Blanqui, Flotte, Albert, and Louis Blanc*—the two last having been members of the Provisional Government. Caussidière was prefect of police.

The Assembly proceeded in the work of framing a constitution, administering the government in the mean time. On the 24th of June, a terrific insurrection broke out, promoted by the leaders of various factions, all desiring the overthrow of the republic which had been inaugurated. Cavaignac, who was minister of war, was appointed dictator, and Paris was declared in a state of siege. The insurgents confined their operations chiefly to the faubourgs St. Jacques and St. Antoine. They got possession of these, and formed skillful and able plans of operation, which had for their ultimate object the surrounding of the city and getting possession of certain important points, including the Chamber— thus securing the government in their own hands.

---

* These men were Socialists, and aimed at a destruction of the government, so that they might bring into effect their peculiar schemes. They were shortly afterward tried at Bourges, and sentenced to long imprisonment or banishment. Louis Blanc and Caussidière escaped to England. The former remains in London; the latter is now a wine-merchant in New York.

Cavaignac proceeded to attack the barricades, thus clearing the streets one by one. The fighting was terrible. For four days the battle continued, the sound of cannon frequently filling the ears of the people all over the city. Night and day the inhabitants were shut up in their houses—ignorant of all, save that the conflict was raging. The women found employment in scraping lint for the wounded. All Paris was a camp. The windows were closed; the soldiers and sentinels passed their watchwords; litters, carrying the dead and wounded, were seen along the streets; the tramp of marching columns and the thunder of rushing cavalry broke upon the ear!

At last the conflict was over; the insurgents were beaten— Cavaignac triumphed. But the victory was dearly purchased. Between two and three thousand persons were killed—and among them, no less than seven general officers had fallen. The insurgents fought like tigers. Many women were in the ranks, using the musket, carrying the banners, rearing barricades, and cheering the fight. Boys and girls mingled in the conflict. The National Guards who combated them, had equal courage and superior discipline. One of the Garde Mobile—Hyacinthe Martin, a youth of fourteen—took four standards from the tops of the barricades. His gallantry excited great interest, and Cavaignac decorated him with the cross of the Legion of Honor. He became a hero of the day, but, sad to relate, being invited to fêtes, banquets, and repasts, his head was turned, and he was soon a ruined profligate.

The leaders in this terrific insurrection were never detected. It is certain that the movement was headed by able men, and directed by skillful engineers. The masses who fought were roused to fury by poverty and distress, by disappointment at finding the national workshops discontinued, and by stimulating excitements furnished by socialist clubs and newspapers. It is computed that forty thousand insurgents were in arms, and eighty thousand government soldiers were brought against them. It may be considered that this struggle was the remote but inevitable result of the course of the Provisional Government in adopting the doctrine of obligation, on the part of the State, to supply work and wages to the people, and in establishing national workshops in pursuance of this idea. Still, it may be said, on the other hand, that nothing but such a step could have enabled the Provisional Government to maintain itself during three months, and give being to an organized Assembly from which a legitimate government could proceed.

The constitution was finished in the autumn, and promulgated on the 19th of November, 1848. On the 10th of December following, the election of President took place, and it appeared that Louis Napoleon had five million out of seven million votes. He was duly inaugurated about a week after the election, and entered upon the high duties which thus devolved upon him.

LETTER LIX.

The Duties of a Consul—Pursuit of a missing Family—Paying for Experience.

MY DEAR C******

Let us now come to the period of 1851, when I entered upon the consulate. Of the space during which I was permitted to hold this office, I have no very remarkable personal incidents to relate. The certifying of invoices, and the legalizing of deeds and powers of attorney, are the chief technical duties of the American Consul at Paris.* If he desires to

---

* Paris is not a seaport, and therefore the numerous consular duties connected with shipping are never required here. On the other hand, it is the literary metropolis of France; and as French consuls are required to collect and furnish geographical, historical, commercial, and statistical information, I found myself constantly applied to by editors

enlarge the circle of his operations, however, he can find various ways of doing it, as for instance, in supplying the wants of distressed Poles, Hungarians, Italians, and others, who are martyrs to liberty, and suppose the American heart and purse always open to those who are thus afflicted : in answering questions from notaries, merchants, lawyers, as to the laws of the different American States upon marriage, inheritance,

---

of papers, authors, bankers, merchants, government officials, for particular facts in regard to the United States. I was exceedingly struck with the general ignorance of all classes, as to our country, its institutions, geography, population, history, &c. I therefore prepared a work, which, with the kind assistance of M. Delbrück, was put into French, and published—it being an octavo volume of about three hundred and seventy-five pages, entitled *Les Etats-Unis d'Amérique.* I had the gratification of seeing it well received on all sides, even by the members of the government, from whom I had complimentary acknowledgments. There is, indeed, a great and growing interest in our country all over Europe, and it seems to be the duty of American officials abroad to take advantage of their opportunities to satisfy and gratify this curiosity by furnishing, in a correct and accessible form, the kind of information that is desired.

The number of Americans in Paris, residents and travelers, varies from one to three thousand. If the Consul is understood to bar out his countrymen, he may see very few of them ; if, on the contrary, he is willing to make himself useful in a neighborly way, many of them will call upon him to take his advice as to schools, physicians, routes of travel, and the like. When there is difficulty, the Consul is the natural resource of his countrymen, especially for those who are without acquaintance. In case of the death of an American, if there is no friend or relative present upon whom the duty devolves, the Consul gives directions as to the funeral, and takes charge of the effects of the deceased.

I have already alluded to French physicians and surgeons, and expressed the opinion that ours, in America, are quite as good. There is, no doubt, great science in the medical and surgical professions of Paris ; but there are two things to be suggested to those who go there for advice. In the first place, these practitioners are very daring in their treatment of strangers, and in the next, their charges to foreigners are usually about double the ordinary rates.

While I was in Paris, a very wealthy and rather aged gentleman from Virginia consulted an eminent surgeon there, as to hydrocele. An op-

and the like; in advising emigrants whether to settle in Iowa, or Illinois, or Missouri, or Texas; in listening to inquiries made by deserted wives as to where their errant husbands may be found, who left France ten or twenty or thirty years ago, and went to America, by which is generally understood St. Domingo or Martinique. A considerable business may be done in lending money to foreigners, who pretend to have been naturalized in the United States, and are therefore entitled to consideration and sympathy, it being of course well understood that money lent to such persons will never be repaid. Some time and cash may also be invested in listening to the stories and contributing to the wants of promising young American artists, who are striving to get to Italy, to pursue their studies—such persons usually being graduates of the London school of artful dodgers. Some waste leisure and a good deal of postage may be disposed of in correspondence with ingenious Americans—inventors and discoverers—as for instance, with a man in Arkansas or Minnesota, who informs you that he has

---

eration was recommended and performed, entirely against the advice of a Virginia physician who chanced to be in Paris, and was consulted. In thirty days the gentleman died. He had intrusted his affairs to me, and I paid his bills. The charge of the surgeon was five thousand francs! The bills of the nurses, hotels, attendants, &c., were of a similar character. A young physician, who had been employed fourteen days as nurse, estimated his services at fifteen hundred francs! I make these remarks, that my countrymen going to Paris for medical or surgical advice, may be duly warned against placing themselves in the hands of rash and unprincipled practitioners. A great name in Paris is by no means a guarantee of that care, prudence, and conscientiousness, which belong to the physician at home.

contrived a new and infallible method of heating and ventilating European cities, and wishes it brought to the notice of the authorities there, it being deemed the duty of the American Consul to give attention to such matters. These monotonies are occasionally diversified by a letter from some unfortunate fellow-countryman who is detained at Mazas or Clichy, and begs to be extricated; or some couple who wish to be put under the bonds of wedlock, or some enterprising wife, all the way from Tennessee, in chase of a runaway husband, or some inexperienced but indignant youth who has been fleeced by his landlord.

Mixed up with these amusements, there sometimes comes an order from the government at home, to obtain a certain document, or to give information as to some institution, or perhaps to make some investigation. The following copy of a letter to the State Department at Washington describes an instance of the latter :

PARIS, February 10, 1853.

To HON. EDWARD EVERETT, Secretary of State.

Sir—Your letter of the 30th December, inclosing one from Hon. Jeremiah Clemens, asking information as to the family of André Hentz, was duly received.

Soon after its receipt, I proceeded to No. 9, Rue St. Appoline, Paris, the last known residence of Madame Hentz, but I could obtain no traces of her or her family. I then wrote to the Mayor of Conflans St. Honorine, where she once lived, and received a reply which directed me to make inquiry at the neighboring village of Grenelle. Thither I proceeded, and applied as advised, to No. 5 Rue Fondry. Here I failed, but was led to suppose that I might get a clew at No. 115 Rue Vieille du Temple, Paris. I returned thither, and on application at the place indicated, was told that no person by the name of Hentz had ever lived there. On going out, I observed that the numbering over the door was freshly painted, and soon discovered that the whole numbering of the street had recently been changed. I now sought the old No. 115, and was here informed that I might perhaps find the person I was looking after at No. 6 Rue Thorigny. I proceeded thither, but was informed that M. Hentz was not there, but perhaps might be found at No. 4. Finally, at No. 4, on the fifth story, I found Henry Hentz and his mother, in rather humble but very neat apartments, and apparently in comfortable circumstances. I told them the object of my visit, and they promised immediately to write to Mr. André Hentz, of whom they had lost all trace, and of whom they were rejoiced to receive intelligence.

I write these particulars, supposing they may be interesting to Mr. Clemens's client.

> I am, with great respect, yours, &c.,
> S. G. GOODRICH.

Another incident may amuse you. I one day received a number of a Journal published in Paris, entitled "Archives des Hommes du Jour," that is, Memoirs of Men of the Time, accompanied by a polite note saying that the editors would be happy to insert in their pages a biographical memoir of myself. They had taken the liberty to sketch the beginning of the desired article, but the particular facts of my life they politely begged me to supply.

Supposing this to be one of those applications which are by no means uncommon, I handed to my friend, M. Jules Delbrück, the letter, with two or three American books, which contained notices of myself, and asked him to write the memoir as desired. This he did, and it was duly sent to the editors of the Hommes du Jour. In due time a proof was sent, and at the same time one of the editors, a very smiling gentleman, came and desired to know how many copies of this memoir of myself I should desire! I replied, very innocently, that I should like one or two. The gentleman lifted his eyebrows, and said suggestively—

" Five hundred is the usual number!"

I now for the first time began to suspect a trap, and replied—

" You expect me to take five hundred copies?"

" Every gentleman takes at least that; sometimes a thousand."

" And you expect me to pay for them?"

" Oui, monsieur!"

" Well, how much do you expect for five hundred copies?"

" A franc each is the usual price; but we will say three hundred and fifty francs for the whole."

" I understand you now: I furnished the article in question at your request; it was for your benefit, not mine. It is of no advantage to me. If you expected to be paid for it, you should have told me so; you would then have been saved the trouble of pursuing the matter any further."

The stranger remonstrated, but I firmly refused to

give him an order for any copies of the publication in question, and supposed I had got rid of the application. A few days afterward, however, I received a long letter from the editors, to which, after some reflection, I sent the following answer:

PARIS, February 7, 1853.

To the Editors of the " Archives des Hommes du Jour."

Gentlemen—I have received, besides several other letters from you, one of the 3d instant, which seems to demand an answer.

Some weeks since, you addressed me a complimentary note, saying that you proposed to insert in the Archives des Hommes du Jour, a biographical sketch of myself, and desired me to fill up with facts an outline which you sent me.

You gave me no intimation that you expected me to pay for the proposed insertion. Nothing in the specimen of the Journal you sent, led me to suspect that there was any lurking signification beneath your polite proposal. I judged of the matter by my own experience, and very innocently supposing that I was merely fulfilling a comity due to men of letters, I complied with your request by getting a friend to furnish the facts you desired.

I have since learned that my experience in the United States has not instructed me in all the customs of Paris.

When the article in question was in proof, a gentleman, professing to be your representative, called on me, and proposed to furnish me with five hundred copies of the sketch, " at the exceedingly low price of three hundred and fifty francs!" I replied that I did not require nor desire any copies of the work; that while I appreciated the politeness of the editors of the Journal, I had not sought the insertion of the biography, and knew of no earthly interest of mine that could be promoted by it. I further stated that my sense of propriety would be shocked at the idea of rendering pecuniary compensation for a eulogistic notice of myself. For all these reasons I declined accepting the proposition, and the more emphatically, as it was very strongly urged upon me.

All this was of course communicated to you: nevertheless, in the letter referred to, you insist upon my paying for the insertion, and for five hundred extra copies, printed by you, after I had positively refused to take them.

Your claim is urged on two grounds: first, that you have expended money, and conferred on me a benefit; and, second, that what you ask is sanctioned by high example, and the practice of years, and has therefore the force of an agreement between you and me.

To this I beg to reply, of course judging from my point of view, that I can not admit that you have done me a service. It seems to me rather an occasion of humiliation to see one's self praised in a journal, which must be regarded as a collection of eulogistic biographies, paid for by the parties eulogized. Whatever may be the rank of the names, by the side of mine, the impression upon my mind is that of degradation.

In reply to your argument that I am bound by usage, permit me to say that in order to make your logic effective, you should show that the usage referred to is public and not secret, and furthermore that it is a commendable usage.

Now, in this case, the practice of your journal is not stated, nor intimated, either in the title-page or preface, or upon the cover, nor did you state any thing of the kind in your note to me. My literary experience has never furnished me with an example of a work conducted on these principles.

Perhaps it would be inconvenient to label your work according to its true character, and that may be a reason with you for concealing it, but at the same time it excludes all idea of mutuality of understanding between you and me, and puts an end to your claim founded upon implied agreement. The consent of both parties is essential to a compact: in this case, you have only the consent of yourselves.

As to the character of the usage you adopt, I am aware that

you cite high authority. You assure me that the "Emperor of France," the "Queen of Spain," "Our holy Father the Pope," "Ministers of religion, Marshals of the empire, Councillors of State, with others down to the pettiest Consul," have all complied with your custom, and paid for their eulogies which appear in your ten annual volumes of the "Archives des Hommes du Jour!" Had you not asserted this as a matter of fact, I should have denied it as impossible, as a shame to literature, a scandal against great names, a defamation of society and civilization in France and in Europe. As you affirm it, however, I pronounce no harsh judgment, and content myself by saying that while I allow others to form standards of conduct for themselves, I must claim and exercise the same privilege for myself.

The custom you insist upon, therefore, can form no rule for me. I can not consent to pay for the insertion of the memoir, as done in my behalf; certainly not for any extra copies of the article itself. I inclose to you, however, one hundred and fifty francs as penance for my ignorance and simplicity in this transaction, with the request that, if convenient, my name may be altogether obliterated from your journal.

I beg you to observe that in all this, I do not seek to impugn your principles or your conduct: I simply state my own opinions, and explain myself by reference to these, without insisting that from your point of view you may not be as correct as I am, from mine. Men's principles may differ, yet there is no necessity that irritation should follow.

I am sorry that any occasion should arise for so long and so formal a letter as this: I trust, however, that it will prove satisfactory, and I am, very respectfully, yours,

S. G. GOODRICH.

LETTER LX.

Character of the French Republic—Its Contrast with the American Republic—Aspect of the Government in France—Louis Napoleon's ambitious Designs—He Flatters the Army—Spreads Rumors of Socialist Plots—Divisions in the National Assembly—A Levee at the Elysée—The Coup d'Etat—Character of this Act—Napoleon's Government—Feelings of the People.

My dear C******

From the memoranda furnished in my preceding letter, you will comprehend the duties which devolve upon the American Consul at Paris, and will have glimpses of some of the particular incidents which befell me while I was there in that capacity. I must now give you a rapid sketch of certain public events which transpired at that period, and which will ever be regarded as among the most remarkable in modern history.

I have told you how Louis Napoleon, in consequence of the Revolution of 1848, became President of the Republic. When I arrived in Paris, in April, 1851, he was officiating in that capacity, his residence being the little palace of the Elysée Bourbon, situated between the Faubourg St. Honoré and the Champs Elysées. The National Assembly, consisting of seven hundred and fifty members, held their sessions at the building called the Chamber of Deputies.* The

---

* The National Assembly held its sessions in a temporary building erected in the courtyard of the Chamber of Deputies, proper. This

government had been in operation somewhat over
two years.

At this period France was a republic, but you will
not understand that its government bore any great
resemblance to our own, save in name. The Constitution had indeed been framed by a Convention,
called a Constituent Assembly, chosen for that purpose by the people : this had been submitted to them
and ratified by them ; and furthermore, the members
of the executive and legislative departments had all
been elected by general suffrage. The government,
therefore, rested upon the principle of popular sovereignty, but still, it was without those checks and
balances belonging to our system, and to which we
attribute its success. Ours is a Federal Republic,
a union of States, each a distinct, independent, and
sovereign power, save only as to national matters,
which are given over to the charge of a General
Government. This cantonal arrangement, which is
the great bulwark of our liberty, was wholly wanting in the French Constitution. All the powers of
government—legislative and executive—for the entire kingdom, were centralized at Paris. There were
no safeguards interposed between this supreme, un-
checked authority, and the people, and the result
showed that this defect was fatal. Our general gov-

---

was popularly called Pasteboard Hall. Louis Napoleon ordered it to
be demolished soon after the promulgation of his Constitution, some
weeks subsequent to the Coup d'Etat.

ernment may attempt usurpation, but it will immediately be arrested by the State governments; our general government may go to pieces, but the fabric of State government remains to shelter the people from anarchy. Our legislative department is furthermore divided into two bodies—the House and the Senate, and these operate as checks upon each other. Unhappily, the French system had neither of these provisions, and as the republic had swallowed up despotism, so despotism in turn speedily devoured the republic.

To the casual observer, the external aspect of things was not very different from what it had been under the monarchy of Louis Philippe. It is true that the palace of the Tuileries was vacant; no royal coaches were seen dashing through the avenues; no image and superscription of majesty frowned upon you from the public monuments, which, on the contrary, everywhere proclaimed " liberty, equality, fraternity." But still, the streets were filled with soldiers as before. Armed sentinels were stationed at the entrances of all the public buildings. The barracks were as usual swarming with soldiers, and large masses of horse and foot were frequently trained at the Champ de Mars and at Satory. Martial reviews and exercises were, indeed, the chief amusement of the metropolis. The President's house was a palace, and all around it was bristling with bayonets. It was obvious that whatever name the government might bear, military force lay at the bottom of it, and if to-day this might be its defense, to-morrow it might also be its overthrow.

It is now ascertained that Louis Napoleon, from the beginning, had his mind fixed upon the restoration of the empire. In accepting the presidency of the republic, and even in swearing fidelity to the Constitution, he considered himself only as mounting the steps of the imperial throne. The French have so long been accustomed to military despotism, that they have no idea of government without it. The people there have not the habit, so universal with us, of obeying the law, through a sense of right; they must always have before them the cannon and the bayonet, to enforce obedience. The framers of the new Constitution, either having no conception of a government unsupported by an army, or having no faith that the French nation would observe laws resting only upon moral obligation, gave to the chief magistrate the actual command of a large body of troops. With a view to prepare them to serve him, in time of need, the President flattered the officers and cajoled the men in various ways, even ordering them in one instance to be served with champagne!

In order to prepare the nation for the revolution which he meditated, Louis Napoleon caused agitating and alarming rumors to be circulated, of a terrible plot, planned by the democrats, republicans, and socialists of France, the object of which was to overturn the whole fabric of society, to destroy religion, to sweep away the obligations of marriage, to strip the rich of their property, and make a general distribution of it among the masses. Other conspiracies, having similar designs, were said to exist in all the surrounding countries of Europe, and the time was now near at hand when the fearful explosion would take place. The police of France, subject to the control and direction of the President, were instructed to discover evidences of this infernal plot, and they were so successful, that the public mind was filled with a vague but anxious apprehension that society was reposing upon a volcano, which might soon burst forth and overwhelm the whole country in chaos.

The National Assembly conducted in a manner to favor these deep, sinister schemes of the President. They were divided into four or five factions, and spent their time chiefly in angry disputes and selfish intrigues. A portion of them were monarchists, and though they had acquired their seats by pledges of devotion to the republic, they were now plotting its overthrow, a part being for the restoration of the Orleanists and a part for the Bourbons. Another faction was for Louis Napoleon, and actively promoted his schemes. By the Constitution he was ineligible for a second term, and his friends were seeking the means of overcoming this difficulty, and giving him a re-election, by fair means or foul. The liberals were divided into several shades of opinion, some being republicans, after the model of General Cavaignac; some being democrats, like Victor Hugo; and some socialists, after the fashion of Pierre Leroux. In such a state of things, there was a vast deal of idle debate, while the substantial interests of the country seemed, if not totally forgotten, at least secondary to the interests of parties, and the passions and prejudices of individuals.

Thus, although France was a republic, it was obvious that the government had fallen into selfish hands, and must perish. Louis Napoleon was only waiting a favorable moment to enter upon his schemes for its destruction. His plans rapidly advanced to maturity. The terror he had excited of a grand socialist convulsion, naturally prepared the people of property to look with favor upon any strong arm that might save them from such a catastrophe; the people at large, even the masses, the friends of the republic, were disgusted at the useless discussions, frothy declamations, and factious intrigues of the Assembly. Louis Napoleon watched his opportunity, and at last, every thing seeming to favor his scheme, he entered upon it with a degree of boldness which has few parallels in history.

I remember that on a certain Monday evening, the 1st of December, 1852, I was present at the Elysée, and was then first introduced to Louis Napoleon. I found him to be an ordinary-looking person, rather under size, but well formed, having a large nose, rather large fishy eyes, and a dull expression. The room was tolerably full, the company consisting, as is usual in such cases, of diplomats, military officers, and court officials, with a sprinkling of citizens in black coats—for hitherto the requisition of a court uniform had not been imposed. This, you will remember, was under the Republic; the rule which raised the black coat to a question of state, grew out of the Empire. Nevertheless, I was forcibly struck by the preponderance of soldiers in the assembly, and I said several times to my companions, that it seemed more like a camp than a palace. The whole scene was dull; the President himself appeared preoccupied, and was not master of his usual urbanity; Gen. Magnan walked from room to room with a ruminating air, occasionally sending his keen glances around, as if searching for something which he could not find. There was no music, no dancing. That gayety which almost always pervades a festive party in Paris, was wholly wanting. There was no ringing laughter, no merry hum of conversation. I noticed all this, but I did not suspect the cause. At eleven o'clock the assembly broke up, and the guests departed. At twelve, the conspirators, gathered for their several tasks, commenced their operations.

About four in the morning, the leading members of the Assembly were seized in their beds, and hurried to prison. Troops were distributed at various points, so as to secure the city. When the light of day came, proclamations were posted at the corners of the streets announcing to the citizens that the National Assembly was dissolved, that universal suffrage was decreed, that the Republic was established! Such was the general unpopularity of the Assembly, that the first impression of the people was that of delight at its overthrow. Throughout the first day, the streets of Paris were like a swarming hive, filled with masses of people, yet for the most part in good-humor. The second day they had reflected, and began to frown, but yet there was no general spirit of revolt. A few barricades were attempted, but the operators were easily dispersed. The third day came, and although there was some agitation among the masses, there was evidently no preparation, no combination for general resistance. As late as ten o'clock in the forenoon, I met one of the republicans whom I knew, and asked him what was to be done. His reply was:

"We can do nothing: our leaders are in prison; we are bound hand and foot. I am ready to give my life at the barricades, if with the chance of benefit; but I do not like to throw it away. We can do nothing!"

Soon after this, I perceived heavy columns of troops, some four thousand men, marching through the Rue de la Paix, and then proceeding along the Boulevards toward the Porte St. Denis. These were soon followed by a body of about a thousand horse I was told that similar bodies were moving to the

same point through other avenues of the city. In a
short time the whole Boulevard, from the Rue de la
Paix to the Place de la Bastille, an extent of two
miles, was filled with troops. My office was on the
Boulevard des Italiens, and was now fronted by a
dense body of lancers, each man with his cocked
pistol in his hand. Except the murmur of the horses'
hoofs, there was a general stillness over the city. The
sidewalks were filled with people, and though there
was no visible cause for alarm, there was still a vague
apprehension which cast pallor and gloom upon the
faces of all.

Suddenly a few shots were heard in the direction
of the Boulevard Montmartre, and then a confused
hum, and soon a furious clatter of hoofs. A moment
after, the whole body of horse started into a gallop,
and rushed by as if in flight; presently they halted,
however, wheeled slowly, and gradually moved back,
taking up their former position. The men looked
keenly at the houses on either side, and pointed
their pistols threateningly at all whom they saw at
the windows. It afterward appeared, that when the
troops had been drawn out in line and stationed
along the Boulevard, some half dozen shots were
fired into them from the tops of buildings and from
windows; this created a sudden panic; the troops
ran, and crowding upon others, caused the sudden
movement I have described. In a few moments,
the heavy, sickening sound of muskets came from

the Porte St. Denis.   Volley succeeded volley, and after some time the people were seen rushing madly along the pavements of the Boulevard as if to escape. The gate of our hotel was now closed, and at the earnest request of the throng that had gathered for shelter in the court of the hotel, I put out the "Stars and Stripes"—the first and last time that I ever deemed it necessary.   The dull roar of muskets, with the occasional boom of cannon, continued at intervals for nearly half an hour.   Silence at last succeeded, and the people ventured into the streets.

About four in the afternoon, I walked for a mile along the Boulevard.   The pavements were strewn with the fragments of shattered windows, broken cornices, and shivered doorways.   Many of the buildings, especially those on the southern side of the street, were thickly spattered with bullet-marks, especially around the windows.   One edifice was riddled through and through with cannon-shot.   Frequent spots of blood stained the sidewalk, and along the Boulevard Montmartre, particularly around the doorways, there were pools like those of the shambles; it being evident that the reckless soldiers* had shot down in heaps the fugitives who, taken by surprise,

---

* The soldiers fired upon all they saw in the streets.   An old woman going along with a loaf of bread, had a bullet put through her; an apothecary, who ventured to appear at his door, instantly received a ball in his forehead.   Files of soldiers poured their volleys upon the innocent people passing along the Boulevard; shots were fired at the windows of private houses; seven persons were killed in a bookseller's shop.   One of my friends saw seventeen dead bodies in one gutter.

strove to obtain shelter at the entrances of the hotels upon the street. It was a sight to sicken the heart, especially of an American, who is not trained to these scenes of massacre. Toward evening a portion of the troops moved away; the rest remained, and bivouacked in the streets for the night. At ten o'clock, I again visited the scene, and was greatly struck with the long line of watch-fires, whose fitful lights, reflected by dark groups of armed men, only rendered the spectacle more ghastly and gloomy.

Of the whole number killed in Paris during this, the third day of the Coup d'Etat, we have no certain account: it is generally estimated at from one thousand to fifteen hundred. I have told you that the press was silenced, save two or three papers, which told the whole story so as to justify the conduct of Louis Napoleon. These represented that the National Assembly were plotting for his overthrow by violent means, and thus would make it appear that his conduct was not only justifiable as an act of self-preservation, but necessary in view of the public good. It is important to state, however, that although the agents of the usurper seized upon the papers of the suspected members at their own houses, and at a moment of surprise, no sufficient proofs have yet been adduced of the alleged treason of the Assem-

---

These persons thus slaughtered were not rioters, working at barricades; they were mostly gentlemen, and hence it was called the massacre of the "kid gloves." The soldiers had undoubtedly been stimulated by liquor to qualify them to perform this work of butchery.

bly.   The apologists of the Coup d'Etat have further declared that the massacre along the Boulevards which I have described, was a measure of stern necessity, in order to repress the insurgent socialists. The fact seems rather to be that it was a cool and calculated slaughter of innocent persons, in order to show the power and spirit of the Dictator, and to strike with paralyzing fear those who should venture to oppose him.

The morning came, and the triumph of the reign of terror was complete.   What was enacted in Paris, was imitated all over France.   Nearly every department was declared in a state of siege; revolt was punished with death, and doubt or hesitation with imprisonment.   Forty thousand persons were hurried to the dungeons, without even the form or pretense of trial.   All over the country the press was silenced, as it had been in Paris, save only a few obsequious prints, which published what was dictated to them.   These declared that all this bloodshed and violence were the necessary result of the socialist conspiracy, which threatened to overturn society; happily, as they contended, Louis Napoleon, like a beneficent providence, had crushed the monster, and he now asked the people to ratify what he had done, by making him President for ten years.   In the midst of agitation, delusion, and panic, the vote was taken, and the usurpation was legalized by a vote of eight millions of suffrages!   The nominal Republic, but real Dic-

tatorship, thus established, was soon made to give
way to the Empire; the ambitious plotter reached the
imperial throne, and now stands before the world as
Napoleon III.!

It is impossible for us Americans to look upon the
conduct of the chief actor in this startling drama,
but with reprobation. We regard constitutions, ratified by the people, as sacred; we consider oaths to
support them as pledges of character, faith, honor,
truth—all that belongs to manhood. We look upon
blood shed for mere ambition, as murder. The American people must be totally changed in religion, morals, feelings, and political associations, before they
could cast their votes for a ruler whose lips were
stained with perjury, and whose hands were red
with the slaughter of their fellow-citizens. But the
French nation is of a different moral constitution;
their tastes, experience, souvenirs, are all different.
They are accustomed to perfidy on the part of their
rulers; violence and crime, wrought for ambition,
have stained the paths of every dynasty that has ruled
over them for a space of fourteen centuries. France
is trained to these things, and hence the public taste,
the prevailing sentiments of society, are not greatly
shocked at them. The people there do not reckon
with a successful usurper as they would with an ordinary man acting in the common business of life;
when they see him installed in the Tuileries they
forget his treacheries and his massacres—the means

by which he attained his power—and cry "Vive l'Empereur!" Even the Church now looks upon Louis Napoleon's conduct with approbation, and burns incense and sings Te Deums in his behalf, as the savior of religion, family, society.

And it must be admitted that, since his acquisition of a throne, Louis Napoleon has conducted the government with ability, and he has certainly been seconded by fortune. He married a lady who, after becoming an empress, shed luster upon her high position by her gentle virtues and gracious manners. He engaged in the Eastern War, and has triumphed. He has greatly improved and embellished the capital, and made Paris the most charming city in the world; nowhere else does life seem to flow on so cheerfully and so tranquilly as here. He has gradually softened the rigors of his government—and though some noble spirits still pine in exile,* he has taken frequent ad-

---

* The number of individuals exiled by the Coup d'Etat amounted to several thousands—some of the more obnoxious persons being sent to Cayenne, Noukahiva, and Lambessa in Algeria. Others were only banished from France; a portion of these have since had permission to return. Among those still excluded is Victor Hugo, no doubt the most eloquent writer and orator now living. He has continued to make the island of Jersey his residence. Two other exiles of some note are Ledru Rollin and Louis Blanc, members of the Provisional Government, and whose misconduct contributed largely to the overthrow of the republic. These have remained in England. Lamoricière, Changarnier, Charras, and Bedeau, all distinguished officers, are in Belgium or Germany.

Cavaignac, who was imprisoned with other members of the Assembly, was speedily released. He is believed to be a sound republican, somewhat according to our American ideas. He is permitted to reside in France, but takes no part in public affairs. Lamartine, a fine poet,

LONDON SOCIETY

vantage of opportunity to diminish the number. The people of France, at the present time, appear to be satisfied with the government, and probably a very large majority, could the question be proposed to them, would vote for its continuance.

Beneath this smooth and tranquil surface there may be, and no doubt is, a smouldering fire of discontent, and which will seek the first opportunity to explode. Louis Napoleon rules only by the vigorous and watchful power of despotism, and it is not in the nature of the French people to endure this for a long period of time. The existing empire can hardly be perpetuated beyond the life of him who has created it; indeed, its present strength lies much more in the fear of anarchy, which is certain to follow if that be removed, than from any love for the system itself, or of him who has imposed it upon the country.

---

a captivating orator, an elegant writer, and withal a man whose heart is full of every noble sentiment, escaped the indignity of imprisonment, and he too is allowed to live in his native land. But his lips are sealed as to every political question, and his only communication with his countrymen and with mankind is through literature, carefully divested of every thought and feeling pertaining to current politics. Every author in France, indeed, wears a muzzle which only permits him to breathe such thoughts as cannot offend the powers that be.

LETTER LXI.

Meeting in Paris to commemorate the Death of Clay and Webster—Termination of my Consular Duties—Character of the French Nation—The Black-coat Circular.

My dear C******

As this chapter must bring me to the end of my residence in Paris, you will permit me to crowd into it a variety of topics, without regard to chronological order or continuity of narrative.

In the autumn of 1852, the news came that Daniel Webster was no more. Under any circumstances, the decease of such a person would cause a deep and pervading emotion, but the manner of Mr. Webster's death imparted to it a peculiar degree of interest. The closing scene was, in fact, appropriate to his character, his noble person, his gigantic intellect, his great fame. It was remarked by an eminent statesman in England, that Mr. Webster's was the most sublime death of modern times. The European papers were filled with details of the event. The Americans in Paris, on hearing the tidings, deemed it proper to assemble for the purpose of giving expression to their emotions. As Mr. Clay had died only a few months before, it was resolved at the same time to pay due homage to his memory.

The meeting, consisting of several hundred persons, mostly Americans, was held in the splendid salon of

the Cercle des Deux Mondes, Boulevard Montmartre.
Mr. Rives, our minister, made an eloquent and touching address, delineating the remarkable qualities of
these two men, and comparing Mr. Clay to the Mississippi, which spreads its fertilizing waters over the
boundless regions of the West, and Mr. Webster to
the resistless Niagara, emptying seas at a plunge, and
shaking all around with its echoing thunders. Mr.
Barnard, our minister to the Court of Berlin, paid a
full and hearty tribute to the memory of Mr. Webster;
he was followed by Mr. George Wood, of New York,
and Franklin Dexter, of Boston, who also made eloquent and feeling addresses. M. Bois Lecompte,
former minister of France to the United States, and
well acquainted with the two great men whose death
we had met to commemorate, closed with a beautiful
eulogy upon each.

In the summer of 1853, I was politely advised from
the State Department that President Pierce had appointed my successor in the consulate. Thus, having
held the place a little over two years, on the 1st of
August, 1853,* I was restored to the privileges of

---

* I shall, I trust, be excused for inserting in a note the following,
which I take from Galignani's Paris Messenger of December 15th, 1854:

MR. GOODRICH, THE LATE CONSUL OF THE UNITED STATES OF AMERICA AT
PARIS.—The Americans in Paris lately presented to Mr. Goodrich a
medallion executed in *vermeil*, by the distinguished artist, Adam-Salo-
mon, with the following inscription encircling an admirable portrait of
the consul, in relief—

"*To S. G. Goodrich, Consul of the United States of America at Paris,
presented by his countrymen in that City, August 1st, 1853.*"

private citizen life. As I had various engagements which forbade me immediately to leave France, I hired a small house in Courbevoie, which I made my residence till my departure for America in the summer of 1855.

This naturally brings me to the close of my story,

The following correspondence, which took place between the parties, is creditable to all concerned:

"PARIS, September 5th, 1854.

"To S. G. GOODRICH, ESQ.—

"It is my very agreeable duty to present you, herewith, a medallion, executed at the request of a number of your American friends at Paris. It is destined alike as a token of personal respect, and an expression of the universal gratification among your countrymen at the manner in which you discharged your duties while consul of the United States here. Not content with a merely formal fulfillment of your official obligations, you made your position eminently agreeable and useful to your countrymen, and at the same time rendered it subservient to the best interests of our common country. On these points there is but one opinion; and, therefore, in making this offering, in behalf of your numerous friends, I am instructed to add their congratulations that nothing can deprive you of the good-will and good opinion so legitimately obtained. I am, sir, respectfully yours,

"FRANCIS WARDEN."

"PARIS, September 16th, 1854.

"*My Dear Sir:*—I have this day had the pleasure of receiving your letter, with the accompanying testimonial of personal regard and approbation of my official conduct, presented by you in behalf of my American friends in Paris. I need not say that I receive these unexpected tokens of kindness with great satisfaction, rendered doubly gratifying by the fact that they come when all know that I have only the humble thanks of a private citizen to give in return. While I thus acknowledge and cherish the compliment my friends have paid me, I feel bound to say that I had been already compensated for any personal sacrifices I had made to obligations lying beyond the mere routine of official duty, while I held the consulate in Paris. During that period, a space of little over two years, more than five hundred letters of introduction were presented to me, and I received at my house several thousands of my countrymen, strangers in this city; yet the instances were extremely rare in which an American trespassed either upon my time or my feelings. On the conso far as it relates to France. Were it pertinent to my design, I should give you some sketches of the French people—of their character and manners, which, in their minuter shadings, are not well appreciated in the United States. We readily comprehend England and the English people, because their language, their institutions, their genius, are similar to our own; but in France we find a different language, a different religion, different institutions—in short, a different civilization. In England, Sunday is a holy day, in France a holiday, and this fact is a sort of index to the difference between these two countries in regard to opinion, society, life. In England, the future exercises a powerful influence over the mind; in France, it is thought best to enjoy the present; England would improve the world, France would embellish it; England founds colonies, plants nations, establishes the useful arts; France refines manners, diffuses the fine arts, and spreads taste and elegance over Christendom. In England the people live in separate buildings, apart from one another, each man claiming that his house is his castle; in France,

---

trary, I was day by day more than rewarded for any services rendered, by the agreeable intercourse of persons so universally intelligent, so little requiring, and so instinctively perceiving and observing the proprieties of every situation in which they were placed. I take great pleasure in recording a fact so creditable to our countrymen, even though it may deprive me of all claims to the merits which the kindness of my friends assigns to my conduct. I have the honor to be,

"With great respect, yours, &c.,
" FRANCIS WARDEN, ESQ.   "S. G. GOODRICH."

they live congregated in hotels, one family above another, like the different layers of honeycomb in a hive. The Englishman finds his chief happiness at his fireside, the Frenchman in the sympathy of congregated masses. In England, the best points of the people are seen in the domestic circle; in France, in the salon. In all these things, English ideas are germain to our own, and hence we readily understand them, enter into them, appreciate them. As to France, it is otherwise; words there have a different sense, things a different use from that we are accustomed to, and hence, in order to understand the genius of the French nation and to do full justice to it, it is necessary to consider them from their point of view. After all that has been said and done, a work describing French society, manners, and institutions, is still a desideratum. This can not be supplied by the hasty sketches of racing travelers; it must be the work of a laborious and careful student, who unites experience and observation to a large and liberal philosophy, which on the one hand can resist the artifices of taste and the blandishments of luxury, and on the other, appreciate good things, even though they may not bear the patent-mark of his own prepossessions. Of course, you will not expect me to begin such a work in the closing pages of these fugitive letters.*

---

* I had intended to say a few words in respect to the leading literary persons of France, at the present day, but in entering upon the

I duly received your letter asking my opinion upon the "black-coat question." Mr. Marcy's celebrated circular respecting diplomatic and consular costume was not issued, or at least did not reach me, till after I had ceased to exercise the consular functions; nevertheless, as I had some opportunity to form a

---

subject I find it too extensive. I may, however, name in a single paragraph, Alexandre Dumas, whose versatility, fecundity, and capacity for labor are without parallel, and whose genius has placed him at the head of living novelists and dramatists, in spite of his notorious charlatanry and love of publicity; Adolphe Dumas, his son, whose three plays illustrative of the manners of equivocal society and of the life of abandoned women has made him rich at the age of thirty-one—a fact very suggestive as to the state of Parisian society; Lamartine, whose humble apartments in the Rue de la Ville l'Evèque are constantly filled with the admiring friends of the impoverished poet and the disowned politician; Alphonse Karr, whose caustic satires upon vice, folly, and prevalent abuses, published once a week, have made him a valuable reformer; Ampère, the traveler and linguist, whose work upon the United States is perhaps the most just that has yet been written by a foreigner; Emile de Girardin, whose innovation in editorial writing—consisting of the constant recurrence of the *alinéa*, or paragraph, each one of which contains a distinct proposition, deduced from the previous one and leading directly to that which follows—was one of the features of the Presse which produced its immense popularity; Scribe, the indefatigable playwright and librettist; Méry, the poet-laureate or court poetaster; Ponsard, whose two comedies in verse, "L'Honneur et l'Argent" and "La Bourse," are rapidly carrying him to a chair in the Academy; Béranger, hale and active at the age of seventy-six, and the most popular man in France; Gustave Planche, the critic and the terror of authors; Jules Janin, the dramatic critic, whose long labors have been totally unproductive of good to either actor or dramatist; Madame de Girardin—recently deceased—whose one act drama of "La Joie fait Peur" is the most profound piece of psychological dissection in existence; and Madame Dudevant, alias George Sand, whose power of painting the finer and more hidden emotions of the soul is unrivaled.

I must add a word in respect to Madame Ristori, the Italian tragedienne who has recently caused such a thrill of excitement in Paris. She is in nothing more remarkable than in her contrast to Rachel. The latter is the pupil of art, the former of nature. Rachel always plays the same part in the same manner. Every tone, every gesture is studied profoundly,

judgment of the measure, I freely give you my impressions upon the subject.

You understand that the State Department, at different periods, has made certain regulations in respect to the diplomatic and consular service, so far even as to prescribe their official dress. The main body of these rules, as they had existed for many years, was drawn up, I believe, by Mr. Livingston, while Secretary of State under Gen. Jackson. The diplomatic dress consisted of a blue coat and blue pantaloons decorated with gold embroidery, and a white waistcoat. It had a general resemblance to the diplomatic costume of other countries, though it was of the simplest form. The consular dress was similar, though the naval button of the United States was prescribed, and the whole costume had a sort of naval air. Diplomats and consuls wore small swords, but no epaulets.

Nevertheless, Mr. Marcy, soon after his accession to the State Department, under President Pierce, issued a circular requiring consuls to give up these costumes altogether; as to diplomats, it was recommended, though not enjoined, that they should appear before

---

and always comes in at the same time and place. Ristori enters into the play with her whole soul, and acts as her feelings dictate. She is of somewhat light complexion, with hazel eyes and brown hair; she has correct features, and off the stage is of grave, lady-like manners and appearance. On the stage she seems to work miracles. I have seen her in Marie Stuart, while on her knees at confession, by a slight continued movement upward make the audience feel as if she were actually ascending to heaven, personally and before their eyes!

foreign courts in simple black. This was urged on the ground that plainness of attire was proper to the representatives of a republic, and it was to be regretted that we had ever departed from the simplicity adopted by Dr. Franklin in appearing before the court of Louis XVI.

It would seem that these are very narrow grounds for a departure from the usages of the civilized world, our own government among the number, and in which Jefferson and Monroe, Adams and Jay, Ellsworth and King, had participated. All these, aye and Dr. Franklin* too, notwithstanding the current notion that he forced his Quaker clothes upon the court of Louis XVI., wore their court costume, simply because custom required it. There is no doubt that they were more respected, and served their country with more effect than they would have done, had they insisted upon shocking the public

---

* It is said, and I believe truly, that Dr. Franklin's appearance at the court of Louis XVI. in a plain suit of drab cloth, and which for a brief space intoxicated the giddy beau monde of Paris, was accidental: his court suit not arriving in time, and the king, who waited anxiously to receive him, requesting that he would come as he was. Whether this was so or not, I believe there is no doubt that Dr. Franklin afterward adopted a court suit, consisting of a black velvet embroidered coat, and black small-clothes, with a small sword. Dr. Franklin was a man of too much sense to undertake to shock established tastes by an offensive departure from what was esteemed propriety. All the portraits of him taken while he was our ambassador at the French court, show that he was accustomed to dress handsomely. I have a copy of one by Greuze, which represents him in a green silk dressing-gown, edged with fur, a light-colored satin waistcoat, with a frill at the bosom. Such a dress, for an elderly gentleman in his study, would now-a-days be considered almost foppish.

taste by what would have been deemed an indecorum if not an indecency—that is, appearing in common clothes on occasions in which etiquette demanded a special and appropriate attire.

·As to the assumption that simplicity of attire is characteristic of republicans, I think there is less of reason in it than of cant. It happens that the particular form of our government excludes all distinctions of rank, and hence the badges which designate these, would be without meaning among us. But with this single exception, we in the United States are as much given to display in dress and equipage as any other people on the globe. We have our military and naval costumes, and these are among the richest in the world : foppery is one of the notorious qualities of all our militia companies. Both our men and women think more of display in dress than those of other nations. When our people get to Europe, they distinguish themselves by going to the height of fashion in all things. At the court introductions in Paris, I always remarked that the Americans —men as well as women—were more sumptuously, and it may be added, more tastefully, attired than most others. Even at the new imperial court of Paris, the American ladies not only stood first in point of beauty, but also in the display of mantles, trains, and diamonds. New Orleans, Virginia, Pennsylvania, New York, Boston, had each its representative, and splendid specimens they were. If the American

Minister had come to introduce these, his countrywomen, to their imperial majesties, and had claimed the privilege of wearing a black coat because simplicity belongs to republicans, I imagine that every observer would have marked the contrast between the pretense and the performance.

Thus, though we may be republicans, we are in fact a sumptuous people, addicted to display, and exceedingly fond of being in the midst of stars and garters. We think the more of these things, doubtless, for the very reason that they are strange to our manners. Every American who goes to London or Paris, wishes to be introduced at court, and seems to feel that this is his privilege. It is not so with any other nation; no English man or woman, in Paris, asks to be presented at the Tuileries, unless it be a person of high social or official rank.

These being characteristics of our people, and perfectly well understood abroad, Mr. Marcy's black-coat circular created no little surprise. It was generally regarded as a mere appeal to the lower classes in America, who might be supposed to entertain the sentiments of the sans-culottes, and as such, it was treated with little respect. Nevertheless, had the government *prescribed* a black dress, for its diplomats, no court in Europe would have made the slightest objection. Such a measure would no doubt have subjected us to criticism, perhaps to ridicule, as a matter of taste; it would have been offensive, inasmuch as it would have seemed designed as a rebuke of the manners and customs of older and more refined nations than ourselves. We should have been considered as reading a lecture to European courts, in this wise—"Look at us, republicans, and behold how we despise the trappings of royalty, and the gaud of courts; look at our black coats, and go ye and do likewise!" Nevertheless, it is perfectly well understood in Europe that any government may regulate the costume of its representatives, and had Mr. Marcy's circular made it obligatory upon the American diplomatic corps to wear black, or white, or red, or any other color, not the slightest exception would have been taken to it by any court in the world.

This, however, was not the course adopted by the government; they merely recommended, they did not prescribe, the black coat. The situation of all our ministers, chargés, and secretaries, therefore, at once became extremely awkward.* The diplomatic business

---

* The desire of our ministers to satisfy the government at home, as well as to take advantage of the popular outburst in favor of the black coat, and at the same time to avoid the ridicule which they knew would attach to their appearing in a common dress at court, led to humiliating devices. Mr. Soulé adopted the shad-bellied, black velvet embroidered coat and small-clothes of the Municipal Council of Paris, said also to have been used by Dr. Franklin. Mr. Buchanan wore a black or blue coat, white waistcoat, small-clothes, silk stockings, a sword, and chapeau bras! Mr. Dallas is understood to have adopted the same costume. If we sympathize with these gentlemen for being forced into such humiliating subterfuges, we ought to bestow more serious condemnation upon those who led them into temptation. In some of the northern courts of Europe, I believe our diplomats have adopted the simple black coat.

I understand that the Consul of Alexandria, whose functions are part-of all countries is transacted between the ambassador and the ministers, and when these persons meet, there is no ceremony. They come together like merchants or lawyers, in their ordinary dress. All the actual business of a foreign minister may therefore be transacted without any particular costume.

But sovereigns surround themselves with a certain etiquette, and they require all who approach them to conform to this. When Queen Victoria invites persons to visit her, it is of course upon condition that they adopt the usages of the court. No one, whatever his rank or station, can claim exemption from this rule. It must be remembered that on all such occasions, the invitation is considered a compliment, and hence well-bred persons, who take advantage of it, feel constrained, by self-respect and a sense of propriety, scrupulously to regard and fulfill the conditions upon which this invitation is bestowed.

Now, it must be remembered that what is called a court costume, is only required of a minister on occasions of mere ceremony or festivity, when he appears by invitation of the sovereign. If he comes, it is not to transact business, but for amusement. He

---

ly diplomatic, wears a blue coat with thirty-one stars, wrought in gold, on the collar. This is a beautiful idea, and might suggest to our government a very simple and appropriate consular and diplomatic costume. Some costume—distinct and national and perfectly understood in all countries—is really important, as well for our consuls as diplomats. Those who insist upon the black coat, show a total ignorance of the duties and position of our public officers abroad, and of the nations among whom they officiate.

may stay away, and nothing belonging to his diplomatic affairs will suffer. Why, then, if he accepts the invitation, should he not conform to the prescribed usages of the court? It is generally considered evidence of a want of gentlemanly breeding, an act of positive vulgarity, for any person to take advantage of a polite invitation, and refuse to conform to the conditions imposed by the host. Above all, it would seem that an ambassador, representing a nation before a foreign court, should be scrupulous to observe the known and established rules of decorum.

It must be remembered that propriety of costume —that is, a dress suited to the taste and fashion prevailing where it is worn, is in all civilized countries a matter of decency. It has been so among all refined nations, and from the earliest ages. One of the most solemn of our Saviour's parables is founded upon a breach of decorum in regard to costume—the appearance of a man at the wedding of the king's son, without a wedding garment. Similar ideas are just as current among us as elsewhere. If a clergyman were to go into the pulpit dressed in a military coat, it would shock the whole audience, and be considered an insult alike to them and to the clerical profession. If a lady issues cards of invitation to a ball, and a man, who takes advantage of the invitation, comes in a sailor's roundabout, he would be held as an ill-bred fellow, and as such would be turned out of doors. He may plead that he had simply cut off the tail of his coat, and as he considered an artificial appendage of this kind derogatory to a free-born man, his principles forbade him to wear it. The answer is, you are welcome to carry out your principles, but if you accept an invitation given to you out of politeness, it is expected and required that you conform to the known usages and decencies of society.

Now in monarchical countries long usage has established it in the public mind, that to appear at court* without a court costume, would be a species of indecency, an offense against the company present, as well as the parties giving the invitation. We may rail at it as much as we please in this country, yet we can not alter the fact I state.

Taking the matter in this point of view, let us consider the situation of our diplomatic representatives under Mr. Marcy's circular. Had the black coat been prescribed, as I have said before, there would have been an end of the matter. Our ministers and chargés would have been dressed in black, that is, like the servants of a café, while all around

---

* In general, a person who should attempt to enter at a court reception, without a proper costume, would be stopped at the door : if he should, by accident, gain admittance, he would probably be invited to leave the room. A professional dress, as that of a soldier, a clergyman, &c., is considered a proper costume at Paris, and I believe at most other courts. If a person is not professional, he must wear either the prescribed costume of his own country, or that of the court to which he is introduced The British minister will introduce no one at a foreign court, who has not been previously presented to the Queen at home.

them would have appeared in appropriate costumes; and thus, in the midst of an assemblage, consisting of the most exalted rank, the highest refinement, the most distinguished ability—the representative of the United States would either have passed unnoticed as a servant, or been remarked upon as an object of ridicule, perhaps of contempt. That would have been all.

But this condition of things was not vouchsafed to our ministers: if they obeyed the circular, and carried the black coat to court, it was known to be in some degree voluntary, and was so far the more offensive on the part of the individual wearing it. Mr. Sanford, our Chargé at Paris, acting from a just regard to the wishes of his government, tried the experiment under many advantages. He was a young gentleman of good address, and held a respectable position in the higher circles of society connected with the court. He was admitted to the Tuileries in his black suit, but was of course an object of much observation and comment. His character — personal and official—protected him from indignity, either of word or look, but the act was considered offensive as well in the palace as in the various branches of society in connection with it. About this time Louis Napoleon was forming his new imperial court, and seeking to give it every degree of splendor. He had prescribed rich costumes for his officers, military and civil, and had directed that their wives

should appear in their most splendid attire. All
the persons connected with the court entered into
this spirit. For the American Chargé to present
himself in simple black, at this particular time,
looked like rebuke, and was, I believe, regarded in
this light. Had Mr. Sanford continued in his office
at Paris, and had he persevered, he would, perhaps,
by his amiable personal character and pleasing address, have removed these difficulties, though it is
quite as possible that he might have found his situation intolerable, not from open affront, but from those
sly yet galling attacks, which the polished habitués
of courts know so well how to make, even in the midst
of smiles and seeming caresses. As it happened, Mr.
Mason soon after arrived in Paris as full minister,
and appreciating the result of Mr. Sanford's experiment, adopted the usual diplomatic costume.

For my own part, I can not see the utility of making ourselves disagreeable, and at the same time
jeoparding the real interests of our country, in such
a matter as that of the dress of our diplomatic representatives. Our policy should be to cultivate peace
with all the world, but it would seem of late that our
desire is rather to array all the nations against us.
Within the last three years we have lost nearly all our
friends in Europe. The Ostend Congress, with its startling doctrines, produced a deep and pervading feeling
of reprehension, and the circulars of " Citizen Saunders" created still more lively emotions of irritation

and resentment.*   The character and conduct of several of our consuls and diplomats, in different parts of Europe, together with our Secretary's well-meant attempts to improve the taste of the European courts in the matter of dress, have all contributed to degrade the American name in foreign countries.

Such are, briefly, my views of Mr. Marcy's diplomatic circular. It seems to have been ill advised, and though its motive was no doubt good, it must have been adopted without full inquiry into the subject. Had the State Department taken the precaution to address our ministers and consuls on the subject, the answer would have been such as to have prevented the ridicule brought upon the country by this measure. The present state of things is embarrassing to our foreign ministers, and derogatory to the country. The true plan is to adopt some simple and appropriate costume, and make it obligatory. If the black coat is to be preferred, then let it be prescribed, so

---

* Mr. Saunders' Circulars were addressed, one to the President of the Swiss Cantons and the other to the French people—the latter being of a very incendiary character. These were translated into various languages, and scattered all over Europe, by the Italian and French exiles in London. I saw one of these, with a preface by Saffi, in which he stated that the writer, Citizen Saunders, was *Consul General* of the United States in Great Britain, that he was very intimate with Mr. Buchanan, the American minister at London, and thus conveying the idea that he spoke officially, in some degree, for the United States. A certain authority was lent to these documents by the statement that they were circulated in France under the seal of the American Legation in London. To judge of the effect produced by all this, let us consider what would be the feeling of our people, if some foreign official should undertake to teach us our duty, and should even call upon us to cut the throats of our rulers !

that the responsibility may fall on the government and not on him who wears it. And one thing more: let us be consistent; if republicanism requires simplicity, and black is to be our national color, let the "fuss and feathers" of the army and navy be dismissed, and the general as well as the private soldier appear in "the black coat!"

LETTER LXII.

Visit to Italy—Florence—Rome—Naples.

MY DEAR C******

In the autumn of 1854 I set out with my family for a brief visit to Italy. With all my wanderings I had never seen this far-famed land, and as I was not likely ever to have another opportunity, I felt it to be a kind of duty to avail myself of a few unappropriated weeks, for that object.

It is not my purpose to give you the details of my travels or my observations. A mere outline must suffice. Embarking in a steamer at Marseilles, we soon reached Genoa. Here we went ashore for a few hours, and then returning to our vessel, proceeded on to Leghorn. Taking the railroad at this place, we wound among the hills, and, having passed Pisa, catching a glimpse of its Leaning Tower, arrived at Florence. In this journey of five days, we had passed from Paris to the center of Italy.

Florence* is situated in a small but fertile valley, on either side of which rise a great number of precipitous hills; behind these is a succession of still greater elevations, with rocky summits reaching at last to the Apennines on the north, and other ranges on the south and west. A narrow stream, poetically called the "yellow Arno" or "golden Arno," but in honest phrase, the muddy Arno, flows nearly through the center of the city. This is bordered by stone quays, leaving a space of about three hundred feet in width, sometimes full and sometimes only a bed of gravel, along which winds the stream shrunken into an insignificant rivulet. The Arno is in fact a sort of mountain torrent; its source is nearly five thousand feet above the level of the sea, yet its whole course is but seventy-five miles. The steep acclivities around Florence suddenly empty the rains into its channel, and it often swells in the course of a few hours to inundation; it subsides as speedily, and in summer almost disappears amid the furrows of its sandy bed.

If we were to judge Florence by a modern standard, we might pronounce it a dull, dismal-looking

---

* Florence has a population of one hundred and ten thousand inhabitants, but it is so compactly built as to occupy a very small territorial space. It is surrounded by a wall, partly of brick and partly of stone, and yet so feeble and dilapidated, as to be wholly useless, except for the purposes of police. It has six gates, duly guarded by military sentries. It is the capital of Tuscany, which is called a Grand Duchy, the Grand Duke, its present ruler, Leopold II., being an Austrian prince. The government is a rigid despotism, sustained by means of a few thousand Austrian troops, and the moral influence of the authority of Austria itself, ever ready to rush to the aid of the government.

place, marred by dilapidation, degraded by tyranny, and occupied by a degenerate people. But when we enter its galleries of art,* when we survey its monuments of architecture, and when we view all these in connection with its history, we speedily discover it to be an inexhaustible mine, alike instructive to the philosopher and the man of taste.

I dare not begin upon the curiosities with which this city is filled: I must leave them to be described by others. The hills around the city are equally interesting, studded as they are with edifices, connected with the names of Michael Angelo, Galileo, Dante, Lorenzo de' Medici, and others, all full of historical associations or recollections of science and art. At the distance of about five miles is Fiésole, now an insignificant village, situated on the top of a steep hill, rising a thousand feet above the bed of the valley. This you ascend by a winding road, built with immense labor, a portion of it cut in the solid rock. This place was the cradle of Florence, its history reaching back three thousand years, into the thick mists of antiquity.

---

* The principal gallery, the Ufizzi, contains the statue of the Venus de' Medici, the group of Niobe, and the most extensive collection of paintings and statuary illustrative of the history and progress of art, in the world. The collection in the Pitti Palace, the residence of the Grand Duke, is less extensive, but it is beautifully arranged, and comprises many gems of art, especially in painting and mosaic. Mr. Powers and Mr. Hart, American sculptors, celebrated for their busts in marble, are established in this city. Here we met Buchanan Read, who had just finished his charming poem, The New Pastoral; at the same time he was acquiring hardly less celebrity by his pencil.

Here are Cyclopean walls, constructed by the early inhabitants to protect themselves at a period when all Italy was in the possession of bands of brigands and robbers, and when every town and village was a fortress. From this point you look down upon Florence, which almost seems at your feet; you have also a commanding view of the whole adjacent country. If you inquire the names of places that attract your attention, you will be carried back to periods anterior to the building of Rome. The guide will point you to the track of Hannibal through the marshes of the Arno, then a wilderness without inhabitants, amid which the Carthaginian general lost a number of elephants, and whose tusks are even at this day dug up from their deep beds in the soil. Allow me to give you a somewhat prosy description in rhyme of this wonderful and suggestive place— the best in the world to study early Roman geography and history—which I wrote on the spot, and which has at least the merit of being brief :

> This is Fiésole—a giant mound,
> With fellow-giants circling phalanx'd round ;
> Hoary with untold centuries they rest,
> Yet to the top with waving olives dress'd,
> While far beyond in rugged peaks arise
> The dark-blue Apennines against the skies.
> In this deep vale, with sentried hills around,
> Set foot to foot, and all with villas crown'd,
> Fair Florence lies—its huge Duomo flinging
> E'en to Fiésole its silvery ringing.

ROME. The Pope and his train passing the ruins of the Forum. Vol 2. p. 525.

Ah, what a varied page these scenes unfold—
How much is written, yet how much untold!
Here on this mound, the huge Cyclopean wall—
Its builders lost in Time's unheeding thrall—
Speaks of whole nations, ages, kingdoms, races,
Of towers and cities, palaces and places—
Of wars and sieges, marches, battles, strife,
The hopes and fears—the agonies of life—
All pass'd away, their throbbing weal and woe,
E'er Rome was built, three thousand years ago!

On the twenty-second day of February we entered
Rome, and found the peach-trees in blossom. The
modern city is in no respect remarkable. Its walls
are of some strength, but readily yielded to the attack of the French army in 1849. Its present population is one hundred and seventy-five thousand.
All the streets are narrow, and even the far-famed
Corso is not over fifty feet wide. In general, the
buildings appear to be of modern date, with here and
there some grand monument of antiquity peering out
from the midst of more recent structures. On the
whole, the aspect of this "Queen of the World" is
eminently sad, degenerate, and disheartening.

The more imposing relics of antiquity, the Forum,
the Palace of the Cæsars, the Coliseum, the Baths of
Caracalla, though within the walls, are still on the
southern side of the city, and beyond the present center of population. All these are gigantic structures,
but mostly of a barbarous character. They show the
amazing power and wealth of the emperors who con-

structed these works, but they also display the actual poverty of art, for there is not one of them that can furnish a useful suggestion to even a house-carpenter. The vain and transitory nature of the ideas and institutions which gave birth to these miracles of labor, strikes the reflecting mind with a deep and painful sense of humiliation. The Coliseum, the most sublime monument of accumulated human toil, regarded as to its gigantic proportions, was erected for amusements now held to be alike cruel and revolting; the baths of Caracalla—whole acres covered with mounds of brick—were constructed to minister to fashionable luxuries, which at the present day would be regarded as infamous. In modern times, the same accommodations would be obtained with one-twentieth part of the labor expended upon these establishments. The vanity, the boasting, the ostentation of conquerors, which gave birth to the triumphal arches, would at this day be looked upon with universal contempt. The temples were erected to gods, which have vanished into thin air. The Aqueducts, whose ruins stretch across the gloomy Campagna, looking like long lines of marching mastodons, were erected in ignorance of that familiar fact, visible to any one who looks into a teapot, that water will rise to its level !

The great lesson to be learned at Rome is that of humility. I know not which is most calculated to sink the pride of man, pagan Rome, sublime in the grandeur of its tyranny, its vices, and its falsehoods, or Christian Rome, contemptible in its littleness, its tricks, and its artifices, which would disgrace the commonest juggler.

I speak not now of the treasures of art,* collected to repletion in the public and private galleries of this wonderful city. These are endless in extent and variety. Among them are the finest paintings of Raphael, and the best sculptures of Michael Angelo, as well as the Dying Gladiator and the Apollo Belvidere. Here, also, is that rich, gorgeous palace, called St. Peter's Church. But still, Rome, on the whole, seems to me the most melancholy spot on earth. Here is a city which once contained three or four millions of

---

* Rome is not only a depository of exhaustless stores of relics of art, and curiosities illustrative of history, but it is the great studio of living artists from all parts of Europe. Both painting and sculpture are pursued here with eminent success. The Angel of the Resurrection in the studio of Tenerani, is the most beautiful and sublime piece of sculpture I ever beheld. Gibson, an Englishman, takes the lead among foreigners, his best things consisting of reliefs, which are beautiful indeed. His Venus is English, but fine. He has tried coloring statuary, after the manner of the ancients, but it is not approved. Our American Crawford ranks very high for invention and poetic expression. He has shown a capacity beyond any other American sculptor, for groups on a large scale. Bartholomew, of Connecticut, is a man of decided genius, and is rapidly attaining fame. Ives, Mosier, Rogers—all our countrymen—are acquiring celebrity.

Among the foreign painters, the most celebrated is Overbeck, a German. He chooses religious subjects, and is a little pre-Raphaelitish in his style. Page, Terry, Chapman, are all highly appreciated, both at home and abroad. I here met the landscape painter, George L. Brown, whom I employed twenty years ago, for a twelvemonth, as a wood-engraver. He has studied laboriously of late, and his pictures are beautiful. When he was a boy, he painted a picture, the first he ever finished. Isaac P. Davis, of Boston, a well-known amateur, called to see it, and asked the price. Brown meant to say fifty cents, but in his confusion said fifty dollars. It was taken by Mr. Davis at this price: so the wood-cutter became a landscape painter !

inhabitants, now shrunk and wasted to a population of less than two hundred thousand, and these living upon the mere ruins of the past. The Christian Church is but little better than a collection of bats and owls, nestling in the ruinous structures erected for the gods and goddesses of heathen antiquity.

Nor is this the most appalling fact here presented to the traveler. Around this place is a belt of undulating land called the Campagna, eight or ten miles in width, fertile by nature, and once covered with a busy population; this has become desolate, and is now tenanted only by sheep and cattle. The air is poisoned, and man breathes it at his peril. To sleep in it is death. And this change has come over it while it claims to be the very seat and center of Christianity, the residence of the Successor of the Apostles, the Head of the Catholic Church, the Representative of Christ on earth, the Spiritual Father of a hundred and fifty millions of souls! Is not this mysterious, fearful?

We reached Naples about the first of April. Here the character of the climate and of the people becomes thoroughly Italian. The Bay of Naples can not be too much praised. Not only do the prominent objects—the crescent-shaped city, rising terrace above terrace on the north; Vesuvius, with its double cone in the east, and the islands of Capri and Ischia at the south—form a beautiful boundary to the view, but the water and the sky and the air have all a liveliness, a cheerfulness, which calls upon the heart to be gay. The Neapolitan is, in truth, constantly preached to by nature, to sing and dance and be happy. It is impossible for any one to resist this influence of the climate—of the earth and the sea and the air—in this region of enchantment. It appears that the ancient Romans felt and yielded to its force. In the vicinity was Puzzuoli, a renowned watering-place, the hills around being still studded with the vestiges of villas once inhabited by the Roman patricians; near by was Cumæ, long a seat and center of taste and luxury; close at hand was Baiæ, the Baden Baden of fashion in the time of Cicero—its ruins abundantly attesting the luxury as well as the licentiousness of those days. In the mouth of the bay was Capri, chosen by Tiberius as the scene of his imperial orgies, in consideration of its delicious climate and picturesque scenery. The whole region is indeed covered over with monuments of Rome in the day of its glory, testifying to the full appreciation of the beauties of the sky and the climate, on the part of its patrician population.

As to the city of Naples itself I shall not speak; though its people, its institutions, its repositories of art, its Museum of vestiges taken from the buried cities of Pompeii and Herculaneum, would furnish interesting subjects of description. I have only to add that after a stay of a month, I left it with reluctance, and returned to Paris. When I arrived, the

Great Exposition was on the eve of being opened.
I remained till July, and had several opportunities to
examine this marvelous array of the world's art and
industry.   On the fourth of the same month I departed for the United States, and arriving in New
York, found anchorage for myself and family in that
city.

———————◆———————

LETTER LXIII.

Leave-taking—Improvement everywhere—In Science—Geology, Chemistry,
Agriculture, Manufactures, Astronomy, Navigation, the Domestic Arts—
Anthracite Coal—Traveling—Painting—Daguerreotypes—The Electric
Telegraph—Moral Progress—In Foreign Countries: in the United States.

MY DEAR C*******

I have now come to my farewell.   Leave-takings
are in general somewhat melancholy, and it is best to
make them as brief as possible.   Mine shall consist
of a single train of thought, and that suggestive of
cheerful rather than mournful feelings.   Like a traveler approaching the end of his journey, I naturally
cast a look backward, and surveying the monuments
which rise up in the distance, seek to estimate the
nature and tendency of the march of events which I
have witnessed, and in which I have participated.

One general remark appears to me applicable to
the half century over which my observation has extended, which is, that everywhere there has been improvement.   I know of no department of human

knowledge, no sphere of human inquiry, no race of men, no region of the earth, where there has been retrogradation. On the whole, the age has been alike fruitful in discovery, and the practical, beneficial results of discovery. Science has advanced with giant strides, and it is the distinguishing characteristic of modern science that it is not the mere toy of the philosopher, nor the hidden mystery of the laboratory, but the hard-working servant of the manufactory, the workshop, and the kitchen. Geology not only instructs us in the sublime history of the formation of the earth, but it teaches us to understand its hidden depths, and to trace out and discover its mineral treasures. Chemistry, the science of atoms, teaching us the component parts of matter, as well as the laws of affinity and repulsion, has put us in possession of a vast range of convenient knowledge now in daily and familiar use in the domestic arts. We have even express treatises upon the "Chemistry of Common Life." Astronomy has not only introduced to us new planets and the sublime phenomena of the depths hitherto beyond our reach, but it has condescended to aid in perfecting the art of navigation, and thus contributed to make the sea the safe and familiar highway of the nations.

We can best appreciate the progress of things around us, by looking at particular facts. Take anthracite coal, for instance, which, when I was a boy, was unknown, or only regarded as a black, shining, useless stone; now six millions of tons are annually dug up and distributed. Think of the labor that is performed by this mass of matter, that had slumbered for ages—hidden, senseless, dead, in the bosom of the earth! It now not only cooks our food and warms our houses so as in winter to give us the climate of summer, but the sleeper, waked from its tomb, like a giant impatient of the time he has lost, turns the whizzing wheel of the factory, sends the screaming locomotive on its way, drives the steamboat foaming through the waves. This single mineral now performs, every day, the labor of at least a hundred thousand men!

On every hand are the evidences of improvement. What advances have been made in agriculture—in the analysis of soils, the preparation of manures, the improvement of implements, from the spade to the steam-reaper; in the manufacture of textile fabrics by the inventions of Jacquard and others in weaving, and innumerable devices in spinning; in the working of iron—cutting, melting, molding, rolling, shaping it like dough, whereby it is applied to a thousand new uses; in commerce and navigation, by improved models of ships, improved chronometers, barometers, and quadrants—in chain-pumps and wheel-rudders; in printing, by the use of the power-press, throwing off a hundred thousand impressions instead of two thousand in a day; in the taking of likenesses by the daguerreotype, making the Sun himself the painter of miniatures; in microscopes, which have revealed new

worlds in the infinity of littleness, as well as in tele-
scopes which have unfolded immeasurable depths of
space before hidden from the view   How has traveling been changed, from jolting along at the rate of six
miles an hour over rough roads in a stage-coach, to
the putting one's self comfortably to bed in a steamboat and going fifteen miles an hour; or sitting down
in a railroad car at New York to read a novel, and
before you have finished, to find yourself at Boston!
The whole standard of life and comfort has been
changed, especially in the cities.   The miracles of
antiquity are between each thumb and finger now; a
friction-match gives us fire and light, the turn of a
cock brings us water, bright as from Castalia.   We
have summer in our houses, even through the rigors
of winter.   We light our streets by gas, and turn
night into day.   Steam brings to the temperate zone
the fresh fruits of the tropics; ether mitigates the agonies of surgical operations; ice converts even the
fires of Sirius into sources of luxury.

These are marvels, yet not the greatest of marvels.
Think—instead of dispatching a letter in a mail-bag,
with the hope of getting an answer in a month—of
sending your thoughts alive along a wire winged with
electricity, to New Orleans or Canada, to Charleston or
St. Louis, and getting a reply in the course of a few
hours!   This is the miracle of human inventions, the
crowning glory of art, at once the most ingenious, the
most gratifying, the most startling of discoveries.   I

know of nothing in the whole range of human contri-
vances which excites such exulting emotions in the
mind of man, as the electric telegraph.*   It is giving
wings of light to the mind, and here on earth impart-
ing to the soul, some of the anticipated powers which
imagination tells us the spirit may exercise in the

---

* The original profession of Samuel Finley Morse, the inventor of the
electric telegraph, was that of an historical painter. He went to Europe
for the purpose of perfecting himself in this, the second time, in 1824. In
the autumn of 1832 he was returning in a ship from Havre, when the subject of electro-magnetism one day became the theme of conversation at
the lunch-table. The fact that an electric spark could be obtained from
a magnet, had led to the new science of magneto-electricity. Reflecting
upon this, the idea of making electricity the means of telegraphic communication struck him with great force. It appears that in this conception he had been anticipated by scientific men, but nothing had been
effected toward realizing it.   Mr. Morse, after earnest and absorbing
reflection upon this subject during his voyage, on his arrival set himself
to the task of making it practical, and the plan he finally discovered and
laid before the world was entirely original with him. All telegraphists
before used evanescent signs ; his system included not only the use of a
new agent, but a self-recording apparatus, adding to the celerity of lightning almost the gift of speech. This was a new and wonderful art—that
of a speaking and printing telegraph !
    It would be interesting, if I had space, to trace this invention through
all its alternations in the mind, feelings, and experiments of its producer.
I can only say that after encountering and overcoming innumerable obstacles, the instrument was made to work on a small but decisive scale,
in 1835. In 1837 he established his apparatus at Washington, and, as
every thing seemed to promise success, he made an arrangement with a
member of Congress (F. O. J. Smith) to take an interest in the patent,
and to proceed forthwith to Europe to secure patents there. This was
done, and Mr. Morse soon joined his associate in England. The expedition resulted only in long embarrassment and disaster to the inventor.
Having returned to the United States, and successfully struggling with
obstacles and adversities, he finally obtained the assistance of the government, and a line of telegraph was built from Washington to Baltimore. After some mistakes and many failures, the work proved successful, effective experiments having been made in 1844. The first
sentence sent over the line is said to have been dictated by Miss Anna
Ellsworth, daughter of H. L. Ellsworth, then commissioner of patents—

world above! Having achieved so much, who shall dare to set limits to the power of human invention?

And in the moral world, the last fifty years appear to me to have shown an improvement, if not as marked, yet as certain and positive, as in the material world. Everywhere, as I believe, the standard of humanity is more elevated than before. About a century ago, an eminent New England divine, afterward president of Yale College, sent a barrel of rum to Africa by a Rhode Island captain, and got in return a negro boy, whom he held as a slave, and this was not an offence. I know of a distinguished D. D. who was a distiller of New England rum half a century ago, and with no loss of reputation. The rules by which we try candidates for office are much more rigid than formerly. Church discipline among all sects is more severe, while sectarian charity is greatly enlarged. Christian missions are among the established institutions of society; education is everywhere improved and extended. If in some things, with the increase of wealth and luxury, we have degenerated, on the whole there has been an immense

---

" What hath God wrought?" It was indeed a natural and beautiful idea, at the moment that man had opened a new and startling development of the works of the Almighty. The means of instantly transmitting intelligence through space, seems to illustrate not only the omnipotence, but the omniscience and omnipresence of God.

Thus the telegraph was established, and though Mr. Morse has encountered opposition, rivalry, and almost fatal competition, he is generally admitted throughout the world to be the true inventor of this greatest marvel of art, the electric telegraph.

advance, as well in technical morals as in those large humanities which aim at the good of all mankind.

If we cast our eyes over foreign lands, we shall see a similar if not an equal progress in all that belongs to the comforts and the charities of life. Despotism still reigns over a large part of the world, but its spirit is mitigated, its heart softened. Dungeons and chains are not now the great instruments of government. There is everywhere—more especially in all parts of Christendom—a feeling of responsibility on the part of even kings and princes, to the universal principles of justice and humanity. There is a moral sense, a moral law among mankind, which tyrants dare not set at defiance!

Such has been the tendency of things within the half century which has passed under my observation. If, then, I am an optimist, it is as much from reason and reflection as from sentiment. In looking at the political condition of our country, there are no doubt threatening clouds in the sky, and mutterings of ominous thunders in the distance. I have, however, known such things before; I have seen the country shaken to its center by the fierce collisions of parties, and the open assaults of the spirit of disunion. But these dangers passed away. Within my memory, the States of the Union have been doubled in number, and the territory of the Union has been trebled in extent! This I have seen; and as such has been the past, so may be, and so I trust will be, the future. Farewell!

APPENDIX.

NOTE I.

List of Works of which S. G. Goodrich is the Editor or Author.

My experience, as an author, has been not a little singular, in one respect. While on the other side of the Atlantic my name has been largely used, as a passport to the public, for books I never wrote—attempts have been made in this country to deprive me of the authorship of at least a hundred volumes which I did write. It requires some patience to reflect upon this with equanimity; to see myself, falsely, saddled with the paternity of things which are either stupid, or vulgar, or immoral—or perhaps all together; and then to be deprived, also by falsehood, of the means of effectually throwing them off by appealing to genuine works—which have obtained general favor—through a suspicion cast into the public mind, that I am a mere pretender, and that the real authorship of these works belongs to another person.

This, however, has been, and perhaps is my position, at least with some portion of the public. I have thought it worth while, therefore, to print a catalogue of my genuine works, and also a list of the false ones, issued under my name, with such notes as seem necessary to set the whole matter clearly before the public.

The following list comprises all my works to the best of my recollection.

MISCELLANEOUS

	Date of publication.	No. vols.
The Token—A New Year's and Christmas Present	1828	14

> [The first volume was issued in 1828, and it was continued, yearly, till 1842—15 years. 18mo. and 12mo. Edited by me, except that in 1829 it was edited by N. P. Willis. Among the contributors to this work were, E. Everett, Bishop Doane, A. H. Everett, J. Q. Adams, H. W. Longfellow, I. McLellan, Jr., N. Hawthorne, Miss Sedgwick, Mrs. Sigourney, Willis Gaylord Clark, N. P. Willis, J. Neale, Grenville Mellen, Geo. Lunt, John Pierpont, Caleb Cushing, H. Pickering, Miss Leslie, T. H. Gallaudet, Mrs. Child, F. W. P. Greenwood, Rev. T. Flint, H. F. Gould, W. L. Stone, H. T. Tuckerman, Madame Calderon de la Barca, O. W. Holmes, Mrs. Seba Smith, Mrs. Osgood, Mrs. Lee, J. Inman, Horace Greeley, I. C. Pray, Orville Dewey, O. W. B. Peabody, James Hall, Mrs. Hale, Mrs. Hoffland, J. T. Fields, Miss M. A. Browne, R. C. Waterston, Nath. Greene, H. H. Weld, G. C. Verplanck, T. S. Fay, J. O. Rockwell, Charles Sprague, etc.]

538 APPENDIX—NOTES.

	Date of publication.	No. vols
A History of All Nations, from the Earliest Period to the Present Time—In which the History of every Nation, Ancient and Modern, is separately given. Large 8vo., 1200 pp.	1849	1

[In the compilation of this work I had the assistance of Rev. Royal Robbins, of Berlin, Conn., Rev. W. S. Jenks, and Mr. S. Kettell, of Boston, and F. B. Goodrich, of New York.]

A Pictorial Geography of the World. Large 8vo., 1000 pp.	1840	1

[The first edition of this work was published in 1831, but being found imperfect, was revised and remodeled at this date. In the original work I had the assistance of J. O. Sargent and S. P. Holbrook, Esqs., and Mr. S. Kettell: the new edition was mainly prepared by T. S. Bradford, Esq.]

Sow Well and Reap Well, or Fireside Education. 12mo.	1838	1
A Pictorial History of America. 8vo.	1845	1
Winter Wreath of Summer Flowers. 8vo. Colored Engravings	1853	1
The Outcast, and other Poems. 12mo	1841	1
Sketches from a Student's Window. 12mo	1836	1
Poems. 12mo	1851	1
Ireland and the Irish. 12mo	1842	1
Five Letters to my Neighbor Smith	1839	1
Les Etats Unis d'Amérique. 8vo	1852	1

[This was published in Paris.]

The Gem Book of British Poetry. Sq. 8vo.	1854	1
Recollections of a Lifetime: or, Men and Things I have Seen. In a series of Familiar Letters—Historical, Biographical, Anecdotical, and Descriptive: addressed to a Friend. 12mo. (In press.)	1857	2
The Picture Play-Book	1855	1

SCHOOL BOOKS.

Ancient History, from the Creation to the Fall of Rome. 12mo	1846	1
Modern History, from the Fall of Rome to the present time. 12mo	1847	1
History of North America—Or, The United States and adjacent Countries. 18mo	1846	1
History of South America and the West Indies. 18mo.	1846	1

	Date of publication.	No. vols.
History of Europe. 18mo	1848	1
History of Asia. 18mo	1848	1
History of Africa. 18mo	1850	1

[In the compilation of the preceding six volumes, excluding North America, I had large assistance from Mr. S. Kettell.]

A Comprehensive Geography and History, Ancient and Modern. 4to	1849	1
The National Geography. 4to	1849	1
A Primer of History, for Beginners at Home and School. 24mo	1850	1
A Primer of Geography, for Home and School—With Maps.	1850	1
A Pictorial History of the United States. 12mo	1846	1
A Pictorial History of England. 12mo	1846	1
A Pictorial History of France. 12mo	1846	1
A Pictorial History of Greece. 12mo	1846	1
A Pictorial History of Rome. 12mo	1848	1

[In the preparation of the preceding five volumes, I had assistance from Dr. Alcott, Mr. J. Lowell, &c. I was largely assisted in the preparation of Rome by Mr. S. Kettell.]

A Pictorial Natural History. 12mo	1842	1
The Young American: Or, A Book of Government and Law. 12mo	1842	1
The Malte-Brun School Geography. 16mo	1830	1
Maps for the same. 4to	1830	1
The Child's Own Book of Geography; or the Western Hemisphere—With Maps. Sq. 12mo. (Out of print.)	1834	1
The Child's Own Book of Geography; or the Eastern Hemisphere—With Maps. Square 12mo. (Out of print.)	1834	1
Goodrich's First Reader. 18mo	1846	1
Goodrich's Second Reader. 18mo	1846	1
Goodrich's Third Reader. 18mo	1846	1
Goodrich's Fourth Reader. 12mo	1846	1
Goodrich's Fifth Reader. 12mo	1846	1

TALES UNDER THE NAME OF PETER PARLEY.

The Tales of Peter Parley about America. Square 16mo.	1827	1
Do. do. Europe. do	1828	1
Peter Parley's Winter-Evening Tales. do	1829	1

	Date of publication.	No. vols.
Peter Parley's Juvenile Tales. Square 16mo.........	1830	1
The Tales of Peter Parley about Africa. Square 16mo.	1830	1
Do. do. Asia. do......	1830	1
Peter Parley's Tales about the Sun, Moon, and Stars. Square 16mo...................................	1830	1
Peter Parley's Tales of the Sea. Square 16mo........	1831	1
Peter Parley's Tales about the Islands in the Pacific Ocean. Square 16mo..........................	1831	1
Peter Parley's Method of Telling about Geography. Square 16mo...................................	1830	1

[This work was remodeled and reproduced in 1844, under the name of "Parley's Geography for Beginners, at Home and School." Two millions of copies of it were sold: the publisher paid me three hundred dollars for the copyright, and made his fortune by it.]

	Date of publication.	No. vols.
Peter Parley's Tales about the World. Square 16mo. (Out of print.).................................	1831	1
Peter Parley's Tales about New York. Square 16mo. (Out of print.)..................................	1832	1
Peter Parley's Tales about Great Britain—Including England, Scotland, and Ireland. Square 16mo. (Out of print.)..................................	1834	1
Parley's Picture Book. Square 16mo................	1834	1
Parley's Short Stories for Long Nights. Square 16mo.	1834	1
Peter Parley's Book of Anecdotes. do.....	1836	1
Parley's Tales about Animals. 12mo..............	1831	1
Persevere and Prosper: Or, The Siberian Sable-Hunter. 18mo...................................	1843	1
Make the Best of It: Or, Cheerful Cherry, and other Tales. 18mo.................................	1843	1
Wit Bought: Or, The Adventures of Robert Merry. 18mo...................................	1844	1
What to do, and How to do it: Or, Morals and Manners. 18mo...................................	1844	1
A Home in the Sea: Or, The Adventures of Philip Brusque. 18mo..............................	1845	1
Right is Might, and other Sketches. 18mo..........	1845	1
A Tale of the Revolution, and other Sketches. 18mo..	1845	1
Dick Boldhero, or the Wonders of South America. 18mo...................................	1846	1
Truth-Finder: Or, Inquisitive Jack. 18mo.........	1846	1

	Date of publication.	No. vols.

Take Care of No. 1: Or, The Adventures of Jacob Karl.
18mo... 1850....1
Tales of Sea and Land.......... .... 1846....1
Every-Day Book. Sq. 16mo. (Out of print.)........ 1835....1
Parley's Present for All Seasons. 12mo........... 1853....1
Parley's Wanderers by Sea and Land. 12mo......... 1854....1
Parley's Fagots for the Fireside. 12mo.............. 1854....1
Parley's Balloon Travels of Robert Merry and his Young
Friends in various parts of Europe. 12mo........ 1856....1
Parley's Adventures of Gilbert Goahead. 12mo....... 1856....1
Parley's Adventures of Billy Bump, all the way from
Sundown to California. (In press.).............. 1857....1
Parley's Balloon Travels of Robert Merry and his Young
Friends in the Holy Land and other parts of Asia.
12mo. (In press.)............................. 1857....1

PARLEY'S HISTORICAL COMPENDS.

Peter Parley's Universal History on the basis of Geog-
raphy. Large sq. 16mo....................... 1837....2
Peter Parley's Common School History. 12mo........ 1837....1
The First Book of History for Children and Youth.
Large sq. 12mo .... 1831....1
The Second Book of History—Designed as a Sequel to
the First Book of History. Large sq. 12mo........ 1832....1
The Third Book of History—Designed as a Sequel to
the First and Second Books of History. Sq. 12mo.. 1833....1

[The two preceding volumes were compiled under my direction, and were then remodeled by me, but were not
published, nor were they intended to appear, as by Peter Parley; they have, however, passed under that name
for several years.]

Parley's Tales about Ancient Rome, with some account
of Modern Italy. Sq. 16mo .... 1832....1
Parley's Tales about Ancient and Modern Greece. Sq.
16mo.. 1833....1
Histoire des Etats-Unis d'Amérique. Published in Paris
and the United States. 12mo. .... 1853....1
Petite Histoire Universelle. Published in Paris and the
United States. 12mo. .... 1853....1

[In the preparation of some of these, I had the aid of N.
Hawthorne, and J. O. Sargent, Esqs., &c.]

PARLEY'S MISCELLANIES.

PARLEY'S CABINET LIBRARY: 20 vols., small 12mo., as follows:

BIOGRAPHICAL DEPARTMENT.

	Date of publication.	No. vols.
1. Lives of Famous Men of Modern Times	1844–5	1
2. Lives of Famous Men of Ancient Times	"	1
3. Curiosities of Human Nature	"	1
4. Lives of Benefactors	"	1
5. Lives of Famous American Indians	"	1
6. Lives of Celebrated Women	"	1

HISTORICAL DEPARTMENT.

7. Lights and Shadows of American History	"	1
8. Lights and Shadows of European History	"	1
9. Lights and Shadows of Asiatic History	"	1
10. Lights and Shadows of African History	"	1
11. History of the American Indians	"	1
12. Manners, Customs, and Antiquities of the American Indians	"	1

MISCELLANEOUS.

13. A Glance at the Sciences	"	1
14. Wonders of Geology	"	1
15. Anecdotes of the Animal Kingdom	"	1
16. A Glance at Philosophy	"	1
17. Book of Literature, with Specimens	"	1
18. Enterprise, Industry, and Art of Man	"	1
19. Manners and Customs of Nations	"	1
20. The World and its Inhabitants	"	1

Parley's Panorama: Or, the Curiosities of Nature and Art, History and Biography. Large 8vo., double columns	1849	1
Parley's Geography for Beginners. Sq. 16mo	1844	1

[This is a reproduction and remodeling of "Parley's Method of Telling about Geography, for Children."]

Parley's Farewell. Large sq. 16mo. (Out of print.)	1836	1
Parley's Arithmetic. Sq. 16mo	1833	1
Parley's Spelling-Book. (Out of print.)	1833	1
Parley's Book of the United States. Sq. 16mo	1833	1

	Date of publication.	No. vols.
Géographie Elémentaire. 8vo.	1854	1
[Published at Paris.]		
Elementary Geography. 8vo. With Maps	1854	1
[Published in London.]		
Parley's Present. Small 24mo. (Out of print.)	1836	1
Parley's Dictionaries—Of Botany, of Astronomy, of the Bible, of Bible Geography, of History, of Commerce. Six vols., large sq. 16mo........................	1834	6
Three Months at Sea (an English book, with additions and modifications). Sq. 16mo...................	1832	1
The Captive of Nootka Sound. Sq. 16mo............	1832	1
The Story of Capt. Riley. do.	1832	1
The Story of La Peyrouse. do.	1832	1
The Story of Alexander Selkirk. do.	1833	1
Bible Stories (a London book, with additions). Sq. 16mo	1833	1
Parley's Magazine. Began 1832. Large sq. 12mo.....	1833	1

> [This work was planned and established by me; but after about a year I was obliged to relinquish it, from ill health and an affection of my eyes. It was conducted, without any interest or participation on my part, for about twelve years, when it ceased.]

Merry's Museum and Parley's Magazine. Large sq. 12mo. Commenced 1841	1841	28

> [This work was begun and established by me, under the title of Merry's Museum, but after the discontinuance of Parley's Magazine, the latter title was added. The work continued under my exclusive editorship until I left for Europe in 1850; from that time, while I had a general charge of the work, Rev. S. T. Allen was the home editor. At the close of the fourteenth year (the twenty-eighth semi-annual volume, 1854), my connection with the work entirely ceased.]

Remarks.

I thus stand before the public as the author and editor of about one hundred and seventy volumes—one hundred and sixteen bearing the name of Peter Parley. Of all these, about seven millions of volumes have been sold: about three hundred thousand volumes are now sold annually.

A recent writer in the Boston Courier, has affirmed that the late Mr. S. Kettell was the "*Veritable Peter Parley*"—thereby asserting, in effect, and conveying the impression, that he being the author of

the Parley Books, I, who have claimed them, am an impostor. He
has, moreover, claimed for him, in precise terms, the actual authorship of various works which have appeared under my own proper
name. For reasons which will appear hereafter, I deem it necessary to expose this impudent attempt at imposture—absurd and
preposterous as it appears, upon its very face.

First, as to the Parley Books—it will probably be sufficient for
me to make the following statement. In respect to the thirty-six
volumes of *Parley's Tales*, in the preceding list, the earlier numbers
of which began and gave currency to the entire Parley series, *no
person except myself ever wrote a single sentence.*

As to *Parley's Historical Compends*—some nine or ten volumes—
I had the assistance of N. Hawthorne, and J. O. Sargent, Esqs., and
others; *but Mr. Kettell never wrote a line of any one of them!*

As to *Parley's Miscellanies*—about fifty volumes—I had some
assistance from several persons in about a dozen of them. Mr.
Kettell wrote a few sketches for five or six volumes of the Cabinet
Library, which I adapted to my purpose, and inserted: *this is the
whole extent of his participation in the entire Parley series—one hundred and sixteen volumes!*

☞ *He never wrote, planned, conceived, or pretended to be the author, of a single volume, bearing Parley's name. The pretense thus
set up for him, since his death, is as preposterous as it is impudent
and false. It would be, indeed, about as reasonable to claim for him
the authorship of Don Quixote, or Gil Blas, or Pilgrim's Progress,
as thus to give him the title of the "Veritable Peter Parley."*

The writer above noticed also claims for Mr. Kettell the chief authorship of *Merry's Museum*, extending to about thirty volumes—
large octavo. This claim is disposed of by the following letter from
Rev. S. T. ALLEN—better qualified than any other person to be a
witness in the case.

NEW YORK, Jan. 28, 1856.

S. G. GOODRICH, ESQ:

Dear Sir—I have read the several articles in the Boston Courier, signed "Veritas," claiming for the late Mr. Kettell the authorship of *Peter
Parley's Tales, Merry's Museum*, &c. As you request from me a statement, as to my knowledge on the subject, I cheerfully give it, which
you can publish if you please.

I purchased, with an associate, the entire Merry's Museum in 1848 or
1849, from the beginning in 1841, and have been its publisher until October last; that is, over six years. I have nearly, from that time to the
present, been its editor, wholly or in part. During this period, Mr. Kettell

has never written any thing for the work. It is within my knowledge that he wrote some articles in the earlier volumes, probably in all not exceeding one hundred and eighty to two hundred pages. His principal articles were the "Travels of Thomas Trotter" and "Michael Kastoff;" these possessed no particular merit, and did not aid or advance the reputation of the work.

The articles by you, extending through fifteen volumes, nearly all of which have since been separately published as Peter Parley's Tales, gave life, circulation, and character to the work. I have had large opportunity to judge of this matter, as I have been, for more than six years, in constant communication with the subscribers (ten or twelve thousand in number), and I say, unhesitatingly, that your articles in the Museum have fully sustained your reputation as the ablest, best known, and most popular writer for youth in this country.

I may say, furthermore, that I have lately been in Europe, and it is within my knowledge that Parley's works have been published there, in various languages, and are highly esteemed.

I further state that I have read your reply to the Boston Courier and "Veritas" of January 13th, and so far as my knowledge extends, and especially in respect to Merry's Museum, it is strictly correct.

I need hardly say, in conclusion, therefore, that I consider these claims of the Boston Courier and "Veritas," in favor of Mr. Kettell, as wholly without foundation. *All that can properly be said is, that out of five or six thousand pages of Merry's Museum, he contributed about two hundred pages, marked with no particular excellence.* The only qualification that need be made is, that I have understood that Mr. Kettell had some general superintendence of the work for about six months, while you were absent in Europe; that is, from September, 1847, to March, 1848. Even during this period, Mr. Kettell's labors seem to have been confined to writing a few small articles, and reading the proofs.

Yours respectfully,   STEPHEN T. ALLEN.

☞ *Here, then, are eight and twenty volumes of Merry's Museum, in addition to eighty-eight volumes of Parley's works, rescued from the claims of this wholesale literary burglar.*

Another claim in behalf of Mr. Kettell is, that he was the author of various valuable and important school-books, such as the Pictorial History of the United States, a Pictorial History of Greece, &c., &c., &c. The subjoined letter from Mr. George Savage, of the late firm of Huntington & Savage, and now associated with Mr. J. H. Colton & Co., Map and Geography Publishers in New York, will settle this claim, also.

NEW YORK, Jan. 31, 1856.

MR. GOODRICH:

Dear Sir : I have looked over the several attacks made upon you in the Boston Courier by "Veritas," claiming that Mr. Kettell was the author of several books which bear your name. I am acquainted with the history of several of these works, and, so far as my knowledge extends, the statements of "Veritas" are entirely destitute of foundation. I can speak positively as to four of the books—the Geographies—"Parley's," the "Primer," the "National," and the "Comprehensive," for I am, and have been for some years, their proprietor and publisher. I have also been interested in them from the beginning, and it is within my knowledge that you wrote them wholly and entirely. The statements of "Veritas" as to Mr. Kettell's authorship of the Pictorial History of Greece and the United States, are equally untrue.

"Veritas" quotes a contract between you and Mr. Kettell of May 26, 1846, to show that Mr. Kettell had written some of the "Parley's Compends of History." If he will look at the books referred to in this contract, he will see that your name is given as the author, and not Parley's.

I speak of these works, because I have been engaged in publishing them, or most of them. It is evident that the articles in the Courier are written, throughout, with great rashness ; and though I do not impugn the motives of the writer, I feel free to say that so far as they depend upon him, they seem to me entirely unworthy of confidence.

I have seen your replies, and having had a large knowledge of your operations, I think your statements have been exact, reasonable, and just, and have no doubt the public will think so.

Yours truly,   GEORGE SAVAGE.

Another claim, in behalf of Mr. Kettell, made by this adventurous writer, is, that the *History of All Nations*—a work of 1200 pages, royal 8vo—which appears under my name—was published, with the exception of a few dry pages, " *as it came from Mr. Kettell's graceful and flowing pen !*" In reply, I offer the following letter, to which I invite the special attention of the reader, inasmuch as it not only refutes this audacious pretense, but it explains the nature of my connection with Mr. Kettell, the reason why I employed him, and the nature and extent of the services he rendered me.

NEW YORK, Feb. 3, 1856.

To the Editor of the Boston Courier :

SIR—I have read the controversy which has been progressing for some weeks, in your journal, as to the alleged claims of Mr. Kettell to the authorship of several works which have appeared under my father's name.

These claims, urged after Mr. Kettell's death, and by a person totally irresponsible, seem hardly to merit serious consideration, but as they have been pressed in a spirit of evident hostility and malice, it may be well for me to state what I know upon the subject.

For the last ten years I have been familiar with my father's literary labors. I have seen the greater part of the manuscripts sent to the printing-office, and have read the greater part of the proofs returned, and can bear witness to the accuracy of the statements made in this connection, in my father's letter, published in the New York Times of the 31st December. Having suffered severely from weak eyes for the past twenty-five years, he has been obliged to use the services of others in consulting authorities, and sometimes in blocking out work to be afterward systematized and reduced to order by him. In this, Mr. Kettell was his principal assistant. He wrote always, as I understood it, as an assistant, and in no sense as an author. *His manuscripts were never finished so as to be fit for the press. Their publication, as they were, would have been fatal to the reputation of any man who should have taken the responsibility of them.* It was my father's task, after having planned these works, to read and remodel the rough drafts of Mr. Kettell, to suit them to his own views, and to prepare them for the public eye. This was, in some cases, a more serious and fatiguing labor than it would have been to write the work from the beginning. I may add that at one period Mr. Kettell's manuscripts were referred to me for examination, and that I was empowered to accept or reject them. Somewhat later I had, for a time, occasion to remodel, adapt, and partly to rewrite such portions as were accepted.

I have, naturally, no wish to detract from the merits of Mr. Kettell. But in regard to the *History of All Nations,* a work attributed by " Veritas" to the " graceful and flowing pen of Mr. Kettell," I must state that five persons (Mr. Kettell, Rev. Mr. Robbins, of Berlin, Conn., Rev. Mr. Jenks, of Boston, myself, and my father) were engaged upon it ; the heaviest share—the plan, the fitting, the refining, the systematizing, and the general views—falling upon the latter. Perhaps " Veritas" will pardon me if I claim for myself the entire authorship of seventy-five pages, so confidently attributed by him to the " graceful and flowing pen of Mr. Kettell."

Take notice, Mr. Editor, that I append my real name to this communication. In controversies of this kind, where honor, truth, and the maintenance of a good name are involved, anonymous correspondence is held by the community to argue in its author—meanness, treachery, and cowardice. I think Mr. Kettell, were he living, would be the first to disavow this eager service in his behalf, by his irresponsible advocate.

I am yours respectfully,   F. B. Goodrich.

I believe I may now leave this matter to the judgment of the public, with a few brief observations.

The enormous claims in behalf of Mr. Kettell, set up by the Boston Courier and its anonymous correspondent " Veritas," have been disposed of as follows :

1. Mr. Kettell never wrote a line of the thirty-six volumes of *Parleys' Tales ;* never a line of the ten volumes of *Parley's Historical Compends*, expressly and repeatedly claimed for him ; and of the fifty volumes of *Parley's Miscellanies*, he only wrote a few sketches in half a dozen of them. To pretend, therefore, that he is the "*Veritable Peter Parley*," is as gross an imposture, as to call him the " *Veritable Author*" of Pickwick, or Guy Mannering, or the Spectator.

2. The claim for Mr. Kettell, of the authorship of *Merry's Museum*, —thirty volumes—is reduced to the writing of about two hundred pages of indifferent matter, as a correspondent.

3. His claim to the authorship of the *History of Greece, History of the United States, Parley's Geography*, the *Primer of Geography, National Geography, Comprehensive Geography and History*—positively asserted by " Veritas"—is shown to be false, in the beginning, the middle, and the end.

4. The audacious claim of the entire authorship of the *History of All Nations*, comes to this, that Mr. Kettell was one of four persons who assisted me in the compilation of that work.

5. It appears, inasmuch as my eyes were weak for a series of twenty-five years, rendering it sometimes impossible for me to consult books, that I employed Mr. Kettell to block out several works, according to plans—minutely and carefully prescribed by me—and that the materials thus furnished, were reduced to method, style, and manner by me, so as to suit my own taste ; and that the works were published, as thus remodeled, and not as they were written by him.   It appears, furthermore, that all this was done, with Mr. Kettell's full consent, upon written and explicit agreements, and that he never did plan, devise, contrive, or finally prepare any book published under my name, nor was he, nor did he ever claim to be, the author of any book thus published.

6. It is material to state, distinctly, that while " Veritas" claims for Mr. Kettell the entire authorship of over one hundred and twenty volumes of my works, he (Mr. Kettell) never assisted me, in any way or in any degree, in more than twenty volumes, and these only in the manner above indicated—that is, in blocking out works, mostly historical, under my direction, and to be finished by me.

7. I do not mean by this to depreciate Mr. Kettell's abilities ; but inasmuch as these audacious claims, in his behalf, have been perti-

naciously and impudently urged, it is proper for me, in this formal manner, to reduce them to their true dimensions.

8. While I thus acknowledge the assistance rendered me by Mr. Kettell in my historical compilations, it is proper to state that I had the aid of other persons—some of them of higher name and fame than he. Among my assistants were N. Hawthorne, E. Sargent, J. O. Sargent, S. P. Holbrook, Esqs., Rev. Royal Robbins, Rev. E. G. Smith, Rev. W. S. Jenks, and others. The claims of "Veritas," if admitted, would not only rob me of the authorship of a hundred volumes, which I wrote, but would transfer to Mr. Kettell about twenty volumes, to which several other authors contributed, with greater ability than he.

9. I think it may be safely assumed, that in the history of literature, there is not a more impudent attempt at imposture than this, which originated in the Boston Courier. It is easy to comprehend why the author has not dared to give his name to the public, but has continued to make his attacks behind the mask of an anonymous title. That I deem myself called upon thus to notice him, arises from the fact that he derived a certain color of authority from the Editor of the Courier, and from publishing papers and documents belonging to Mr. Kettell's heirs—though these contributed, in no degree, either to refute the statements here made, or to substantiate any portion of the claims here referred to.

10. Literary history is full of instances in which littleness, allied to malignity, has signalized itself by seeking to deprive authors of their just claims—and while thus doing wrong to their literary labors, attempting also to degrade them in the eyes of the world, as guilty of appropriating to themselves honors which are not legitimately theirs. It is also a vice of base minds to believe imputations of this sort, without evidence, or even against evidence, when once they have been suggested. I do not think it best, therefore, to leave my name to be thus dealt with by future pretenders, who may desire to emulate this Boston adventurer.

SPURIOUS PARLEY BOOKS.

AMERICAN COUNTERFEITS AND IMPOSITIONS.

In the United States, the name of Parley has been applied to several works of which I am not the author, though for the most part, from mistake and not from fraudulent designs. The following are among the number:

		Date of publication.	No. vols.
Parley's Washington. 18mo......................		1832	1
Parley's Columbus. do........................		1832	1
Parley's Franklin. do........................		1832	1

[The name of Parley is not in the title-page of any of these works, but is put upon the back, and they are sold as Parley books, but without authority, though, at the outset, as I believe, with no improper design.]

Parley's Miscellanies. 18mo........................	——....	1
Parley's Consul's Daughter, and other Tales. 18mo...	——....	1
Parley's Tales of Humor. 18mo.....................	——....	1
Parley's Tales of Terror. do......................	——....	1
Parley's Tales for the Times. 18mo	——....	1
Parley's Tales of Adventure. do.................	——....	1

[The publication of this series, under the name of Parley, is, I believe, abandoned, as I remonstrated with the publishers against it, as a fraud upon the public.]

Parley's Picture Books—12 kinds....................	——...	12

[These I have not seen; they are, however, impositions.]

The Rose, by Peter Parley	——....	1
The Bud, by Peter Parley...........................	——....	1
The Mines of different Countries. By Peter Parley...	——....	1
The Garden, by Peter Parley	——....	1
The Gift, by Peter Parley	——....	1
The Flower-Basket, by Peter Parley.................	——....	1
Fairy Tales, by Peter Parley	——....	1

[The preceding seven volumes I have not seen, but I find them in some of the American catalogues.   They are all spurious.]

Parley's Book of Books. Sq. 16mo..................	——....	1

[This book, I believe, consists of extracts from Parley's Magazine.   Its publication in this form, so far as it may convey the idea that it is written by me, is deceptive.]

Parley's Pictorial—A book for Home Education and Family Entertainment. 8vo	——....	1
Parley's Household Library. 8vo	——....	1

[These two works are from old altered plates of Parley's Magazine, and are designed to deceive the public, by making it believe that they are original works, and by the author of Parley's Tales.   They are a gross and shameful imposition.]

ENGLISH COUNTERFEITS AND IMPOSITIONS.

[The London publishers and authors have made a large
business of preparing and publishing Parley books.
Some of these are republications, without change, from
the genuine American editions—to which I make no
objection; some are the genuine works, more or less altered; and many others are counterfeits, every means
being used to pass them off upon the public as by the
original author of Parley's Tales. Among the most
notorious of these are the following:

	Date of publication.	No. vols.
Peter Parley's Annual—A Christmas and New Year's Present. Published by *Darton & Co*	1841	14

[This is a large 16mo., with colored engravings, and has
been continued from 1841 to 1855—14 volumes.]

				Date of publication.	No. vols.
Peter Parley's Royal Victoria Game of the Kings and Queens of England. 18mo. *Darton & Co*				1834	1
Parley's Book of Gymnastics. Sq. 16mo. *Darton & Co.*				1840	1
Parley's Parting Gift.	do.	do.		1846	1
Parley's Book of Industry.	do.	do.		1855	1
Parley's Book of Poetry.	do.	do.		1843	1
Parley's Ireland.	do.	do.		1843	1
Parley's Wonders of Earth, Sea, and Sky. Square 16mo.		do.		1853	1
Parley's Odds and Ends. Square 16mo.		do.		1840	1
Parley's Peeps at Paris.	do.	do.		1848	1
Parley's Prize Book.	do.	do.		1848	1
Parley's School Atlas.	do.	do.		1842	1
Parley's Canada.	do.	do.		1839	1
Parley's China and the Chinese. do.		do.		1844	1
Parley's Child's Own Atlas. Square.		do.		1853	1
Parley's Life and Journey of St. Paul. Square 16mo. *Simpkins*				1845	1
Peter Parley's Lives of the Twelve Apostles. Sq. 16mo. *Bogue*				1844	1
Peter Parley's Visit to London during the Coronation. Sq. 16mo. *Bogue*				1838	1
Peter Parley's Tales of England, Scotland, and Ireland. Sq. 16mo. *Tegg*				1842	1
Peter Parley's Mythology of Greece and Rome. Sq. 16mo. *Tegg*				1841	1
Peter Parley's Tales of Greece, Ancient and Modern. Square 16mo. *Tegg*				1842	1

			Date of publication.	No. vols.
Peter Parley's Tales of Ancient Rome and Modern Italy. Sq. 16mo. *Tegg*			1840	1
Peter Parley's Tales about Christmas. Sq. 16mo. *Tegg.*			1839	1
Peter Parley's Shipwrecks.	do.	do.	1846	1
Parley's Plants.	do.	do.	1839	1
Parley's Modern Geography.	do.	do.	1837	1
Parley's Bible Geography. Sq. 16mo. *J. S. Hodson*			1839	1
Parley's Child's First Step. Sq. 16mo. *Clements*			1839	1

[There are still other counterfeits of Parley's works, issued
by various parties in London. The utter disregard of
truth, honor, and decency, on the part of respectable
British authors and publishers, in this wholesale system
of imposition and injustice, is all the more remarkable,
when we consider that the British public, and especially
the British authors and booksellers, are denouncing us
in America as pirates, for refusing international copyright.

The conduct of all these parties places them, morally,
on a footing with other counterfeiters and forgers: public opinion, in the United States, would consign persons
conducting in this manner, to the same degree of reprobation. Can it be that, in England, a man who utters a
counterfeit five-pound note is sent to Newgate, while
another may issue thousands of counterfeit volumes,
and not destroy his reputation ?]

NOTE II.

Messrs. Low and Co.'s Catalogue.

Since the preceding pages were in type, I have been favored by
Messrs. Samson Low, Son & Co., of London, with the proof-sheets of
their new "AMERICAN CATALOGUE OF BOOKS," in the preface of which
are some interesting statistics of the book-trade in the United States.
From this I make the following extract:

" It seems to be generally agreed that in the twelve years ending
1842, nearly half the publications issued in the United States were
reprints of English books," &c.

"There are no means of verifying this, but the increase and comparative nationality of the literature during the last five years (1850
to 1855) are very striking, testifying at once by its progressive char-

acter to the position, strength, and value of the literature of the country at the present day.

"During 1852, unavoidably including many really published in the preceding six months, we find there were 966 new books and new editions; 312 of which were reprints of English books, and 56 translations from other countries.

"During 1853, 879 new books and new editions, including 298 reprints of English books, and 37 translations.

"During 1854, 765 new books and new editions, of which 277 were reprints of English books, and 41 translations.

"During 1855, 1,092 new books and new editions, including 250 reprints of English books, and 38 translations.

"During the six months to July, 1856, 751 new books and new editions, of which but 102 were reprints of English books, and 26 translations."

This statement, made with great care from published catalogues, notices, and titles of books, coincides in a remarkable degree with the conclusions at which I had arrived, as will be seen at page 389, vol. ii. According to this catalogue of the Messrs. Low, the proportion of British books in our book production is now about twenty to twenty-five per cent. It is to be remarked, however, that a great many new editions of school-books, and popular works of constant and large sale, are produced, of which no public notice is given, and which, therefore, are not included in their estimate, above quoted. If we allow for these editions, we shall see that my estimate of twenty per cent. for the proportion of British literature in our publications at the present time, is fully sustained. The rapid relative increase of American over British mind in our literature, is equally manifest from both statements.

NOTE III.

" *Old Humphrey,*" or *George Mogridge, the first Counterfeiter of the Parley Books.*

I have just met with a book recently issued by the *London Religious Tract Society*, entitled " Memoirs of Old Humphrey," that is, the late George Mogridge, a well-known writer of religious books and essays, especially for the young, for the last thirty years. By a list of his writings, inserted in this volume, it seems he was the person employed by Mr. Thomas Tegg, to write the counterfeit Parley books, of which I have given an account at page 292, vol. ii.

Until now, the real authorship of these volumes has been kept a secret. Tegg disguised the matter by encouraging the idea that he wrote them himself. It appears by the Memoir, above alluded to, that the real author of this imposition, was a person claiming to be very pious, and now that his fraud is known, he becomes the hero of a *religious* tract society !

The false books which he wrote, and which have been palmed off upon the public for twenty years, as written by me, were as follows :

> Peter Parley's Tales of Great Britain.
> —————— Greece, Ancient and Modern.
> —————— Rome and Modern Italy.
> —————— Mythology of Ancient Greece and Rome.
> —————— Geography.
> —————— Tales about Christmas.
> —————— Shipwrecks and Disasters at Sea

Some of these are founded upon genuine books, and some are wholly original ; but they are all written with a sedulous attempt to make them pass as by the veritable author of Parley's Tales. This was the first example of counterfeiting these works, and led to that system of fraud which has caused me so much injury and annoyance.

INDEX.

24*